Frommer's®

Japanese PhraseFinder & Dictionary

1st Edition

D0680891

WILEY

Wiley Publishing, Inc.

Published by:

Wiley Publishing, Inc.

111 River St.
Hoboken, NJ 07030-5774

ISBN-13: 978-0-470-17837-9

Editors: Tomoko Yamaguchi & Yoji Yamaguchi

Series Editor: Maureen Clarke
Photo Editor: Richard H. Fox
Illustrations by Maciek Albrecht

Translation, Copyediting, Proofreading, Production, and Layout by:
Lingo Systems, 15115 SW Sequoia Pkwy, Ste 200, Portland, OR 97224

For information on our other products and services or to obtain technical support,
please contact our Customer Care Department within the U.S. at 800/762-2974, outside the U.S. at 317/572-3993 or fax 317/572-4002.
Wiley also publishes its books in a variety of electronic formats. Some content that
appears in print may not be available in electronic formats.

Manufactured in the United States of America

5 4 3 2 1

Contents

An Invitation to the Reader

In researching this book, we discovered many wonderful saying and terms useful to travelers in Japanese. We're sure you'll find others. Please tell us about them so we can share them with your fellow travelers in upcoming editions. If you were disappointed by any aspect of this book, we'd like to know that, too. Please write to:

Frommer's Japanese PhraseFinder & Dictionary, 1st Edition
Wiley Publishing, Inc.
111 River St. • Hoboken, NJ 07030-5774

An Additional Note

The packer, editors and publisher cannot be held responsible for the experience of readers while traveling. Your safety is important to us, however, so we encourage you to stay alert and aware of your surroundings. Keep a close eye on cameras, purses, and wallets, all favorite targets of thieves and pickpockets.

Frommers.com

Now that you have the language for a great trip, visit our website at **www.frommers.com** for travel information on more than 3,600 destinations. With features updated regularly, we give you instant access to the most current trip-planning information available. At Frommers.com, you'll also find the best prices on airfares, accommodations, and car rentals—and you can even book travel online through our travel booking partners. At Frommers.com, you'll also find:

- Online updates to our most popular guidebooks
- Vacation sweepstakes and contest giveaways
- Newsletter highlighting the hottest travel trends
- Online travel message boards with featured travel discussions

INTRODUCTION: HOW TO USE THIS BOOK

More than 120 million people in Japan are native speakers of Japanese. Many more speak it as a second language. Japanese is a cosmopolitan tongue, heavily influenced by Chinese and receptive to foreign "loan" words (see page 18). Conversely, many Japanese words have entered the English language lexicon, in the worlds of technology, art, food, and more.

Although more and more Japanese—especially younger people and people in larger cities—can speak at least some English, most locals will appreciate your attempt, no matter how limited, to speak their language. Being able to communicate in this rich and historic tongue will prove both challenging and rewarding, and it will also help you to make new friends.

Our intention is not to teach you Japanese; a class or audio program is better for that. Our aim is to provide a portable travel tool that's easy to use on the spot. The problem with most phrasebooks is that you practically have to memorize the contents before you know where to look for a term you need pronto. This phrasebook is designed for fingertip referencing, so you can whip it out and find the words you need fast.

Part of this book organizes terms by chapters, like the sections in a Frommer's guide—getting a room, getting a good meal, etc. Within those divisions, we tried to organize phrases intuitively, according to how frequently most readers would be likely to use them. The most unique feature, however, is the two-way PhraseFinder dictionary in the back, which lists words as well as phrases organized by keyword. Say a taxi driver hands you ¥500 instead of ¥1,000. Look up "change" in the dictionary and discover how to say: "Sorry, but this isn't the correct change."

To make best use of the content, we recommend that you spend some time flipping through it before you depart for your trip. Familiarize yourself with the order of the chapters. Read through the pronunciations section in chapter one and practice pronouncing random phrases throughout the book. Try looking up a few phrases in the phrasebook section as well as in the dictionary. This way, you'll be able to locate phrases faster and speak them more clearly when you need them.

What will make this book most practical? What will make it easiest to use? These are the questions we asked ourselves repeatedly as we assembled these travel terms. Our immediate goal was to create a phrasebook as indispensable as your passport. Our far-ranging goal, of course, is to enrich your experience of travel. And with that, we wish you *Ganbatte kudasai!* (Have a great trip!)

CHAPTER ONE

SURVIVAL JAPANESE

If you tire of toting around this phrasebook, tear out this chapter. You should be able to navigate your destination with only the terms found in the next 32 pages.

BASIC GREETINGS

For a full list of greetings, see p99.

Hello.	こんにちは。 *kon nichi wa.*
How are you?	お元気ですか? *ogenki desu ka.*
I'm fine, thanks	元気です、どうもありがとう。 *genki desu, dōmo arigatō.*
And you?	あなたもお元気ですか? *anata mo ogenki desu ka.*
My name is ____.	____と申します。 *____ to mōshimasu.*
And yours?	あなたのお名前は? *anata no onamae wa.*
It's a pleasure to meet you.	あなたにお会いできて嬉しいです。 *anata ni oai dekite ureshii desu.*
Please.	どうぞ。 *dōzo.*
Thank you.	どうもありがとう。 *dōmo arigatō.*
Yes.	はい。 *hai.*
No.	いいえ。 *iie.*
Okay.	オッケイ。 *okkei.*

No problem.	いいですよ。
	ii desu yo.
I'm sorry, I don't understand.	すみませんが、わかりません。
	sumi masen ga, wakari masen.
Would you speak slower please?	もう少しゆっくり話していただけませんか?
	mō sukoshi yukkuri hanashite itadake masen ka.
Would you speak louder please?	もう少し大きな声で話していただけませんか?
	mō sukoshi ōkina koe de hanashite itadake masen ka.
Do you speak English?	英語を話しますか?
	eigo o hanashi masu ka.
Do you speak any other languages?	他の国の言葉も話しますか?
	hoka no kuni no kotoba mo hanashi masu ka.
I speak ____ better than Japanese.	日本語よりも____の方が うまく話せます。
	nihongo yori mo ____ no hō ga umaku hanase masu.
Would you please repeat that?	もう一度繰り返していただけますか?
	mō ichido kuri kaeshite itadake masu ka.
Would you point that out in this dictionary?	この辞書でそれを指していただけませんか?
	kono jisho de sore o sashite itadake masen ka.

THE KEY QUESTIONS

With the right hand gestures, you can get a lot of mileage from the following list of single-word questions and answers.

Who?	誰?
	dare.
What?	何?
	nani.

When?	いつ？
	itsu.
Where?	どこ？
	doko.
To where?	どこへ？
	doko e.
Why?	なぜ？
	naze.
How?	どう？
	dō.
Which?	どれ？
	dore.
How many? /	いくつ／いくら、どれくらい？
How much?	*ikutsu／ ikura, dorekurai*

THE ANSWERS: WHO
For full coverage of pronouns, see p23.

I	私
	watashi
you	あなた
	anata
him	彼
	kare
her	彼女
	kanojo
us	私たち
	watashi tachi
them	彼ら
	karera

THE ANSWERS: WHEN
For full coverage of time-related terms, see p13.

now	今
	ima
later	後
	ato

in a minute	すぐ
	sugu
today	今日
	kyō
tomorrow	明日
	ashita
yesterday	昨日
	kinō
in a week	1週間後に
	isshū kango ni
next week	来週
	raishū
last week	先週
	senshū
next month	来月
	raigetsu
At ____	____に
	ni
ten o'clock this morning.	今朝の10時
	kesa no jū ji
two o'clock this afternoon.	今日の午後2時
	kyō no gogo ni ji
seven o'clock this evening.	今晩7時
	konban shichi ji

For full coverage of numbers, see p6.

THE ANSWERS: WHERE

here	ここ
	koko
there	そこ
	soko
near	近い
	chikai
closer	もっと近い
	motto chikai

closest	一番近い
	ichiban chikai
far	遠い
	tōi
farther	もっと遠い
	motto tōi
farthest	一番遠い
	ichiban tōi
across from	の向かい
	no mukai
next to	の隣
	no tonari
behind	の後ろ
	no ushiro
straight ahead	ここをまっすぐ
	koko o massugu
left	左
	hidari
right	右
	migi
up	上
	ue
down	下
	shita
lower	もっと低い
	motto hikui
higher	もっと高い
	motto takai
forward	前
	mae
back	後ろ
	ushiro
around	周り
	mawari

across the street	この道の向こう側 *kono michi no mukō gawa*
down the street	この道（の先） *kono michi (no saki)*
on the corner	角に *kado ni*
kitty-corner	斜め向かい *naname mukai*
____ blocks from here	ここから____目の角 *koko kara ____ me no kado*

For a full list of numbers used for blocks, see the section "Generic Inanimate Objects" on p. 11.

THE ANSWERS: WHICH

this one	これ *kore*
that (that one, close by)	それ *sore*
(that one, in the distance)	あれ *are*
these	これら *korera*
those (those there, close by)	それら *sorera*

NUMBERS & COUNTING

one	一 *ichi*	six	六 *roku*
two	二 *ni*	seven	七 *shichi/nana*
three	三 *san*	eight	八 *hachi*
four	四 *shi/yo/yon*	nine	九 *kyū*
five	五 *go*	ten	十 *jū*

eleven	十一 *jū ichi*	thirty	三十 *san jū*
twelve	十二 *jū ni*	forty	四十 *yon jū*
thirteen	十三 *jū san*	fifty	五十 *go jū*
fourteen	十四 *jū shi*	sixty	六十 *roku jū*
fifteen	十五 *jū go*	seventy	七十 *nana jū*
sixteen	十六 *jū roku*	eighty	八十 *hachi jū*
seventeen	十七 *jū shichi/jū nana*	ninety	九十 *kyū jū*
eighteen	十八 *jū hachi*	one hundred	百 *hyaku*
nineteen	十九 *jū kyū*	two hundred	二百 *ni hyaku*
twenty	二十 *ni jū*	one thousand	千 *sen*
twenty-one	二十一 *ni jū ichi*		

COUNTERS

When counting objects, you need to use a counter. In English you simply put a number before the item you wish to count and pluralize it; for example, one car, two cars, etc. In Japanese, which has no plural form, you instead use a separate counter word that varies depending on the type of thing you wish to count. The item being counted comes first, followed by the number, which is in turn followed by the counter word. The counters vary according to the type, shape, or size of each item. The pronunciation of either the number or the counter will vary in some instances. Note that the numbers four (*shi*), seven (*shichi*) and nine (*kyu*) can also be *yon*, *nana*, and *ku* when counting objects.

PEOPLE

one person	一人
	hitori
two people	二人
	futari
three people	三人
	sannin
four people	四人
	yonin
five people	五人
	gonin
six people	六人
	rokunin
seven people	七人
	shichinin / nananin
eight people	八人
	hachinin
nine people	九人
	kyūnin or kunin
ten people	十人
	jyūnin

MECHANICAL OBJECTS

one mechanical object	一台
	ichidai
two mechanical objects	二台
	nidai
three mechanical objects	三台
	sandai
four mechanical objects	四台
	yondai
five mechanical objects	五台
	godai
six mechanical objects	六台
	rokudai
seven mechanical objects	七台
	nanadai

eight mechanical objects	八台	*hachidai*
nine mechanical objects	九台	*kyūdai*
ten mechanical objects	十台	*jyūdai*

FLAT OBJECTS

one flat object	一枚	*ichimai*
two flat objects	二枚	*nimai*
three flat objects	三枚	*sanmai*
four flat objects	四枚	*yonmai*
five flat objects	五枚	*gomai*
six flat objects	六枚	*rokumai*
seven flat objects	七枚	*nanamai*
eight flat objects	八枚	*hachimai*
nine flat objects	九枚	*kyūmai*
ten flat objects	十枚	*jyūmai*

SMALL ANIMALS

one small animal	一匹	*ippiki*
two small animals	二匹	*nihiki*
three small animals	三匹	*sanbiki*

four small animals	四匹
	yonhiki
five small animals	五匹
	gohiki
six small animals	六匹
	roppiki
seven small animals	七匹
	nanahiki
eight small animals	八匹
	happiki
nine small animals	九匹
	kyūhiki
ten small animals	十匹
	jyuppiki

CYLINDRICAL OBJECTS

one cylindrical object	一本
	ippon
two cylindrical objects	二本
	nihon
three cylindrical objects	三本
	sanbon
four cylindrical objects	四本
	yonhon
five cylindrical objects	五本
	gohon
six cylindrical objects	六本
	roppon
seven cylindrical objects	七本
	nanahon
eight cylindrical objects	八本
	hachihon/happon
nine cylindrical objects	九本
	kyūhon
ten cylindrical objects	十本
	jyuppon

GENERIC INANIMATE OBJECTS

one object	一つ	
	hitotsu	
two objects	二つ	
	futatsu	
three objects	三つ	
	mittsu	
four objects	四つ	
	yottsu	
five objects	五つ	
	itsutsu	
six objects	六つ	
	muttsu	
seven objects	七つ	
	nanatsu	
eight objects	八つ	
	yattsu	
nine objects	九つ	
	kokonotsu	
ten objects	十	
	tô	

MEASUREMENTS

Measurements will usually be metric, though you may need a few American measurement terms.

inch	インチ
	inchi
foot	フット
	futto
mile	マイル
	mairu
millimeter	ミリメートル
	miri mētoru
centimeter	センチメートル
	senchi mētoru
meter	メートル
	mētoru

A Little Tip

Double consonants in Japanese are *kk, ss, tt* and *pp*. They are pronounced as a single consonant preceded by a short pause. For example:

bikkuri *(bee-(k)-koo-ree)*
zasshi *(zah-(s)-shee)*
matte! *(mah-(t)-teh!)*
ippai *(ee-(p)-pah-ee)*

kilometer	キロメートル *kiro mētoru*
hectare	ヘクタール *hekutāru*
squared	平方形の *hēhōkei no*
short	短い *mijikai*
long	長い *nagai*

VOLUME

milliliters	ミリリットル *miri rittoru*
liter	リットル *rittoru*
kilo	キロ *kiro*
ounce	オンス *onsu*
cup	カップ *kappu*
pint	パイント *painto*
quart	クォート *kuōto*

gallon	ガロン
	garon

QUANTITY

some	いくつか (の) / いくらか (の)
	ikutsuka (no) / ikuraka (no)
none	少しもない、全くない
	sukoshi mo nai, mattaku nai
all	すべて / すべての
	subete/subete no
many / much	沢山の
	takusan no
a little bit (can be used for quantity or for time)	少し
	sukoshi
dozen	ダース
	dāsu

SIZE

small	小さい
	chiisai
the smallest (literally "the most small")	もっとも小さい
	mottomo chīsai
medium	中位の
	chū kurai no
big	大きい
	ōkii
fat	太った
	futotta
wide	広い
	hiroi
narrow	狭い
	semai

TIME

Time in Japanese is referred to, literally, by the hour. What time is it? translates literally as "What hour is it?"
For full coverage of number terms, see p6.

HOURS OF THE DAY

What time is it?	今何時ですか？
	ima nan ji desu ka.
At what time?	何時に？
	nan ji ni.
For how long?	どのくらい？
	dono kurai.
It's one o'clock.	1 時です。
	ichi ji desu.
It's two o'clock.	2 時です。
	ni ji desu.
It's two thirty.	2 時半（2 時 30 分）です。
	ni ji han (ni ji san juppun) desu.
It's two fifteen.	2 時 15 分です。
	ni ji jū go fun desu.
It's a quarter to three.	2 時 45 分です。
	ni ji yon jū go fun desu.
It's noon.	正午です。
	shōgo desu.
It's midnight.	真夜中です。
	mayonaka desu.
It's early.	早いです。
	hayai desu.
It's late.	遅いです。
	osoi desu.
in the morning	午前
	gozen
in the afternoon	午後
	gogo
at night	夜
	yoru
dawn	夜明け
	yo ake

A.M.	午前	
	gozen	
P.M.	午後	
	gogo	

DAYS OF THE WEEK

Sunday	日曜日	
	nichi yō bi	
Monday	月曜日	
	getsu yō bi	
Tuesday	火曜日	
	ka yō bi	
Wednesday	水曜日	
	sui yō bi	
Thursday	木曜日	
	moku yo bi	
Friday	金曜日	
	kin yō bi	
Saturday	土曜日	
	do yō bi	
today	今日	
	kyō	
tomorrow	明日	
	ashita	
yesterday	昨日	
	kinō	
the day before yesterday	おととい	
	ototoi	
one week	一週間	
	isshū kan	
next week	来週	
	raishū	
last week	先週	
	senshū	

DAYS OF THE MONTH

When saying or writing the date in Japanese, the month always precedes the day.

1	1日 *tsuitachi*	17	17日 *jūshichi nichi*
2	2日 *futsuka*	18	18日 *jūhachi nichi*
3	3日 *mikka*	19	19日 *jūku nichi*
4	4日 *yokka*	20	20日 *hatsuka*
5	5日 *itsuka*	21	21日 *nijūichi nichi*
6	6日 *muika*	22	22日 *nijūni nichi*
7	7日 *nanoka*	23	23日 *nijūsan nichi*
8	8日 *yōka*	24	24日 *nijūyokka*
9	9日 *kokonoka*	25	25日 *nijūgo nichi*
10	10日 *tōka*	26	26日 *nijūroku nichi*
11	11日 *jūichi nichi*	27	27日 *nijūshichi nichi*
12	12日 *jūni nichi*	28	28日 *nijūhachi nichi*
13	13日 *jūsan nichi*	29	29日 *nijūku nichi*
14	14日 *jūyokka*	30	30日 *sanjū nichi*
15	15日 *jūgonichi*	31	31日 *sanjūichi nichi*
16	16日 *jūroku nichi*		

MONTHS OF THE YEAR

January
一月
ichi gatsu

February
二月
ni gatsu

March
三月
san gatsu

April
四月
shi gatsu

May
五月
go gatsu

June
六月
roku gatsu

July
七月
shichi gatsu

August
八月
hachi gatsu

September
九月
ku gatsu

October
十月
jū gatsu

November
十一月
jū ichi gatsu

December
十二月
jū ni gatsu

SEASONS OF THE YEAR

spring
春
haru

summer
夏
natsu

autumn
秋
aki

winter
冬
fuyu

"JAPLISH"

Gairaigo is not to be confused with what is often known as 'Japlish,' or badly misused English that is sometimes incomprehensible and often hilarious. While the prevalence of Japlish is decreasing as English is more widely used in Japan, it is still not unusual to encounter signs warning you to "Take care of your feet" (i.e., watch your step) or department store specials on "flying pans."

Another form of Japlish is English words that are used strictly for their sound or even visual appearance as text, without regard for their literal meanings. This is a common practice among packagers and manufacturers. A popular soft drink bears the name Poccari Sweat; presumably, it does not reveal anything about the ingredients.

Gairaigo (Japanese Loan Words)

Gairaigo refers to Japanese terms that originated from words in foreign languages, mostly English. Though similar in pronunciation to the words of origin, their relationships to the original meanings are sometimes obscure. Here are some examples.

aisu (アイス) : i.e., 'ice'; ice cream, ice pop
baikingu (バイキング): i.e., 'Viking'; buffet, smorgasbord
bebiikaa (ベビーカー): i.e., 'baby car'; stroller, carriage
depâto (デパート): i.e., 'department'; department store
eakon (エアコン): i.e., 'air con'; air conditioning
furiidaiyaru (フリーダイヤル): i.e., 'free dial'; toll-free call
igirisu (イギリス): i.e., Inglez in Portuguese; Englishperson; the UK
kasutera (カステラ): i.e., castela in Dutch; sponge cake
saabisu (サービス): i.e., 'service'; gratis, free-of-charge
sumaato (スマート): i.e., 'smart' (British); slender, svelte
tabako (タバコ): i.e., 'tobacco'; cigarette

JAPANESE GRAMMAR BASICS

Compared to Western languages, little is known about the origins of Japanese or its connections to other tongues. The most popular theory places it in the family that includes Turkish, Mongolian, and Korean. Another theory links it to Polynesian and other languages in the South Pacific. In its present form, Japanese consists of native words as well as loan words from Chinese and Western languages such as English, Portuguese, and German (see page 18).

PRONUNCIATION

Most Japanese syllables consist of either a single vowel, or a consonant + a vowel.

Vowels are either short or long. The sound does not change, only the length of the syllable. However, a short or long vowel can change the meaning of a word entirely. For instance, *shujin* (husband) vs. *shūjin* (prisoner).

PRONUNCIATION GUIDE

Vowels

a: ah like the a in father; hana *(hah-nah)*
ā: elongated a (aah); okāsan *(oh-kaah-sahn)*
i: ee like the ee in feed; migi *(mee-ghee)*
ī: elongated i (eee); kīroi *(keee-ro-ee)*
u: oo like the u in blue; sugu *(soo-ghoo)*
ū: elongated u (ooo); kukan *(kooo-kah-n)*
e: eh like the e in bed; te *(teh)*
ē: elongated e (eeh); dēta *(deeh-tah)*
o: oh like the o in rose; omoi *(oh-moh-ee)*
ō: elongated o (ooh); ōkii *(ooh-kee-ee)*

Vowel Combinations

ai: kaidan *(kah-ee-dah-n)*
ae: mae *(mah-eh)*
ao: aoba *(ah-oh-bah)*
au: kau *(kah-oo)*
ue: tsukue *(tsoo-koo-eh)*

oi: oi *(oh-ee)*
oe: koe *(koh-eh)*

Consonants

k: as in English, like the k in kick; kekkon *(keh-k-koh-n)*
g: as in English, like the g in gum; genkan *(geh-n-kah-n)*
s: as in English, like the s in see; sara *(sah-rah)*
j: as in English, like the j in jump; jikan *(jee-kah-n)*
z: as in English, like the z in zoo; zubon *(zoo-boh-n)*
t: as in English, like the t in time; takai *(tah-kah-ee)*
d: as in English, like the d in dog; daikon *(dah-ee-koh-n)*
n: as in English, like the n in name, or at the end of a word, run;
          naka *(nah-kah)*, hon *(hoh-n)*
h: as in English, like the h in home; hashi *(hah-shee)*
b: as in English, like the b in baby; ban *(bah-n)*
p: as in English, like the p in pepper; pan *(pah-n)*
f: softer than English f and closer to h, like hf; fūsen *(hfoo-seh-n)*
m: as in English, like the m in man; manzoku
          (mah-n-zoh-koo)
y: as in English, like the consonant y in yes; yama *(yah-mah)*
r: closer to English l than r; tap the roof of your palate with
          your tongue; raku *(rah-koo)*
w: as in English, like the w in woman; wakai
          (wah-kah-ee)

Consonant Combinations

ky: ki *(kee)* + ya *(yah)*, yu *(yoo)* or yo *(yoh)*, pronounced almost
          simultaneously; kyaku *(kee-yah-koo)*, Kyōto *(kee-yooh-toh)*,
          kyūkei *(kee-yooo-keh-ee)*
sh: as in English, like sh in she; shabu-shabu *(shah-boo shah-boo)*
ch: as in English, like the ch in cherry; chōcho *(chooh choh)*
tsu: like ts at the end of hats in English, followed by u, although
          the u is nearly silent when it is followed by a consonant;
          tsukuru *(ts(oo)-koo-roo)*

ry: this is possibly the most difficult sound for non-native
speakers to pronounce; ri *(ree)* + ya *(yah)*, yu *(yoo)* or yo
(yoh), pronounced almost simultaneously, remembering
the r is closer to the English l; ryaku *(ree-yah-koo)*, ryūkō
(ree-yooo-kooh); ryōri *(ree-yooh-ree)*

WORD PRONUNCIATION

Japanese has no accented syllables, unlike English, which has
accented and unaccented syllables (e.g., Is THIS the FACE
that LAUNCHED a THOUsand SHIPS?). In spoken Japanese,
all syllables receive the same level of stress. Some commonly
mispronounced Japanese words or names

	Incorrect	Correct
karate	*kah RAH-tee*	*kah-rah-teh*
sashimi	*sah-SHEE-mee*	*sah-shee-mee*
sayōnara	*SAH-yoh-NAH-rah*	*sah-yooh-nah-rah*
sukiyaki	*SOO-kee-YAH-kee*	*soo-kee-yah-kee*
Toyota	*toh-YOH-tah*	*toh-yoh-tah*

SENTENCE CONSTRUCTION

The basic sentence construction in English is:
    subject – verb – object
    i.e. I read a book.

In Japanese, the basic sentence structure is:
    subject – object – verb
    i.e. Watashi wa hon o yomimashita.

The position of subject and object can alternate (Hon o watashi
wa yomimashita), but the verb always goes at the end of the
sentence.
    Subjects and objects are distinguished in the sentence by
particles, or case markers, which follow them.

Particles

wa / ga (no English equivalent) subject **wah / gah**
   Watashi wa ringo o tabemashita.
   I ate an apple.
   Watashi ga ringo o tabemashita.
   It is I who ate the apple.

o (no English equivalent) direct object **oh**
   Jane wa hon o kaimashita.
   Jane bought a book.

Particles also specify such things as to, from, when and where an event is taking place.

de (in, by, with, at) how, where, in what **deh** circumstance
   Te de sētā o araimashita
   I washed the sweater by hand.
   Mary wa doitsu de kenkyū shite imasu
   Mary is doing research in Germany.
   Watashi wa mainichi basu de kayotteimasu.
   I commute by bus everyday.

e (to, toward) direction toward **eh**
   Otōsan wa nyū yōku e ikimasu ka?
   Is your father going to New York?

ka (or) or **kah**
   Kurīmu ka sato wa ikaga desu ka?
   Would you like cream or sugar?

kara (from) starting point **kah-rah**
   Kare wa bosuton kara unten shitekimashita.
   He drove from Boston.

made (up to, until) destination, end point **mah-deh**
   Kuji kara goji made shigoto o shimasu
   I work from nine until five.

ni (to, on, at) target; direction; when **nee**
> **Okāsan ni hana o agemashita.**
> I gave my mother flowers.
> **Watashitachi wa furansu ni ryokō ni ikimasu.**
> We are traveling to France.
> **Asa rokuji ni okiru yotei desu.**
> I plan to get up at six o'clock.

to (and) and **toh**
> **Onīsan to Onēsan wa hawai ni sunde imasu.**
> My older brother and older sister live in Hawaii.

PERSONAL PRONOUNS

I, me	watashi	wah-tah-shee
I, me	boku (male, informal)	boh koo
I, me	atashi (female, informal)	ah-tah-shee
we, us	watashitachi	wah-tah-shee-tah-chee
you (sing.)	anata	ah-nah-tah
you (pl.)	anatatachi	ah-nah-tah-tah-chee
he, him	kare	kah-reh
she, her	kanojo	kah-noh-joh
they, them	karera	kah-reh-rah

Anata (you) is rarely used and can sound presumptuous and unnatural in the wrong context. For second-person direct address (you familiar), the safest bet is to use a proper name (either given or surname, depending on your relationship to that person) + *san*. With small children, *san* becomes *chan* or *kun* (see page 25). Or, if you are asking a question, you can drop the pronoun altogether and use just the interrogative verb form:
> e.g., *Anata ga kimasu ka? Kimasu ka?*
> Are you coming?

POSSESSIVE PRONOUNS

I becomes my, he becomes his and she becomes hers, etc., by adding the particle no (noh) after the pronoun.

I (watashi)	my (watashi no)	watashi no kaban (my bag)
he (kare)	his (kare no)	kare no tokei (his watch)
she (kanojo)	her (kanojo no)	kanojo no kuruma (her car)
we (watashitachi)	our (watashitachi no)	watashitachi no resutoran (our restaurant)
they (karera)	their (karera no)	karera no ie (their home)

A Little Tip

Japanese people introduce themselves with the surname first, followed by the given name (e.g., Watanabe Ken, instead of Ken Watanabe). However, it isn't necessary for non-Japanese to follow suit (e.g., "I'm Smith John"), as most people understand the difference in Japanese and Western conventions.

FORMS OF ADDRESS

As in English, the way you address another person in Japanese depends on your relationship, the context, and your relative social status. But for the most part, the question in English is whether to use a person's first name or last, in Japanese it is a bit more intricate. The honorific title is a suffix that is attached to a person's name (either given or surname).

Title	Appropriate for
-chan *(chah-n)*	young children; used with given name
-kun *(koo-n)*	boys' given name, 'subordinate' males
-sama *(sah-mah)*	after superior's, VIP's or customer's surname; also used in letters
-san *(sah-n)*	the most common and safest option, especially when meeting someone for the first time; can be used with either the given name or surname

As mentioned on page 23, the use of *anata* is not advisable in most situations. To politely address people whose names you do not know, you can use titles based on age and gender. See introductions on page 101.

AGE & GENDER-BASED FORMS OF ADDRESS
bōya *(booh-yah)* young boy
o-bocchan *(oh-boh-t-chah-n)* young boy
ojō-san *(oh-jooh-sah-n)* young girl
onī-san *(oh-neee-sah-n)* young man; lit. 'big brother'
onē-san *(oh-neeh-sah-n)* young woman; lit. 'big sister'
oji-san *(oh-jee-sah-n)* middle-aged man; lit. 'uncle'
oba-san *(oh-bah-sah-n)* middle-aged woman; lit. 'aunt'
ojī-san *(oh-jeee-sah-n)* elderly man; lit. 'grandfather'
obā-san *(oh-baah-sah-n)* elderly woman; lit. 'grandmother'

PROFESSIONAL TITLES
buchō *(boo-chooh)* department manager
kachō *(kah-chooh)* section chief; manager
kōchō *(kooh-chooh)* school principal
sensei *(seh-n-seh-ee)* teacher, professor; also, doctor
shachō *(shah-chooh)* company president
tenchō *(teh-n-chooh)* store manager

VERBS

Unlike verbs in other languages, Japanese verbs are not conjugated according to person, gender, or number. Whether the subject is I, he, she, or they, the verb to walk is always *aruku*. Verbs are conjugated to show tense, negation, and level of completion or duration, as well as the status of the speaker or subject. In informal situations with family or friends, the plain, or dictionary, form of a verb is appropriate. In more formal settings, the polite, or *–masu*, form is called for.

Verbs consist of what is called a stem form, plus an ending. They are categorized according to the endings of their plain forms. The stem form does not change, except in the case of irregular verbs. They are conjugated by changing the endings, or adding a suffix.

'U' Verbs

These are verbs that end with 'u,' or [stem form] + u. They are conjugated by dropping the u and changing the syllable that immediately precedes it.

HANASU: 'to speak'

Plain present	hanasu	hah-nah-soo
Plain past	hanashita	hah-nah-shee-tah
Plain present negative	hanasanai	hah-nah-sah-nah-ee
Plain past negative	hanasanakatta	hah-nah-sah-nah-kah-t-tah
Polite present affirmative	hanashimasu	hah-nah-shee-mah-soo
Polite past affirmative	hanashimashita	hah-nah-shee-mah-shee-tah
Polite present negative	hanashimasen	hah-nah-shee-mah-seh-n
Polite past negative	hanashimasen deshita	hah-nah-shee-mah-seh-n deh-shee-tah

KIKU: to hear, listen

Plain present	kiku	kee-koo
Plain past	kiita	kee-ee-tah
Plain present negative	kikanai	kee-kah-nah-ee
Plain past negative	kikanakatta	kee-kah-nah-kah-t-tah
Polite present affirmative	kikimasu	kee-kee-mah-soo
Polite past affirmative	kikimashita	kee-kee-mah-shee-tah
Polite present negative	kikimasen	kee-kee-mah-seh-n
Polite past negative	kikimasen deshita	kee-kee-mah-seh-n deh-shee-tah

'Ru' Verbs

These are verbs that end with '*ru*', or [stem form] + *ru*. They are conjugated by dropping the *ru*.

TABERU: 'to eat'

Plain present	taberu	tah-beh-roo
Plain past	tabeta	tah-beh-tah
Plain present negative	tabenai	tah-beh-nah-ee
Plain past negative	tabenakatta	tah-beh-nah-kah-t-tah
Polite present affirmative	tabemasu	tah-beh-mah-soo
Polite past affirmative	tabemashita	tah-beh-mah-shee-tah
Polite present negative	tabemasen	tah-beh-mah-seh-n
Polite past negative	tabemasen deshita	tah-beh-mah-seh-n deh-shee-tah

MIRU: 'to see'

Plain present	miru	mee-roo
Plain past	mita	mee-tah
Plain present negative	minai	mee-nah-ee
Plain past negative	minakatta	mee-nah-kah-t-tah
Polite present affirmative	mimasu	mee-mah-soo
Polite past affirmative	mimashita	mee-mah-shee-tah
Polite present negative	mimasen	mee-mah-seh-n
Polite past negative	mimasen deshita	mee-mah-seh-n deh-shee-tah

IRREGULAR VERBS

These are verbs whose stem and ending change in conjugation.

SURU: 'to do'

Plain present	suru	soo-roo
Plain past	shita	shee-tah
Plain present negative	shinai	shee-nah-ee
Plain past negative	shinakatta	shee-nah-kah-t-tah
Polite present affirmative	shimasu	shee-mah-soo
Polite past affirmative	shimashita	shee-mah-shee-tah
Polite present negative	shimasen	shee-mah-seh-n
Polite past negative	shimasen deshita	shee-mah-seh-n deh-shee-tah

KURU: 'to come'

Plain present	kuru	koo-roo
Plain past	kita	kee-tah
Plain present negative	konai	koh-nah-ee
Plain past negative	konakatta	koh-nah-kah-t-tah
Polite present affirmative	kimasu	kee-mah-soo
Polite past affirmative	kimashita	kee-mah-shee-tah
Polite present negative	kimasen	kee-mah-seh-n
Polite past negative	kimasen deshita	kee-mah-seh-n deh-shee-tah

Te (or de) Form

By itself, this verb form is used as an informal request. It is commonly combined with other verbs or suffixes. To denote either past or present, the second, or auxiliary, verb is conjugated.

U Verbs

OYOGU	**oyoide** *(oh-yoh-ee-deh)*	Swim.
KAKU	**kaite** *(kah-ee-teh)*	Write it.

Ru Verbs

OKIRU	**okite** *(oh-kee-teh)*	Wake up.
NERU	**nete** *(neh-teh)*	Go to sleep.

Irregular Verbs

SURU	**shite** *(shee-teh)*	Do.
KURU	**kite** *(kee-teh)*	Come.

Te + IMASU: present progression; "to be doing"
Densha o matte imasu.   I am waiting for a train.
Terebi o mite imasu.   He is watching TV.
Kaban o sagashite imasu.   She is looking for her bag.

Te + KUDASAI: Please (do something); polite request
Namae o kaite kudasai   Please write your name.
Hayaku okite kudasai.   Please wake up early.
Yoku benkyō shite kudasai. Please study well.

Te + AGEMASU: to do something for someone else; a favor to someone else.
Musume ni puresento o katte agemasu.
I will buy my daughter a present.
Gohan o tsukutte agemashita.
I made dinner (for them).
Akachan no furo o junbi shite agemasu.
I will draw the baby's bath.

Note: The *te agemasu* can sound patronizing unless it's used in a proper way. For instance, to say "I bought my daughter a present", *katte agemasu* is OK, but if it is your mother, you would not use the te-agemasu form. Instead, you would simply say *Haha ni purezento o kaimashita.* (I bought my mother a present.) It should be used very carefully when speaking to someone senior or superior to you, or even among equals. It is best to avoid using it whenever in doubt.

Te + MORAU: someone doing something for you; a favor received
Kare ni kuruma o aratte moraimasu.
He is going to wash my car.
Kanojo ni doa o akete moraimashita.
She opened the door for me.
Haha ni shukudai o mite moratte imasu.
My mother is checking my homework.

DESU: to be

The word *desu* is a combination of the particle *de*, the verb *aru* (to exist) and the polite ending *masu*. It is used to express condition or identity, and like all verbs, appears at the end of a sentence.

Plain present	da	dah
Plain past	datta	dah-t-tah
Plain present negative	ja nai	jah-nah-ee
Plain past negative	ja nakatta	jah-nah-kah-t-tah
Polite present affirmative	desu	deh-soo
Polite past affirmative	deshita	deh-shee-tah
Polite present negative	de wa arimasen	deh-wah-ah-ree-mah-seh-n
Polite past negative	de wa arimasen deshita	deh-wah-ah-ree-mah-seh-n deh-shee-tah

ADJECTIVES

In Japanese the adjective appears either before the noun it is modifying, or at the end of the sentence preceding the word desu in conjugated form. For instance,

Sore wa takai tokei desu.
That's an expensive watch.
Sono tokei wa takai desu.
The watch is expensive.

There are two types of adjectives—the *I* adjectives, which are adjectives that end in i, and the *na* adjectives, which are combined with the suffix *–na* when modifying a noun (e.g., *jōzu na hito*, a skilled person). One exception is the word *kirei*, which means pretty or neat. Although it ends with the letter *i*, it is conjugated as a *na* adjective.

I-Adjective
warui: 'bad'

Plain present	warui	wah-roo-ee
Plain past	warukatta	wah-roo-kah-t-tah
Plain present negative	warukunai	wah-roo-koo-nah-ee
Plain past negative	warukunakatta	wah-roo-koo-nah-kah-t-tah
Polite present affirmative	warui desu	wah-roo-ee deh-soo
Polite past affirmative	warukatta desu	wah-roo-kah-t-tah deh-soo
Polite present negative	waruku arimasen	wah-roo-koo ah-ree-mah-seh-n
Polite past negative	waruku arimasen deshita	wah-roo-koo ah-ree-mah-seh-n deh-shee-tah

Na-Adjective
damena: 'failed'

Plain present	dame na	dah-meh nah
Plain past	dame datta	dah-meh dah-t-tah
Plain present negative	dame janai	dah-meh jah nah-ee
Plain past negative	dame janakatta	dah-meh jah nah-kah-t-tah
Polite present affirmative	dame desu	dah-meh deh-soo
Polite past affirmative	dame deshita	dah-meh deh-shee-tah
Polite present negative	dame de wa arimasen	dah-meh deh-wah ah-ree-mah-seh-n
Polite past negative	dame de wa arimasen deshita	dah-meh deh-wah ah-ree-mah-seh-n deh-shee-tah

CHAPTER TWO

GETTING THERE & GETTING AROUND

This section deals with every form of transportation. Whether you've just reached your destination by plane or you're renting a car to tour the countryside, you'll find the phrases you need in the next 27 pages.

AT THE AIRPORT

I am looking for _____	_____はどこですか。
	_____ wa doko desu ka.
a porter.	ポーター
	pōtā
the check-in counter.	チェックイン カウンター
	chekku in kauntā
the ticket counter.	チケット カウンター
	chiketto kauntā
arrivals.	到着ロビー
	tōchaku robī
departures.	出発ロビー
	shuppatsu robī
gate number _____.	_____番ゲート
	_____ban gēto

For full coverage of numbers, see p6.

the waiting area.	待合室
	machiai shitsu
the men's restroom.	男性用トイレ
	dansei yō toire
the women's restroom.	女性用トイレ
	josei yō toire
the police station.	警察の派出所
	keisatsu no hashutsusho
a security guard.	警備員
	keibi in

the smoking area.	喫煙所
	kitsuen jo
the information booth.	案内窓口
	annai madoguchi
a public telephone.	公衆電話
	kōshū denwa
an ATM.	ATM 機
	ATM ki
baggage claim.	手荷物引き渡し所
	tenimotsu hikiwatashi jo
a luggage cart.	荷物運搬カート
	nimotsu unpan kāto
a currency exchange.	外貨両替所
	gaika ryōgae jo
a café.	喫茶店
	kissaten
a restaurant.	レストラン
	resutoran
a bar.	バー
	bā
a bookstore or newsstand.	本屋か新聞雑誌売り場
	hon ya ka shinbun zasshi uriba
a duty-free shop.	免税店
	menzei ten
Is there Internet access here?	ここにはインターネットに接続できるところがありますか？
	koko niwa intānetto ni setsuzoku dekiru tokoro ga arimasu ka.
I'd like to page someone.	呼び出し放送をしていただけますか。
	yobidashi hōsō o shite itadake masu ka.
Do you accept credit cards?	クレジットカードは使えますか？
	kurejitto kādo wa tsukae masu ka

CHECKING IN

I would like a one-way ticket to ____.	____行きの片道航空券を買いたいのですが。
	____ yuki no katamichi kōkūken o kaitai no desuga.
I would like a round trip ticket to ____.	____行きの往復航空券を買いたいのですが。
	____ yuki no ōfuku kōkūken o kaitai no desuga.
How much are the tickets?	その航空券の値段はいくらですか？
	sono kōkūken no nedan wa ikura desu ka.
Do you have anything less expensive?	もう少し安いのはありませんか？
	mō sukoshi yasui nowa arimasen ka.
How long is the flight?	飛行時間はどのくらいですか？
	hikō jikan wa dono kurai desu ka.

For full coverage of number terms, see p6.
For full coverage of time, see p13.

What time does flight ____ leave?	____便は何時に出発しますか？
	____ bin wa nanji ni shuppatsu shimasu ka.
What time does flight ____ arrive?	____便は何時に到着しますか？
	____ bin wa nanji ni tōchaku shimasu ka.
Do I have a connecting flight?	接続便はありますか？
	setsuzoku bin wa arimasu ka.
Do I need to change planes?	飛行機を乗り換える必要がありますか？
	hikōki o norikaeru hitsuyō ga arimasu ka.
My flight leaves at __:__.	私のフライトは __:__ に出発します。
	watashi no furaito wa __:__ ni shuppatsu shimasu.

For full coverage of numbers, see p6.

GETTING THERE

Common Airport Signs

到着	Arrivals
出発	Departures
ターミナル	Terminal
ゲート	Gate
チケット取扱い	Ticketing
税関	Customs
手荷物引き渡し所	Baggage Claim
押す	Push
引く	Pull
禁煙	No Smoking
入口	Entrance
出口	Exit
男性用	Men's
女性用	Women's
シャトルバス	Shuttle Buses
タクシー	Taxis

What time will the flight arrive?	その便は何時に到着しますか？ *sono bin wa nanji ni tōchaku shimasu ka.*
Is the flight on time?	その便は定刻通りに出発しますか？ *sono bin wa teikoku dōri ni shuppatsu shimasu ka.*
Is the flight delayed?	その便は予定より遅れていますか？ *sono bin wa yotei yori okurete imasu ka.*
From which terminal is flight _____ leaving?	_____便の出発ターミナルはどれですか？ *_____ bin no shuppatsu tāminaru wa dore desu ka.*

From which gate is flight ____ leaving?	____便の出発ゲートは何番ですか？
	____ bin no shuppatsu gēto wa nan ban desu ka.
How much time do I need for check-in?	チェックインの手続きにどのくらい時間がかかりますか？
	chekku in no tetsuzuki ni dono kurai jikan ga kakarimasu ka.
Is there an express check-in line?	特別優先チェックインカウンターはありますか？
	tokubetsu yūsen chekku in kauntā wa arimasu ka.
Is there electronic check-in?	自動チェックイン機はありますか？
	jidō chekku in ki wa arimasu ka.

Seat Preferences

I would like ____ ticket(s) in ____	____の航空券を____枚ください。
	____ no kōkūken o ____ mai kudasai.
first class.	ファースト クラス
	fāsuto kurasu
business class.	ビジネス クラス
	bijinesu kurasu
economy class.	エコノミー クラス
	ekonomī kurasu
I would like ____	____ がいいのですが。
	____ ga ii no desuga.
Please don't give me ____	____ 以外のものをください。
	____ igai no mono o kudasai.
a window seat.	窓側の座席
	mado gawa no zaseki
an aisle seat.	通路側の座席
	tsūro gawa no zaseki
an emergency exit row seat.	非常用出口に一番近い座席
	hijōyō deguchi ni ichiban chikai zaseki

a bulkhead seat.	仕切り壁前の座席
	shiki kabe mae no zaseki
a seat by the restroom.	トイレ近くの座席
	toire chikaku no zaseki
a seat near the front.	前方の座席
	zenpō no zaseki
a seat near the middle.	中央部の座席
	chūōbu no zaseki
a seat near the back.	後方の座席
	kōhō no zaseki
Is there a meal on the flight?	機内食は出ますか?
	kinaishoku wa demasu ka.
I'd like to order ____	____をください。
	____ o kudasai.
a vegetarian meal.	ベジタリアン料理
	bejitarian ryōri
I am traveling to ____.	____に旅行に行きます。
	____ ni ryokō ni ikimasu.
I am coming from ____.	____から来ます。
	____ kara kimasu.
I arrived from ____.	____から到着しました。
	____ kara tōchaku shimashita.

For full coverage of country terms, see English / Japanese dictionary.

I'd like to change / cancel / confirm my reservation.	予約の変更 / 取り消し / 確認をしたいのですが。
	yoyaku no henkō / torikeshi / kakunin o shitai no desuga.
I have ____ bags to check.	預ける荷物は ____ 個あります。
	azukeru nimotsu wa ____ ko arimasu.

For full coverage of numbers, see p6.

Passengers with Special Needs

Is that wheelchair accessible?	車椅子で入れますか？
	kurumaisu de haire masu ka.
May I have a wheelchair / walker please?	車椅子か歩行器をお借りできますか？
	kurumaisu ka hokō ki o okari dekimasu ka.
I need some assistance boarding.	搭乗するのを 手伝っていただきたいのですが。
	tōjō suru no o tetsudatte itadakitai no desuga.
I need to bring my service dog.	介護犬を連れて行く必要があります。
	kaigo ken o tsurete iku hitsuyō ga arimasu.
Do you have services for the hearing impaired?	聴覚障害者のためのサービスはありますか？
	chōkaku shōgaisha no tame no sābisu wa arimasu ka.
Do you have services for the visually impaired?	視覚障害者のためのサービスはありますか？
	shikaku shōgaisha no tame no sabisu wa arimasu ka.

Trouble at Check-In

How long is the delay?	どのくらい遅れていますか？
	donokurai okurete imasu ka.
My flight was late.	飛行機の出発が遅れました。
	hikōki no shuppatsu ga okure mashita.
I missed my flight.	飛行機に乗り遅れました。
	hikōki ni nori okure mashita.
When is the next flight?	次の便はいつ出発しますか？
	tsugi no bin wa itsu shuppatsu shimasu ka.

May I have a meal voucher?	食事利用券をいただけますか。
	shokuji riyō ken o itadake masu ka.
May I have a room voucher?	客室利用券をいただけますか。
	kyakushitsu riyō ken o itadake masu ka.

AT CUSTOMS / SECURITY CHECKPOINTS

I'm traveling with a group.	団体で旅行しています。
	dantai de ryokō shite imasu.
I'm on my own.	個人で旅行しています。
	kojin de ryokō shite imasu.
I'm traveling on business.	仕事で来ています。
	shigoto de kite imasu.
I'm on vacation.	休暇中です。
	kyūka chū desu.
I have nothing to declare.	申告するものはありません。
	shinkoku suru mono wa arimasen.
I would like to declare ____.	____を申告します。
	____ *o shinkoku shimasu.*
I have some liquor.	お酒を買いました。
	osake o kai mashita.
I have some cigars.	タバコを買いました。
	tabako o kai mashita.
They are gifts.	これらはもらい物です。
	kore wa morai mono desu.
They are for personal use.	個人用です。
	kojin yō desu.
That is my medicine.	それは私の薬です。
	sore wa watashi no kusuri desu.
I have my prescription.	処方薬を持っています。
	shohōyaku o motte imasu.
My children are traveling on the same passport.	子供たちもこのパスポートで旅行しています。
	kodomotachi mo kono pasupōto de ryokō shite imasu.

I'd like a male / female officer to conduct the search.

検査するのは男性 / 女性の係員にしていただきたいです。
kensa suru nowa dansei / josei no kakari in ni shite itadaki tai desu.

Trouble at Security
Help me. I've lost _____

_____を失くしてしまったのですが、探すのを手伝っていただけませんか。
_____ o nakushite shimatta no desuga, sagasu no o tetsudatte itadake masen ka.

my passport.
私のパスポート
watashi no pasupōto

my boarding pass.
私の搭乗券
watashi no tojoken

Listen Up: Security Lingo

靴を脱いでください。 *kutsu o nuide kudasai.*	Please remove your shoes.
上着 / セーターを脱いでください。 *uwagi / sētā o nuide kudasai.*	Remove your jacket / sweater.
身に付けている貴金属をはずしてください。 *mi ni tsukete iru kikinzoku o hazushite kudasai.*	Remove your jewelry.
カバンをベルトコンベヤーに載せてください。 *kaban o beruto konbeyā ni nosete kudasai.*	Place your bags on the conveyor belt.
横に移動してください。 *yoko ni idō shite kudasai.*	Step to the side.
手で身体検査を行います。 *te de shintai kensa o okonai masu.*	We have to do a hand search.

my identification.	私の身分証明書 *watashi no mibun shōmei sho*
my wallet.	私の財布 *watashi no saifu*
my purse.	私のハンドバッグ *watashi no hando baggu*
Someone stole my purse / wallet!	誰かに財布を盗まれました! *dareka ni saifu o nusumare mashita.*

IN-FLIGHT

It's unlikely you'll need much Japanese on the plane, but these phrases will help if a bilingual flight attendant is unavailable or if you need to talk to a Japanese-speaking neighbor.

I think that's my seat.	それは私の席だと思いますが。 *sore wa watashi no seki dato omoi masuga.*
May I have ____ ?	____をいただけますか? *____ o itadake masu ka.*
water	水 *mizu*
sparkling water	炭酸水 *tansan sui*
orange juice	オレンジ ジュース *orenji jūsu*
soda	ソーダ *sōda*
diet soda	ダイエット ソーダ *daietto sōda*
a beer	ビール *bīru*
wine	ワイン *wain*

For a complete list of drinks, see p79.

a pillow	枕
	makura
a blanket	毛布
	mōfu
a hand wipe	お絞り
	oshibori
headphones	ヘッドホーン
	heddo hōn
a magazine or newspaper	雑誌か新聞
	zasshi ka shinbun

When will the meal be served?
食事はいつ出ますか?
shokuji wa itsu demasu ka.

How long until we land?
あとどれくらいで着きますか?
ato dore kurai de tsuki masu ka.

May I move to another seat?
別の席に移ってもいいですか?
betsu no seki ni utsuttemo iidesu ka.

How do I turn the light on / off?
どうやって点灯 / 消灯しますか。
dōyatte tentō / shōtō shimasu ka.

Trouble In-Flight

These headphones are broken.
このヘッドホーンは壊れています。
kono heddo hōn wa kowarete imasu.

I spilled.
私がこぼしました。
watashi ga koboshi mashita.

My child spilled.
私の子供がこぼしました。
watashi no kodomo ga koboshi mashita.

My child is sick.
子供の具合が悪いのですが。
kodomo no guai ga waruino desuga.

I need an airsickness bag.
飛行機酔いの袋をいただけますか。
hikōki yoi no fukuro o itadeke masuka.

I smell something strange.	変なにおいがします。 *henna nioi ga shimasu.*
That passenger is behaving suspiciously.	あの乗客の様子が変です。 *ano jōkyaku no yōsu ga hen desu.*

BAGGAGE CLAIM

Where is baggage claim for flight ____?	____便の手荷物引き渡し所はどこ ですか？ *____ bin no tenimotsu hikiwatashi jo wa doko desu ka.*
Would you please help with my bags?	荷物を手伝っていただけませんか？ *nimotsu o tetsudatte itadake masen ka.*
I am missing ____ bags.	荷物が ____ つ見つかりません。 *nimotsu ga ____ tsu mitsukari masen.*

*For a full list of numbers used for bags, see the section "Generic
Inanimate Objects on p.11.*

My bag is ____	私の荷物 ____ *watashi no nimotsu ____*
lost.	が失くなりました。 *ga nakunari mashita.*
damaged.	が損傷しました。 *ga sonshō shi mashita.*
stolen.	が盗まれました。 *ga nusumare mashita.*
a suitcase.	はスーツケースです。 *wa sūtsukēsu desu.*
a briefcase.	はブリーフケースです。 *wa burīfukēsu desu.*
a carry-on.	は機内持込み用です。 *wa kinai mochikomi yō desu.*
a suit bag.	はスーツバッグです。 *wa sūtsubaggu desu.*

a trunk.	はトランクです。
	wa toranku desu.
golf clubs.	はゴルフクラブです。
	wa gorufu kurabu desu.

For full coverage of color terms, see English / Japanese Dictionary.

hard.	は硬いです。
	wa katai desu.
made out of ____	____製です。
	____ *sei desu.*
canvas.	キャンバス地
	kyanbasu ji
vinyl.	ビニール
	binīru
leather.	皮
	kawa
hard plastic.	硬いプラスチック
	katai purasuchikku
aluminum.	アルミニウム
	aruminiumu

RENTING A VEHICLE

Is there a car rental agency in the airport?	空港内にレンタカー会社はありますか?
	kūkō nai ni rentakā gaisha wa arimasu ka.
I have a reservation.	予約してあります。
	yoyaku shite arimasu.

Vehicle Preferences

I would like to rent ____	____を借りたいのですが。
	____ *o karitai no desuga.*
an economy car.	エコノミー車
	ekonomī sha
a midsize car.	中型車
	chūgata sha

a sedan.	セダン
	sedan
a convertible.	オープンカー
	ōpun kā
a van.	バン
	ban
a sports car.	スポーツカー
	supōtsu kā
a 4-wheel-drive vehicle.	**4輪駆動車**
	yon rin kudō sha
a motorcycle.	バイク
	baiku
a scooter.	スクーター
	sukūtā
Do you have one with _____?	**_____が付いているのはありますか?**
	_____ ga tsuite iru nowa arimasu ka.
air conditioning	エアコン
	eakon
a sunroof	サンルーフ
	san rūfu
a CD player	**CD**プレーヤー
	CD purēyā
satellite radio	**衛星ラジオ**
	eisei rajio
satellite tracking	**衛星追跡システム**
	eisei tsuiseki shisutemu
an onboard map	**地図**
	chizu
a DVD player	**DVD**プレーヤー
	DVD purēyā
child seat	チャイルドシート
	chairudo shīto
Do you have a _____?	**_____はありますか?**
	_____ wa arimasu ka.

smaller car	もっと小さい車 *motto chiisai kuruma*
bigger car	もっと大きい車 *motto ōkii kuruma*
cheaper car	もっと安い車 *motto yasui kuruma*

Do you have a non-smoking car?
禁煙車はありますか?
kinen sha wa arimasu ka.

I need an automatic transmission.
オートマチック車が欲しいのですが。
ōtomachikku sha ga hoshii no desuga.

A standard transmission is okay.
マニュアル車でもいいです。
manyuaru sha demo ii desu.

May I have an upgrade?
アップグレードできますか?
appu gurēdo dekimasu ka.

Money Matters

What's the daily / weekly / monthly rate?
日/週/月単位の料金はいくらですか?
nichi/shū/tsuki tan i no ryōkin wa ikura desu ka.

How much is insurance?
保険はいくらかかりますか?
hoken wa ikura kakari masu ka.

Are there other fees?
その他にもかかる料金はありますか?
sono hoka nimo kakaru ryōkin wa arimasu ka.

Is there a weekend rate?
週末料金はありますか?
shūmatsu ryōkin wa arimasu ka.

Technical Questions

What kind of fuel does it take?
使用燃料の種類は何ですか?
shiyō nenryō no shurui wa nan desu ka.

Do you have the manual in English?	英語のマニュアルはありますか？
	eigo no manyuaru wa arimasu ka.
Do you have a booklet in English with the local traffic laws?	この地方の交通規則が英語版はありますか？
	kono chihō no kōtsū kisoku ga eigoban wa arimasu ka.

Technical Issues

Fill it up with ____	____で満タンにしてください。
	kono chihō no kōtsū kisoku ga ____ de mantan ni shite kudasai.
Regular	レギュラー・ガソリン
	regyurā gasorin
Diesel	ディーゼル
	dīzeru
Unleaded	無鉛ガソリン
	muen gasorin
The ____ doesn't work.	____が機能しません。
	____ga kinō shimasen.

See diagram on p49 for car parts.

It is already dented.	すでに凹みがあります。
	sudeni hekomi ga arimasu.
It is scratched.	傷があります。
	kizu ga arimasu.
The windshield is cracked.	フロントガラスにヒビが入っています。
	furonto garasu ni hibi ga haitte imasu.
The tires look low.	タイヤの空気圧が低いようです。
	taiya no kūkiatsu ga hikui yō desu.
It has a flat tire.	タイヤがパンクしています。
	taiya ga panku shite imasu.
Whom do I call for service?	サービスを頼むには誰に電話をかければよいですか？
	sābisu o tanomu niwa dare ni denwa o kakereba yoi desuka.
It won't start.	エンジンがかかりません。
	enjin ga kakari masen.

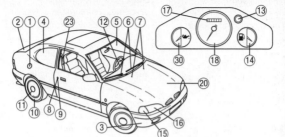

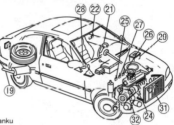

1. ガソリンタンク gasorin tanku
2. トランク toranku
3. バンパー banpā
4. 窓 mado
5. フロントガラス furonto garasu
6. ワイパー waipā
7. フロントガラス ウォッシャー
   furonto garasu wosshā
8. ドア doa
9. ロック rokku
10. タイヤ taiya
11. ホイールキャップ hoīru kyappu
12. ハンドル handoru
13. 非常灯 hijō tō
14. 燃料メーター nenryō mētā
15. ウィンカー winkā
16. ヘッドライト heddo raito
17. 走行距離計 sōkō kyori kei

18. 速度計 sokudo kei
19. マフラー mafurā
20. ボンネット bon netto
21. ハンドル handoru
22. バックミラー bakku mirā
23. シートベルト shīto beruto
24. エンジン enjin
25. アクセル akuseru
26. クラッチ kuracchi
27. ブレーキ burēki
28. サイドブレーキ saido burēki
29. バッテリー batterī
30. オイルゲージ oiru gēji
31. ラジエーター rajiētā
32. ファン ベルト fan beruto

It's out of gas.	ガソリンが入っていません。
	gasorin ga haitte imasen.
The Check Engine light is on.	エンジンのチェックランプが点灯しています。
	enjin no chekku ranpu ga tentō shite imasu.
The oil light is on.	オイル ランプが点灯しています。
	oiru ranpu ga tentō shite imasu.
The brake light is on.	ブレーキ ランプが点灯しています。
	burēki ranpu ga tentō shite imasu.
It runs rough.	走る時激しく振動します。
	hashiru toki hageshiku shindō shimasu.
The car is over-heating.	車がオーバーヒートしています。
	kuruma ga ōbāhīto shite imasu.

Asking for Directions

Excuse me, please.	ちょっとすみませんが。
	chotto sumimasen ga.
How do I get to ____?	____への行き方を教えていただけますか。
	____eno ikikata o oshiete itadake masu ka.
Go straight.	まっすぐ行きます。
	massugu iki masu.
Turn left.	左に曲がります。
	hidari ni magari masu.
Continue right.	そのまま右に進みます。
	sonomama migi ni susumi masu.
It's on the right.	右側にあります。
	migi gawa ni arimasu.
Can you show me on the map?	地図で示していただけませんか?
	chizu de shimeshite itadake masen ka.
How far is it from here?	ここからどれくらいの距離がありますか?
	kokokara dore kurai no kyori ga arimasu ka.

Is this the right road for ____?	____へ行きたいのですがこの道で合っていますか？
	____ e ikitai no desu ga kono michi de atte imasu ka.
I've lost my way.	道に迷ってしまいました。
	michi ni mayotte shimai mashita.
Would you repeat that?	もう一度言っていただけませんか？
	mō ichido itte itadake masen ka.
Thanks for your help.	どうもありがとうございました。
	dōmo arigatō gozai mashita.

For full coverage of direction-related terms, see p4.

Sorry, Officer

What is the speed limit?	制限速度は何キロですか？
	seigen sokudo wa nan kiro desu ka.
I wasn't going that fast.	それほどスピードは出していませんでした。
	sorehodo supīdo wa dashite imasen deshita.
How much is the fine?	罰金はいくらですか？
	bakkin wa ikura desu ka.

Road Signs

制限速度	Speed Limit
停止	Stop
道を譲る	Yield
危険	Danger
行き止まり	No Exit
一方通行	One Way
進入禁止	Do Not Enter
道路閉鎖中	Road Closed
有料	Toll
現金のみ	Cash Only
駐車禁止	No Parking
駐車料金	Parking Fee
車庫	Parking Garage

Where do I pay the fine?	罰金はどこで払えばよいですか？ *bakkin wa doko de haraeba yoi* *desu ka.*
Do I have to go to court?	裁判所に行かなければなりませんか？ *saibansho ni ikanakereba narimasen* *ka.*
I had an accident.	事故に遭いました。 *jiko ni ai mashita.*
The other driver hit me.	相手の運転手が私にぶつかりました。 *aite no untenshu ga watashi ni* *butsukari mashita.*
I'm at fault.	私に落ち度があります。 *watashi ni ochido ga arimasu.*

BY TAXI

Where is the taxi stand?	タクシー乗り場はどこにありますか？ *takushī noriba wa doko ni arimasu* *ka.*

Listen Up: Taxi Lingo

乗ってく下さい！ *notte kudasai.*	Get in!
荷物はそこに置いてください。 私がやります。 *nimotsu wa soko ni oite kudasai.* *watashi ga yarimasu.*	Leave your luggage. I got it.
何人乗りますか？ *nan nin norimasu ka.*	How many passengers?
お急ぎですか？ *oisogi desu ka.*	Are you in a hurry?

Is there a limo / bus / van for my hotel?	ホテルまで行ってくれるリムジンバス / バス / バンはありますか？
	hotel made itte kureru rimujin basu/ basu / ban wa arimasuka.
I need to get to ____.	____に行きたいのですが。
	____ ni ikitai no desuga.
How much will that cost?	料金はいくらくらいかかりますか？
	ryōkin wa ikura kurai kakari masu ka.
How long will it take?	どのくらい時間がかかりますか？
	dono kurai jikan ga kakari masu ka.
Can you take me / us to the train / bus station?	駅 / バス停までお願いします。
	eki / basutei made onegai shimasu.
I am in a hurry.	ちょっと急いでいるんです。
	chotto isoide iru n desu.
Slow down.	速度を落としてください。
	sokudo o otoshite kudasai.
Am I close enough to walk?	ここからだと歩いていけますか？
	kokokara dato aruite ikemasu ka.
Let me out here.	ここで降ろしてください。
	koko de oroshtie kudasai.
That's not the correct change.	おつりが間違っています。
	otsuri ga machigatte imasu.

BY TRAIN

How do I get to the train station?	駅へはどう行きますか。
	eki ewa dō iki masu ka.
Would you take me to the train station?	駅までお願いします。
	eki made onegai shimasu.
How long is the trip to ____?	____まではどのくらいかかりますか？
	____ made wa dono kurai kakari masu ka.
When is the next train?	次の電車はいつ来ますか？
	tsugi no densha wa itsu kimasu ka.
Do you have a schedule / timetable?	時刻表はありますか？
	jikoku hyo wa arimasu ka.

Do I have to change trains?	電車を乗り換える必要がありますか？ *densha o norikaeru hitsuyō ga arimasu ka.*
a one-way ticket	片道切符 *katamichi kippu*
a round-trip ticket	往復切符 *ōfuku kippu*
Which platform does it leave from?	何番線から発車しますか？ *nan ban sen kara hassha shimasu ka.*
Is there a bar car?	ビュッフェはありますか？ *byuffe wa arimasu ka.*
Is there a dining car?	食堂車はありますか？ *shokudō sha wa arimasu ka.*
Which car is my seat in?	私の座席は何号車にありますか？ *watashi no zaseki wa nangōsha ni arimasu ka.*
Is this seat taken?	この席は空いていますか？ *kono seki wa aite imasu ka.*
Where is the next stop?	次の停車駅はどこですか？ *tsugi no teisha eki wa doko desu ka.*
How many stops to ____?	____までは停車駅が何個ありますか？ *____ made wa teisha eki ga nan ko arimasu ka.*
What's the train number and destination?	電車の番号と行き先は何ですか？ *densha no bangō to ikisaki wa nan desu ka.*

BY BUS

How do I get to the bus station?	バス停に行く道を教えていただけませんか。 *basutei ni iku michi o oshiete itadake masen ka.*
Would you take me to the bus station?	バス停まで連れて行っていただけませんか? *basutei made tsurete itte itadake masen ka.*
May I have a bus schedule?	バスの時刻表をもらえますか? *basu no jikokuhyō o moraemasu ka.*
Which bus goes to ____?	____行きのバスはどれですか? *____ yuki no basu wa dore desuka.*
Where does it leave from?	それはどこから発車しますか? *sore wa doko kara hassha shimasu ka.*
How long does the bus take?	このバスでどのくらいかかりますか? *kono basu de dono kurai kakari masu ka.*
How much is it?	それはいくらですか? *sore wa ikura desu ka.*
Is there an express bus?	特急バスはありますか? *tokkyū basu wa arimasu ka.*
Does it make local stops?	各停留所に停車しますか? *kaku teiryūjo ni teisha shimasu ka.*
Does it run at night?	夜間も運行しますか? *yakan mo unkō shimasu ka.*

When does the next bus leave?	次のバスはいつ 発車しますか？
	tsugi no basu wa itsu hassha shimasu ka.
a one-way ticket	片道切符
	katamichi kippu
a round-trip ticket	往復切符
	ōfuku kippu
How long will the bus be stopped?	このバスはどのくらいの時間停車しますか？
	kono basu wa dono kurai no jikan teisha shimasu ka.
Is there an air conditioned bus?	冷房のあるバスはありますか？
	reibō no aru basu wa arimasu ka.
Is this seat taken?	この席は空いていますか？
	kono seki wa aite imasu ka.
Where is the next stop?	次の停留所はどこですか？
	tsugi no teiryūjo wa doko desu ka.
Please tell me when we reach ____.	____に着いたら教えていただけますか。
	____ ni itsuitara oshiete itadake masu ka.
Let me off here.	ここで降ろしてください。
	koko de oroshite kudasai.

BY BOAT OR SHIP

Would you take me to the port?	港までお願いします。
	minato made onegai shimasu.
When does the ship sail?	この船はいつ出航しますか？
	kono fune wa itsu shukkō shimasu ka.
How long is the trip?	目的地まではどのくらいかかりますか？
	mokutekichi made wa dono kurai kakari masu ka.
Where are the life preservers?	救命用具はどこにありますか？
	kyūmei yōgu wa doko ni arimasu ka.

I would like a private cabin.	船室は個室にしてください。 *senshitsu wa koshitsu ni shite kudasai.*
Is the trip rough?	航行中揺れますか？ *kōkōchū yuremasu ka?*
I feel seasick.	船酔いしたみたいです。 *funayoi shita mitai desu.*
I need some seasick pills.	船酔いに効く薬がほしいのですが。 *funayoi ni kiku kusuri ga hoshii no desuga.*
Where is the bathroom?	トイレはどこですか？ *toire wa doko desu ka.*
Does the ship have a casino?	船内にカジノはありますか？ *sennai ni kajino wa arimasu ka.*
Will the ship stop at ports along the way?	途中で停まる港はありますか？ *tochū de tomaru minato wa arimasu ka.*

BY SUBWAY

Where's the subway station?	地下鉄の駅はどこにありますか？ *chikatetsu no eki wa doko ni arimasu ka.*
Where can I buy a ticket?	切符はどこで買えますか？ *kippu wa doko de kaemasu ka.*
Could I have a map of the subway?	地下鉄の地図をいただけますか？ *chikatetsu no chizu o itadake masu ka.*
Which line should I take for ____?	____へ行くにはどの線に乗ればいいですか？ *____ e iku niwa dono sen ni noreba ii desu ka.*
Is this the right line for ____?	____へ行きたいのですがこの線でいいですか？ *____ e ikitai no desuga kono sen de ii desu ka.*

Which stop is it for ____?	____へ行くにはどの駅で降りればいいですか？
	____ e iku niwa dono eki de orireba ii desu ka.
How many stops is it to ____?	____まで停車駅は何個ありますか？
	____ made teisha eki wa nan ko arimasu ka.
Is the next stop ____?	次の駅は____ですか？
	tsugi no eki wa ____ desu ka.
Where are we?	ここはどこですか？
	koko wa doko desu ka.

SUBWAY TICKETS

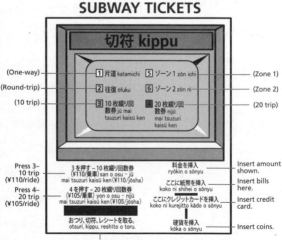

切符 kippu

(One-way)   1 片道 katamichi   5 ゾーン 1 zōn ichi   (Zone 1)
(Round-trip) 2 往復 ōfuku   6 ゾーン 2 zōn ni   (Zone 2)
(10 trip)   3 10 枚綴り回数券 jū mai tsuzuri kaisū ken   8 20 枚綴り回数券 nijū mai tsuzuri kaisū ken   (20 trip)

Press 3–   3 を押す－10 枚綴り回数券   料金を挿入   Insert amount
10 trip   (¥110/乗車) san o osu－jū   ryōkin o sōnyu   shown.
(¥110/ride) mai tsuzuri kaisū ken (¥110/jōsha)
                                           ここに紙幣を挿入   Insert bills
Press 4–   4 を押す－20 枚綴り回数券   koko ni shihei o sōnyu   here.
20 trip   (¥105/乗車) yon o osu－nijū
(¥105/ride) mai tsuzuri kaisū ken (¥105/jōsha)   ここにクレジットカードを挿入   Insert credit
                                           koko ni kurejitto kādo o sōnyu   card.

             おつり、切符、レシートを取る。   硬貨を挿入   Insert coins.
             otsuri, kippu, reshīto o toru.   kōka o sōnyu

(Take change, tickets, receipt)

Where do I change to ____?	____へ行くにはどこで乗り換えればよいですか？
	____ e iku niwa doko de norikaereba yoi desu ka.
What time is the last train to ____?	____ 行きの最終電車は何時ですか？
	____ yuki no saishū densha wa nanji desu ka.

CONSIDERATIONS FOR TRAVELERS WITH SPECIAL NEEDS

Do you have wheelchair access?	車椅子で移動できますか？
	kurumaisu de idō dekimasu ka.
Do you have elevators? Where?	エレベータはありますか？ どこですか。
	erebētā wa arimasu ka. doko desu ka.
Do you have ramps? Where?	スロープはありますか？ どこですか。
	surōpu wa arimasu ka. doko desu ka.
Are the restrooms wheelchair accessible?	トイレには車椅子で入れますか？
	toire niwa kurumaisu de hairemasu ka.
Do you have audio assistance for the hearing impaired?	聴覚障害者のための補聴アシスタンスがありますか？
	chōkaku shōgaisha no tame no hochō ashisutansu ga arimasu ka.
I am deaf.	私は耳が聞こえません。
	watashi wa mimi ga kikoe masen.
May I bring my service dog?	介護犬を連れて行ってもいいですか？
	kaigo ken o tsurete ittemo ii desu ka.
I am blind.	私は目が見えません。
	watashi wa me ga mie masen.
I need to charge my power chair.	電動車椅子を充電する必要があります。
	dendō kurumaisu o jūden suru hitsuyō ga arimasu.

CHAPTER THREE

LODGING

This chapter will help you find the right accommodations, at the right price, and the amenities you might need during your stay.

ROOM PREFERENCES

Please recommend ____

_____を選んでいただけますか。
_____o erande itadake masu ka.

a clean hostel.
清潔なホステル
seiketsu na hosuteru

a moderately priced hotel.
手頃な値段のホテル
tegoro na nedan no hoteru

a moderately priced B&B.
手頃な値段のB & B
tegoro na nedan no B ando B

a good hotel / motel.
良いホテル / モーテル
yoi hoteru / mōteru

Does the hotel have ____?
そのホテルに____はありますか？
sono hoteru ni _____ wa arimasu ka.

a pool
プール
pūru

a casino
カジノ
kajino

suites
スイートルーム
suīto rūmu

a balcony
バルコニー
barukonī

a fitness center
ジム
jimu

a spa
スパ
supa

a private beach
プライベート ビーチ
puraibēto bīchi

a tennis court	テニスコート
	tenisu kōto
I would like a room for _____.	_____の部屋をお願いします。
	_____ *no heya o onegai shimasu.*

For full coverage of number terms, see p6.

I would like _____	_____がいいのですが。
	_____ *ga ii no desuga.*
a king-sized bed.	キングサイズのベッド
	kingu saizu no beddo
a double bed.	ダブル サイズのベッド
	daburu saizu no beddo
twin beds.	ツイン サイズのベッド
	tsuin saizu no beddo
adjoining rooms.	続き部屋
	tsuzuki beya
a smoking room.	喫煙できる部屋
	kitsuen dekiru heya
a non-smoking room.	禁煙の部屋
	kin en no heya

Listen Up: Reservations Lingo

ただいま空室がございません。	We have no vacancies.
tadaima kūshitsu ga gozaimasen.	
何日ご滞在ですか?	How long will you be staying?
nan nichi gotaizai desu ka.	
喫煙または禁煙のどちらがよろしいですか?	Smoking or non smoking?
kitsuen matawa kin en no dochira ga yoroshii desu ka.	

a private bathroom.	プライベート バスルーム *puraibēto basurūmu*
a shower.	シャワー *shawā*
a bathtub.	浴槽 *yokusō*
air conditioning.	エアコン *eakon*
television.	テレビ *terebi*
cable.	ケーブル *kēburu*
satellite TV.	衛星テレビ *eisei terebi*
a telephone.	電話 *denwa*
Internet access.	インターネット接続 *intānetto setsuzoku*
high-speed Internet access.	高速インターネット接続 *kōsoku intānetto setsuzoku*
a refrigerator.	冷蔵庫 *reizōko*
a beach view.	ビーチの見える *bīchi no mieru*
a city view.	街の景色の見える *machi no keshiki no mieru*
a kitchenette.	簡易キッチン *kan i kicchin*
a balcony.	バルコニー *barukonī*
a suite.	スイートルーム *suīto rūmu*
a penthouse.	ペントハウス *pento hausu*

I would like a room _____	_____部屋をお願いしたいのですが。
	_____ heya o onegai shitai no desuga.
on the ground floor.	**1階にある**
	ikkai ni aru
near the elevator.	**エレベーターに近い**
	erevētā ni chikai
near the stairs.	**階段に近い**
	kaidan ni chikai
near the pool.	**プールに近い**
	pūru ni chikai
away from the street.	**道路から離れた**
	dōro kara hanareta
I would like a corner room.	**角部屋をお願いしたいのですが。**
	kado beya o onegai shitai no desuga.
Do you have _____?	**_____はありますか?**
	_____ wa arimasu ka.
a crib	**ベビーベッド**
	bebī beddo
a foldout bed	**折りたたみ式ベッド**
	oritatami shiki beddo

FOR GUESTS WITH SPECIAL NEEDS

I need a room with _____	_____部屋をお願いします。
	_____ heya o onegai shimasu.
wheelchair access.	**車椅子で移動できる**
	kurumaisu de idō dekiru
services for the visually impaired.	**視覚障害者のための設備のある**
	shikaku shōgaisha no tame no setsubi no aru.
services for the hearing impaired.	**聴覚障害者のための設備のある**
	chōkaku shōgaisha no tame no setsubi no aru

| I am traveling with a service dog. | 介護犬を連れているのですが。
kaigo ken o tsurete iru no desuga. |

MONEY MATTERS

I would like to make a reservation.	予約をしたいのですが。 *yoyaku o shitai no desuga.*
How much per night?	一泊の料金はいくらですか？ *ippaku no ryōkin wa ikura desu ka.*
Do you have a ____?	____はありますか？ *____ wa arimasu ka.*
weekly / monthly rate	週 / 月単位の料金 *shū / tsuki tan i no ryōkin*
a weekend rate	週末料金 *shūmatsu ryōkin*
We will be staying for ____ days / weeks.	____日間 / 週間滞在する予定です。 *____ nichikan / shūkan taizai suru yotei desu.*

For full coverage of number terms, see p6.

| When is checkout time? | チェックアウトの時間はいつですか？
chekku auto no jikan wa itsu desu ka. |

For full coverage of time-related terms, see p13.

Do you accept credit cards / travelers checks?	クレジットカード/トラベラーズ チェックは使えますか？ *kurejitto-kādo/toraberāzu-chekku wa tsukae masu ka.*
May I see a room?	お部屋を見せていただけますか？ *oheya o misete itadake masu ka.*
How much are taxes?	税金はいくらですか？ *zeikin wa ikura desu ka.*
Is there a service charge?	サービス料はありますか？ *sābisu ryō wa arimasu ka.*
I'd like to speak with the manager.	マネージャーとお話ししたいのですが。 *manējā to ohanashi shitai no desuga.*

IN-ROOM AMENITIES

I'd like to place an international call.

国際電話をかけたいのですが。
kokusai denwa o kaketai no desuga.

I'd like to place a long-distance call.

市外電話をかけたいのですが。
shigai denwa o kaketai no desuga.

I'd like directory assistance in English.

英語の番号案内にかけたいのですが。
eigo no bangō annai ni kaketai no desuga.

I'd like room service.

ルームサービスをお願いします。
rūmu sābisu o onegai shimasu.

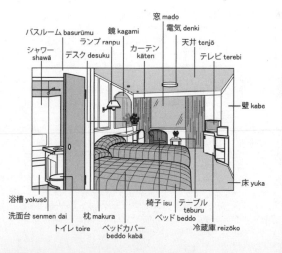

シャワー shawā
バスルーム basurūmu
ランプ ranpu
デスク desuku
鏡 kagami
カーテン kāten
窓 mado
電気 denki
天井 tenjō
テレビ terebi
壁 kabe
床 yuka
浴槽 yokusō
洗面台 senmen dai
枕 makura
トイレ toire
ベッドカバー beddo kabā
椅子 isu
ベッド beddo
テーブル tēburu
冷蔵庫 reizōko

I'd like maid service.	メードのサービスをお願いします。
	mēdo no sābisu o onegai shimasu.
I'd like the front desk	フロントデスクをお願いします。
	furonto desuku o onegai shimasu.
Do you have room service?	ルームサービスはありますか?
	rūmu sābisu wa arimasu ka.
When is the kitchen open?	食事は何時からできますか?
	shokuji wa nanji kara deki masu ka.
When is breakfast served?	朝食は何時ですか?
	chōshoku wa nan ji desu ka.

For full coverage of time-related terms, see p13.

Do you offer massages?	マッサージのサービスはありますか?
	massāji no sābisu wa arimasu ka.
Do you have a lounge?	ラウンジはありますか?
	raunji wa arimasu ka.
Do you have a business center?	ビジネスセンターはありますか?
	bijinesu sentā wa arimasu ka.
Do you serve breakfast?	朝食は出ますか?
	chōshoku wa demasu ka.

Instructions for Dialing the Hotel Phone

他の部屋に電話をかけるには部屋番号をダイヤルします。 *hoka no heya ni denwa o kakeru niwa, heya bangō o daiyaru shimasu.*	To call another room, dial the room number.
市内電話をかけるには、最初に9をダイヤルします。 *shinai denwa o kakeru niwa, saisho ni kyū o daiyaru shimasu.*	To make a local call, first dial 9.
オペレーターを呼びだすには、0をダイヤルします。 *operētā o yobi dasu niwa, zero o daiyaru shimasu.*	To call the operator, dial 0.

Do you have Wi-Fi?	ワイヤーレスインターネット はありますか？
	waiyāresu intānetto wa arimasu ka.
May I have a newspaper in the morning?	朝、新聞をもらえますか？
	asa, shinbun o morae masu ka.
Do you offer a tailor service?	仕立屋のサービスはありますか？
	shitateya no sābisu wa arimasu ka.
Do you offer laundry service?	ランドリー サービスはありますか？
	randorī sābisu wa arimasu ka.
Do you offer dry cleaning?	ドライ クリーニングのサービスはありますか？
	dorai kurīningu no sābisu wa arimasu ka.
May we have ____?	____いただけませんか？
	____ *itadake masen ka.*
clean sheets today	今日、きれいなシーツ
	kyō, kirei na shītsu
more towels	タオルをもっと
	taoru o motto
more toilet paper	トイレット ペーパーをもっと
	toirctto pēpā o motto
extra pillows	枕をもっと
	makura o motto
Do you have an ice machine?	製氷機はありますか？
	seihyō ki wa arimasu ka.
Did I receive any ____?	私に____はありますか？
	watashi ni ____ wa arimasu ka.
messages	伝言
	dengon
mail	手紙
	tegami
faxes	ファックス
	fakkusu
A spare key, please.	スペアー キーをください。
	supeā kī o kudasai.

More hangers please.	ハンガーをもっとください。
	hangā o motto kudasai.
I am allergic to down pillows.	私は羽毛の枕にアレルギー反応が起きます。
	watashi wa umō no makura ni arerugī hannō ga okimasu.
I'd like a wake up call.	モーニングコールをお願いします。
	mōningu kōru o onegai shimasu.

For full coverage of time-related terms, see p13.

Do you have alarm clocks?	目覚まし時計はありますか？
	mezamashi dokei wa arimasu ka.
Is there a safe in the room?	室内に金庫はありますか？
	shitsu nai ni kinko wa arimasu ka.
Does the room have a hair dryer?	室内にヘアードライヤーはありますか？
	shitsu nai ni heā doraiyā wa arimasu ka.

HOTEL ROOM TROUBLE

May I speak with the manager?	マネージャーとお話したいのですが。
	manējā to ohanashi shitai no desuga.
The television does not work.	テレビが見れないんです。
	terebi ga mirenai n desu.
The telephone does not work.	電話が使えないんです。
	denwa ga tsukaenai n desu.
The air conditioning does not work.	エアコンがきかないんです。
	eakon ga kikanai n desu.
The Internet access does not work.	インターネットの接続ができないんです。
	intānetto no setsuzoku ga dekinai n desu.
The cable TV does not work.	ケーブルテレビが見れないんんです。
	kēburu terebi ga mirenai n desu.

There is no hot water.

お湯が出ないんです。
oyu ga denai n desu.

The toilet is over-flowing!

トイレの水が溢れているんです！
toire no mizu ga afurete irun desu.

This room is _____

この部屋は _____
kono heya wa _____

  too noisy.

  騒音がひど過ぎます。
  sōon ga hido sugi masu.

  too cold.

  寒すぎます。
  samu sugi masu.

  too warm.

  暖か過ぎます。
  atataka sugi masu.

This room has _____

この部屋に_____がいます。
kono heya ni_____ ga imasu.

  bugs.

  虫
  mushi

  mice.

  ねずみ
  nezumi

I'd like a different room.

別の部屋に替えていただけませんか。
betsu no heya ni kaete itadake masen ka.

Do you have a bigger room?

これより大きい部屋はあり ますか？
kore yori ōkii heya wa arimasu ka.

I locked myself out of my room.	ドアに鍵がかかってしまい部屋に入ることができないんです。
	doa ni kagi ga kakatte shimai heya ni hairu koto ga deki nai n desu.
Do you have any fans?	扇風機はありますか？
	senpūki wa arimasu ka.
The sheets are not clean.	シーツが汚れています。
	shītsu ga yogorete imasu.
The towels are not clean.	タオルが汚れています。
	taoru ga yogorete imasu.
The room is not clean.	部屋が汚れています。
	heya ga yogorete imasu.
The guests next door / above / below are being very loud.	隣 / 上の階 / 下の階の部屋がとてもうるさいんです。
	tonari / ue no kai / shita no kai no heya ga totemo urusai n desu.

CHECKING OUT

I think this charge is a mistake.	この請求額は間違っていると思います。
	kono seikyū gaku wa machigatte iru to omoi masu.
Please explain this charge to me.	なぜこの請求額になるのか説明していただけますか。
	naze kono seikyūgaku ni naru noka setsumei shite itadake masu ka.
Thank you, we enjoyed our stay.	楽しく滞在しました。ありがとうございました。
	tanoshiku taizai shimashita. arigatō gozaimashita.
The service was excellent.	サービスがとてもよかったです。
	sābisu ga totemo yokatta desu.
The staff is very professional and courteous.	スタッフはとてもプロフェッショナルで親切です。
	sutaffu wa totemo purofesshonaru de shinsetsu desu.

Please call a cab for me.	タクシーを呼んでいただけますか。 *takushī o yonde itadake masu ka.*
Would someone please get my bags?	どなたか 私の荷物を取ってきていた だけませんか？ *donata ka watashi no nimotsu o totte kite itadake masen ka.*

HAPPY CAMPING

I'd like a site for ____	____場所が欲しいんですが。 _____ *basho ga hoshii n desuga.*
a tent.	テントを張る *tento o haru*
a camper.	キャンパーのための *kyanpā no tame no*
Are there ____?	ここに ___はありますか？ *koko ni ____ wa arimasu ka.*
bathrooms	トイレ *toire*
showers	シャワー *shawā*
Is there running water?	ここに水道水はありますか？ *koko ni suidōsui wa arimasu ka.*
Is the water drinkable?	この水は飲めますか？ *kono mizu wa nome masu ka.*
Where is the electrical hookup?	電気の接続部はどこにありますか？ *denki no setsuzoku bu wa doko ni arimasu ka.*

CHAPTER FOUR

DINING

This chapter includes a menu reader and the language you need to communicate in a range of dining establishments and food markets.

FINDING A RESTAURANT

Would you recommend a good ____ restaurant?	よい____を教えていただけませんか? *yoi ____ o oshiete itadake masen ka.*
local	地元のレストラン *jimoto no resutoran*
Chinese	中華料理店 *chūka ryōri ten*
family	ファミリーレストラン *famirī resutoran*
French	フレンス料理のレストラン *furansu ryōri no resutoran*
Indian	インド料理のレストラン *indo ryōri no resutoran*
Italian	イタリア料理のレストラン *itaria ryōri no resutoran*
gastropub / dining bar (izakaya)	居酒屋 *izakaya*
Japanese	和食の店 *washoku no mise*
Korean	韓国料理店 *kankoku ryōri ten*
pizza	ピザ屋 *piza ya*
steakhouse	ステーキハウス *sutēki hausu*

Thai	タイ料理の店 *tai ryōri no mise*
vegetarian	ベジタリアンのレストラン *bejitarian no resutoran*
Western	洋食屋 *yō shoku ya*
buffet	バイキング *baikingu*
inexpensive (budget)	あまり高くないレストラン *amari takaku nai resutoran*

Which is the best restaurant in town?
この街で最高のレストランはどれですか?
kono machi de saikō no resutoran wa dore desu ka

Is there a late-night restaurant nearby?
この近くに深夜営業しているレストランはありますか?
kono chikaku ni shinya eigyō shite iru resutoran wa arimasu ka.

Is there a restaurant that serves breakfast nearby?
この近くに朝食を出すレストランはありますか?
kono chikaku ni chōshoku o dasu resutoran wa arimasu ka.

Is it very expensive?
値段は高いですか?
nedan wa takai desu ka.

Do I need a reservation?
予約が必要ですか?
yoyaku ga hitsuyō desu ka.

Do I have to dress up?
正装しなければなりませんか。
seisō shinakere ba nari masen ka.

Do they serve lunch?
ランチはやってますか?
ranchi wa yatte masu ka.

What time do they open for dinner?
ディナーは何時からですか?
dinā wa nan ji kara desu ka.

For lunch?
ランチは何時からですか?
ranchi wa nan ji kara desu ka.

What time do they close?	何時に閉店しますか？ *nan ji ni heiten shimasu ka.*
Do you have a take out menu?	持帰り用のメニューはありますか？ *mochi kaeri yō no menyū wa arimasu ka.*
Do you have a bar?	バーはありますか？ *bā wa arimasu ka.*
Is there a café nearby?	この近くに喫茶店はありますか？ *kono chikaku ni kissa ten wa arimasu ka.*

GETTING SEATED

Are you still serving?	まだ開いていますか？ *mada aite imasu ka.*
How long is the wait?	どのくらい待ちますか？ *dono kurai machi masu ka.*
Do you have a no-smoking section?	禁煙席はありますか？ *kin en seki wa arimasu ka.*
A table for ____, please.	____人座れるテーブルをお願いします。 *____ nin suwareru tēburu o onegai shimasu.*

For a full list of numbers, see p6.

Do you have a quiet table?	静かなテーブル席はありますか？ *shizukana tēburu seki wa arimasu ka.*
May we sit outside / inside please?	外 / 中に座ってもいいですか？ *soto / naka ni suwattemo ii desu ka.*
May we sit at the counter?	カウンターに座ってもいいですか？ *kauntā ni suwatte mo ii desu ka.*
A menu please?	メニューを見せてください。 *menyū o misete kudasai.*

Listen Up: Restaurant Lingo

喫煙席と禁煙席、どちらがよろし
いですか?
*kitsu en seki to kin en seki ,
dochira ga yoroshii desu ka.*

Smoking or
nonsmoking?

上着とネクタイが要ります。
uwagi to nekutai ga iri masu.

You'll need a tie and
jacket.

申し訳ございませんが 半ズボン
ではお入りいただけません。
*mōshiwake gozai masen
ga han zubon dewa o hairi
itadake masen*

I'm sorry, no shorts are
allowed.

何かお飲み物をお持ちしまし
ょうか?
*nani ka onomimono o omochi
shima shō ka.*

May I bring you
something to drink?

ワイン リストをご覧になりま
すか?
*wain risuto o goran ni
narimasu ka.*

Would you like to see
a wine list?

当店のスペシャルをご説明しま
しょうか?
*tōten no supesharu o
gosetsumei shima shō ka.*

Would you like to hear
our specials?

ご注文はお決まりですか?
gochūmon wa okimari desu ka

Are you ready to order?

申し訳ございませんが、クレジッ
トカードが拒否されました。
*mōshiwake gozai masen ga,
kurejitto kādo ga kyohi sare
mashita.*

I'm sorry, sir, your credit
card was declined.

ORDERING

Do you have a special tonight?	今夜はスペシャルはありますか？ *konya wa supesharu wa arimasu ka.*
What do you recommend?	何がお勧めですか？ *nani ga osusume desu ka.*
May I see a wine list?	**ワインリストを見せていただけますか？** *wain risuto o misete itadake masu ka.*
Do you serve wine by the glass?	**グラスワインはありますか？** *gurasu wain wa arimasu ka.*
May I see a drink list?	飲み物のメニューを見せていただけますか？ *nomi mono no menyū o misete itadake masu ka.*
I would like it cooked ____	____でお願いします。 ____ *de onegai shimasu.*
rare.	レア *rea*
medium rare.	ミディアム レア *midiamu rea*
medium.	ミディアム *midiamu*
medium well.	ミディアム ウェル *midiamu weru*
well.	ウェルダン *werudan*
charred.	ベリーウェル *berī weru*
Do you have a ____ menu?	____向けメニューはありますか？ ____ *muke menyū wa arimasu ka.*
vegetarian	ベジタリアン *bejitarian*
children's	子供 *kodomo*

What is in this dish?	この料理には何が入っていま *kono ryōri niwa nani ga haitte* *ka.*
How is it prepared?	どのように調理されていますか？ *donoyō ni chōri sarete imasu ka.*
What kind of oil is that cooked in?	これにはどんなオイルが 使われていますか？ *kore niwa donna oiru ga* *tsukawarete imasu ka.*
Do you have any low-salt dishes?	減塩の料理はありますか？ *gen en no ryōri wa arimasu ka.*
On the side, please.	横に添えてください。 *yoko ni soete kudasai.*
May I make a substitution?	ほかのものに替えていいですか？ *hoka no mono ni kaete ii desu ka.*
I'd like to try that.	それを食べてみます。 *sore o tabete mimasu.*
Is that fresh?	それは新鮮ですか？ *sore wa shinsen desu ka.*
Excuse me! (to summon a waiter)	すみません！ *sumi masen.*
Extra butter, please.	バターをもう少しください。 *batā o mō sukoshi kudasai.*
No butter, thanks.	バターは要りません。 *batā wa iri masen.*
No cream, thanks.	クリームは要りません。 *kurīmu wa iri masen.*
Dressing on the side, please.	ドレッシングを横に添えてください。 *doressingu o yokoni soete kudasai.*
No salt, please.	塩を入れないでください。 *shio o ire naide kudasai.*
May I have some oil, please?	油をもらえますか？ *abura o morae masu ka.*

パンをもう少しいただけますか。
pan o mō sukoshi itadake masu ka.

私は牛乳が飲めません。
watashi wa gyūnyū ga nome masen.

牛乳が入っていないものでは何がお勧めですか？
gyūnyū ga haitte inai mono dewa nani ga osusume desu ka.

I am allergic to _____

_____にアレルギーがあります。
_____ ni arerugī ga arimasu.

seafood.

魚介類
gyokairui

shellfish.

貝類
kai rui

nuts.

ナッツ類
nattsu rui

peanuts.

ピーナッツ
pīnattsu

Water _____, please.

_____水をお願いします。
_____ mizu o onegai shimasu.

with ice

氷の入っている
kōri no haitte iru

without ice

氷の入っていない
kōri no haitte inai

I'm sorry, I don't think this is what I ordered.

すみませんが、これは私が注文したのと違うようです。
sumi masen ga, kore wa watashi ga chūmon shita no to chigau yō desu.

My meat is a little over / under cooked.

肉が少し焼きすぎています / よく焼けていません。
niku ga sukoshi yake sugite imasu / yoku yakete imasen.

My vegetables are a little over / under cooked.	野菜が少し煮えすぎています / よく煮えていません。 *yasai ga sukoshi nie sugite imasu / yoku niete imasen.*
There's a bug in my food!	食べ物の中に虫が入っています! *tabemono no naka ni mushi ga haitte imasu.*
May I have a refill?	お代わりをいただけますか? *okawari o itadake masu ka.*
A dessert menu, please.	デザートのメニューを見せてください。 *dezāto no menyū o misete kudasai.*

DRINKS

alcoholic	アルコール *arukōru*
neat / straight	ストレートで *sutorēto de*
on the rocks	ロックで *rokku de*
with (seltzer or soda) water	(炭酸水またはソーダ) 水で *(tansansui / sōda) sui de*
draft beer	生ビール *nama bīru*
bottle beer	ビンビール *bin bīru*
wine	ワイン *wain*
house wine	ハウスワイン *hausu wain*
sweet wine	甘口ワイン *amakuchi wain*
dry white wine	辛口白ワイン *karakuchi shiro wain*

rosé	ロゼ *roze*
scotch	スコッチ *sukocchi*
red wine	赤ワイン *aka wain*
whiskey	ウイスキー *uisukī*
sparkling sweet wine	甘口スパークリング ワイン *amakuchi supākuringu wain*
chuhai	酎ハイ *chūhai*
liqueur	リキュール *rikyūru*
brandy	ブランデー *burandē*
cognac	コニャック *konyakku*
gin	ジン *jin*
vodka	ウオッカ *uokka*
rum	ラム *ramu*
nonalcoholic	ノンアルコールの *non arukōru no*
hot chocolate	ホット チョコレート *hotto chokorēto*
lemonade	レモネード *remonēdo*
milkshake	ミルクセーキ *miruku sēki*
milk	ミルク *miruku*

tea	紅茶 *kōcha*
coffee	コーヒー *kōhī*
cappuccino	カプチーノ *kapuchīno*
espresso	エスプレッソ *esupuresso*
iced coffee	アイス コーヒー *aisu kōhī*
fruit juice	フルーツ ジュース *furūtsu jūsu*

For a full list of fruits, see p93.

SETTLING UP

I'm stuffed.	お腹が一杯です。 *onaka ga ippai desu.*
The meal was excellent.	とてもおいしかったです。 *totemo oishikatta desu.*
There's a problem with my bill.	お勘定が違うようなんですが。 *okanjō ga chigau yō nan desuga.*
My compliments to the chef!	シェフにとてもおいしかったと伝えてください! *shefu ni totemo oishikatta to tsutaete kudasai.*
Check, please.	お勘定をお願いします。 *okanjō o onegai shimasu.*

MENU READER

Japanese cuisine is far more varied than the offerings of most overseas Japanese restaurants, ranging from astronomically expensive haute cuisine to street food. While this is not a comprehensive guide, it will give you some idea of the diversity of the foods of Japan.

KAISEKI (懐石、会席)

These elaborate multi-course meals are becoming increasingly popular in the US. There are two types of *kaiseki*. One is based on the traditional *cha-kaiseki* (茶懐石), or food served during the traditional tea ceremony. Similar to the French menu *dégustation*, it involves multiple courses of small but elaborate dishes that vary according to season. The courses are predetermined; you do not order individual items. It is usually served at high-end Japanese restaurants known as *ryōtei* (料亭) and *kappō* (割烹), although nowadays, the word has become a catch-all name for any high-end tasting menu, so it is not unusual to find places offering French *kaiseki* menus.

The other form of *kaiseki* (会席) is served at banquets and is tailored toward drinking, featuring many dishes that go well with alcohol, which include *sashimi*, *tempura*, *aemono* and *sunomono*. The first part consists of an appetizer (*zensai*, 前菜), clear soup (*suimono*, 吸い物), and sashimi. The second part includes dishes that are grilled (*yakimono*, 焼物), steamed (*mushimono*, 蒸物), simmered (*nimono*, 煮物) and deep-fried (*agemono*, 揚物). An alternative to these would be a one-pot stew (*nabemono*, 鍋物). A salad, either vinegared (*sunomono*, 酢の物) or marinated (*aemono*, 和え物), also comes with this course. The final part is a course of boiled plain rice (*gohan*, 御飯), miso soup (*miso shiru*, 味噌汁), and pickles (*tsukemono*, 漬け物), served with green tea and some kind of fresh fruit.

BENTO (弁当)

Typically prepared for school and office lunchboxes, the bento is a boxed meal consisting of rice, pickles, and assorted finger foods. These can be found at any convenience store, supermarket or kiosk at a large train station. Bento sold at train stations are called *ekiben* (駅弁), and often contain some local flavor.

TEISHOKU (定食)

Teishoku are inexpensive set meals, usually consisting of meat or fish, some sides, soup and rice, which are all served at once. Restaurants that specialize in them, *teishoku-ya*, are comparable to luncheonettes or diners in the US.

IF YOU KNEW SUSHI

The popular combo of raw fish and vinegar-seasoned rice comes from an ages old means of preserving fish. Sushi comes in a variety of forms:

Nigirizushi (握りずし): a small handful of rice topped with fish or other seafood and a dab of wasabi paste; also sometimes known as *Edomae* (江戸前) sushi.

Makizushi (巻ずし): rice and fillings rolled inside a wrapping of dried seaweed (*nori*) with the use of a flexible bamboo mat. The best-known example is *tekkamaki* (てっか巻き), or raw tuna.

Chirashizushi (散らしずし): sometimes called *barazushi* (ばらずし), or literally 'scattered sushi.' It consists of various, usually colorful, toppings attractively arranged on top of a bed of seasoned rice. Unlike *nigirizushi* or *makizushi*, which can be eaten by hand, it must be eaten with utensils.

inarizushi (いなりずし): sushi rice stuffed into pockets of sweetened thin, deep-fried tofu called *abura-age* (あぶらあげ). *Inari* is a Shinto deity who is associated with foxes. Foxes were believed to have a fondness for *abura-age*, hence the name.

oshizushi (おしずし): A style of sushi that originated in Osaka, it consists of sushi rice and fish pressed into a rectangular box and then cut into slices. The best-known version is *battera*, which is rice topped with seasoned mackerel and a thin slice of *konbu* (昆布).

FOOD TERMS

CONDIMENTS / SAUCES / SPICES
furikake ふりかけ: topping for hot rice, usually ground dried fish and nori, with salt
goma 胡麻: sesame
karashi からし: Japanese mustard
kinako 黄粉: soybean flour
kōshinryō 香辛料: spice
mirin みりん: sweet liquid flavoring
miso 味噌: fermented soybean paste
ponzu ぽん酢: condiment of citrus juice, vinegar and soy sauce
shōyu 醤油: soy sauce
tare たれ: sauce
tōgarashi 唐辛子: chili pepper
wasabi わさび: Japanese horseradish

GARNISHES / SIDES
fukujinzuke 福神漬け: pickled vegetables
gari がり: thinly sliced vinegared ginger
hijiki ひじき: seaweed
kinpira gobō きんぴらごぼう: burdock

konbu 昆布: kelp
nattō 納豆: fermented soybeans
nori のり: dried laver
shōga 生姜: ginger
takuan 沢庵: pickled daikon radish
tsukemono 漬け物: pickles
umeboshi 梅干し: pickled japanese plum
wakame わかめ: seaweed

GRAINS / RICE / RICE DISHES

chāhan チャーハン: fried rice
donburi 丼: bowl of rice topped with food
genmai 玄米: brown rice
gohan 御飯: cooked rice
gomoku meshi 五目飯: rice dish with chicken and assorted vegetables
kama meshi 釜飯: rice cooked in a large pot over a hearth
katsudon カツ丼: pork donburi
kayu 粥: rice porridge
kome 米: rice
meshi 飯: informal term for food or meal
mochi もち: rice cake
mugi 麦: grain; usually refers to barley
ojiya おじや: rice gruel; also called zōsui (雑炊)
oyako donburi 親子丼: chicken and egg donburi

MEATS / POULTRY

butaniku 豚肉: pork
gibie ジビエ: wild game in season
gyūniku 牛肉: beef
hitsuji 羊: lamb
horumon ホルモン: offal, variety meats
kamo 鴨: duck

katsu カツ: breaded and deep-fried meat, fish or chicken

motsu もつ: giblets, viscera

niku 肉: meat

nikujaga 肉じゃが: simmered dish of meat, potatoes and vegetables

shamo しゃも: gamecock, game fowl

tamago 卵 or 玉子: egg

toriniku 鳥肉: chicken meat

NOODLES

kitsune soba / udon きつねそば/うどん: noodles served with abura-age

rāmen ラーメン: Chinese-style noodles served in stock

soba そば: buckwheat noodles

sōmen 素麺: thin wheat noodles

udon うどん: soft, thick wheat noodles

udonsuki うどんすき: udon cooked in clear soup with vegetables and chicken or fish

SEAFOOD

aji あじ: horse mackerel

anago 穴子: saltwater conger eel

ankō あんこう: angler fish

awabi あわび: abalone

ayu 鮎: freshwater sweetfish

dojō どじょう: loach, a freshwater fish

ebi えび: prawn, shrimp, lobster

fugu ふぐ: puffer, blowfish

hamaguri はまぐり: clam

hamo はも: freshwater eel

hokke ほっけ: mackerel

hotategai 帆立て貝: scallop

ika いか: squid

ikura イクラ: salmon eggs
inada いなだ: young yellowtail tuna, also called hamachi (はまち)
iwashi いわし: sardine
kai 貝: mollusk
kaki かき: oyster
kamaboko 蒲鉾: processed fish paste
kani かに: crab
karasumi からすみ: dried mullet roe
katsuo かつお: bonito
katsuobushi カツオ節: dried bonito
kazunoko 数の子: herring roe
kegani 毛がに: hairy crab
koi 鯉: carp
maguro まぐろ: northern bluefin tuna
mentaiko 明太子: salted, spicy pollack roe
saba さば: chub mackerel
sakana 魚: fish
sanma さんま: Pacific saury
sake さけ: salmon
shirako 白子: soft roe; fish semen
suppon すっぽん: snapping turtle
surume するめ: dried squid
tai 鯛: sea bream; red snapper
tako たこ: octopus
takoyaki たこやき: grilled chopped octopus in batter
tara たら: cod
toro とろ: fatty tuna meat
unagi うなぎ: sea-born eel that migrates to freshwater
uni うに: sea urchin

SOUPS / STEWS / STOCK

chirinabe ちり鍋: *nabemono* of meat or fish, tofu and vegetables served with dipping sauce

dashi だし: soup stock made with fish and kelp

miso shiru 味噌汁: miso soup

mizutaki 水炊き: chicken *nabemono*

nabemono 鍋物: one-pot dish; stew

suimono 吸い物: clear soup

sumashijiru すまし汁: clear soup

zōni ぞうに: *mochi* in soup

SWEETS / SNACKS / DESSERTS

anko あんこ: sweet red bean paste

annindōfu 杏仁豆腐: almond jelly

kasutera カステラ: Castella cake

manjū まんじゅう: steamed bun with sweet or savory filling

senbei 煎餅: rice cracker

taiyaki たいやき: sweet cake shaped like a sea bream

wagashi 和菓子: Japanese confections, cakes, candy, cookies

yōkan 羊羹: sweet red bean jelly

TEA

bancha 番茶: common green tea

cha 茶: tea

genmaicha 玄米茶: green tea with roasted rice grains added for flavor

hōjicha 焙じ茶: roasted green tea

maccha 抹茶: powdered green tea

mugicha 麦茶: barley tea

sencha 煎茶: higher-quality green tea usually reserved for guests

SPECIALTIES

fucha ryōri 普茶料理: Zen Buddhist vegetarian cuisine

izakaya 居酒屋: Japanese gastropub or dining bar

kabayaki かばやき: grilled fish or eel basted in a thick, sweet sauce

kappō 割烹: upscale Japanese restaurant

kushiyaki 串焼き: spit-roasting

kyō ryōri 京料理: Kyoto-style cuisine

oden おでん: Japanese hodgepodge

okonomiyaki お好み焼き: savory pancake

omakase おまかせ: chef's menu

osechi ryōri おせち料理: food for celebrating the New Year

robatayaki ろばたやき: grilled food prepared in front of you

ryōtei 料亭: upscale Japanese restaurant

shabu-shabu しゃぶしゃぶ: *nabemono* of thinly sliced meat and vegetables served with dipping sauce

shōjin ryori 精進料理: vegetarian cuisine derived from the diet of Buddhist monks

sukiyaki すきやき: *nabemono* of meat and vegetables

sumibiyaki 炭火焼き: charcoal grilling

tempura 天ぷら: battered and deep-fried seafood and vegetables

teppanyaki 鉄板焼き: meat and vegetables grilled on an iron hot plate in front of you, à la Benihana

yakiniku 焼き肉: meat grilled on a griddle, usually over charcoal

yakitori 焼き鳥: chicken meat and parts grilled on a skewer

BUYING GROCERIES

In Japan, groceries can be bought at convenience stores, neighborhood stores, or large supermarkets.

AT THE SUPERMARKET

Where can I find ____?	____はどこににありますか？
	____ wa doko ni arimasu ka.
spices	スパイス
	supaisu
toiletries	化粧品
	keshōhin
paper plates and napkins	紙皿とナプキン
	kamizara to napukin
canned goods	缶詰
	kanzume
snack food	軽食
	keishoku
baby food	ベビーフード
	bebī fūdo
water	水
	mizu
juice	ジュース
	jūsu
bread	パン
	pan
cheese	チーズ
	chīzu
fruit	果物
	kudamono
cookies	クッキー
	kukkī

AT THE BUTCHER SHOP

Is the meat fresh?	この肉は新鮮ですか？
	kono niku wa shinsen desu ka.

Do you sell fresh ____ ?	新鮮な____はありますか？
	shinsen na ____ wa arimasu ka.
beef	牛肉
	gyūniku
pork	豚肉
	butaniku
lamb	子羊の肉
	kohitsuji no niku
Is the ____ fresh?	この____は新鮮ですか？
	kono ____ wa shinsen desu ka.
fish	魚
	sakana
seafood	シーフード
	shīfūdo
angler fish	あんこう
	ankō
abalone	あわび
	awabi
bonito	かつお
	katsuo
carp	鯉
	koi
clam	はまぐり
	hamaguri
crab	かに
	kani
mollusk	貝
	kai
octopus	たこ
	tako
oyster	かき
	kaki
Pacific saury	さんま
	sanma

prawn; shrimp	えび *ebi*
puffer; blowfish	ふぐ *fugu*
red snapper; sea bream	鯛 *tai*
salmon	さけ *sake*
salmon eggs	イクラ *ikura*
sardine	いわし *iwashi*
sea urchin	うに *uni*
scallop	帆立て貝 *hotategai*
tuna, yellowtail	いなだ or はまち *inada or hamachi*
tuna, northern bluefin	まぐろ *maguro*
tuna belly	とろ *toro*
May I smell it?	そのにおいをかいでもいいですか? *sono nioi o kaide mo ii desu ka.*
Would you please ____ ?	____いただけませんか? *____ itadake masen ka.*
filet it	おろして *oroshite*
debone it	骨を取り除いて *hone o tori nozoite*
remove the head and tail	頭と尻尾を取り除いて *atama to shippo o tori nozoite*

AT THE PRODUCE STAND / MARKET

Fruits

persimmon	柿
	kaki
cherry	さくらんぼ
	sakuranbo
Japanese citron	柚子
	yuzu
banana	バナナ
	banana
apple	りんご
	ringo
grapes	ぶどう
	budō
orange	オレンジ
	orenji
lime	ライム
	raimu
lemon	レモン
	remon
mango	マンゴー
	mangō
melon	メロン
	meron
cantaloupe	マスクメロン
	masuku meron
watermelon	スイカ
	suika
honeydew	甘露メロン
	kanro meron
cranberry	クランベリー
	kuran berī

peach	もも	
	momo	
apricot	杏	
	anzu	
strawberry	いちご	
	ichigo	
blueberry	ブルーベリー	
	burūberī	
kiwi	キーウィー	
	kīwī	
pineapple	パイナップル	
	painappuru	
blackberries	ブラックベリー	
	burakkuberī	
grapefruit	グレープフルーツ	
	gurēpufurūtsu	
tangerine	みかん	
	mikan	
plum	プラム	
	puramu	
pear	梨	
	nashi	

Vegetables

Japanese radish	大根
	daikon
red bean	小豆
	azuki
soybean	枝豆
	edamame
winter mushroom	榎
	enoki
burdock	ごぼう
	gobō

pumpkin	かぼちゃ
	kabocha
mushroom	きのこ
	kinoko
chestnut	くり
	kuri
black bean	黒豆
	kuromame
Matsutake mushroom	松茸
	matsutake
leek	ねぎ
	negi
Japanese green pepper	ピーマン
	pīman
lotus root	れんこん
	renkon
sweet potato	さつまいも
	satsumaimo
Shītake mushroom	しいたけ
	shītake
bamboo shoot	竹の子
	takenoko
lettuce	レタス
	retasu
spinach	ほうれん草
	hōrensō
avocado	アボガド
	abogado
artichoke	アーティチョーク
	ātichōku
beans	豆
	mame
green beans	青豆
	ao mame

tomato	トマト
	tomato
potato	じゃがいも
	jagaimo
onion	たまねぎ
	tamanegi
celery	セロリ
	serori
broccoli	ブロッコリー
	burokkorī
cauliflower	カリフラワー
	karifurawā
carrot	にんじん
	ninjin
corn	とうもろこし
	tōmorokoshi
cucumber	きゅうり
	kyūri
bean sprouts	もやし
	moyashi
okra	おくら
	okura
bamboo shoots	たけのこ
	takenoko
eggplant	なす
	nasu
yam	やまいも
	yamaimo
squash	うり
	uri

Fresh Herbs and Spices

black pepper	くろこしょう
	kuro koshō

salt	塩
	shio
basil	バジル
	bajiru
parsley	パセリ
	paseri
garlic	にんにく
	nin niku
sugar	砂糖
	satō

CHAPTER FIVE

SOCIALIZING

Whether you're meeting people in a bar or a park, you'll find the language you need, in this chapter, to make new friends.

GREETINGS

Hello.	こんにちは。 *kon nichi wa.*
How are you?	お元気ですか？ *ogenki desu ka.*
Fine, thanks.	元気です。どうもありがとう。 *genki desu. dōmo arigatō.*
And you?	あなたもお元気ですか？ *anata mo ogenki desu ka.*
I'm exhausted from the trip.	旅行で疲れました。 *ryokō de tsukare mashita.*
I have a headache.	頭痛がしています。 *zutsū ga shite imasu.*
I'm terrible.	体の調子が悪いです。 *karada no chōshi ga warui desu.*
I have a cold.	カゼを引きました。 *kaze o hiki mashita.*
Good morning.	おはようございます。 *ohayō gozai masu.*
Good evening.	こんばんは。 *kon ban wa.*
Good afternoon.	こんにちは。 *kon nichi wa.*
Good night.	おやすみなさい。 *oyasumi nasai.*

Listen Up: Common Greetings

お会いできて嬉しいです。 *oai dekite ureshii desu.*	It's a pleasure.
とても嬉しいです。 *totemo ureshii desu.*	Delighted.
ご用を承ります。／ご希望通りに。 *goyō o uke tamawari masu. /* *gokibō dōrini.*	At your service. / As you wish.
嬉しいです。 *ureshii desu.*	Charmed.
ごきげんよう。 *gokigen yō.*	Good day. (shortened)
こんにちは。 *kon nichi wa.*	Hello.
お元気ですか? *ogenki desu ka.*	How's it going?
最近どう? *saikin dō?*	What's up?
何をしているのですか? *nani o shite iru no desu ka*	What's going on?
さよなら! *sayonara*	Bye!
さようなら。 *sayōnara*	Goodbye.
それじゃ、また後で。 *soreja, mata ato de.*	See you later.

OVERCOMING THE LANGUAGE BARRIER

I don't understand.	わかりません。 *wakari masen.*
Please speak more slowly.	もっとゆっくり話してください。 *motto yukkuri hanashi te kudasai.*
Please speak louder.	もっと大きな声で話してください。 *motto ōkina koe de hanashi te kudasai.*
Do you speak English?	英語を話しますか？ *eigo o hanashi masu ka.*
I speak ＿＿＿ better than Japanese.	日本語より＿＿＿の方がうまく話せます。 *nihongo yori ＿＿＿ no hō ga umaku hanase masu.*
Please spell that.	つづりを言ってもらえますか。 *tsuzuri o itte morae masu ka.*
Please repeat that?	もう一度お願いします。 *mō ichido onegai shimasu.*
How do you say ＿＿＿?	＿＿＿は何と言いますか？ *＿＿＿ wa nan to iimasu ka.*
Would you show me that in this dictionary?	それをこの辞書で示してもらえますか。 *sore o kono jisho de shimeshite morae masu ka.*

GETTING PERSONAL

People in Japan are generally friendly, but more formal than Americans or Europeans.

INTRODUCTIONS

What is your name?	あなたの名前は何ですか？
	anata no namae wa nan desu ka.
My name is ___.	私は____です。
	watashi wa _____ desu.
I'm very pleased to meet you.	お会いできて嬉しいです。
	oai dekite ureshii desu.
May I introduce my ____	私の____を紹介します。
	watashi no ____ o shōkai shimasu.
How is your ___?	____はお元気ですか？
	_____ wa ogenki desu ka.
wife	奥さん
	oku san
husband	ご主人
	go shujin
child	お子さん
	oko san
friends	お友達
	o tomodachi
boyfriend / girlfriend	ボーイフレンド / ガールフレンド
	bōi furendo / gāru furendo
family	ご家族
	go kazoku
mother	お母さん
	oka san
father	お父さん
	otō san

brother / sister	ご兄弟 / ご姉妹
	go kyōdai / go shimai
friend	お友達
	o tomodachi
neighbor	ご近所の方
	go kinjo no kata
boss	上司
	jōshi
cousin	いとこ
	itoko
aunt / uncle	おばさん / おじさん
	oba san / oji san
fiancée / fiancé	婚約者
	kon yaku sha
partner	パートナー
	pātonā
niece / nephew	姪御さん / 甥御さん
	meigo san / oigo san
parents	ご両親
	go ryōshin
grandparents	お祖父さん、お祖母さん
	ojīsan, obāsan
Are you married / single?	ご結婚していますか / 独身ですか？
	go kekkon shite imasu ka / dokushin desu ka.
I'm married.	結婚しています。
	kekkon shite imasu.
I'm single.	独身です。
	dokushin desu.
I'm divorced.	離婚しました。
	rikon shima shita.

I'm a widow / widower.	未亡人 / やもめです。
	mibōjin / yamome desu.
We're separated.	別居しています。
	bekkyo shite imasu.
I live with my boyfriend / girlfriend.	ボーイフレンド / ガールフレンドと一緒に暮らしています。
	bōi furendo / gāru furendo to issho ni kurashite imasu.
How old are you?	何歳ですか?
	nan sai desu ka.
How old are your children?	お子さんは何歳ですか?
	oko san wa nan sai desu ka.
Wow! That's very young.	まあ! とてもお若いですね。
	ma! totemo owakai desu ne.
No you're not! You're much younger.	違いますよ! あなたの方がずっと若いです。
	chigai masuyo. anata no hō ga zutto wakai desu.
Your wife / daughter is beautiful.	あなたの奥さん / お嬢さんは美人ですね。
	anata no oku san / ojō san wa bijin desu ne.
Your husband / son is handsome.	あなたのご主人 / 息子さんはハンサムですね。
	anata no goshujin / musuko san wa hansamu desu ne.
What a beautiful baby!	可愛い赤ちゃんですね!
	kawaii aka chan desu ne.
Are you here on business?	ここへは商用で来られましたか?
	koko ewa shōyō de korare mashita ka.
I am vacationing.	私は休暇で来ました。
	watashi wa kyūka de kimashita.

I'm attending a conference.	会議に参加します。
	kaigi ni sanka shimasu.
How long are you staying?	どのくらい滞在しますか？
	dono kurai taizai shimasu ka.
What are you studying?	何を勉強していますか？
	nani o benkyō shite imasu ka.
I'm a student.	私は学生です。
	watashi wa gakusei desu.
Where are you from?	どこから来ましたか？
	doko kara kimashita ka.

PERSONAL DESCRIPTIONS

blond(e)	金髪
	kinpatsu
brunette	ブルネット
	burunetto
redhead	赤毛
	aka ge
straight hair	直毛
	choku mō
curly hair	巻き毛
	maki ge
kinky hair	ちじれ毛
	chijire ge
long hair	長い髪
	nagai kami
short hair	短い髪
	mijikai kami
tanned	日焼けした
	hiyake shita
pale	青白い
	ao jiroi
mocha-skinned	茶色い皮膚
	chairoi hifu
black	黒人
	koku jin

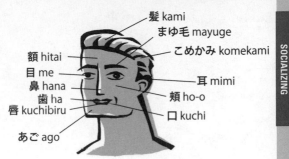

髪 kami
まゆ毛 mayuge
こめかみ komekami
額 hitai
目 me
鼻 hana
歯 ha
唇 kuchibiru
あご ago
耳 mimi
頬 ho-o
口 kuchi

white	白人
	haku jin
Asian	アジア人
	ajia jin
African-American	アフリカ系アメリカ人
	afurika kei amerika jin
caucasian	白人
	hakujin
biracial	人種の混じった
	jinshu no majitta
tall	背が高い
	se ga takai
short	背が低い
	se ga hikui
thin	痩せている
	yasete iru
fat	太っている
	futotte iru
blue eyes	青い目
	aoi me
brown eyes	茶色い目
	chairoi me

green eyes	緑の目
	midori no me
hazel eyes	薄茶色の目
	usucha iro no me
eyebrows	まゆ毛
	mayu ge
eyelashes	まつ毛
	matsu ge
freckles	そばかす
	sobakasu
moles	ほくろ
	hokuro
face	顔
	kao

DISPOSITIONS & MOODS

sad	悲しい
	kanashii
happy	嬉しい
	ureshii
angry	怒っている
	okotte iru
tired	疲れている
	tsukarete iru
anxious	心配している
	shinpai shite iru
confused	混乱している
	konran shite iru
enthusiastic	熱心である
	nesshin de aru

Listen Up: Nationalities

私は台湾人です。 *watashi wa taiwan jin desu.*	I'm Taiwanese.
私はチベット人です。 *watashi wa chibetto jin desu.*	I'm Tibetan.
私は韓国人です。 *watashi wa kankoku jin desu.*	I'm Korean.
私はフィリピン人です。 *watashi wa firipin jin desu.*	I'm Filipino.
私は中国人です。 *watashi wa chūgoku jin desu.*	I'm Chinese.
私はマカオ人です。 *watashi wa makao jin desu.*	I'm Macanese.
私はタイ人です。 *watashi wa tai jin desu.*	I'm Thai.
私はマレーシア人です。 *watashi wa marēshiya jin desu.*	I'm Malaysian.
私はベトナム人です。 *watashi wa betonamu jin desu.*	I'm Vietnamese.
私はネパール人です。 *watashi wa nepāru jin desu.*	I'm Nepalese.
私はラオス人です。 *watashi wa raosu jin desu.*	I'm Laotian.
私はヒンズー人です。 *watashi wa hinzū jin desu.*	I'm Indian.
私はビルマ人です。 *watashi wa biruma jin desu.*	I'm Burmese.
私はイタリア人です。 *iwatashi wa itaria jin desu.*	I'm Russian.
私は日本人です。 *watashi wa nihon jin desu.*	I'm Japanese.

For a full list of nationalities, see English / Japanese dictionary.

PROFESSIONS

What do you do for a living?	仕事は何をされていますか？ *shigoto wa nani o sarete imasu ka.*
Here is my business card.	私の名刺をお渡しします。 *watashi no meishi o owatashi shimasu.*
I am _____	私は_____です。 *watashi wa _____ desu.*
a doctor.	医者 *isha*
an engineer.	エンジニア *enjinia*
a lawyer.	弁護士 *bengoshi*
a salesperson.	販売員 *hanbai in*
a writer.	作家 *sakka*
an editor.	編集者 *henshū sha*
a designer.	デザイナー *dezainā*
an educator.	教育者 *kyōiku sha*
an artist.	芸術家 *geijutsu ka*
a craftsperson.	職人 *shoku nin*
a homemaker.	主婦 *shufu*
an accountant.	会計士 *kaikei shi*
a nurse.	看護師 *kango shi*

a musician.	音楽家 *ongaku ka*
a military professional.	職業軍人 *shokugyō gunjin*
a government employee.	公務員 *kōmu in*

DOING BUSINESS

I'd like an appointment.	面会の約束をしたいのですが。 *menkai no yakusoku o shitai no desuga.*
I'm here to see ____.	____に会いに来ました。 *____ ni ai ni ki mashita.*
May I photocopy this?	これをコピーしてもいいですか？ *kore o kopi shitemo ii desu ka.*
May I use a computer here?	ここでコンピュータを使用できますか？ *koko de konpyūtā o shiyō deki masu ka.*
What's the password?	パスワードは何ですか？ *pasuwādo wa nan desu ka.*
May I access the Internet?	インターネットにアクセスできますか？ *intānetto ni akusesu deki masu ka.*
May I send a fax?	ファックスを送信できますか？ *fakkusu o sōshin deki masu ka.*
May I use the phone?	電話を使用できますか？ *denwa o shiyō deki masu ka.*

PARTING WAYS

Keep in touch.	連絡を取り合いましょう。 *renraku o toriai mashō.*
Please write or email.	手紙かEメールをください。 *tegami ka E mēru o kudasai.*

Here's my phone number.	私の電話番号をお渡しします。 *watashi no denwa bangō o* *owatashi shimasu.*
Call me.	私に電話をください。 *watashi ni denwa o kudasai.*
May I have your phone number / e-mail please?	あなたの電話番号 / E メールアドレス をいただけますか? *anata no denwa bangō / E mēru* *adoresu o itadake masu ka.*
May I have your card?	あなたの名刺をいただけますか? *anata no meishi o itadake masu ka.*
Give me your address and I'll write you.	あなたの住所を教えてください。手紙 を書きます。 *anatao no jūsho o oshiete kudasai.* *tegami o kaki masu.*

TOPICS OF CONVERSATION

As in the United States or Europe, the weather and current affairs are common conversation topics.

THE WEATHER

It's so _____	とても_____。 *totemo _____ .*
Is it always so _____ ?	いつもそんなに_____か? *itsumo sonna ni _____ ka.*
sunny	晴れています *harete imasu*
rainy	雨が降ります *amega furi masu*
cloudy	曇っています *kumotte imasu*
humid	湿気が多いです *shikke ga ōidesu*

warm	暖かいです *atatakai desu*
cool	涼しいです *suzushii desu*
windy	風が強いです *kaze ga tsuyoi desu*
Do you know the weather forecast for tomorrow?	明日の天候予報を知っていますか? *ashita no tenki yohō o shitte imasu ka.*

THE ISSUES

What do you think about ____?	____についてどう思いますか? *____ ni tsuite dō omoi masu ka.*
democracy	民主主義 *minshu shugi*
socialism	社会主義 *shakai shugi*
American Democrats	アメリカの民主党 *amerika no minshutō*
American Republicans	アメリカの共和党 *amerika no kyōwatō*
monarchy	君主政治 *kunshuseiji*
the environment	環境 *kankyō*
climate change	気候変動 *kikōhendō*
the economy	経済 *keizai*
What political party do you belong to?	あなたはどの政党に属していますか? *anata wa dono seitō ni zokushi imasu ka.*

What did you think of the election in ____?	____の選挙についてどう思いましたか。
	_____ no senkyo ni tsuite dō omoi mashita ka.
What do you think of the war in ____?	____の戦争についてどう思いますか?
	_____ no sensō ni tsuite dō omoi masu ka.

RELIGION

Do you go to church / temple / mosque?	教会 / 寺院 / モスクへ行きますか?
	kyōkai / jiin / mosuku e ikimasu ka.
Are you religious?	宗教を信仰していますか?
	shūkyō o shinkō shiteimasu ka.
I'm ____ / I was raised ____	私は____です / 私は____として育ちました。
	watashi wa _____ desu / watashi wa _____ toshite sodachi mashita.
Protestant.	プロテスタント
	purotesutanto
Catholic.	カトリック
	katorikku
Jewish.	ユダヤ教徒
	yudaya kyōto
Muslim.	イスラム教徒
	isuramu kyōto
Buddhist.	仏教徒
	bukkyōto
Greek Orthodox.	ギリシャ正教徒
	girisha seikyōto
Hindu.	ヒンズー教徒
	hinzū kyōto
agnostic.	不可知論者
	fuka chiron sha
atheist.	無神論者
	mu shinron sha

I'm spiritual but I don't attend services.	私は信心深いですが、教会の礼拝には参加しません。
	watashi wa shinjin bukai desuga, kyōkai no reihai niwa sanka shimasen.
I don't believe in that.	それは信じません。
	sore wa shinji masen.
That's against my beliefs.	それは私の信仰に反します。
	sore wa watashi no shinkō ni hanshi masu.
I'd rather not talk about it.	そのことについては話したくありません。
	sono koto ni tsuite wa hanashi taku arima sen.

GETTING TO KNOW SOMEONE

Following are some conversation starters.

MUSICAL TASTES

What kind of music do you like?	どのような音楽が好きですか？
	dono yo na ongaku ga suki desu ka.
I like ＿＿＿	＿＿＿が好きです。
	＿＿＿ *ga suki desu.*
rock 'n' roll.	ロックンロール
	rokkun rōru
hip hop.	ヒップ ホップ
	hippu hoppu
techno.	テクノ
	tekuno
soul.	ソウル
	sōru
classical.	クラシック
	kurashikku
jazz.	ジャズ
	jazu

country and western.	カウントリー アンド ウェスタン *kantorī ando uesutan*
reggae.	レゲー *regē*
calypso.	カリプソ *karipuso*
opera.	オペラ *opera*
show-tunes / musicals.	映画音楽 / ミュージカル *eiga ongaku / myūjikaru*
New Age.	ニューエイジ *nyū eiji*
pop.	ポップ *Poppu*

HOBBIES

What do you like to do in your spare time?	開いている時間には何をするのが好きですか? *aite iru jigan niwa nani o suru noga suki desu ka.*
I like ____	____のが好きです。 *____ no ga suki desu.*
playing guitar.	ギターを弾く *gitā o hiku*
piano.	ピアノを弾く *piano o hiku*

For other instruments, see the English / Japanese dictionary.

painting.	絵を描く *e o kaku*
drawing.	スケッチする *sukecchi suru*
dancing.	ダンスをする *dansu o suru*
reading.	本を読む *hon o yomu*

watching TV.	テレビを見る
	terebi o miru
shopping.	買い物をする
	kaimono o suru
going to the movies.	映画を観に行く
	eiga o mini iku
hiking.	ハイキングをする
	haikingu o suru
camping.	キャンプをする
	kyanpu o suru
hanging out.	ぶらぶらする
	bura bura suru
traveling.	旅行する
	ryokō suru
eating out.	外食する
	gaishoku suru
cooking.	料理をする
	ryōri o suru
sewing.	裁縫をする
	saihō o suru
sports.	スポーツをする
	supōtsu o suru
Do you like to dance?	踊るのは好きですか?
	odoru nowa suki desu ka.
Would you like to go out?	外に出かけたいですか?
	soto ni dekake tai desu ka.
May I buy you dinner sometime?	いつか夕食をご馳走させてください。
	itsuka yūshoku o gochisō sasete kudasai.
What kind of food do you like?	どんな料理が 好きですか?
	donna ryōri ga suki desu ka.

For a full list of food types, see Dining in Chapter 4.

Would you like to go ____?	____行きたいですか？
	_____ ikitai desu ka.
to a movie	映画を観に
	eiga o mini
to a concert	コンサートに
	konsāto ni
to the zoo	動物園に
	dōbutsu en ni
to the beach	ビーチに
	bīchi ni
to a museum	美術館に
	bijutsu kan ni
for a walk in the park	公園に散歩しに
	kōen ni sapo shini
dancing	ダンスをしに
	dansu o shini
Would you like to get ____?	____に行きたいですか？
	_____ ni ikitai desu ka.
lunch	お昼ごはんを食べ
	ohiru gohan o tabe
coffee	コーヒーを飲み
	kōhī o nomi
dinner	夕食を食べ
	yūshoku o tebe
What kind of books do you like to read?	どんな本を読むのが好きですか？
	donna hon o yomu noga suki desu ka.
I like ____	____が好きです。
	_____ ga suki desu.
mysteries.	ミステリー
	misuterī
Westerns.	西部劇物
	seibu geki mono
dramas.	劇の脚本
	geki no kyakuhon

novels.	小説 *shōsetsu*
biographies.	伝記物 *denki mono*
auto-biographies.	自叙伝 *jijoden*
romance.	恋愛小説 *renai shōsetsu*
history.	歴史物 *rekishimono*

CHAPTER SIX
MONEY & COMMUNICATIONS

This chapter covers money, the mail, phone, Internet service, and other tools you need to connect with the outside world.

MONEY

Do you accept ____ ?	____は使えますか？
	____ *wa tsukae masu ka.*
Visa / MasterCard / Discover / American Express / Diners' Club credit cards	ビザカード / マスターカード / ディスカバー / アメリカン エキスプレス / ダイナーズ クラブ クレジットカード
	biza kādo/ masutā kādo / disukabā / amerikan ekisupuresu / dainazu kurabu kurejitto kādo
bills	紙幣
	shihei
coins	硬貨
	kōka
travelers checks	トラベラーズ チェック
	toraberāzu chekku
money transfer	振り込み
	furikomi
May I wire transfer funds here?	ここから電信振り込みできますか？
	koko kara denshin furikomi deki masu ka.
Would you please tell me where to find ____ ?	____はどこにありますか。
	____ *wa doko ni arimasu ka.*
a bank	銀行
	ginkō

a credit bureau	クレジット部 *kurejitto bu*
an ATM	**ATM** *ATM*
a currency exchange	通貨両替所 *tsūka ryōgae jo*
A receipt, please.	レシートをください。 *reshīto o kudasai.*
Would you tell me _____ ?	_____は何ですか。 *_____ wa nan desu ka.*
the exchange rate for dollars to _____	ドルから_____への交換レート *doru kara _____ eno kōkan rēto*
the exchange rate for pounds to _____	ポンドから_____への変換レート *pondo kara _____ eno kōkan rēto*
Is there a service charge?	サービス料は取られますか？ *sābisu ryō wa torare masu ka.*
May I have a cash advance on my credit card?	このクレジットカードでキャッシングできますか？ *kono kurejitto kādo de kyasshingu deki masu ka.*
Will you accept a credit card?	クレジットカードを使えますか？ *kurejitto kādo o tsukae masu ka.*
May I have smaller bills, please.	両替してもらえますか。 *ryōgae shite morae masu ka.*
Can you make change?	おつりをもらえますか？ *otsuri o morae masu ka.*
I only have bills.	お札しかありません。 *osatsu shika ari masen.*
Some coins, please.	小銭もまぜてください。 *kozeni mo mazete kudasai.*

Listen Up: Bank Lingo

ここに署名してください。 *koko ni shomei shite kudasai.*	Please sign here.
レシートのお返しです。 *reshīto no okaeshi desu.*	Here is your receipt.
身分証明書を見せてください。 *mibun shōmeisho o misete kudasai.*	May I see your ID, please?
トラベラーズ チェックが使えます。 *toraberāzu chekku ga tsukaemasu.*	We accept travelers checks.
現金のみです。 *genkin nomi desu.*	Cash only.

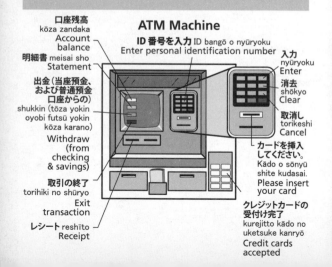

口座残高
kōza zandaka
Account balance

明細書 meisai sho
Statement

出金(当座預金、および普通預金口座からの)
shukkin (tōza yokin oyobi futsū yokin kōza karano)
Withdraw (from checking & savings)

取引の終了
torihiki no shūryo
Exit transaction

レシート reshīto
Receipt

ATM Machine

ID 番号を入力 ID bangō o nyūryoku
Enter personal identification number

入力
nyūryoku
Enter

消去
shōkyo
Clear

取消し
torikeshi
Cancel

カードを挿入してください。
Kādo o sōnyū shite kudasai.
Please insert your card

クレジットカードの受付け完了
kurejitto kādo no uketsuke kanryō
Credit cards accepted

PHONE SERVICE

Where can I buy or rent a cell phone?

携帯電話はどこで借りるか買うことが できますか?
keitai denwa wa dokode kariru ka kau koto ga deki masu ka.

What rate plans do you have?

どんな料金プランがありますか?
donna ryōkin puran ga arimasu ka.

Is this good throughout the country?

これは国中どこでも通用しますか?
kore wa kunijū dokodemo tsūyō shimasu ka.

May I have a prepaid phone?

プリペイドの電話をください。
puri peido no denwa o kudasai.

Where can I buy a phone card?

テレフォンカードはどこで買えますか?
terefon kādo wa doko de kae masu ka.

May I add more minutes to my phone card?

テレフォンカードにもっと時間を追加 できますか?
terefon kādo ni motto jikan o tsuika deki masu ka.

MAKING A CALL

May I dial direct?

直通電話はできますか?
chokutsū denwa wa deki masu ka.

Operator please.

オペレーターをお願いします。
operētā o onegai shimasu.

I'd like to make an international call.

国際電話をかけたいのですが。
kokusai denwa o kake tai no desuga.

I'd like to make a collect call.

コレクトコールをお願いします。
korekuto kōru o onegai shimasu.

I'd like to use a calling card.

コーリングカードを使います。
kōringu kādo o tsukai masu.

COMMUNICATIONS

Listen Up: Telephone Lingo

もしもし。
moshi moshi.

Hello?

お電話番号をお願い
します。
*odenwa bangō o
onegai shimasu.*

What number?

申し訳ございませんが、
相手先の電話は話し
中です。
*mōshiwake gozai
masen ga, aite saki no
denwa wa hanashi chū
desu.*

I'm sorry, the line
is busy.

一度切ってからおかけ直
しください。
*ichido kitte kara mata
okake naoshi kudasai.*

Please, hang up and redial.

申し訳ございませんが、
どなたも電話にでられ
ません。
*mōshiwake gozai
masen ga, donata
mo denwa ni derare
masen.*

I'm sorry, nobody is answering.

カードの残り時間は10
分です。
*kādo no nokori jikan
wa juppun desu.*

Your card has ten minutes left.

Bill my credit card.	私のクレジットカードに請求してください。 *watashi no kurejitto kādo ni seikyū shite kudasai.*
May I bill the charges to my room?	私の部屋に請求してもらえますか？ *watashi no heya ni seikyū shite morae masu ka.*
May I bill the charges to my home phone?	これはわたしの家の電話に請求していただけますか？ *kore wa watashi no ie no denwa ni seikyū shite itadake masu ka.*
Information, please.	インフォメーションをお願いします。 *infomēshon o onegai shimasu.*
I'd like the number for ___.	___ の番号をお願いします。 *___ no bangō o onegai shimasu.*
I just got disconnected.	電話が切れてしまいました。 *denwa ga kirete shimai mashita.*
The line is busy.	只今話し中です。 *tadaima hanashi chū desu.*
I lost the connection.	電話が切れてしまいました。 *denwa ga kireteshimai mashita.*

INTERNET ACCESS

Where is an Internet café?	インターネット カフェはどこにありますか？
	intānetto kafe wa doko ni arimasu ka.
Is there a wireless hub nearby?	この近くにワイヤーレス ハブはありますか？
	kono chikaku ni waiyā resu habu wa arimasu ka.
How much do you charge per minute / hour?	1分／1時間いくらですか？
	ippun / ichi jikan ikura desu ka.
Can I print here?	ここで印刷できますか？
	koko de insatsu deki masu ka.
Can I burn a CD?	CD に書き込めますか？
	CD ni kaki kome masu ka.
Would you please help me change the language preference to English?	言語を英語に変えるのを手伝っていただけませんか？
	gengo o eigo ni kaeru no o tetsudatte itadake masen ka.
May I scan something?	何かスキャンしてもいいですか？
	nanika sukyan shitemo ii desu ka.
Can I upload photos?	写真をアップロードできますか？
	shashin o appu rōdo deki masu ka.

Do you have a USB port so I can download music?

音楽をダウンロードできる USB ポートはありますか？

ongaku o daun rōdo dekiru USB pōto wa arimasu ka.

Do you have a machine compatible with iTunes?

iTune と互換性のある機械はありますか？

iTune to gokansei no aru kikai wa arimasu ka.

Do you have a Mac?

Mac はありますか？

Makku wa arimasu ka.

Do you have a PC?

PC はありますか？

PC wa arimasu ka.

Do you have a newer version of this software?

このソフトウェアの新しいバージョンはありますか？

kono sofuto uea no atarashii bājon wa arimasu ka.

Do you have broadband?

ブロードバンドはありますか？

burōdo bando wa arimasu ka.

How fast is your connection speed here?

この回線速度は何ですか？

kono kaisen sokudo wa nan desu ka.

GETTING MAIL

Where is the post office?

郵便局はどこにありますか？

yūbin kyoku wa doko ni arimasu ka.

May I send an international package?

外国に小包を送れますか？

gaikoku ni kozutsumi o okure masu ka.

Do I need a customs form?

関税申告用紙に記入しなければなりませんか？

kanzei shinkoku yōshi ni kinyū shi nakere ba nari masen ka.

Do you sell insurance for packages?

小包に保険をかけられますか？

kozutsumi ni hoken o kakerare masu ka.

Please, mark it fragile.	「割れ物注意」の印を付けてください。 *「waremono chūi」no shirushi o* *tsukete kudasai.*
Please, handle with care.	丁寧に扱ってください。 *teinei ni atsukatte kudasai.*
Do you have twine?	ひもはありますか? *himo wa arimasu ka.*
Where is a DHL office?	DHL はどこにありますか? *DHL wa doko ni arimasu ka.*

Listen Up: Postal Lingo

次の方どうぞ! *tsugi no kata dōzo.*	Next!
ここに置いてください。 *koko ni oite kudasai.*	Please, set it here.
どのクラスですか? *dono kurasu desu ka.*	Which class?
どのサービスになさいますか? *dono sābisu ni nasai masu ka.*	What kind of service would you like?

Do you sell stamps?	切手を売っていますか？
	kitte o utte imasu ka.
Do you sell postcards?	はがきを売っていますか？
	hagaki o utte imasu ka.
May I send that first class?	それをファースト クラスで送れますか？
	sore o fāsuto kurasu de okure masu ka.
How much to send that express / air mail?	それを 速達 / 航空便で送るといくらかかりますか？
	sore o sokutatsu / kōkū bin de okuru to ikura kakari masu ka.
Do you offer overnight delivery?	翌日配達のサービスはありますか？
	yokujitsu haitatsu no sābisu wa arimasu ka.
How long will it take to reach the United States?	何日くらいでアメリカに届きますか？
	nan nichi kurai de amerika ni todoki masu ka.
I'd like to buy an envelope.	封筒を 1 枚ください。
	fūtō o ichi mai kudasai.
May I send it airmail?	それを航空便で送ってください。
	sore o kōkū bin de okutte kudasai.
I'd like to send it certified / registered mail.	それを配達証明郵便 / 書留郵便で送ってください。
	sore o haitatsu shōmei yūbin / kakitome yūbin de okutte kudasai.

CHAPTER SEVEN
CULTURE

CINEMA

Is there a movie theater nearby?	この近くに映画館はありますか？ *kono chikakuni eiga kan wa arimasu ka.*
What's playing tonight?	今夜上映されるのは何ですか？ *kon ya jōei sareru nowa nan desu ka.*
Is that in English or Japanese?	それは英語ですか、それとも日本語ですか？ *sore wa eigo desuka, sore tomo nihongo desu ka.*
Are there English subtitles?	英語の字幕は出ますか？ *eigo no jimaku wa demasu ka.*
Is the theater air conditioned?	館内は冷房が効いていますか？ *kan nai wa reibō ga kiite imasu ka.*
How much is a ticket?	チケットはいくらですか？ *chiketto wa ikura desu ka.*
Do you have a _____ discount?	_____割引きはありますか？ _____ *waribiki wa arimasu ka.*
senior	高齢者 *kōreisha*
student	学生 *gakusei*
children's	児童 *jidō*
What time is the movie showing?	映画は何時に始まりますか？ *eiga wa nanji ni hajimeri masu ka.*
How long is the movie?	上映時間はどのくらいですか？ *jōei jikan wa dono kurai desu ka.*

May I buy tickets in
advance?

前もってチケットを買えますか?
mae motte chiketto o kae masu ka.

Is it sold out?

売り切れですか?
urikire desu ka.

When does it begin?

いつ始まりますか?
itsu hajimari masu ka.

PERFORMANCES

Do you have ballroom
dancing?

社交ダンスは開かれますか?
shakō dansu wa hirakare masu ka.

Are there any plays
showing right now?

現在上演されている劇はありますか?
*genzai jōen sarete iru geki wa
arimasu ka.*

Where can I buy tickets?

チケットはどこで買えますか?
chiketto wa doko de kae masu ka.

Are there student discounts?

学生割引きはありますか?
gakusei waribiki wa arimasu ka.

I need ____ seats.

____席ください。
____ seki kudasai.

For a full list of numbers, see p6.

An aisle seat.

通路側の座席。
tsūro gawa no zaseki.

Orchestra seat, please.

オーケストラ席をお願いします。
ōkesutora seki o onegai shimasu.

What time does the play
start?

劇は何時に始まりますか?
geki wa nanji ni hajimari masu ka.

Is there an intermission?

途中で休憩はありますか?
tochū de kyūkei wa arimasu ka.

Do you have an opera
house?

オペラハウスはありますか?
opera hausu wa arimasu ka.

Is there a local symphony?

地方交響楽団はありますか?
chihō kōkyō gakudan wa arimasu ka.

CULTURE

Listen Up: Box Office Lingo

何をご覧になりますか？ *nani o goran ni nari masu ka.*	What would you like to see?
何枚ですか？ *nan mai desu ka.*	How many?
大人２枚ですか？ *otona nimai desu ka.*	For two adults?
バターは？塩は？ *batā wa? shio wa?*	With butter? Salt?
ほかにも何かございますか？ *hoka nimo nani ka gozai masu ka.*	Would you like anything else?

May I purchase tickets over the phone?

電話でチケットを買えますか？
denwa de chiketto o kae masu ka.

What time is the box office open?

チケット売り場は何時に開きますか？
chiketto uriba wa nanji ni hiraki masu ka.

I need space for a wheelchair, please.

車椅子が入れるくらいの空間が必要です。
kuruma isu ga haireru kurai no kūkan ga hitsuyō desu.

Do you have private boxes available?

ボックス席はありますか？
bokkusu seki wa arimasu ka.

Is there a church that gives concerts?

コンサートを催す教会はありますか？
konsāto o moyōsu kyōkai wa arimasu ka.

A program, please.	プログラムをください。
	puroguramu o kudasai.
Please show us to our seats.	座席まで案内していただけますか。
	zaseki made annai shite itadake
	masu ka.

MUSEUMS, GALLERIES & SIGHTS

Do you have a museum guide?	美術館ガイドはいますか？
	bijutsukan gaido wa Imasu ka.
Do you have guided tours?	ガイドが付いて説明しますか？
	gaido ga tsuite setsumei shimasu ka.
What are the museum hours?	美術館の開館時間は何時から何時までですか。
	bijutsukan no kaikan jikan wa nanji kara nanji made desu ka.
Do I need an appointment?	予約が必要ですか？
	yoyaku ga hitsuyō desu ka.
What is the admission fee?	入場料はいくらですか？
	nyūjō ryō wa ikura desu ka.
Do you have ____?	____はありますか？
	____ wa arimasu ka.
student discounts	学生割引き
	gakusei waribiki
senior discounts	高齢者割引き
	kōreisha waribiki

Do you have services for the hearing impaired?

聴覚障害者のためのサービスはありますか？

chōkaku shōgaisha no tame no sābisu wa arimasu ka.

Do you have audio tours in English?

英語の音声ガイドはありますか？

eigo no onsei gaido wa arimasu ka.

CHAPTER EIGHT

SHOPPING

This chapter covers the phrases you'll need to shop in a variety of settings, from the mall to street vendors. We also threw in the terminology you'll need to visit the barber or hairdresser.

For coverage of food and grocery shopping, see p90.

GENERAL SHOPPING TERMS

Please tell me _____	_____を教えてください。
	_____ o oshiete kudasai.
how to get to a mall?	ショッピングセンターへの行き方
	shoppingu sentā eno iki kata
the best place for shopping?	ショッピングに一番よいところ
	shoppingu ni ichiban yoi tokoro
how to get downtown?	繁華街への行き方
	hanka gai eno iki kata
Where can I find a _____?	_____はどこにありますか?
	_____ wa doko ni arimasu ka.
shoe store	靴屋
	kutsu ya
men's / women's / children's clothing store	紳士 / 婦人 / 子供服の店
	shinshi / fujin / kodomo fuku no mise
designer fashion shop	デザイナー ブランドの店
	dezainā burando no mise
vintage clothing store	ビンテージ物を売っている洋服屋
	bintēji mono o utteiru yōfuku ya
jewelry store	宝石店
	hōseki ten
bookstore	本屋
	hon ya
toy store	おもちゃ屋
	omocha ya

stationery store	文房具店
	bunbōgu ten
antique shop	骨董品店
	kottōhin ten
cigar shop	タバコ屋
	tabako ya
souvenir shop	お土産屋
	omiyage ya
Where can I find a flea market?	フリーマーケットはどこでやっていますか?
	furī māketto wa doko de yatte imasu ka.

CLOTHES SHOPPING

I'd like to buy ____	____を買いたいのですが。
	____ *o kaitai no desuga.*
men's shirts.	紳士用のシャツ
	shinshi yō no shatsu
women's shoes.	婦人用の靴
	fujin yō no kutsu
children's clothes.	子供服
	kodomo fuku
toys.	オモチャ
	omocha

For a full list of numbers, see p6.

I'm looking for a size ____	____サイズを探しています。
	____ *saizu o sagashite imasu.*
small.	S
	esu
medium.	M
	emu
large.	L
	eru

イヤリング
iyaringu

腕時計
ude dokei

ワンピース
wan pīsu

シャツ
shatsu

ネクタイ
nekutai

ジャケット
jaketto

ベルト
beruto

ズボン
zubon

靴
kutsu

extra-large.	LL
	eru eru
I'm looking for ___ .	____を探しています。
	_ _ o sagashite imasu.
a silk blouse.	シルクのブラウス
	shiruku no burausu
cotton pants.	コットンのズボン
	kotton no zubon
a hat.	帽子
	bōshi
sunglasses.	サングラス
	san gurasu
underwear.	下着
	shitagi
cashmere.	カシミヤの
	kashimiya no
socks.	靴下
	kutsu shita
sweaters.	セーター
	sētā

Listen Up: Market Lingo

品物を扱う前に(店の人に)た ずねてください。*shinamono o atsukau mae ni (miseno hito ni) tazunete kudasai.*	Please ask (the store employee) for help before handling goods.
____ 円のお返しです。 *____ en no okaeshi desu.*	Here is your change.
2 つで 40 円です。 *futatsu de yon jū en desu.*	Two for forty, sir.

No thanks, maybe I'll come back.	いいえ、いりません。でもまた後で戻っ てくるかもしれません。 *iie, iri masen. demo mata ato de modotte kuru kamo shirema sen.*
Would you take ¥____?	____ 円で買えますか? *____ en de kae masu ka.*

For a full list of numbers, see p6.

That's a deal!	では買います! *dewa kai masu.*
Do you have a less expensive one?	もう少し安いのはありますか? *mō sukoshi yasui nowa arimasu ka.*
Is there tax?	税金はかかりますか? *zeikin wa kakari masu ka.*
May I have the VAT forms?	VAT付加価値税用紙をください。 *VAT fuka kachi zei yōshi o kudasai.*

BOOKSTORE / NEWSSTAND SHOPPING

Is there a _____ nearby?	この近くに_____はありますか？
	kono chikaku ni _____ wa arimasu ka.
a bookstore	本屋
	hon ya
a newsstand	新聞売り場
	shinbun uriba
Do you have _____ in English?	英語の_____はありますか？
	eigo no _____ wa arimasu ka.
books	本
	hon
newspapers	新聞
	shinbun
magazines	雑誌
	zasshi
books about local history	地方の歴史に関する本
	chihō no rekishi ni kansuru hon
picture books	絵本
	ehon

SHOPPING FOR ELECTRONICS

Can I play this in the United States / United Kingdom?	これはアメリカ／イギリスでつかえますか？
	kore wa amerika / igirisu de tsukae masu ka.
Will this game work on my game console in the United States / United Kingdom?	このゲームは、アメリカ／イギリスにある私のゲーム機で使用できますか？
	kono gēmu wa, amerika/igirisu ni aru watashi no gēmu ki de shiyō dekimasu ka.

Do you have this in a
U.S. / U.K. market format?

これと同じものでアメリカ／イギリス対
応のものがありますか？

*koreto onaji mono de amerika/
igirisu taiō no mono ga arimasu ka.*

Can you convert this to a
U.S. / U.K. market format?

これはアメリカ／イギリスの形式に変
換できますか？

*kore wa amerika/igirisu no keishiki
ni henkan deki masu ka.*

Will this work with a
110 VAC adapter?

これは110VのACアダプターで動き
ますか？

*kore wa hyaku jū boruto no AC
adaputā de ugoki masu ka.*

Do you have an adapter
plug for 110 to 220?

110から220に変換するのアダプター
プラグはありますか？

*hyaku jū kara ni hyaku ni jū ni
henkan suru adaputā puragu wa
arimasu ka.*

Do you sell electronics
adapters here?

電子アダプターは売っていますか？

denshi adaputā wa utte imasu ka.

Is it safe to use my laptop
with this adapter?

このアダプターで私のラップトップを使
っても大丈夫ですか？

*kono adaputā de watashi no rappu
toppu o tsukattemo daijōbu desu
ka.*

If it doesn't work, may I
return it?

もし使えなかった場合返品できます
か？

*moshi tsukaenakatta baai henpin
deki masu ka.*

May I try it here in the
store?

これをここで試してみることはできま
すか？

*kore o koko de tameshite miru koto
wa deki masu ka.*

AT THE BARBER / HAIRDRESSER

Do you have a style guide?	スタイル ブックはありますか？
	sutairu bukku wa arimasu ka.
A trim, please.	髪をそろえてください。
	kami o soroete kudasai.
I'd like it bleached.	ブリーチしてください。
	burīchi shite kudasai.
Would you change the color ____?	____色に変えてください。
	____ iro ni kaete kudasai.
darker	もっと濃い
	motto koi
lighter	もっと明るい
	motto akarui
Would you just touch it up a little?	少し修正してください。
	sukoshi shūsei shite kudasai.
I'd like it curled.	カールしてください。
	kāru shite kudasai.
Do I need an appointment?	予約する必要がありますか？
	yoyaku suru hitsuyō ga arimasu ka.
Shampoo, cut, and perm.	シャンプー、カット、パーマ。
	shanpū, katto, pama.
Do you do permanents?	パーマはできますか？
	pāma wa deki masu ka.
May I make an appointment?	予約できますか？
	yoyaku deki masu ka.
Please use low heat.	低温でお願いします。
	teion de onegai shimasu.
Please don't blow dry it.	ブローしないでください。
	burō shinaide kudasai.
Please dry it curly / straight.	カール / ストレートにドライしてください。
	kāru / sutorēto ni dorai shite kudasai.

Would you fix my braids?	編んだ髪を直してください。 *anda kami o naoshite kudasai.*
Would you fix my highlights?	ハイライトを直してください。 *hai raito o naoshite kudasai.*
Do you wax?	ワックスはできますか？ *wakkusu wa deki masu ka.*
Please wax my ____	私の____をワックスしてください。 *watashi no ____ o wakkusu shite kudasai.*
legs.	足 *ashi*
bikini line.	ビキニの線 *bikini no sen*
eyebrows.	まゆ毛 *mayu ge*
under my nose.	鼻の下 *hana no shita*
Please trim my beard.	ひげを揃えてください。 *hige o soroete kudasai.*
A shave, please.	剃ってください。 *sotte kudasai.*
Use a fresh blade please.	良く切れる刃を使ってください。 *yoku kireru ha o tsukatte kudasai.*
Sure, cut it all off.	はい、全部切ってください。 *hai, zenbu kitte kudasai.*

CHAPTER NINE
SPORTS & FITNESS

GETTING FIT

Is there a gym nearby?	この近くにジムはありますか？ *kono chikaku ni jimu wa arimasu ka.*
Do you have free weights?	フリーウェイトはありますか？ *furī ueito wa arimasu ka.*
I'd like to go for a swim.	泳ぎに行きたいのですが。 *oyogi ni ikitai no desuga.*
Do I have to be a member?	会員でなければなりませんか？ *kai in de nakere ba narima sen ka.*
May I come here for one day?	一日ここに来ることはできますか？ *ichi nichi koko ni kuru koto wa deki masu ka.*
How much does a membership cost?	会員になるにはいくらかかりますか？ *kaiin ni naru niwa ikura kakari masu ka.*
I need to get a locker please.	ロッカーを使いたいのですが。 *rokkā o tsukai tai no desuga.*
Do you have a lock?	鍵はありますか？ *kagi wa arimasu ka.*

Do you have a treadmill?	トレッドミルはありますか？
	toreddo miru wa arimasu ka.
Do you have a stationary bike?	エアロ バイクはありますか？
	earo baiku wa arimasu ka.
Do you have handball / squash courts?	ハンドボール / スカッシュ コートはありますか？
	hando bōru / sukasshu kōto wa arimasu ka.
Are they indoors?	それは屋内にありますか？
	sore wa okunai ni arimasu ka.
I'd like to play tennis.	テニスをしたいのですが。
	tenisu o shitai no desuga.
Would you like to play?	プレイしませんか？
	purei shima sen ka.
I'd like to rent a racquet.	ラケットを借りたいのですが。
	raketto o kari tai no desuga.
I need to buy some ____	____を買わなければなりません。
	____ o kawa nakere ba nari masen.
new balls.	新しいボール
	atarashii bōru
safety glasses.	セーフティーグラス
	sēfutī gurasu
May I rent a court for tomorrow?	明日、コートを借りたいのですが。
	ashita, kōto o karitai no desuga.
May I have clean towels?	きれいなタオルをいただけますか。
	kirei na taoru o itadake masu ka.
Where are the showers / locker-rooms?	シャワー / ロッカールームはどこにありますか？
	shawā/rokkā rūmu wa doko ni arimasu ka.

Do you have a workout room for women only?

女性専用のワークアウト ルームはありますか?

josei senyō no wāku auto rūmu wa arimasu ka.

Do you have aerobics classes?

エアロビクスのクラスはありますか?

earobikusu no kurasu wa arimasu ka.

Do you have a women's pool?

女性用のプールはありますか?

josei yō no pūru wa arimasu ka.

Let's go for a jog.

ジョギングに行きましょう。

jogingu ni iki ma shō.

That was a great workout.

とてもよい運動でした。

totemo yoi undō deshita.

CATCHING A GAME

Where is the stadium?

スタジアムはどこですか?

sutajiamu wa doko desu ka.

Where can I see a cockfight?

闘鶏はどこで見ることがますか?

tōkei wa doko de miru koto ga deki masu ka.

Do you have a bullfight?

闘牛は行われますか?

tōgyū wa okonaware masu ka.

Who is your favorite toreador / matador?	好きな闘牛士は誰ですか? *suki na tōgyūshi wa dare desu ka.*
Who is the best goalie?	最高のゴールキーパーは誰ですか? *saikō no gōru kīpā wa dare desu ka.*
Are there any women's teams?	女性チームはありますか? *josei chīmu wa arimasu ka.*
Do you have any amateur / professional teams?	アマチュア / プロのチームはありますか? *amachua / puro no chīmu wa arimasu ka.*
Is there a game I could play in?	私も参加できるゲームはありますか? *watashi mo sanka dekiru gēmu wa arimasu ka.*
Which is the best team?	最高のチームはどれですか? *saikō no chīmu wa dore desu ka.*
Will the game be on television?	この試合はテレビでも放送されますか? *kono shiai wa terebi demo hōsō sare masu ka.*
Where can I buy tickets?	チケットはどこで買えますか? *chiketto wa doko de kae masu ka.*
The best seats, please.	一番よい席をお願いします。 *ichiban yoi seki o onegai shimasu.*
The cheapest seats, please.	一番安い席をお願いします。 *ichiban yasui seki o onegai shimasu.*
How close are these seats?	これらの席はどれくらい近いですか? *korera no seki wa dore kurai chikai desu ka.*
May I have box seats?	ボックス シートをいただけますか? *bokkusu shīto o itadake masu ka.*

Wow! What a game!	うわぁ! すごい試合だ!
	uwa! sugoi shiai da.
Go Go Go!	行け、行け、行け!
	ike, ike, ike!
Oh No!	あ、だめだ!
	a, dame da!
Give it to them!	彼らにあげろ!
	karera ni agero!
Go for it!	がんばれ!
	ganbare!
Score!	入れろ!
	irero!
What's the score?	何点ですか?
	nan ten desu ka.
Who's winning?	どっちが勝ってますか?
	docchi ga katte masu ka.

HIKING

Where can I find a guide to hiking trails?	ハイキング トレイルのガイドはどこで見つけられますか?
	haikingu toreiru no gaido wa doko de mitsuke rare masu ka.
Do we need to hire a guide?	ガイドを雇う必要がありますか?
	gaido o yatou hitsuyō ga arimasu ka.
Where can I rent equipment?	装具はどこで借りられますか?
	sōgu wa doko de kari rare masu ka.
Do they have rock climbing there?	そこにはロック クライミングがありますか?
	soko niwa rokku kuraimingu ga arimasu ka.
We need more ropes and carabiners.	ロープとカラビナがもっと必要です。
	rōpu to karabina ga motto hitsuyō desu.
Where can we go mountain climbing?	どこで登山ができますか?
	doko de tozan ga deki masu ka.

Are the routes _____ ?
ルートは_____ されていますか?
rūto wa _____ sarete imasu ka.

  well marked
  標識が完備
  hyōshiki ga kanbi

  in good condition
  整備
  seibi

What is the altitude there?
標高はいくらですか?
hyōkō wa ikura desu ka.

How long will it take?
どのくらい時間がかかりますか?
dono kurai jikan ga kakari masu ka.

Is it very difficult?
とても難しいですか?
totemo muzukashii desu ka.

I'd like a challenging climb - but I don't want to take oxygen.
登りがいのある山は好きですが、酸素補給器は携帯したくありません。
nobori gai no aru yama wa suki desuga, sanso hokyūki wa keitai shitaku arima sen.

I want to hire someone to carry my excess gear.
残りの装具を運んでくれる人を雇いたいのですが。
nokori no sōgu o hakonde kureru hito o yatoi tai no desuga.

We don't have time for a long route.	長いルートを行く時間はありません。 nagai rūto o iku jikan wa arima sen.
I don't think it's safe to proceed.	先に進むのは安全ではないと思います。 saki ni susumu nowa anzen dewa nai to omoi masu.
Do we have a backup plan?	第２プランはありますか？ dai ni puran wa arimasu ka.
If we're not back by tomorrow, send a search party.	私たちが明日までに戻らなければ、捜索隊を送ってください。 watashi tachi ga ashita made ni modora nakere ba, sōsaku tai o okutte kudasai.
Are the campsites marked?	キャンプサイトには標識が整備されていますか？ kyanpu saito niwa hyōshiki ga seibi sarete imasu ka.
Can we camp off the trail?	トレイル外でキャンプはできますか？ toreiru gai de kyanpu wa deki masu ka.
Is it okay to build fires here?	ここで火をおこしてもいいですか？ koko de hi o okoshite mo ii desuka.
Do we need permits?	許可が要りますか？ kyoka ga iri masu ka.

For more camping terms, see p71.

BOATING OR FISHING

When do we sail?	いつ出航しますか？ *itsu shukkō shimasu ka.*
Where are the life preservers?	救命用具はどこにありますか？ *kyūmei yōgu wa doko ni arimasu ka.*
Can I purchase bait?	えさを買えますか？ *esa o kae masu ka.*
Can I rent a pole?	釣竿を借りられますか？ *tsurizao o kari rare masu ka.*
How long is the voyage?	航海はどれくらいですか？ *kōkai wa dorekurai desu ka.*
Are we going up river or down?	川を上りますかそれとも下りますか？ *kawa o nobori masu ka, soretomo kudari masu ka.*
How far are we going?	どのくらい遠くまで行きますか？ *dono kurai tōku made iki masu ka.*
How fast are we going?	どのくらいの速度で行きますか？ *dono kurai no sokudo de iki masu ka.*
How deep is the water here?	ここの水深はどのくらいありますか？ *koko no suishin wa dono kurai arimasu ka.*
I got one!	かかった！ *kakatta!*

I can't swim.	泳げません。
	oyoge masen.
Can we go ashore?	岸に上がれますか？
	kishi ni agare masu ka.

For more boating terms, see p56.

DIVING

I'd like to go snorkeling.	スノーケルをしたいのですが。
	sunōkeru o shitai no desuga.
I'd like to go scuba diving.	スキューバダイビングをしたいので すが。
	sukyūba daibingu o shitai no desuga.
I have a NAUI / PADI certification.	私は NAUI / PADI の資格証明書を持 っています。
	watashi wa NAUI / PADI no shikaku shōmei sho o motte imasu.
I need to rent gear.	道具を借りる必要があります。
	dōgu o kariru hitsuyō ga arimasu.
We'd like to see some shipwrecks if we can.	できれば難破船を見たいです。
	deki reba nanpa sen o mitai desu.
Are there any good reef dives?	さんご礁のあるダイビング場所はあり ますか？
	sango shō no aru daibingu basho wa arimasu ka.
I'd like to see a lot of sea-life.	海の生き物をたくさん見たいです。
	umi no ikimono o takusan mitai desu.
Are the currents strong?	潮の流れは強いですか？
	shio no nagare wa tsuyoi desu ka.
How clear is the water?	海の中の透明度はどうですか？
	umi no naka no tōmeido wa dō desu ka.

I want / don't want to go with a group.	グループで行きたい / 行きたくない です。
	gurūpu de ikitai / ikitaku nai desu.
Can we charter our own boat?	私たちだけで行くボートをチャーター できますか？
	watashi tachi dake de iku bōto o chātā deki masu ka.

SURFING

I'd like to go surfing.	サーフィンをしたいのですが。
	sāfin o shitai no desuga.
Are there any good beaches?	よいビーチはありますか？
	yoi bīchi wa arimasu ka.
Can I rent a board?	ボードを借りることはできますか？
	bōdo o karirukoto wa deki masu ka.
How are the currents?	潮の流れはどうですか？
	shio no nagare wa dō desu ka.
How high are the waves?	波の高さはどれくらいですか？
	nami no takasa wa dore kurai desu ka.
Is it usually crowded?	たいていいつも混んでいますか？
	taitei itsumo konde imasu ka.
Are there facilities on that beach?	そのビーチにシャワーやトイレはあり ますか？
	sono bīchi ni shawā ya toire wa arimasu ka.
Is there wind surfing there also?	そこにはウィンド サーフィンもありま すか？
	soko niwa uindo sāfin mo arimasu ka.

GOLFING

I'd like to reserve a tee-time, please.	ティー タイムの予約をお願いします。 *tī taimu no yoyaku o onegai shimasu.*
Do we need to be members to play?	会員でないとプレイできませんか？ *kaiin de nai to purē deki masen ka.*
How many holes is your course?	このコースは何ホールありますか？ *kono kōsu wa nan hōru arimasu ka.*
What is par for the course?	このコースのパーはいくつですか？ *kono kōsu no pā wa ikutsu desu ka.*
I need to rent clubs.	クラブを借りなければなりません。 *kurabu o kari nakereba narimasen.*
I need to purchase a sleeve of balls.	ボール一箱買わなければなりません。 *bōru hito hako kawa nakereba narimasen.*
I need a glove.	手袋が必要です。 *tebukuro ga hitsuyō desu.*
I need a new hat.	新しい帽子が必要です。 *atarashii bōshi ga hitsuyō desu.*
Do you require soft spikes?	ソフトスパイクを履かなければなりませんか？ *sofuto supaiku o haka nakere ba narima sen ka.*
Do you have carts?	カートはありますか？ *kāto wa arimasu ka.*

I'd like to hire a caddy.	キャディを雇いたいのですが。
	kyadī o yatoi tai no desuga.
Do you have a driving range?	ゴルフ練習場はありますか？
	gorufu renshū jō wa arimasu ka.
How much are the greens fees?	グリーン料金はいくらですか？
	gurīn ryōkin wa ikura desu ka.
Can I book a lesson with the pro?	プロレッスンの予約はできますか？
	puro ressun no yoyaku wa deki masu ka.
I need to have a club repaired.	クラブの修理が必要です。
	kurabu no shūri ga hitsuyō desu.
Is the course dry?	コースは乾いていますか？
	kōsu wa kawaite imasu ka.
Are there any wildlife hazards?	野生動物に遭遇する危険はありますか？
	yasei dōbutsu ni sōgu suru kiken wa arimasu ka.
How many meters is the course?	このコースは一周何メートルありますか？
	kono kōsu wa isshū nan mētoru arimasu ka.
Is it very hilly?	急な斜面が多いですか？
	kyū na shamen ga ōi desu ka.

CHAPTER TEN

NIGHTLIFE

For coverage of movies and cultural events, see p128, Chapter Seven, "Culture."

CLUB HOPPING

Where can I find _____ ?	_____はどこにありますか？ _____ wa doko ni arimasu ka.
a good nightclub	よいナイトクラブ *yoi naito kurabu*
a club with a live band	ライブ演奏のあるクラブ *raibu ensō no aru kurabu*
a reggac club	レゲー クラブ *regē kurabu*
a hip hop club	ヒップホップ クラブ *hippu hoppu kurabu*
a techno club	テクノ クラブ *tekuno kurabu*
a jazz club	ジャズ クラブ *jazu kurabu*
a country western club	カントリー ウエスタン クラブ *kantori uesutan kurabu*
a gay / lesbian club	ゲイ / レスビアン クラブ *gei / resubian kurabu*
a club where I can dance	踊れるクラブ *odoreru kurabu*
a club with Spanish / Mexican music	スペイン / メキシコ音楽が聴ける クラブ *supein / mekishiko ongaku ga kikeru kurabu*
the most popular club in town	街で一番人気があるクラブ *machi de ichiban ninki ga aru kurabu*

a singles bar	独身が集まるバー
	dokushin ga atsumaru bā
a piano bar	ピアノ バー
	piano bā
the most upscale club	最高級バー
	sai kōkyū bā
What's the hottest bar these days?	最近最も人気があるのはどんなバーですか？
	saikin mottomo ninki ga aru nowa donna bā desu ka.
What's the cover charge?	カバー チャージはいくらですか？
	kabā chāji wa ikura desu ka.
Do they have a dress code?	服装に規則はありますか？
	fukusō ni kisoku wa arimasu ka.
Is it expensive?	値段は高いですか？
	nedan wa takai desu ka.
What's the best time to go?	いつ行くのが一番いいですか？
	itsu iku noga ichiban ii desu ka.
What kind of music do they play there?	どんな音楽を演奏していますか？
	donna ongaku o ensō shite imasu ka.
Is it smoking?	タバコを吸えますか？
	tabako o sue masu ka.
Is it nonsmoking?	禁煙ですか？
	kin en desu ka.
I'm looking for ____	____を探しています。
	____ o sagashite imasu.
a good cigar shop.	よいタバコ屋
	yoi tabako ya
a pack of cigarettes.	タバコ１箱
	tabako hito hako

I'd like _____	_____ ください。 _____ *kudasai.*
a drink please.	飲み物を *nomi mono o*
a bottle of beer please.	ビールを1本 *bīru o ippon*
a beer on tap please.	生ビールを *nama bīru o*
a shot of _____ please.	_____ を1杯 _____ *o ippai*

For a full list of drinks, see p79.

Make it a double please!	ダブルにしてください！ *daburu ni shite kudasai.*
With ice, please.	水を入れてください。 *kōri o irete kudasai.*
And one for the lady / the gentleman!	1つはこのご婦人／男性に！ *hitotsu wa kono gofujin / dansei ni.*
How much for a bottle / glass of beer?	ビール1本／1杯はいくらですか？ *bīru ippon / ippai wa ikura desu ka.*

NIGHTLIFE

Do You Mind If I Smoke?

タバコはありますか？ *tabako wa arimasuka.*	Do you have a cigarette?
火はありますか？ *hi wa arimasuka.*	Do you have a light?
火をおかししましょうか？ *hi o okashi shimashō ka.*	May I offer you a light?
禁煙です。 *kin en desu.*	Smoking not permitted.

I'd like to buy a drink for that woman / man over there.

あそこの女性 / 男性に私のおごりで一杯あげてください。

asoko no josei / dansei ni watashi no ogori de ippai agete kudasai.

A pack of cigarettes, please.

タバコを１箱ください。

tabako o hito hako kudasai.

Do you have a lighter or matches?

ライターかマッチを持ってますか?

raitā ka macchi o motte masu ka.

Do you smoke?

タバコを吸いますか?

tabako o suimasu ka.

Would you like a cigarette?

タバコ１本いかがですか?

tabako ippon ikaga desu ka.

May I run a tab?

つけにしていいですか?

tsuke ni shite ii desu ka.

What's the cover?

カバーチャージはいくらですか?

kabā chāji wa ikura desu ka.

ACROSS A CROWDED ROOM

Excuse me; may I buy you a drink?

あのー、私のおごりで１杯いかがですか?

anō, watashi no ogori de ippai ikaga desu ka.

You look amazing.	すてきですね。
	suteki desu ne.
You look like the most interesting person in the room.	あなたはここで一番魅力的です。
	anata wa koko de ichiban miryoku teki desu.
Would you like to dance?	ダンスしませんか？
	dansu shima sen ka.
Do you like to dance fast or slow?	ダンスは速いのとスローなのとどちらが好きですか？
	dansu wa hayai noto surōna noto dochira ga suki desu ka.
Give me your hand.	手をかしてください。
	te o kashite kudasai.
What would you like to drink?	飲み物は何がいいですか？
	nomi mono wa nani ga ii desu ka.
You're a great dancer.	踊りが上手ですね。
	odori ga jōzu desu ne.
I don't know that dance!	あれは私の知らないダンスです！
	are wa watashi no shira nai dansu desu
Do you like this song?	この歌は好きですか？
	kono uta wa suki desu ka.
You have nice eyes!	あなたの目はとても素敵ですね！
	anata no me wa totemo suteki desu ne.

For a full list of features, see p105.

For a full list of features, see p105.

May I have your phone number?	あなたの電話番号を教えてくれますか？
	anata no denwa bangō o oshiete kureru masu ka.

NIGHTLIFE

IN THE CASINO

How much is this table?	このテーブルでは最低いくらのかけ ですか? *kono tēburu dewa saitei ikura no kake desu ka.*
Deal me in.	私も入れてください。 *watashi mo irete kudasai.*
Put it on red!	赤に置いてください! *aka ni oite kudasai.*
Put it on black!	黒に置いてください! *kuro ni oite kudasai.*
Let it ride!	つづけるよ! *tsuzukeru yo!*
21!	21! *nijū ichi!*
Snake-eyes!	スネークアイだ! *sunēku ai da!*
Seven.	7。 *shichi/nana.*

For a full list of numbers, see p6.

Damn, eleven.	残念、11 だ。 *zannen, jū ichi da.*
I'll pass.	パスします。 *pasu shimasu.*
Hit me!	もう 1 枚! *mō ichi mai.*
Split.	2 手に分けるよ。 *futa te ni wakeru yo.*
Are the drinks complimentary?	飲み物はタダですか? *nomi mono wa tada desu ka.*
May I bill it to my room?	わたしの部屋につけてくれますか? *watashi no heya ni tsukete kure masu ka.*

I'd like to cash out.	清算してください。
	seisan shite kudasai.
I'll hold.	パスします。
	pasu shimasu.
I'll see your bet.	それにあわせます。
	sore ni awasemasu.
I call.	コール。
	kōru.
Full house!	フルハウス!
	furu hausu.
Royal flush.	ロイヤル フラッシュ。
	roiyaru furasshu.
Straight,	ストレート。
	sutoreto.

NIGHTLIFE

CHAPTER ELEVEN

HEALTH & SAFETY

This chapter covers the terms you'll need to maintain your health
and safety—including the most useful phrases for the pharmacy,
the doctor's office, and the police station.

AT THE PHARMACY

Please fill this prescription.	この薬を処方してください。 *kono kusuri o shohō shite kudasai.*
Do you have something for ____ ?	____に効く薬はありますか？ ____ *ni kiku kusuri wa arimasu ka.*
a cold	カゼ *kaze*
a cough	咳 *seki*
I need something ____	____が欲しいのですが。 ____ *ga hoshii no desuga.*
to help me sleep.	眠れるようになるもの *nemureru yōni naru mono*
to help me relax.	気を静められるもの *ki o shizume rareru mono*
I want to buy ____	____をください。 ____ *o kudasai.*
condoms.	コンドーム *kondōmu*
an antihistamine.	抗ヒスタミン剤 *kō hisutamin zai*
antibiotic cream.	抗生物質クリーム *kōsei busshitsu kurīmu*
aspirin.	アスピリン *asupirin*

non-aspirin pain reliever.	アスピリン以外の鎮痛剤
	asupirin igai no chintsūzai
medicine with codeine.	コデインを含む薬
	kodein o fukumu kusuri
insect repellant.	虫除けローション
	mushi yoke rōshon
I need something for _____	_____に効くものが欲しいのですが。
	_____ ni kiku mono ga hoshii no desuga.
corns.	うおのめ
	uonome
congestion.	充血
	jūketsu
warts.	いぼ
	ibo
constipation.	便秘
	benpi
diarrhea.	下痢
	geri
indigestion.	消化不良
	shōka furyō
nausea.	吐き気
	hakike
motion sickness.	乗り物酔い
	norimono yoi
seasickness.	船酔い
	funayoi
acne.	ニキビ
	nikibi

AT THE DOCTOR'S OFFICE

I would like to see _____	_____に診ていただきたいのですが。
	_____ ni mite itadaki tai no desuga.
a doctor.	医者
	isha

HEALTH & SAFETY

a chiropractor.	カイロプラクター
	kairo purakutā
a gynecologist.	婦人科医
	fujinka i
an eye / ears & nose / throat specialist.	眼科 / 耳鼻科 / 咽喉科医
	ganka / jibika / inkōka i
a dentist.	歯医者
	haisha
an optometrist.	検眼師
	kenganshi
Do I need an appointment?	予約が必要ですか？
	yoyaku ga hitsuyō desu ka.
I have an emergency.	緊急なんです。
	kinkyū nan desu.
My prescription has run out and I need a refill.	薬がなくなってしまったので薬をいただきたいのですが。
	kusuri ga nakunatte shimatta node kusuri o itadakitai no desuga.
Please call a doctor.	医者を呼んでください。
	isha o yonde kudasai.
I need an ambulance.	救急車を呼んでください。
	kyūkyū sha o yonde kudasai.

SYMPTOMS

For a full list of body parts, see p165.

My ____ hurts.	____が痛いんです。
	____ *ga itain desu.*
My ____ is stiff.	____が凝っています。
	____ *ga kotte imasu.*
I think I'm having a heart attack.	心臓発作を起こしたみたいです。
	shinzō hossa o okoshita mitai desu.
I can't move.	動けません。
	ugoke masen.
I fell.	転びました。
	korobi mashita.

I fainted.	気を失いました。 *ki o ushinai mashita.*
I have a cut on my ____.	____を切りました。 *____ o kiri mashita.*
I have a headache.	頭痛がします。 *zutsū ga shimasu.*
My vision is blurry.	物がぼやけて見えます。 *mono ga boyakete mie masu.*
I feel dizzy.	めまいがします。 *memai ga shimasu.*
I think I'm pregnant.	妊娠したみたいなんです。 *ninshin shita mitai nan desu.*
I don't think I'm pregnant.	妊娠ではないと思います。 *ninshin dewa nai to omoi masu.*
I'm having trouble walking.	歩行が困難なんです。 *hokō ga konnan nan desu.*
I can't get up.	立ち上がれません。 *tachi agare masen.*

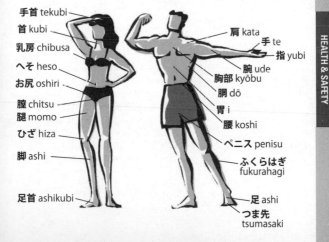

手首 tekubi
首 kubi
乳房 chibusa
へそ heso
お尻 oshiri
膣 chitsu
腿 momo
ひざ hiza
脚 ashi
足首 ashikubi

肩 kata
手 te
指 yubi
腕 ude
胸部 kyōbu
胴 dō
胃 i
腰 koshi
ペニス penisu
ふくらはぎ fukurahagi
足 ashi
つま先 tsumasaki

I was mugged.	襲われました。
	osoware mashita.
I was raped.	強姦されました。
	gōkan sare mashita.
A dog attacked me.	犬に襲われました。
	inu ni osoware mashita.
A snake bit me.	蛇にかまれました。
	hebi ni kamare mashita.
I can't move my ____ without pain.	____を動かすと痛みます。
	____ o ugokasu to itami masu.

MEDICATIONS

I need morning-after pills.	モーニング アフター ピルが欲しいのですが。
	mōningu afutā piru ga hoshii no desuga.
I need birth control pills.	避妊薬が欲しいのですが。
	hinin yaku ga hoshii no desuga.
I lost my eyeglasses and need new ones.	眼鏡をなくしたので、新しいのが必要なんですが。
	megane o nakushita node, atarashii noga hitsuyō nan desuga.
I need new contact lenses.	新しいコンタクトレンズが必要なんですが。
	atarashii kontakuto renzu ga hitsuyō nan desuga.
I need erectile dysfunction pills.	勃起不全改善薬が欲しいのですが。
	bokki fuzen kaizen yaku ga hoshii no desuga.
Please fill this prescription.	処方箋がほしいのですが。
	shohōsen ga hoshii no desuga.

I need a prescription for ____.	_____の薬を処方してほしいので すが。
	_____ no kusuri o shoho shite hoshii no desuga.
I am allergic to ____	私は____にアレルギーがあります。
	watashi wa____ ni arerugī ga arimasu.
penicillin.	ペニシリン
	penishirin
antibiotics.	抗生物質
	kōsei busshitsu
sulfa drugs.	サルファー剤
	sarufā zai
steroids.	ステロイド
	suteroido
I have asthma.	私は喘息を持っています。
	watashi wa zensoku o motte imasu.

DENTAL PROBLEMS

I have a toothache.	歯が痛みます。
	ha ga itami masu.
I chipped a tooth.	歯が欠けました。
	ha ga kake mashita.
My bridge came loose.	ブリッジがゆるんできました。
	burijji ga yurunde kimashita.
I lost a crown.	歯にかぶせていたものがとれてしまい ましたしました。
	ha ni kabusete ita mono ga torete shimai mashita.
I lost a denture plate.	義歯がとれてしまいました。
	gishi ga torete shimai mashita.

AT THE POLICE STATION

I'm sorry, did I do something wrong?	すみません、私がなにか悪いことをしましたか？
	sumima sen, watashi ga nani ka warui koto o shimashita ka.
I am ____	私は____です。
	watashi wa ____ desu.
an American.	アメリカ人
	amerika jin
British.	イギリス人
	igirisu jin
a Canadian.	カナダ人
	kanada jin
Irish.	アイルランド人
	airurando jin
an Australian.	オーストラリア人
	ōsutoraria jin
a New Zealander.	ニュージーランド人
	nyūjīrando jin
The car is a rental.	車はレンタカーです。
	kuruma wa rentakā desu.
Do I pay the fine to you?	罰金を払うのですか？
	bakkin o harau no desu ka.
Do I have to go to court?	裁判所に行かなければなりませんか？
	saiban sho ni ikana kereba narima sen ka.
When?	いつですか？
	itsu desu ka.
I'm sorry, my Japanese isn't very good.	すみません、日本語はあまり上手に話せません。
	sumima sen, nihon go wa amari jōzuni hanase masen.

Listen Up: Police Lingo

免許証、登録証、保険証を見せてください。 *menkyo shō, tōroku shō, hoken shō o misete kudasai.*	Your license, registration and insurance, please.
罰金は 1000 円です。私に直接払ってもかまいません。 *bekkin wa sen en desu. watashi ni chokusetsu harattemo kamai masen.*	The fine is ¥1000. You can pay me directly.
パスポートを見せてください。 *pasupōto o misete kudasai.*	Your passport please?
どこに行くんですか? *doko ni ikun desu ka.*	Where are you going?
なぜそんなに急いでいますか? *naze sonnani isoide imasu ka.*	Why are you in such a hurry?

I need an interpreter.	通訳が必要です。 *tsūyaku ga hitsuyō desu.*
I'm sorry, I don't understand the ticket.	すみません、このチケットの意味がわかりません。 *sumima sen, kono chiketto no imi ga wakari masen.*
May I call my embassy?	私の国の大使館に電話をかけてもいいですか? *watashi no kuni no taishi kan ni denwa o kaketemo ii desu ka.*
I was robbed.	強盗に遭いました。 *gōtō ni ai mashita.*
I was mugged.	襲われました。 *osoware mashita.*

HEALTH & SAFETY

I was raped.	強姦されました。
	gōkan sare mashita.
Do I need to make a report?	警察に届け出る必要がありますか？
	keisatsu ni todokeru hitsuyō ga arimasu ka.
Somebody broke into my room.	誰かが私の部屋に侵入しました。
	dareka ga watashi no heya ni shin nyū shima shita.
Someone stole my purse / wallet.	誰かが私のハンドバッグ/財布を盗みました。
	dareka ga watashi no hando baggu/ saifu o nusumi mashita.

ENGLISH–JAPANESE

DICTIONARY KEY

n	noun	*s*	singular
v	verb	*pl*	plural
adj	adjective		
prep	preposition		
adv	adverb		

Japanese verbs are conjugated only to indicate tense (see p26). They are listed here in present tense form.

For food terms, see the Menu Reader (p82) and Grocery section (p90) in Chapter 4, Dining.

A

able, to be able to (can) *v* で きる dekiru

above *adj* 上の ue no p70

accept, to accept *v* 受け入れる uke ireru

Do you accept credit cards? クレジットカードを使えます か? kurejitto kādo o tsukae masu ka. p34

accident *n* 事故 jiko p52

I've had an accident. 事故に あいました。 jiko ni ai mashita. p52

account *n* 口座 kōza p120

I'd like to transfer to / from my checking / savings account. 当座預金/普通預金 口座へ/から振り替えたいので すが。 tōza-yokin/futsū-yokin e/kara furikaete tai no desuga.

acne *n* にきび nikibi p163

across *prep* の向こう側 no mukō gawa p6

across the street この道の向こう 側 kono michi no mukō gawa p6

actual *adj* 実際の jissai no

adapter plug *n* アダプター プラ グ adaputā puragu

address *n* 住所 jūsho p110

What's the address? 住所は何ですか? jūsho wa nan desu ka.

admission fee *n* 入場料 nyūjōryō p131

in advance 前もって mae motte p129

African-American *adj* アフリ カ系アメリカ人の afurika kei amerika jin no p105

afternoon *n* 午後 gogo p14

in the afternoon 午後に gogo ni

age *n* 歳 toshi

What's your age? 何歳です か? nan sai desu ka.

agency *n* 会社 kaisha p45

car rental agency レンタ カー 会社 rentakā gaisha

agnostic *adj* 不可知論の fukachiron no

air conditioning n 冷房 reibō
p128 /エアコン eakon p46,
62, 68

**Would you lower / raise
the air conditioning?** 冷房
を下げて/上げていただけませ
んか? reibō o sagete/agete
itadake masen ka.

airport n 空港 kūkō

I need a ride to the airport.
空港まで乗って行く必要があ
ります。kūkō made notte iku
hitsuyō ga arimasu.

**How far is it from the
airport?** 空港からどのくらい
のところにありますか? kūkō
kara dono kurai no tokoro ni
arimasu ka.

airsickness bag n 飛行機酔い
の袋 hikōki yoi no fukuro p43

aisle n 通路 tsūro

alarm clock n 目覚まし時計
mezamashi tokei p68

alcohol n アルコール arukōru p79

Do you serve alcohol?
アルコールは出していますか?
arukōru wa dashite imasu ka.

I'd like nonalcoholic beer.
アルコール抜きのビールをく
ださい。arukōru nuki no bīru
o kudasai.

all n すべて subete p13

all adj すべての subete no p13

all of the time いつも itsumo

That's all, thank you. 以上で
す。どうもありがとう。ijō desu.
dōmo arigatō.

allergic adj アレルギー体質の /
アレルギー反応の arerugī han
nō no p68

I'm allergic to ____. 私
は____にアレルギーがありま
す。watashi wa ____ ni arerugī
ga arimasu.p78,167 See
p78 and 167 for common
allergens.

altitude n 標高 hyōkō p148

aluminum n アルミニウム
aruminiumu

ambulance n 救急車 kyūkyūsha

American adj アメリカの、アメ
リカ人の amerika no, amerika
jin no

amount n 量 ryō

angry adj 怒った okotta

animal n 動物 dōbutsu

another adj 別の betsu no p43

answer n 答え kotae

**answer, to answer (phone
call, question)** v 答える
kotaeru

Answer me, please. 答えてく
ださい。kotaete kudasai.

antibiotic n 抗生物質 kōsei
busshitsu

I need an antibiotic. 抗生物
質をください。kōsei busshitsu
o kudasai.

antihistamine n 抗ヒスタミン剤
kōhisutamin zai p162

anxious adj 心配な shinpai na /
心配している shinpai shiteiru
p106

any adj 何か nanika /何も
/nanimo

anything n 何でも nan demo

anywhere adv どこへも doko emo

April n 四月 shi gatsu p17

appointment n 予約 yoyaku p141,164

Do I need an appointment? 予約が必要ですか? yoyaku ga hitsuyō desu ka. p164

are v See be, to be.

Argentinian adj アルゼンチンの、アルゼンチン人の aruzenchin no, aruzenchin jin no

arm n 腕 ude p165

arrive, to arrive v 到着する tōchaku suru p35, 36

arrival(s) n 到着 tōchaku

animal n 動物 dōbutsu

exhibit of art 美術品の展示 bijutsu hin no tenji

art adj 芸術の geijutsu no

art museum n 美術館 bijutsu kan

artist n 美術家 bijutsu ka

Asian adj アジアの、アジア人の ajia no, ajia jin no p105

ask for (request) v 頼む tanomu

ask a question v 質問する shitsumon suru

aspirin n アスピリン asupirin p162

assist v 手伝う tetsudau p39

assistance n 手伝い tetsudai/アシスタンス ashisutansu p59

asthma n 喘息 zensoku p167

I have asthma. 喘息があります。zensoku ga arimasu./喘息を持っています。zensoku o motte imasu. p167

atheist n 無神論者 mushinron sha p113

ATM n ATM機 ATM ki

I'm looking for an ATM. ATM機を探しています。ATM ki o sagashite imasu.

attend v 参加する sanka suru p104 /出席する shusseki suru

audio adj 音声の onsei no p132

August n 八月 hachi gatsu p17

aunt n おば oba / おばさん obasan p102

Australia n オーストラリア ōsutoraria

Australian adj オーストラリアの、オーストラリア人の ōsutoraria no, ōsutoraria jin no

autumn n 秋 aki p17

available adj 使用可能な shiyō kanō na

B

baby n 赤ちゃん aka chan p103/ベビー bebī p90

baby adj 赤ちゃんの aka chan no

Do you sell baby food? ベビーフードは売っていますか? bebī fūdo wa utte imasu ka.

babysitter n ベビーシッター bebī shittā

Do you have babysitters who speak English? 英語を

話すベビーシッターはいますか? eigo o hanasu bebī shittā wa imasu ka.

back n 背中 senaka

My back hurts. 背中が痛みます。 senaka ga itami masu.

back rub n 背中をさする senaka o sasuru

backed up (toilet) adj つまっている tsumatte iru

The toilet is backed up. トイレがつまっています。 toire ga tsumatte imasu.

bag n 袋

airsickness bag 飛行機酔いの袋 hikōki yoi no fukuro p43

My bag was stolen. 私のバックが盗まれました。 watashi no baggu ga nusumare mashita.

I lost my bag. 私はバックを失くしました。 watashi wa baggu o nakushi mashita.

bag v 袋に入れる fukuro ni ireru

baggage n 手荷物 tenimotsu p34, 44

baggage adj 手荷物の tenimotsu no

baggage claim 手荷物引き渡し所 tenimotsu hikiwatashi jo p44

bait n えさ esa

balance (on bank account) n 残高 zandaka p120

balance v バランスを取る baransu o toru

balcony n バルコニー barukonī p60

ball (sport) n ボール bōru

ballroom dancing n 社交ダンス shakō dansu p129

band (musical ensemble) n 演奏 ensō p155

band-aid n vendaje m, バンドエイド bando eido

bank n 銀行 ginkō p118

Can you help me find a bank? 銀行はどこにあるか教えていただけますか? ginkō wa doko ni aruka oshiete itadake masu ka.

bar n バー bā

barber n 理髪店 rihatsu ten

bass (instrument) n バス basu

bath n お風呂 ofuro

bathroom (restroom) n トイレ toire p33, 59

Where is the nearest public bathroom? ここから一番近い公衆トイレはどこにありますか? koko kara ichiban chikai kōshū toire wa doko ni arimasu ka.

bathtub n 浴槽 yokusō p62

bathe, to bathe oneself v お風呂に入る ofuro ni hairu

battery (for flashlight) n 電池 denchi

battery (for car) n バッテリー batterī

bee n ハチ hachi

I was stung by a bee. ハチに刺されました。 hachi ni sasare mashita.

be, to be (temporary state, condition, mood) v である de aru

be, to be (permanent quality) v である de aru

beach n ビーチ bīchi p62, 116, 152

beach v ビーチに乗り上げる bīchi ni noriageru

beard n ひげ hige

beautiful adj きれいな kireina p137

bed n ベッド beddo p61

beer n ビール bīru p42, 79

  beer on tap 生ビール nama bīru p79

begin v 始まる hajimaru p129

behave v 振る舞う furumau

behind adv 後ろの ushiro no p5

below adv 下の shita no p70

belt n ベルト beruto p41

  conveyor belt ベルトコンベヤー beruto konbeyā

berth n 寝台 shindai

best 最高の saikō no

bet, to bet v かける kakeru

better より良い yori yoi

big adj 大きい ōkii p13

bilingual adj 二ヶ国語を話す ni kakoku go o hanasu

bill (currency) n 紙幣 shihei p118

bill v 請求する seikyū suru p123

biography n 伝記 denki

biracial adj 人種の混じった jinshu no majitta p105

bird n 鳥 tori

birth control n 避妊 hinin

I'm out of birth control pills. 避妊薬がなくなりました。 hinin yaku ga nakunari mashita.

I need more birth control pills. もっと避妊薬が必要 です。 motto hinin yaku ga hitsuyō desu.

bit (small amount) n 少し sukoshi

black adj 黒い kuroi /黒人 koku jin p104

blanket n 毛布 mōfu p43

bleach n ブリーチ burīchi

blind adj 目の見えない me no mienai

block n 角 kado p6 /ブロック burokku

blond(e) adj 金髪の kinpatsu no p104

blouse n ブラウス burausu p135

blue adj 青い aoi p105

blurry adj ぼやけた boyaketa p165

board n 搭乗 tōjō p39

  on board 搭乗して tōjō shite

board v 入港する nyūkō suru

boarding pass n 搭乗券 tōjō ken p41

boat n ボート bōto

Bolivian adj ボリビアの、ボリビア 人の boribia no, boribia jin no

bomb n 爆弾 bakudan

book n 本 hon p117, 139

bookstore n 本屋 hon ya p133

boss n 上司 jōshi

bottle n ビン bin

May I heat this (baby) bottle someplace? どこかでこのビンを温めることができますか? dokoka de kono bin o atatameru koto ga deki masu ka.

box (seat) n ボックス席 bokkusu seki p130/ボックスシート bokkusu sīto p146

box office n チケット売り場 chiketto uriba

boy n 男の子 otoko no ko

boyfriend n ボーイフレンド bōi furendo p101

braid n 編んだ髪 anda kami p142

braille, American n 点字、アメリカの tenji, amerika no

brake n ブレーキ burēki p50

emergency brake 非常ブレーキ hijō burēki

brake v ブレーキをかける burēki o kakeru

brandy n ブランデー burandē p80

bread n パン pan p78, 90

break v 壊れる kowareru

breakfast n 朝食 chōshoku p66

What time is breakfast? 朝食は何時ですか? chōshoku wa nan ji desu ka.

bridge (across a river, dental) n 橋 hashi /歯の矯正ブリッジ ha no kyōsei burijji p167

briefcase n ブリーフケース burīfu kēsu p44

bright adj 明るい akarui

broadband n ブロードバンド burōdo bando

bronze adj ブロンズ製の buronzu sei no

brother n 兄弟 kyōdai / ご兄弟 go kyōdai p102

brown adj 茶色の cha iro no p106

brunette n ブルネット burunetto p104

Buddhist n 仏教徒 bukkyōto p113

budget n 予算 yosan

buffet n バイキング baikingu

bug n 虫 mushi

bull n 雄牛 oushi

bullfight n 闘牛 tōgyū

bullfighter n 闘牛士 tōgyū shi

burn v 焼く yaku/焼きつける yaki tsukeru

Can I burn a CD here? ここで CD に焼きつけ(書込み)できますか? koko de CD ni yakitsuke (kakikomi) deki masu ka. p124

bus n バス basu p53, 55

Where is the bus stop? バス停はどこにありますか? basu tei wa doko ni arimasu ka.

Which bus goes to ____? ____行きのバスはどれですか。____ yuki no basu wa dore desu ka. p55

business n ビジネス bijinesu p37, 40

business adj 商用で shōyō de p103

business center ビジネス センター bijinesu sentā p66

busy adj 客の多い kyaku no ōi **(restaurant)**, 話し中で hanashi chū de **(phone)**

butter *n* バター batā p77
buy, to buy *v* 買う kau **p121, 129, 134**

C

café *n* 喫茶店 kissa ten p34, 74
  Internet café インターネット カフェ intânetto kafe p124
call, to call *v* 呼ぶ yobu (shout) 電話をかける denwa o kakeru (phone) p66
camp, to camp *v* キャンプをする kyanpu o suru **p115**
camper *n* キャンパー kyanpā p71
camping *adj* キャンプの kyanpu no
  Do we need a camping permit? キャンプをする許可が必要ですか? kyanpu o suru kyoka ga hitsuyō desu ka.
campsite *n* キャンプサイト kyanpu saito **p149**
can *n* 缶詰 kanzume
can (able to) *v* できる dekiru
Canada *n* カナダ kanada
Canadian *adj* カナダの、カナダ人の kanada no, kanada jin no
cancel, to cancel *v* 取り消す tori kesu **p38**
  My flight was canceled. 私のフライトはキャンセルされました。watashi no furaito wa kyanseru saremashita.
canvas *n* キャンバス kyanbasu (for painting) /キャンバス地 kyanbasu ji **p45** (material)
cappuccino *n* カプチーノ kapuchīno

car *n* 車 kuruma
  car rental agency レンタ カー会社 rentakā gaisha
  I need a rental car. レンタカーが必要です。rentakā ga hitsuyō desu.
card *n* カード kādo p34
  Do you accept credit cards? クレジットカードを使えますか? kurejitto kādo o tsukae masu ka. p34
  May I have your business card? あなたの名刺をいただけますか? anata no meishi o itadake masu ka.
car seat (child's safety seat) *n* チャイルドシート chairudo shīto
  Do you rent car seats for children? チャイルドシートをレンタルしていますか? chairudo shīto o rentaru shite imasu ka.
carsickness *n* 車酔い kuruma yoi
cash *n* 現金 genkin p138
  cash only 現金のみ genkin nomi p120
cash, to cash *v* 現金に換える genkin ni kaeru
  to cash out (gambling) 清算する seisan suru p161
cashmere *n* カシミヤ kashimiya
casino *n* カジノ kajino p60
cat *n* ねこ neko
Catholic *adj* カトリック教の katorikku kyō no p113

cavity (tooth cavity) n 虫歯 mushiba

I think I have a cavity. 虫歯があるようなんです。 mushiba ga aru yō nandesu.

CD n CD p46, 124

CD player n CD プレーヤー CD purēyā p46

celebrate, to celebrate v 祝う iwau

cell phone n 携帯電話 keitai denwa p121

centimeter n センチメートル senchi mētoru

chamber music n 室内楽 shitsunai gaku

change (money) n おつり otsuri

I'd like change, please. おつりをください。 otsuri o kudasai.

This isn't the correct change. このおつりは正しくありません。 kono otsuri wa tadashiku arimasen.

change (to change money, clothes) v 交換する kōkan suru

changing room n 更衣室 kōi shitsu

charge, to charge (money) v 請求する seikyū suru p123

charge, to charge (a battery) v 充電する jūden suru p59

charmed adj 魅了された miryō sareta

charred (meat) adj ベリーウェルで berī weru de p76

charter, to charter v チャーターする chātā suru p152

cheap adj 安い yasui p47, 146

check n 小切手 kogitte / チェック chekku p64, 118

Do you accept travelers' checks? トラベラーズ チェックを使えますか? toraberāzu chekku o tsukae masu ka. p64

check, to check v 調べる shiraberu

checked (pattern) adj チェックの chekku no

check-in n チェックイン chekku in p33

What time is check-in? チェックインは何時ですか? chekku in wa nan ji desu ka.

check-out n チェックアウト chekku auto

check-out time チェックアウトの時間 chekku auto no jikan

What time is check-out? チェックアウトは何時ですか? chekku auto wa nan ji desu ka.

check out, to check out v チェックアウトする chekku auto suru p64

cheese n チーズ chīzu p90

chicken n チキン chikin

child n 子供 kodomo p43

children n 子供たち kodomo tachi p40, 76

Are children allowed? 子供もいいですか? kodomo mo ii desu ka.

Do you have children's programs? 子供用のプログラムはありますか? kodomo yō no puroguramu wa arimasu ka.

ENGLISH–JAPANESE

Do you have a children's menu? 子供用のメニューはありますか? kodomo yō no menyū wa arimasu ka.

Chinese *adj* 中国の、中国人の chūgoku no, chūgoku jin no p107

chiropractor *n* カイロプラクター kairo purakutā p164

church *n* 教会 kyōkai p112

cigar *n* 葉巻 hamaki

cigarette *n* タバコ tabako

  a pack of cigarettes タバコ1箱 tabako hito hako

cinema *n* 映画館 eiga kan

city *n* 市 shi/ 街 machi p62

claim *n* 請求 seikyū

  I'd like to file a claim. 賠償を請求します。 baishō o seikyū shimasu.

clarinet *n* クラリネット kurarinetto

class *n* クラス kurasu p37

  business class ビジネスクラス bijinesu kurasu

  economy class エコノミークラス ekonomī kurasu

  first class ファーストクラス fāsuto kurasu

classical (music) *adj* クラシックの kurasshikku no

clean *adj* 清潔な seiketsu na

clean, to clean *v* 掃除する sōji suru

  Please clean the room today. 今日、部屋を掃除してください。 kyō, heya o sōji shite kudasai.

clear *v* 明らかにする akiraka ni suru

clear *adj* 透明な tōmei na p151

climbing *n* 登山 tozan p147

climb, to climb *v* 登る noboru

  to climb a mountain 山に登る yama ni noboru

  to climb stairs 階段を昇る kaidan o noboru

close, to close *v* 閉じる tojiru

close (near) 近い chikai p4

closed *adj* 閉じた tojita

cloudy *adj* 曇った kumotta p111

clover *n* クローバー kurōbā

go clubbing, to go clubbing *v* クラブに踊りに行く kurabu ni odori ni iku

coat *n* コート kōto p135

cockfight *n* 闘鶏 tōkei

coffee *n* コーヒー kōhī p81

  iced coffee アイスコーヒー aisu kōhī

cognac *n* コニャック konyakku p80

coin *n* 硬貨 kōka

cold *n* カゼ kaze p98, 162

  I have a cold. カゼを引きました。 kaze o hiki mashita.

cold *adj* 寒い samui p166

  I'm cold. 寒いです。 samui desu.

  It's cold out. 外は寒いです。 soto wa samui desu.

coliseum *n* 大劇場 daigeki jō

collect *adj* 受信人払いの jushin nin barai no

I'd like to place a collect call. コレクト コールをお願いします。korekuto kōru o onegai shimasu.

collect, to collect v 集める atsumeru

college n 大学 daigaku

Colombian adj コロンビアの、コロンビア人の koronbia no, koronbia jin no

color n 色 iro

color v 色をぬる iro o nuru

computer n コンピューター konpyūtā

concert n コンサート konsāto p116

condition n 状態 jōtai

in good / bad condition 良い/悪い状態 yoi/warui jōtai

condom n コンドーム kondōmu p162

condor n コンドル kondoru

confirm, to confirm v 確認する kakunin suru p38

I'd like to confirm my reservation. 予約を確認したいのですが。yoyaku o kakunin shitai no desuga.

confused adj 混乱した konran shita

congested adj 混雑した konzatsu shita

connection speed n 回線速度 kaisen sokudo p125

constipated adj 便秘した benpi shita

I'm constipated. 便秘しています。benpi shite imasu.

contact lens n コンタクト レンズ kontakuto renzu m

I lost my contact lens. コンタクト レンズをなくしました。kontakuto renzu o nakushi mashita.

continue, to continue v 続ける tsuzukeru

convertible n オープンカー ōpun kā

cook, to cook v 料理する ryōri suru

I'd like a room where I can cook. 料理することができる部屋をお願いします。ryōri suru koto ga dekiru heya o onegai shimasu.

cookie n クッキー kukkī p90

copper adj 銅製の dōsei no

corner n 隅 sumi

on the corner 隅の

correct v 直す naosu

correct adj 正しい tadashii

Am I on the correct train? 私は正しい電車に乗っていますか? watashi wa tadashii densha ni notte imasu ka.

cost, to cost v 金額がかかる kingaku ga kakaru

How much does it cost? それはいくらしますか? sore wa ikura shimasu ka. p137

Costa Rican adj コスタリカの、コスタリカ人の kosutarika no, kosutarika jin no

costume n 衣装 ishō

cotton n 綿 men / コットン kotton p135

cough n 咳 seki p162

cough v 咳をする seki o suru p162

counter (in bar) n カウンター kauntā p74

country-and-western n カントリーアンドウエスタン kantorī ando wesutan p114

court (legal) n 裁判所 saiban sho p52, 168,

court (sport) n コート kōto

courteous adj ていねいな teinei na / 親切な shinsetsuna p70

cousin n いとこ Itoko

cover charge (in bar) n カバーチャージ kabā chāji p156, 158

cow n 牛 ushi

crack (in glass object) n ヒビ割れ hibi ware

craftsperson n 職人 shoku nin p109/工芸家 kōgeika

cream n クリーム kurīmu p77

credit card n クレジット カード kurejitto kādo p119

Do you accept credit cards? クレジットカードを使えますか? kurejitto kādo o tsukae masu ka. p119

crib n ベビーベッド bebī beddo p63

crown (dental) n 歯にかぶせているもの ha ni kabusete iru mono

curb n 縁石 enseki

curl n カール kāru

curly adj カールした kāru shita p142

currency exchange n 両替 ryōgae p34, 119

Where is the nearest currency exchange? ここから一番近い両替所はどこにありますか? koko kara ichiban chikai ryōgae jo wa doko ni arimasu ka.

current (water) n 潮の流れ shio no nagare

customs n 税関 zeikan p36 / 関税 kanzei p125

cut (wound) n 切り傷 kiri kizu

I have a bad cut. 私はひどい切り傷があります。watashi wa hidoi kirikizu ga arimasu.

cut, to cut v 切る kiru p142

cybercafé n サイバー カフェ saibā kafe

Where can I find a cybercafé? サイバー カフェはどこにありますか? saibā kafe wa doko ni arimasu ka.

D

damaged adj 損傷した sonshō shita p44

Damn! expletive しまった! shimatta / 残念! zan nen

dance v 踊る odoru / ダンスをする dansu o suru p116, 159

danger n 危険 kiken p51

dark n 暗がり kuragari

dark adj 暗い kurai

daughter n 娘 musume / お嬢さん ojōsan p103

day n 日 hi

the day before yesterday おととい ototoi p15

these last few days ここ 2 - 3日 koko nisan nichi

dawn n 夜明け yoake p14

at dawn 夜明けに yoake ni

deaf adj 耳が聞こえない mimi ga kikoenai

deal (bargain) n 取り引き torihiki

What a great deal! なんてすばらしい取引だ! nante subarashii torihiki da.

deal (cards) v 配る kubaru

Deal me in. 私も入れてください。 watashi mo irete kudasai.

December n 十二月 jū ni gatsu p17

declined adj 拒否された kyohi sareta

Was my credit card declined? 私のクレジットカードが拒否されたのですか? watashi no kurejitto kādo ga kyohi saretano desu ka.

declare v 申告する shinkoku suru p40

I have nothing to declare. 申告するものはありません。 shinkoku suru mono wa arimasen.

deep adj 深い fukai p150

delay n 遅れ okure p44

How long is the delay? どのくらいの遅れですか? dono kurai no okure desuka. p39

delighted adj 嬉しい ureshii

democracy n 民主主義 minshu shugi

dent v へこむ hekomu p48

He / She dented the car. 彼 / 彼女が車をへこませました。 kare / kanojo ga kuruma o hekomase mashita.

dentist n 歯医者 haisha p164

denture n 義歯 gishi

denture plate 義歯 gishi

departure n 出発 shuppatsu

designer n デザイナー dezainā p109

dessert n デザート dezāto p79

dessert menu デザートのメニュー dezāto no menyū

destination n 行き先 yuki saki

diabetic adj 糖尿病の tōnyōbyō no

dial (a phone) v 電話をかける denwa o kakeru / ダイヤルする daiyaru suru p66

dial direct 直通番号にかける chokutsū bangō ni kakeru

diaper n おむつ omutsu

Where can I change a diaper? おむつはどこで替えられますか? omutsu wa doko de kaerare masu ka.

diarrhea n 下痢 geri p163

dictionary n 辞書 jisho

different (other) adj 異なる kotonaru / 違う chigau p137/ 別の betsuno p69

difficult adj 困難な konnan na / 難しい muzukashii p148

dinner n 夕食 yūshoku p117

directory assistance (phone)
n 番号案内 bangō annai

disability *n* 障害 shōgai

disappear *v* 消える kieru

disco *n* ディスコ disuco p114

disconnected *adj* 切断された
setsudan sareta

> **Operator, I was
> disconnected.** オペレータさ
> ん、電話が切れてしまいました。
> opērēta san, denwa ga kirete
> shimai mashita.

discount *n* 値引き nebiki

> **Do I qualify for a discount?**
> 私は値引きの対象になりま
> すか? watashi wa nebiki no
> taishō ni narimasuka.

dish *n* 料理 ryōri p77

dive *v* もぐる moguru

> **scuba dive** スキューバダイブ
> sukyūba daibu p151

divorced *adj* 離婚した rikon
shita

dizzy *adj* めまいがする memai
ga suru p165

do, to do *v* する suru

doctor *n* 医者 isha p108, 163

doctor's office *n* 医院 iin

dog *n* 犬 inu p166

> **service dog** 介護犬 kaigo ken
> p39, 59, 64

dollar *n* ドル doru

door *n* ドア doa

double *adj* ダブルの daburu no
p61, 157

> **double bed** ダブルベッド
> daburu beddo p61

double vision 二重映像 nijū
eizō

down *adj* 下に shita ni

download *v* ダウンロードする
daunrōdo suru **p125**

downtown *n* 繁華街 hanka
gai p133

dozen *n* ダース dāsu p13

drain *n* 排水 haisui

drama *n* 劇の脚本 geki no
kyakuhon

drawing (work of art) *n* 絵 e

dress (garment) *n* ドレス doresu

dress (general attire) *n* 服装
fukusō p156

> **What's the dress code?** 服装
> の規則は何ですか? fukusō no
> kisoku wa nan desu ka.

dress *v* 着る kiru

> **Should I dress up for that
> affair.** そこでは正装しなけれ
> ばなりませんか? soko dewa
> seisō shinakereba nari masen
> ka.

dressing (salad) *n* ドレッシング
doressingu

dried *adj* 乾燥した kansō shita

drink *n* 飲み物 nomi mono p75,
76, 157

> **I'd like a drink.** 飲み物をくだ
> さい。nomi mono o kudasai.

drink, to drink *v* 飲む nomu

drip *v* 滴る shitataru

drive *v* 運転する unten suru

driver *n* 運転手 unten shu p52

driving range *n* ゴルフ練習場
gorufu renshū jō

drum *n* ドラム doramu

dry 乾いた kawaita

  This towel isn't dry. このタオルは乾いていません。kono taoru wa kawaite imasen.

dry, to dry v 乾かす kawakasu

  I need to dry my clothes. 私の服を乾かす必要があります。watashi no fuku o kawakasu hitsuyô ga arimasu.

dry cleaner n ドライクリーナー dorai kurīnā

dry cleaning n ドライクリーニング dorai kurīningu

duck n アヒル ahiru

duty-free adj 免税の menzei no p34

duty-free shop n 免税店 menzei ten p34

DVD n DVD p46

  Do the rooms have DVD players? その部屋には DVD プレーヤーがありますか? sono heya niwa DVD purēyā ga arimasu ka.

  Where can I rent DVDs or videos? DVD またはビデオはどこで借りられますか? DVD matawa bideo wa doko de karirare masu ka.

E

early adj 早い hayai p14

  It's early. 早いです。hayai desu.

eat v 食べる taberu

  to eat out 外食する gaishoku suru

economy n エコノミー ekonomī

Ecuadorian adj エクアドルの、エクアドル人の ekuadoru no, ekuadoru jin no

editor n 編集者 henshū sha p109

educator n 教育者 kyōiku sha p109

eight n 八 hachi p6

eighteen n 十八 jū hachi p7

eighth n 8番目の hachi banme no

eighty n 八十 hachi jū p7

election n 選挙 senkyo p112

electrical hookup n 電気接続部 denki setsuzoku bu p71

elevator n エレベーター erebētā p59, 63

eleven n 十一 jū ichi p7

e-mail n Eメール E mēru p110

  May I have your e-mail address? あなたのEメールアドレスをいただけますか? anata no E mēru adoresu o itadake masu ka.

  e-mail message Eメール メッセージ E mēru messēji

e-mail, to send e-mail v Eメールする ii-mēru suru

embarrassed adj 恥ずかしい hazukashii

embassy n 大使館 taishi kan

emergency n 緊急 kinkyū

emergency brake n 非常ブレーキ hijō burēki

emergency exit n 非常出口 hijō deguchi p37

employee n 従業員 jūgyō in

employer n 雇い主 yatoi nushi

engine *n* エンジン enjin p48

engineer *n* エンジニア enjinia p108

England *n* イギリス igirisu

English *adj* イギリス(の)、イギリス人(の) igirisu no, igirisu jin no p168

Do you speak English? 英語を話しますか? eigo o hanashi masu ka. p2

enjoy, to enjoy *v* 楽しむ tanoshimu

enter, to enter *v* 入る hairu

Do not enter. 進入禁止 shinyū kinshi

enthusiastic *adj* 熱心な nesshin na p106

entrance *n* 入口 iriguchi p36

envelope *n* 封筒 fūtō p127

environment *n* 環境 kankyō

escalator *n* エスカレーター esukarētā

espresso *n* エスプレッソ esupuresso

exchange rate *n* 交換レート kōkan rēto p119

What is the exchange rate for US / Canadian dollars? アメリカドル/カナダドルの交換レートは何ですか? amerika doru/kanada doru no kōkan rēto wa nan desu ka.

excuse (pardon) *v* すみません sumi masen p50, 77

Excuse me. すみません sumi masen

exhausted *adj* 疲れた tsukareta

exhibit *n* 展示 tenji

exit *n* 出口 deguchi p36

not an exit 出口なし deguchi nashi

exit *v* 出る deru

expensive *adj* 高い takai p73, 156

explain *v* 説明する setsumei suru

express *adj* 特急の tokkyū no

express check-in 特別優先チェックイン tokubetsu yūsen chekku in

extra (additional) *adj* 余分の yobun no

extra-large *adj* 特大の tokudai no

eye *n* 目 me p105

eyebrow *n* まゆ毛 mayu ge

eyeglasses *n* 眼鏡 megane

eyelash *n* まつ毛 matsu ge

F

fabric *n* 布 nuno

face *n* 顔 kao p106

faint *v* 気を失う ki o ushinau p165

fall (season) *n* 秋 aki

fall *v* 落ちる ochiru

family *n* 家族 kazoku / ご家族 go kazoku p101

fan *n* 扇風機 senpūki

far 遠くに tōkuni / 遠い tōi p5

How far is it to _____? _____まではどれだけ遠く離れていますか? _____ made wa doredake tōku hanarete imasu ka.

fare *n* 料金 ryōkin

fast *adj* 速い hayai

fat *adj* 太った futotta p13

father *n* 父 chichi / お父さん otōsan p102

faucet *n* 蛇口 jaguchi

fault *n* 落ち度 ochido p52

I'm at fault. 私に落ち度があります。watashi ni ochido ga arimasu. p52

It was his fault. それは彼に落ち度があります。sore wa kare ni ochido ga arimasu.

fax *n* ファックス fakkusu p67

February *n* 二月 ni gatsu p17

fee *n* 料金 ryōkin

female *adj* 女性の josei no

fiancé(e) *n* 婚約者 konyaku sha p102

fifteen *adj* 十五の jūgo no p7

fifth *adj* 五番目の go banme no

fifty *adj* 五十の gojū no p7

find *v* 見つける mitsukeru

fine (for traffic violation) *n* 罰金 bakkin p168

fine 元気な genki na p1

I'm fine. 私は元気です。watashi wa genki desu.

fire! *n* 火事だ! kaji da.

first *adj* 最初の saisho no

fishing pole *n* 釣竿 tsuri zao

fitness center *n* フィットネス センター fittonesu sentā / ジム jimu p60

fit (clothes) *v* ぴったり合う pittari au p136

Does this look like it fits? ぴったり合っているように見えますか? pittari atte iru yō ni miemasu ka.

fitting room *n* 試着室 shichaku shitsu

five *adj* 五つの itsutsu no p11

flight *n* フライト furaito / ___便 , ___bin p35

Where do domestic flights arrive / depart? 国内線の出発/到着場所はどこですか? kokunai sen no shuppatsu / tōchaku basho wa doko desu ka.

Where do international flights arrive / depart? 国際線の出発 / 到着場所はどこですか? kokusai sen no shuppatsu / tōchaku basho wa doko desu ka.

What time does this flight leave? このフライトは何時に出発しますか? kono furaito wa nan ji ni shuppatsu shimasu ka.

flight attendant 飛行機の乗務員 hikōki no jōmuin

floor *n* 階 kai

ground floor 1 階 ikkai p63

second floor 2 階 ni kai

flower *n* 花 hana

flush (gambling) *n* フラッシュ furasshu

flush, to flush *v* 流れる、流す nagareru, nagasu

This toilet won't flush. このトイレは流れません。kono toire wa nagare masen.

flute *n* フルート furūto

food *n* 食べ物 tabe mono

foot (body part, measurement) n 足、フット ashi, futto

forehead n 額 hitai

formula n 粉ミルク kona miruku

Do you sell infants' formula? ベビー用粉ミルクは売っていますか? bebī yō kona miruku wa utte imasu ka.

forty adj 四十の yonjū no p7

forward adj 先へ saki e / 前へ mae e p5

four adj 四つの yottsu no p11

fourteen adj 十四の jūyon no / 十四の jū shi no p7

fourth adj 四番目の yon banme no

one-fourth 四分の一 yon bun no ichi

fragile adj 割れやすい ware yasui /「割れ物注意」「waremono chūi」p126

freckle n そばかす sobakasu

French adj フランスの、フランス人の furansu no, furansu jin no p107

fresh adj 新鮮な shinsen na p77, 90, 91

Friday n 金曜日 kin yō bi p15

friend n 友人 yūjin / 友達 tomodachi p101

front adj 前方の zenpō no p38

front desk フロント デスク furonto desuku p66

front door フロント ドア furonto doa

fruit n 果物 kuda mono p90

fruit juice n フルーツ ジュース furūtsu jūsu

full, to be full (after a meal) adj 満腹になった manpuku ni natta

Full house! n フル ハウス! furu hausu.

fuse n ヒューズ hyūzu

G

gallon n ガロン garon p12

garlic n にんにく nin niku p97

gas n ガソリン gasorin p48

gas gauge 燃料計 nenryō kei

out of gas ガソリンが入っていない gasorin ga haitte inai

gate (at airport) n ゲート gēto p33

German adj ドイツの、ドイツ人の doitsu no, doitsu jin no

gift n 贈り物 okuri mono

gin n ジン jin p80

girl n 女の子 onna no ko

girlfriend n ガールフレンド gāru furendo p101

give, to give v あげる ageru

glass n グラス gurasu p76

Do you have it by the glass? グラスでありますか? gurasu de arimasuka.

I'd like a glass please. グラスで一つお願いします。gurasu de hitotsu onegai shimasu.

glasses (eye) n 眼鏡 megane

I need new glasses. 新しい眼鏡が必要です。atarashii megane ga hitsuyō desu.

glove n 手袋 tebukuro p153

go, to go v 行く iku

goal (sport) n ゴール gōru

goalie n ゴールキーパー gōru kīpā p146

gold adj 金製の kin sei no

golf n ゴルフ gorufu p45

golf, to go golfing v ゴルフを する gorufu o suru

good adj よい yoi p60, 72

goodbye n さようなら sayōnara p99

grade (school) n 学年 gakunen

gram n グラム guramu

grandfather n 祖父 sofu / お祖 父さん ojīsan p102

grandmother n 祖母 sobo /お 祖母さん obāsan p102

grandparent n 祖父母 sofubo

grape n ぶどう budō

gray adj 灰色の hai iro no

great adj 立派な rippa na

Greek adj ギリシャの、ギリシャ 人の girisha no, girisha jin no

Greek Orthodox adj ギリシャ 正教の girisha seikyō no p113

green adj 緑色の midori iro no p106

groceries n 食料品 shokuryō hin

group n グループ gurūpu p152

grow, to grow (get larger) v 育つ sodatsu

> **Where did you grow up?** ど こで育ちましたか? doko de sodachi mashita ka.

guard n ガード gādo

security guard セキュリティ ガ ード sekyuritī gādo / 警備員 keibi in p33

Guatemalan adj グアテマラの、 グアテマラ人の guatemara no, guatemara jin no p107

guest n お客 okyaku

guide (of tours) n ガイド gaido p131

guide (publication) n ガイドブッ ク gaido bukku

guide, to guide v 案内する an nai suru

guided tour n ガイド付きツアー gaido tsuki tuā

guitar n ギター gitā p115

gym n ジム jimu p143

gynecologist n 婦人科医 fujinka i

H

hair n 髪の毛 kami no ke

haircut n ヘアーカット heā katto

> **I need a haircut.** 髪の毛を切 りたいのですが。 kami no ke o kiri tai no desuga.
> **How much is a haircut?** カ ットはいくらですか? katto wa ikura desuka.

hairdresser n ヘアードレッサー heā dressā

hair dryer n ヘアードライヤー heā doraiyā p68

half n 半分 hanbun

> **one-half** 二分の一 ni bun no ichi

hallway n 廊下 rōka

hand n 手 te

handicapped-accessible adj 障害者に対応した shōgai sha ni taiō shita

handle, to handle v 扱う atsukau

ENGLISH—JAPANESE

handsome *adj* ハンサムな hansamu na **p103**

hangout (hot spot) *n* 溜まり場 tamari ba

hang out (to relax) *v* よく出入りする yoku deiri suru

hang up (to end a phone call) *v* 切る kiru **p122**

hanger *n* ハンガー hangā

happy *adj* 幸せな shiawase na / 嬉しい ureshii **p106**

hard *adj* 難しい muzukashii (**difficult**) / 堅い katai (**firm**) **p45**

hat *n* 帽子 bōshi

have *v* 持つ motsu

hazel *adj* 薄茶色の usu chairo no **p106**

headache *n* 頭痛 zutsu **p165**

headlight *n* ヘッドライト heddo raito

headphones *n* ヘッドホーン heddo hōn

hear *v* 聞く kiku

hearing-impaired *adj* 聴覚障害の chōkaku shōgai no

heart *n* 心臓 shinzō **p164**

heart attack *n* 心臓発作 shinzō hossa **p164**

hectare *n* ヘクタール hekutāru **p11**

hello *n* こんにちは kon nichi wa **p1**

Help! *n* 助けて! tasukete.

help, to help *v* 助ける tasukeru

hen *n* 雌鶏 mendori

her *adj* 彼女の kanojo no **p3**

herb *n* ハーブ hābu

here *n* ここ koko **p4**

high *adj* 高い takai

highlights (hair) *n* ハイライト hairaito **p142**

highway *n* 高速道路 kōsoku dōro

hike, to hike *v* ハイキングをする haikingu o suru

him *pron* 彼を kare o **p3**

Hindu *adj* ヒンズー教の、ヒンズー人の hinzū kyō no, hinzū jin no **p113**

hip-hop *n* ヒップホップ hippu hoppu

his *adj* 彼の kare no

historical *adj* 歴史的な rekishi teki na

history *n* 歴史 rekishi

hobby *n* 趣味 shumi

hold, to hold *v* 抱く daku

> **to hold hands** 手を握る te o nigiru
> **Would you hold this for me?** これを持っていただけませんか? kore o motte itadakemasen ka.

hold, to hold (to pause) *v* 待つ matsu

> **Hold on a minute!** ちょっと待って! chotto matte.
> **I'll hold.** パスします。pasu shimasu.

hold, to hold (gambling) *v* パスする pasu suru **p161**

holiday *n* 休日 kyūjitsu

home *n* 家 ie

homemaker *n* 主婦 shufu

Honduran *adj* ホンジュラスの、ホンジュラス人の honjurasu no, honjurasu jin no

horn *n* 角 tsuno

horse *n* 馬 uma

hostel *n* ホステル hosuteru p60

hot *adj* 熱い atsui

hot chocolate *n* ホット チョコレート hotto chokorēto p80

hotel *n* ホテル hoteru p53, 60

Do you have a list of local hotels? 地元のホテルの一覧表はありますか? jimoto no hoteru no ichiran hyō wa arimasu ka.

hour *n* 時間 jikan p124, 131

hours (at museum) *n* 時間 jikan

how *adv* いくら ikura *(how much)*, いくつ ikutsu *(how many)* p3, 35

humid *adj* 湿気のある shikke no aru p111

hundred *n* 百 hyaku

hurry *v* 急ぐ p52, 53

I'm in a hurry. 私は急いでいます。watashi wa isoide imasu.
Hurry, please! 急いでください! isoide kudasai.

hurt, to hurt *v* 痛む itamu p164

Ouch! That hurts! 痛い! itai. 痛いです! itai desu.

husband *n* 夫 otto / 主人 shujin/ ご主人 go shujin p101

I

I *pron* 私は watashi wa

ice *n* 氷 kōri p78

identification *n* 身分証明書 mibun shōmei sho p42

inch *n* インチ inchi p11

indigestion *n* 消化不良 shōka furyō

inexpensive *adj* 高くない takaku nai p73

infant *n* 赤ちゃん akachan

Are infants allowed? 赤ちゃんもいいですか? Akachan mo ii desu ka.

information *n* 情報 jōhō

information booth *n* 案内所 an nai jo

injury *n* けが kega

insect repellent *n* 虫除け mushi yoke p163

inside 内部 naibu / 中 naka p74

insult *v* 侮辱する bujoku suru

insurance *n* 保険 hoken p47, 125

iinterest rate *n* 金利 kinri p119

intermission *n* 休憩 kyūkei

Internet *n* インターネット intānetto p34, 62

High-speed Internet 高速インターネット kōsoku intānetto
Do you have Internet access? インターネットに接続できますか? intānetto ni setsuzoku deki masu ka.
Where can I find an Internet café? インターネットカフェはどこにありますか? intā netto kafe wa doko ni arimasu ka.

ENGLISH–JAPANESE

interpreter n 通訳 tsūyaku p168

I need an interpreter. 通訳が必要です。tsūyaku ga hitsuyō desu.

introduce, to introduce v 紹介する shōkai suru p101

I'd like to introduce you to ____. あなたを____に紹介します。anata o ____ ni shōkai shimasu.

Ireland n アイルランド alrurando

Irish adj アイルランドの、アイルランド人の airurando no, alrurando jin no

is v See **be (to be)**.

Italian adj イタリアの、イタリア人の itaria no, itaria jin no p107

J

jacket n 上着 uwagi p41, 75

January n 一月 ichi gatsu p17

Japanese adj 日本の、日本人の nihon no, nihon jin no p107

jazz n ジャズ jazu p114

Jewish adj ユダヤ教の、ユダヤ人の yudaya kyō no, yudaya jin no p113

jog, to run v ジョギングをする joggingu o suru p145

juice n ジュース jūsu p42

June n 六月 roku gatsu p17

July n 七月 shichi gatsu p17

K

keep, to keep v 保つ tamotsu

kid n 子供 kodomo

Are kids allowed? 子供もいいですか？kodomo mo ii desu ka.

Do you have kids' programs? 子供用のプログラムはありますか？kodomo yō no puroguramu wa arimasu ka.

Do you have a kids' menu? 子供用のメニューはありますか？kodomo yō no menyū wa arimasu ka.

kilo n キログラム kiro guramu

kilometer n キロメートル kiro mētoru p11

kind n 種類 shurui **(type)**

What kind is it? それはどんな種類ですか？sore wa donna shurui desu ka.

kiss n キス kisu

kitchen n キッチン kicchin p62

know, to know (something) v 知っている shitte iru

know, to know (someone) v 知っている shitte iru

L

land, to land v 着陸する chakuriku suru / 着く tsuku p43

landscape n 景色 keshiki

language n 言語 gengo

laptop n ラップトップ rappu toppu p140

large adj 大きい ōkii p137

last, to last v 続く tsuzuku

last adv 最後に saigo ni

late adj 遅い osoi p14

Please don't be late. どうか遅れないでください。dōka okure naide kudasai.

later adv あとで ato de

See you later. それじゃ、また後で。soreja, mata ato de.

laundry n 洗濯 sentaku / randorī p67

lavender adj ラベンダー色の rabendā iro no

law n 法律 hōritsu

lawyer n 弁護士 bengo shi p108

least n 最小 saishō

least adj 最も小さい、最も少ない mottomo chiisai, mottomo sukunai

leather n 皮 kawa p45

leave, to leave (depart) v 出発する shuppatsu suru p35

left adj 左の hidari no p5

on the left 左に hidari ni

leg n 脚 ashi

lemonade n レモネード remonēdo

less adj もっと少ない motto sukunia

lesson n レッスン ressun p154

license n 免許証 menkyo shō p169

driver's license 運転免許証 unten menkyo shō

life preserver n 救命用具 kyūmei yōgu

light (lamp) n ランプ ranpu p50

light (for cigarette) n 火 hi p157

May I offer you a light? 火を貸しましょうか? hi o kashima shō ka. **lighter (cigarette)** n ライター raitā p158

like, desire v 望む、nozomu

I would like ___. ___が好きです。___ ga suki desu.

like, to like v 好きである suki de aru

I like this place. 私はここが好きです。watashi wa koko ga suki desu.

limo n リムジン rimujin p53

liquor n 酒 sake p40

liter n リットル rittoru p12

little adj 小さい chiisai (size)、少し sukoshi (amount)

live, to live v 住む sumu

Where do you live? あなたはどこに住んでいますか? anata wa doko ni sunde imasu ka.

living n 生活 seikatsu

What do you do for a living? 何をして生活していますか? nani o shite seikatsu shite imasu ka.

local adj 地方の chihō no p48

lock n 鍵 kagi p143

lock, to lock v 鍵をかける kagi o kakeru

I can't lock the door. ドアに鍵をかけることができません。doa ni kagi o kakeru koto ga dekima sen.

I'm locked out. ドアに鍵がかかってしまい部屋に入ること

ができません。doa ni kagi ga kakatte shimai heya ni hairu koto ga deki masen.

locker *n* ロッカー rokkā **p143**

storage locker 保管ロッカー hokan rokkā

locker room ロッカールーム rokkā rūmu **p144**

long *adv* 長く nagaku

For how long? どれくらい長く? dore kurai nagaku.

long *adj* 長い nagai **p12**

look, to look *v* (to observe) 見る miru

I'm just looking. ただ見ているだけです。tada miteiru dake desu.

Look here! ここを見て! koko o mite.

look, to look *v* (to appear) のように見える no yō ni mieru

How does this look? これはどう見えますか? kore wa dō mie masu ka.

look for, to look for (to search) *v* 探す sagasu

I'm looking for a porter. ポーターを探しています。pōtā o sagashite imasu.

loose *adj* ゆるい yurui **p136**

lose, to lose *v* 失くす nakusu

I lost my passport. 私はパスポートを失くしました。watashi wa pasupōto o nakushi mashita.

I lost my wallet. 私は財布を失くしました。watashi wa saifu o nakushi mashita.

I'm lost. 私は迷ってしまいました。watashi wa mayotte shimai mashita.

loud *adj* うるさい urusai **p70**

loudly *adv* うるさく urusaku

lounge *n* ラウンジ raunji

lounge, to lounge *v* くつろぐ kutsurogu

love *n* 愛 ai

love, to love *v* 愛する ai suru

to love (family) 愛する ai suru

to love (a friend) 愛する ai suru

to love (a lover) 愛する ai suru

low *adj* 低い hikui **p48**

lunch *n* 昼食 chūshoku/ ランチ ranchi **p73**

luggage *n* 荷物 nimotsu **p34, 52**/ 旅行カバン ryokō kaban

Where do I report lost luggage? 旅行カバンの紛失はどこに報告しますか? ryokō kaban no funshitsu wa doko ni hōkoku shimasu ka.

Where is the lost luggage claim? 紛失した旅行カバンを受け取る場所はどこですか? funshitsu shita ryokō kaban o uketoru basho wa doko desu ka.

M

machine *n* 機械 kikai **p125**

made of *adj* から作られた kara tsuku rareta

magazine *n* 雑誌 zasshi

maid (hotel) *n* メード mēdo

maiden *adj* 未婚の mikon no
  That's my maiden name. そ
  れは私の旧姓です。sore wa
  watashi no kyūsei desu.
mail *n* 郵便 yūbin / 手紙 tegami
  p67
  air mail 航空便 kōkūbin
  registered mail 書留 kakitome
mail *v* 郵便で出す yūbin de dasu
make, to make *v* 作る tsukuru
makeup *n* 化粧 keshō
make up, to make up
  (apologize) *v* 埋め合せをす
  る ume awase o suru
make up, to make up (apply
  cosmetics) *v* 化粧をする
  keshō o suru
male *n* 男性 dansei p41
male *adj* 男性の dansei no
mall *n* ショッピングセンター
  shoppingu sentā p133
man *n* 男 otoko
manager *n* マネージャー
  manējā
manual (instruction booklet)
  n マニュアル manyuaru p48
many *adj* 多い ōi / 沢山の
  takusan no p13
map *n* 地図 chizu p46
March (month) *n* 三月 san
  gatsu p17
market *n* マーケット māketto /
  市場 ichiba p134, 137
  flea market フリーマーケット
  furii māketto p134
  open-air market 青空市場
  aozora ichiba

married *adj* 既婚の kikon no
  / 結婚している kekkon shite
  iru p102
marry, to marry *v* 結婚する
  kekkon suru
massage *n* マッサージ massāji
  p66
match (sport) *n* 試合 shiai
match *n* マッチ macchi *n*
  book of matches マッチ
  macchi
match, to match *v* 調和する
  chōwa suru
  Does this _____ match my
  outfit? この_____は私の服
  と合いますか kono _____ wa
  watashi no fuku to aimasu ka?
May (month) *n* 五月 go gatsu
  p17
may *v aux* してよい shite yoi
  May I _____? _____してもよ
  いですか? _____ shitemo yoi
  desu ka.
meal *n* 食事 shokuji p40, 43
meat *n* 肉 niku p78, 90
meatball *n* ミートボール mīto
  bōru
medication *n* 薬物治療
  yakubutsu chiryō
medium (size) *adj* ミディアム
  midiamu
medium rare (meat) *adj* ミディ
  アム レア midiamu rea p76
medium well (meat) *adj* ミデ
  ィアム ウェル midiamu weru
  p76
member *n* 会員 kai in
menu *n* メニュー menyū p74,
  76

May I see a menu?
メニューを見せていただけませんか? menyū o misete itadakemasen ka.

children's menu 子供用のメニュー kodomo yō no menyū

diabetic menu 糖尿病患者用の tōnyōbyō kanja yō no menyū

kosher menu コーシャ料理のkōsha ryōri no menyū

metal detector n 金属探知機 kinzoku tanchi ki

meter n メートル mētoru p11

Mexican adj メキシコの、メキシコ人の mekishiko no, mekishiko jin no

middle adj 中間の chūkan no

midnight n 真夜中 mayonaka

mile n マイル mairu p11

military n 軍 gun

milk n 牛乳 gyūnyū / ミルク miruku p78, 80

milk shake ミルクセーキ miruku sēki

milliliter n ミリリットル miri rittoru

millimeter n ミリメートル miri mētoru

minute n 分 fun

in a minute すぐに sugu ni

miss, to miss (a flight) v 乗りそこなう nori sokonau p39

missing adj 見つからない mitsukara nai

mistake n 間違い machigai p70

moderately priced adj 手頃な値段の tegoro na nedan no p60

mole (facial feature) n ほくろ hokuro

Monday n 月曜日 getsu yō bi p15

money n お金 okane

money transfer 振込 furikomi

month n see months of the year p17

morning n 朝 asa / 午前 gozen p14, 67

in the morning 午前 gozen

mosque n モスク mosuku

mother n 母 haha / お母さん okāsan p101

mother, to mother v 世話をする sewa o suru

motorcycle n バイク baiku

mountain n 山 yama

mountain climbing 登山 tozan p147

mouse n ねずみ nezumi

mouth n 口 kuchi

move, to move v 動く ugoku

movie n 映画 eiga p115, 116, 128

much n 多量 taryō / 沢山の takusan no p131

mug, to mug (someone) v 襲う osou

mugged adj 襲われた osowareta

museum n 美術館 bijutsu kan p116

music n 音楽 ongaku p114

live music 生演奏 nama ensō

musician n ミュージシャン myūjishan p109

muslim adj イスラム教の
isuramu kyō no p113

mustache n 口ひげ kuchi hige

mystery (novel) n ミステリー
misuterī

N

name n 名前 namae p101

My name is ___. 私は___と
申します。 watashi wa ___ to
mōshimasu. p1

What's your name? あなた
の名前は何ですか? anata no
namae wa nan desu ka. p101

napkin n ナプキン napukin

narrow adj 狭い semai p13

nationality n 国籍 kokuseki

nausea n 吐き気 hakike p163

near adj 近い chikai p4

nearby adj 近くに chikaku ni
p73

neat (tidy) adj きちんとした
kichin to shita

need, to need v 欲しい hoshii

neighbor n 近所の人 kinjo no
hito / ご近所の方 kinjo no
kata p102

nephew n おい oi / 甥御さん
oigo san p102

network n ネットワーク
nettowāku

new adj 新しい atarashii p125

newspaper n 新聞 shinbun

newsstand n 新聞売り場
shinbun uriba p139

New Zealand n ニュージーラン
ド nyūjīrando

New Zealander adj ニュージー
ランドの、ニュージーランド人の
nyūjīrando no, nyūjīrando jin no

next prep 次 tsugi

next to の次 no tsugi

the next station 次の駅 tsugi
no eki

Nicaraguan adj ニカラグアの、
ニカラグア人の nikaragua no,
nikaragua jin no p107

nice adj すてきな suteki na

niece n めい mei / 姪御さん
meigo san p102

night n 夜 yoru p14

at night 夜に yoru ni

per night 一泊当たり ippaku
atari p64

nightclub n ナイトクラブ naito
kurabu

nine adj 九つの kokonotsu
no p11

nineteen adj 十九の jūkyū
no p7

ninety adj 九十の kyūjū no p7

ninth adj 九番目の kyū banme
no

no adv でない de nai

noisy adj 音がうるさい oto ga
urusai

none n 何もない nanimo nai / 少
しもない sukoshi mo nai、全く
ない mattaku nai p13

nonsmoking adj 禁煙 kin en

nonsmoking area 禁煙場所
kin en basho

nonsmoking room 禁煙室 kin
en shitsu

noon n 正午 shōgo p14

nose *n* 鼻 hana p142

novel *n* 小説 shōsetsu

November *n* 十一月 jū ichi gatsu p17

now *adv* 今 ima p3

number *n* 数字 sūji / 番号 bangō p54, 66, 110

 Which room number? 部屋は何番? heya wa nan ban.

 May I have your phone number? あなたの電話番号を教えていただけますか? anata no denwa bangō o oshiete itadake masu ka.

nurse *n* 看護師 kango shi p109

nurse *v* 授乳する junyū suru

 Do you have a place where I can nurse? 授乳できる場所はありますか? junyū dekiru basho wa arimasu ka.

nursery *n* 託児所 takuji sho

 Do you have a nursery? 託児所はありますか? takuji sho wa arimasu ka.

nut *n* クルミ kurumi

O

o'clock *adv* 時 ji p4

 two o'clock 2 時 ni ji

October *n* 十月 jū gatsu p17

offer, to offer *v* 提供する teikyō suru

officer *n* 係員 kakari in p41

oil *n* 油 abura p77

okay *adv* オッケー okkē

old *adj* 古い furui / __歳の __ sai no p103

olive *n* オリーブ orību

one *adj* 一つの hitotsu no p10

one way (traffic sign) *adj* 一方通行 ippō tsūkō

open (business) *adj* 営業中 eigyō chū

 Are you open? 営業していますか? eigyō shite imasu ka.

opera *n* オペラ opera p114

operator (phone) *n* オペレーター operētā

optometrist *n* 検眼師 kengan shi

orange (color) *adj* オレンジ色の orenji iro no

orange juice *n* オレンジ ジュース orenji jūsu p42

order, to order (demand) *v* 注文する chūmon suru

order, to order (request) *v* 頼む tanomu

organic *adj* 有機の yūki no

Ouch! 痛い! itai.

outside *n* 外 soto p74

overcooked *adj* 焼き(煮)すぎた yaki (ni) sugita

overheat, to overheat *v* オーバーヒートする ōbāhīto suru

 The car overheated. 車がオーバーヒートしました。 kuruma ga ōbāhīto shimashita.

overflowing *adv* あふれて afurete

oxygen tank *n* 酸素タンク sanso tanku

P

package *n* 小包み kozutsumi p125

pacifier *n* おしゃぶり oshaburi

page, to page (someone) *v* 呼び出す yobidasu **p34**

paint, to paint *v* 塗る nuru

painting *n* 絵 e

pale *adj* 青白い ao jiroi **p104**

Panamanian *adj* パナマの、パナマ人の panama no, panama jin no

paper *n* 紙 kami

parade *n* パレード parēdo

Paraguayan *adj* パラグアイの、パラグアイ人の paraguai no, paraguai jin no

parent *n* 親 oya

park *n* 公園 kōen **p116**

park, to park *v* 駐車する chūsha suru

> **no parking** 駐車禁止 chūsha kinshi **p51**
> **parking fee** 駐車料金 chūsha ryōkin **p51**
> **parking garage** 車庫 shako **p51**

partner *n* パートナー pātonā

party *n* 団体 dantai

party *n* パーティー pātī

> **political party** 政党 seitō

pass, to pass *v* パスする pasu suru

> **I'll pass.** パスします。 pasu shimasu. **p160**

passenger *n* 乗客 jōkyaku

passport *n* パスポート pasupōto

> **I've lost my passport.** 私はパスポートを失くしました。 watashi wa pasupōto o nakushi mashita.

pay, to pay *v* 支払う shiharau

> **peanut** *n* ピーナッツ pīnattsu

pedestrian *adj* 歩行者用の hokōsha yō no

pediatrician *n* 小児科医 shōnika i

> **Can you recommend a pediatrician?** お勧めの小児科医はいますか？ osusume no shōnika i wa imasu ka.

permit *n* 許可 kyoka

> **Do we need a camping permit?** キャンプをする許可が必要ですか？ kyanpu o suru kyoka ga hitsuyō desu ka.

permit, to permit *v* 許可する kyoka suru

Peruvian *adj* ペルーの、ペルー人の perū no, perū jin no

phone *n* 電話 denwa **p62**

> **May I have your phone number?** あなたの電話番号を教えていただけますか？ anata no denwa bangō o oshiete itadake masu ka.
>
> **Where can I find a public phone?** 公衆電話はどこにありますか？ kōshū denwa wa doko ni arimasu ka.
>
> **phone operator** 電話オペレーター denwa operētā
>
> **Do you sell prepaid phones?** プリペイド電話を売っていますか？ puripeido denwa o utte imasu ka.

phone *adj* 電話の denwa no

> **Do you have a phone directory?** 電話帳はありますか？ denwa chō wa arimasu ka.

phone call n 電話 denwa
I need to make a collect phone call. コレクト コールをしたいのですが。korekuto kōru o shitai no desuga.
an international phone call 国際電話 kokusai denwa
photocopy, to photocopy v コピーを取る kopī o toru / コピーする kopī suru **p109**
piano n ピアノ piano **p115**
pillow n 枕 makura **p43, 67, 68**
down pillow 羽毛の枕 umō no makura **p68**
pink adj ピンクの pinku no
pint n パイント painto **p12**
pizza n ピザ piza **p72**
place, to place v 置く oku
plastic n プラスチック purasuchikku **p45**
play n プレイ purei
play, to play (a game) v プレイする purei suru
play, to play (an instrument) v 演奏する ensō suru / 弾く hiku **p115**
playground n 遊び場 asobi ba
Do you have a playground? 遊び場はありますか? asobi ba wa arimasu ka.
please (polite entreaty) adv どうぞ dōzo
please, to be pleasing to v 喜ばせる yorokobaseru
pleasure n 喜び yorokobi
It's a pleasure. 嬉しいです。ureshii desu.
plug n コンセント konsento

plug, to plug v 差し込む sashi komu
point, to point v 指す sasu **p2**
**Would you point me in the direction of____? ____の方向に指し示していただけませんか? ____ no hōkō ni sashi shimeshite itadake masen ka.
police n 警察 keisatsu **p33**
police station n 警察署 keisatsu sho / 警察の派出所 keisatsu no hashutsu sho **p33**
pool n プール pūru **p60**
pool (the game) n ビリヤード biriyādo
pop music n ポップ ミュージック poppu myūjikku
popular adj 人気がある ninki ga aru **p155**
port (beverage) n ポートワイン pōto wain
port (for ship) n 港 minato
porter n ポーター pōtā **p33**
portion n 部分 bubun
portrait n 肖像画 shōzō ga
postcard n ポストカード posuto kādo
post office n 郵便局 yūbin kyoku
Where is the post office? 郵便局はどこにありますか? yūbin kyoku wa doko ni arimasu ka.
poultry n 家禽 kakin
pound n ポンド pondo
prefer, to prefer v の方を好む no hō o konomu
pregnant adj 妊娠した ninshin shita

prepared *adj* 準備された junbi sareta

prescription *n* 処方箋 shohōsen / 処方薬 shohōyaku p40

price *n* 価格 kakaku

print, to print *v* 印刷する insatsu suru p124

private berth / cabin *n* 個人客室 kojin kyakushitsu/キャビンkyabin

problem *n* 問題 mondai

process, to process *v* 処理する shori suru

product *n* 製品 seihin

professional *adj* プロフェッショナルな purofesshonaru na

program *n* プログラム puroguramu

  May I have a program? プログラムをいただけますか？ puroguramu o itadake masu ka.

Protestant *n* プロテスタント purotesutanto

publisher *n* 出版社 shuppansha

Puerto Rican *adj* プエルトリコの、プエルトリコ人の puerutoriko no, puerutoriko jin no

pull, to pull *v* 引く hiku p36

pump *n* ポンプ ponpu

purple *adj* 紫の murasaki no

purse *n* 財布 saifu

push, to push *v* 押す osu p36

put, to put *v* 置く oku

Q

quarter *adj* 四分の一 yonbun no ichi

  one-quarter 四分の一 yon bun no ichi

quiet *adj* 静かな shizuka na p74

R

rabbit *n* うさぎ usagi

radio *n* ラジオ rajio

  satellite radio 衛星ラジオ eisei rajio p46

rain, to rain *v* 雨が降る ame ga furu p111

  Is it supposed to rain? 雨が降る予定ですか？ ame ga furu yotei desuka.

rainy *adj* 雨の ame no

  It's rainy. 雨です。ame desu.

ramp, wheelchair *n* スロープ、車椅子 surōpu, kuruma isu p59

rare (meat) *adj* レアの rea no p76

rate (for car rental, hotel) *n* 料金 ryōkin p47, 64

  What's the rate per day? — 日当たりの料金はいくらですか？ ichi nichi atari no ryōkin wa ikura desu ka.

  What's the rate per week? 一週間当たりの料金はいくらですか？ isshūkan atari no ryōkin wa ikura desu ka.

rate plan (cell phone) *n* 料金プラン ryōkin puran

rather *adv* むしろ mushiro

read, to read *v* 読む yomu

really *adv* 本当に hontō ni

receipt *n* レシート reshīto p119, 120

receive, to receive *v* 受け取る uketoru

recommend, to recommend *v* 勧める susumeru

red *adj* 赤の aka no

redhead *n* 赤毛 akage p104

reef *n* さんご礁 sango shō p151

refill (of beverage) *n* el お替わり okawari

refill (of prescription) *n* 補充 hojū

reggae *adj* レゲー regē p114, 155

relative (family) *n* 親戚 shinseki

remove, to remove *v* 取り除く torinozoku / 脱ぐ nugu p41

rent, to rent *v* 借りる kariru

I'd like to rent a car. 車を借りたいのですが。kuruma o karitai no desuga. **p45**

repeat, to repeat *v* 繰り返す kuri kaesu p2

Would you please repeat that? もう一度繰り返していただけますか? mō ichido kuri kaeshite itadake masu ka. p2

reservation *n* 予約 yoyaku

I'd like to make a reservation for ___. ___の予約をしたいのですが。___ no yoyaku o shitai no desuga. p64 See p6 for numbers.

restaurant *n* レストラン resutoran p34

Where can I find a good restaurant? よいレストランはどこにありますか? yoi resutoran wa doko ni arimasu ka.

restroom *n* トイレ toire p33

Do you have a public restroom? 公衆トイレはありますか? kōshū toire wa arimasu ka.

return, to return (to a place) *v* 戻る modoru

return, to return (something to a store) *v* 返品する henpin suru p140

ride, to ride *v* 乗っていく notte iku

right *adj* 右の migi no p5, 50

It is on the right. 右側にあります。migi gawa ni arimasu. p50

Turn right at the corner. 角を右に曲がります。kado o migi ni magari masu.

rights *n pl* 権利 kenri

civil rights 市民の権利 shimin no kenri

river *n* 川 kawa p150

road *n* 道路 dōro

road closed sign *n* 道路閉鎖中 dōro heisa chū p51

rob, to rob *v* 奪う ubau

I've been robbed. 強盗に遭いました。gōtō ni aimashita.

rock and roll *n* ロックンロール rokkun rōru

rock climbing *n* ロッククライミング rokku kuraimingu

rocks (ice) *n* ロック rokku p79

I'd like it on the rocks. ロックでお願いします。rokku de onegai shimasu.

romance (novel) *n* 恋愛小説 ren ai shōsetsu

romantic *adj* ロマンチックな romanchikku na

room (hotel) *n* 部屋 heya

room for one / two 1人 / 2人 部屋 hitori /futari beya

room service ルーム サービス rūmu sābisu

rope *n* ロープ rōpu p147

rose *n* バラ bara

royal flush *n* ロイヤル フラッシュ roiyaru furasshu

rum *n* ラム酒 ramu shu p80

run, to run *v* 走る hashiru

S

sad *adj* 悲しい kanashii p106

safe (for storing valuables) *n* 金庫 kinko p68

Do the rooms have safes? 室内には金庫がありますか? shitsu nai niwa kinko ga arimasu ka. p68

safe (secure) *adj* 安全な anzen na

Is this area safe? この地域は安全ですか? kono chiiki wa anzen desu ka.

sail *n* 航海 kōkai

sail, to sail *v* 航海する kōkai suru

When do we sail? いつ出航しますか? itsu shukkō shimasu ka. p150

salad *n* サラダ sarada

salesperson *n* 販売員 hanbai in p108

salt *n* 塩 shio p97

Is that low-salt? それは減塩ですか? sore wa gen en desu ka.

Salvadorian *adj* サルバドルの、サルバドル人の sarubadoru no, sarubadoru jin no p108

satellite *n* 衛星 eisei p46

satellite radio 衛星ラジオ eisei rajio p46

satellite tracking 衛星追跡 eisei tsuiseki p46

Saturday *n* 土曜日 do yō bi p15

sauce *n* ソース sōsu

say, to say *v* 言う iu p100

scan, to scan *v* (document) スキャンする sukyan suru p124

schedule *n* スケジュール sukejūru

school *n* 学校 gakkō

scooter *n* スクーター sukūtā p46

score *n* 得点 tokuten

Scottish *adj* スコットランドの、スコットランド人の sukottorando no, sukottorando jin no

scratched *adj* 傷のある kizu no aru p48

scratched surface 擦り傷のある表面 suri kizu no aru hyōmen

scuba dive, to scuba dive *v* スキューバ ダイブをする sukyūba daibingu o suru p151

sculpture *n* 彫刻 chōkoku

seafood *n* シーフード shīfūdo p91 / 魚介類 gyokai rui p78

ENGLISH–JAPANESE

search n 検査 kensa

  hand search 手で検査する
  te de kensa suru

search, to search v 調べる
  shiraberu

seasick adj 船酔い funa yoi p57

  I am seasick. 船酔いしま
  した。funa yoi shimashita.
  seasickness pill n 船酔いに
  効く薬 funa yoi ni kiku kusuri

seat n 座席 zaseki p37, 38/ 席
  seki p42, 43, 54

  child seat チャイルドシート
  chairudo shiito p46

second adj 二番目の niban
  me no

  security checkpoint セキュリ
  ティ チェックポイント sekyuritī
  chekku pointo

  security guard セキュリティ ガ
  ード sekyuritī gādo / 警備員
  keibi in p33

sedan n セダン sedan p46

see, to see v 見る miru

  May I see it? 見せていただけま
  すか? misete itadake masu ka.

self-serve adj セルフサービスの
  serufu sābisu no

sell, to sell v 売る uru

seltzer n ソーダ水 sōda sui p79

send, to send v 送る okuru
  p125, 127

separated (marital status) adj
  別れた wakareta / 別居してい
  る bekkyo shite iru p103

September n 九月 ku gatsu
  p17

serve, to serve v 出す dasu

service n サービス sābisu

  out of service 回送 kaisō

services (religious) n 奉仕
  hōshi / 礼拝 reihai p113

service charge n サービス料
  sābisu ryō p64, 119

seven adj 七つの nanatsu no
  p11

seventy adj 七十の nana jū
  no p7

seventeen adj 十七の jūshichi
  no p7

seventh adj 七番目の nana ban
  me no

sew, to sew v 縫う nuu / 裁縫を
  する saihō o suru p116

sex (gender) n 性別 seibetsu

shallow adj 浅い asai

sheet (bed linen) n シーツ shītsu

shellfish n 貝類 kai rui p78

ship n 船 fune p56

ship, to ship v 船で運ぶ fune
  de hakobu

  **How much to ship this to
  ___?** これを___まで船で送る
  にはいくらかかりますか? kore
  o ___ made fune de okuru
  niwa ikura kakari masu ka.

shipwreck n 難破船 nanpa sen

shirt n シャツ shatsu

shoe n 靴 kutsu p41, 133, 134

shop n 店 mise

shop v 買い物をする kaimono o
  suru p115

  **I'm shopping for mens'
  clothes.** 紳士服を買いに来
  ました。shinshi fuku o kai ni
  kimashita.

I'm shopping for womens' clothes. 婦人服を買いに来ました。fujin fuku o kai ni kimashita.

I'm shopping for childrens' clothes. 子供服を買いに来ました。kodomo fuku o kai ni kimashita.

short *adj* 短い mijikai p12

shorts *n* 半ズボン han zubon p75

shot (liquor) *n* 一杯 ippai

shout *v* 大声で呼ぶ ōgoe de yobu

show (performance) *n* ショー shō

What time is the show? ショーは何時ですか? shō wa nanji desuka?

show, to show *v* 見せる miseru

Would you show me? 見せていただけませんか? misete itadake masen ka.

shower *n* シャワー shawā p62

Does it have a shower? それにはシャワーが付いていますか? sore niwa shawā ga tsuite imasu ka.

shower, to shower *v* シャワーを浴びる shawā o abiru

shrimp *n* 海老 ebi p92

shuttle bus *n* シャトル バス shatoru basu

sick *adj* 病気の byōki no

I feel sick. 気分が悪いです。kibun ga warui desu.

side *n* 添え物 soe mono

on the side (e.g., salad dressing) 横に添えて yoko ni soete p77

sidewalk *n* 歩道 hodō

sightseeing *n* 観光 kankō

sightseeing bus *n* 観光バス kankō basu

sign, to sign *v* 署名 shomei p120

Where do I sign? どこに署名すればいいですか? doko ni shomei sureba ii desu ka.

silk *n* シルク shiruku p135

silver *adj* 銀製の gin sei no

sing, to sing *v* 歌う utau

single (unmarried) *adj* 独身の dokushin no p102

Are you single? あなたは独身ですか? anata wa dokushin desu ka.

single (one) *adj* 一つの hitotsu no

single bed シングル ベッド shinguru beddo

sink *n* 洗面台 senmen dai

sister *n* 姉妹 shimai / ご姉妹 go shimai p102

sit, to sit *v* 座る suwaru

six *adj* 六つの muttsu no p11

sixteen *adj* 十六の jūroku no p7

sixty *adj* 六十の rokujū no p7

size (clothing, shoes) *n* サイズ saizu p134

skin *n* 皮膚 hifu

sleeping berth *n* 寝台 shindai

slow *adj* 遅い osoi

slow, to slow v 速度を落とす sokudo o otosu p53

Slow down! 速度を落として ください! sokudo o otoshite kudasai. p53

slow(ly) adv ゆっくり yukkuri

Speak more slowly. もっとゆ っくり話してください。motto yukkuri hanashite kudasai. p100

slum n スラム街 suramu gai

small adj 小さい chiisai p13

smell, to smell v 匂いをかぐ nioi o kagu

smoke, to smoke v タバコを吸 う tabako o suu p158

smoking n 喫煙 kitsu en p61

smoking area 喫煙所 kitsu en jo p34

No Smoking 禁煙 kin en p61

snack n 軽食 keishoku p90

Snake eyes! n スネークアイだ! sunēku ai da. p160

snorkel n スノーケル sunōkeru

soap n 石鹸 sekken

sock n 靴下 kutsu shita

soda n ソーダ sōda p42

diet soda ダイエットソーダ daietto sōda

soft adj 柔らかい yawarakai

software n ソフトウェア sofuto uea

sold out adj 売り切れ urikire

some adj いくつかの ikutsukano

someone n 誰か dare ka p42

something n 何か nani ka / 何 nani p75, 124

son n 息子 musuko / 息子さん musuko san p103

song n 歌 uta p159

sorry adj すみません sumi masen.

I'm sorry. すみません。sumi masen.

soup n スープ sūpu

spa n スパ supa p60

Spain n スペイン supein

Spanish adj スペインの、スペイ ン人の supein no, supein jin no p107

spare tire n スペアタイヤ supea taiya

speak, to speak v 話す hanasu p2

Do you speak English? 英語 を話しますか? eigo o hanashi masu ka. p2

Would you speak louder, please? もっと大きな声で話し てください。motto ōkina koe de hanashite kudasai. / もっと 大きな声で話していただけま せんか。motto ōkina koe de hanashite itadake masen ka. p2

Would you speak slower, please? もっとゆっくり話し てください。motto yukkuri hanashite kudasai. / もっとゆ っくり話していただけません か。motto yukkuri hanashite itadake masen ka. p2

special (featured meal) n スペシャル supesharu

specify, to specify v 具体的に 述べる gutai teki ni noberu

speed limit n 制限速度 seigen sokudo p51

What's the speed limit? 制限
速度は何キロですか? seigen
sokudo wa nan kiro desu ka.
p51

speedometer n 速度計 sokudo kei

spell, to spell v つづる tsuzuru
p100

How do you spell that? つ
づりを言ってください。tsuzuri
o itte kudasai. / つづりを言っ
てもらえますか。tsuzuri o itte
morae masu ka. **p100**

spice n スパイス supaisu

spill, to spill v こぼす kobosu
p43

split (gambling) n 分ける
wakeru

sports n スポーツ supōtsu p116

spring (season) n 春 haru p17

stadium n スタジアム sutajiamu
p145

staff (employees) n スタッフ
sutaffu p70

stamp (postage) n 切手 kitte

stair n 階段 kaidan

Where are the stairs? 階段は
どこですか? kaidan wa doko
desu ka.

Are there many stairs? 階段
の数は多いですか? kaidan no
kazu wa ōi desu ka.

stand, to stand v 立つ tatsu

start, to start (commence) v
始まる hajimaru

start, to start (a car) v 発車さ
せる hassha saseru

state n 状況 jōkyō

station n 駅 eki p53, 57

Where is the nearest____?
ここから一番近い____はど
こですか? koko kara ichiban
chikai ____ wa doko desu ka.

gas station ガソリン スタンド
gasorin sutando

bus station バス停 basu tei

subway station 地下鉄の駅
chikatetsu no eki

train station 駅 eki

stay, to stay v 泊る tomaru / 滞在
する taizai suru **p64, 70**

**We'll be staying for
____ nights.** ____日間滞在
する予定です。____ nichi kan
taizai suru yotei desu. **p64**
Numbers, **p6.**

steakhouse n ステーキハウス
sutēki hausu p72

steal, to steal v 盗む nusumu

stolen adj 盗まれた nusumareta
p44

stop n 駅 eki p58 / 停車駅
teisha eki p58

Is this my stop? ここは私が
降りる駅ですか? koko wa
watashi ga oriru eki desu ka.

I missed my stop. 私は乗り過
ごしてしまいました。watashi
wa nori sugoshite shimai
mashita.

stop, to stop v 停まる tomaru

Please stop. 停まってくださ
い。tomatte kudasai.

STOP (traffic sign) 止まれ
tomare

Stop, thief! 止まれ、泥棒!
tomare, dorobō.

store n 店 mise

straight (hair) adj ストレートの sutorēto no p142/ 直毛 chokumō p104

straight ahead ここをまっすぐ koko o saki massugu p5

straight (drink) ストレートで sutorēto de p79

Go straight. (giving directions) まっすぐ行きます。 massugu ikimasu. p50

straight (gambling) n ストレート sutorēto p161

street n 道 michi p6

across the street この道の向こう側 kono michi no mukō gawa p6

down the street この道(の先) kono michi (no saki) p6

Which street? どの道? dono michi.

How many more streets? あと何本の道がありますか? ato nan bon no michi ga arimasuka?

stressed adj ストレスを感じている sutoresu o kanjite iru

striped adj 縞の shima no

stroller n ベビーカー bebī kā

Do you rent baby strollers? ベビーカーはレンタルできますか? bebī kā wa rentaru deki masu ka.

substitution n 替わりのもの kawari no mono

suburb n 郊外 kōgai

subway n 地下鉄 chikatetsu p57

subway line 地下鉄の路線 chikatetsu no rosen

subway station 地下鉄の駅 chikatetsu no eki

Which subway do I take for ___? ___へはどの地下鉄で行けばよいですか? ___ ewa dono chikatetsu de ikeba yoi desu ka.

subtitle n 字幕 jimaku

suitcase n スーツケース sūtsu kēsu p44

suite n スーツ sūtsu

summer n 夏 natsu p17

sun n 太陽 taiyō

sunburn n 日焼け hiyake

I have a bad sunburn. 私はひどく日焼けしました。watashi wa hidoku hiyake shimashita.

Sunday n 日曜日 nichi yō bi p15

sunglasses n サングラス sangurasu

sunny adj 晴れた hareta p111

It's sunny out. 外は晴れています。 soto wa harete imasu.

sunroof n サンルーフ san rūfu

sunscreen n 日焼け止めクリーム hiyake dome kurīmu

Do you have sunscreen SPF ___? SPF ___ の日焼け止めクリームはありますか? SPF ___ no hiyake dome kurīmu wa arimasu ka. See numbers p6.

supermarket n スーパーマーケット sūpā māketto

surf v サーフィンする sāfin suru p152

surfboard n サーフボード sāfu bōdo

suspiciously adv 怪しそうに ayashisō ni / 様子が変 yōsu ga hen p44

swallow, to swallow v 飲み込む nomi komu

sweater n セーター sētā p41, 135

swim, to swim v 泳ぐ oyogu p143

Can one swim here? ここでは泳げますか? koko dewa oyoge masu ka.

swimsuit n 水着 mizugi

swim trunks n 水泳パンツ suiei pantsu

symphony n 交響楽団 kōkyō gakudan

T

table n テーブル tēburu p74

table for two 2人用のテーブル futari yō no tēburu

tailor n 仕立て屋 shitate ya p67

Can you recommend a good tailor? よい仕立て屋を勧めていただけませんか?yoi shitate ya o susumete itadake masen ka.

take, to take v 連れて行く tsureteiku

Take me to the station. 駅まで連れて行ってください。eki made tsurete itte kudasai.

How much to take me to ____? ____まで行くにはいくらかかりますか? ____ made iku niwa ikura kakari masu ka

takeout menu n 持帰り用のメニュー mochi kaeri yō no menyū

talk, to talk v 話す hanasu

tall adj 高い takai / 背が高い se ga takai p105

tanned adj 日焼けした hiyake shita

taste (flavor) n 味 aji

taste (discernment) n 好み konomi

taste, to taste v 味見する ajimi suru

tax n 税金 zeikin p64, 138

value-added tax (VAT) 付加価値税 fuka kachi zei p138

taxi n タクシー takushī p36, 52

Taxi! タクシー! takushī.

Would you call me a taxi? タクシーを呼んでいただけませんか? takushī o yonde itadake masen ka.

tea n お茶 ocha / 茶 cha p88

team n チーム chīmu p146

Techno n テクノ tekuno p114

television n テレビ terebi

temple n 寺院 jiin p112

ten adj 十の jū no p6

tennis n テニス tenisu p61

tennis court テニスコート tenisu kōto p61

tent n テント tento

tenth adj 十番目の jū ban me no

terminal n (airport) ターミナル tāminaru p36

Thank you. どうもありがとう。dōmo arigatō p1

that (near) adj その sono

that (far away) adj あの ano

theater n 劇場 gekijō

them (m/f) 彼ら（に、を）karera (ni, o) p3

there (demonstrative) *adv* そこに soko ni **(nearby)**, あそこに asoko ni **(far)**

Is / Are there ? ありますか? arimasu ka.

over there あそこに asoko ni

these *adj* これらの korera no p6

thick *adj* 厚い atsui

thin *adj* 薄い usui

third *adj* 3番目の san banme no

thirteen *adj* 十三の jū san no p7

thirty *adj* 三十の sanjū no p7

this *adj* この kono

those *adj* それらの sorerano

thousand 千 sen p7

three 三 san p6

Thursday *n* 木曜日 moku yō bi p15

ticket *n* 切符 kippu / チケット chiketto p33, 35

ticket counter 切符売り場 kippu uriba / チケットカウンター chiketto kauntā

one-way ticket 片道切符 katamichi kippu p56

round-trip ticket 往復切符 ōfuku kippu p56

tight *adj* きつい kitsui p136

time *n* 時間 jikan p64

Is it on time? それは定刻通りですか? sore wa teikoku dōri desu ka.

At what time? 何時に? nan ji ni.

What time is it? 何時ですか? nan ji desu ka.

timetable *n* **(train)** 時刻表 jikoku hyō p53

tip (gratuity) チップ chippu

tire *n* タイヤ taiya p48

I have a flat tire. タイヤがパンクしました。taiya ga panku shima shita.

tired *adj* 疲れた tsukareta/ 疲れている tsukarete iru p106

today *n* 今日 kyō

toilet *n* トイレ toire

The toilet is overflowing. トイレの水が溢れているんです。toire no mizu ga afurete irun desu. p69

The toilet is backed up. トイレがつまっています。toire ga tsumatte imasu.

toilet paper *n* トイレット ペーパー toiretto pēpā

You're out of toilet paper. トイレットペーパーがなくなりました。toiretto pēpā ga naku nari mashita.

toiletries *n* 洗面用品 senmen yōhin p90

toll *n* 使用料 shiyōryō

tomorrow *n* 明日 ashita p4

ton *n* トン ton

too (excessively) *adv* 〜過ぎる 〜sugiru

too (also) *adv* 〜も 〜mo

tooth *n* 歯 ha p167

I lost my tooth. 歯が1本抜けました。ha ga ippon nuke mashita.

toothache *n* 歯痛 haita

I have a toothache. 歯が痛みます。ha ga itami masu.

total n 合計 gōkei

What is the total? 合計でいくらですか? gōkei de ikura desu ka.

tour n ツアー tsuā

Are guided tours available? ガイド付きツアーはありますか? gaido tsuki tsuā wa arimasu ka.

Are audio tours available? 音声ガイド付きツアーはありますか? onsei gaido tsuki tsuā wa arimasu ka.

towel n タオル taoru

May we have more towels? もっとタオルをいただけますか? motto taoru o itadake masu ka.

toy n おもちゃ omocha

toy store n おもちゃ屋 omocha ya

Do you have any toys for the children? 子供のおもちゃはありますか? kodomo no omocha wa arimasu ka.

traffic n 交通 kōtsū

How's traffic? 交通状態はどうですか? kōtsū jōtai wa dō desu ka.

traffic rules 交通規則 kōtsū kisoku

trail n 登山道 tozan dō / トレイル toreiru p149

Are there trails? 登山道はありますか? tozan dō wa arimasuka.

train n 列車 ressha / 電車 densha p53, 54

express train 特急列車 tokkyū ressha

local train 普通列車 futsū ressha

Does the train go to ____? この電車は_____へ行きますか? kono densha wa _____ e ikimasu ka.

May I have a train schedule? 電車の時刻表をいただけますか? densha no jikokuhyō o itadake masu ka.

Where is the train station? 駅はどこにありますか? eki wa doko ni arimasuka.

train, to train v 訓練する kunren suru

transfer, to transfer v 移す utsusu

I need to transfer funds. 振込したいのですが。furikomi shitai no desuga.

transmission n 変速機 hensoku ki

automatic transmission オートマチック ōto machikku

standard transmission マニュアル manyuaru

travel, to travel v 旅行する ryokō suru p38, 40

travelers' check n トラベラーズチェック toraberāzu chekku

Do you cash travelers' checks? トラベラーズチェックを現金に交換できますか? toraberāzu chekku o genkin ni kōkan deki masu ka.

trim, to trim (hair) v 切りそ
ろえる kiri soroeru / そろえる
soroeru **p141**

trip n 旅行 ryokō **p98**

triple adj 3倍の san bai no adj
triple

trumpet n トランペット
tranpetto

trunk n 旅行カバン ryokō kaban
(luggage) **p49**, トランク
toranku (in car)

try, to try (attempt) v 試す
tamesu

try, to try on (clothing) v 試着
する shichaku suru

try, to try (food) v 試食する
shishoku suru

Tuesday n 火曜日 ka yō bi **p15**

turkey n 七面鳥 shichimenchō

turn, to turn v 曲がる magaru
p50

> **to turn left / right** 左 / 右に
> 曲がる hidari / migi ni magaru
> **p50**
>
> **to turn off / on** 消す / 付ける
> kesu / tsukeru

twelve adj 十二の juni no **p7**

twenty adj 二十の nijū no **p7**

twine n 麻ひも asa himo / ひも
himo **p126**

two adj 二つの futatsu no **p10**

U

umbrella n 傘 kasa f

uncle n おじ oji / おじさん ojisan
p102

undercooked adj 完全に煮えて
いない kanzen ni niete iai

understand, to understand v
理解する rikai suru

> **I don't understand.** わかりま
> せん。wakari masen. **p2, 100**
>
> **Do you understand?** わかり
> ますか？ wakari masu ka.

underwear n 下着 shitagi

university n 大学 daigaku

up adv 上に ue ni **p5**

update, to update v 更新する
kōshin suru

upgrade n アップグレード
appugurēdo **p47**

upload, to upload v アップロー
ドする appurōdo suru **p124**

upscale adj 高級な kōkyūna

Uruguayan adj ウルグアイの、
ウルグアイ人の uruguai no、
uruguai jin no **p108**

us pron 私達（に、を）watashi
tachi (ni, o) **p3**

USB port n USB ポート USB
pōto

use, to use v 使う tsukau

V

vacation n バケーション
bakēshon / 休暇 kyūka **p40,
44**

> **on vacation** 休暇で kyūka de
> **to go on vacation** バケーシ
> ョンに出かける bakēshon ni
> dekakeru

vacancy n 空き室 aki shitsu

van n バン ban

VCR n ビデオデッキ bideo dekki

Do the rooms have VCRs?
部屋にはビデオデッキが置いて
ありますか? heya niwa bideo
dekki ga oite arimasu ka.

vegetable *n* 野菜 yasai

vegetarian *n* ベジタリアン
bejitarian p38

vending machine *n* 自動販売
機 jidō hanbai ki

Venezuelan *adj* ベネズエラの、
ベネズエラ人の benezuera no,
benezuera jin no p108

version *n* バージョン bājon

very とても totemo p78

video *n* ビデオ bideo

**Where can I rent videos or
DVDs?** DVD またはビデオは
どこで借りられますか? DVD
matawa bideo wa doko de
karirare masu ka.

view *n* 眺め nagame

beach view ビーチの眺め
bīchi no nagame

city view 市街の眺め shigai no
nagame

vineyard *n* ぶどう園 budō en

vinyl *n* ビニール binīru p45

violin *n* バイオリン baiorin

visa *n* ビザ biza

Do I need a visa? ビザが必要
ですか? biza ga hitsuyō desu
ka.

vision *n* 視力 shiryoku

visit, to visit *v* 訪ねる tazuneru

visually-impaired *adj* 視覚
障害の shikaku shōgai no

vodka *n* ウオッカ uokka p80

voucher *n* 利用券 riyōken p40

W

wait, to wait *v* 待つ matsu p74

Please wait. どうかお待ちくだ
さい。dōka omachi kudasai.

How long is the wait? どの
くらい待ちますか? dono kurai
machi masu ka. p74

waiter *n* ウエイター ueitā

waiting area *n* 待合室 machiai
shitu p33

wake-up call *n* ウェークアップ
コール ueku appu kōru

wallet *n* 財布 saifu p42

I lost my wallet. 私は財布を
失くしました。watashi wa saifu
o nakushi mashita.

Someone stole my wallet.
誰かに財布を盗まれました。
dareka ni saifu o nusumare
mashita. p42

walk, to walk *v* 歩く aruku

walker (ambulatory device)
n 歩行器 hokōki p39

walkway *n* 歩道 hodō

moving walkway 自動移動通
路 jidō idō tsūro

want, to want *v* 〜欲しい 〜
hoshii

war *n* 戦争 sensō p112

warm *adj* 暖かい atatakai p111

watch, to watch *v* 観察する
kansatsu suru

water *n* 水 mizu p42

Is the water potable? この水
は飲めますか? kono mizu wa
nome masu ka.

Is there running water? ここ
に水道水はありますか? koko
ni suidōsui wa arimasu ka.
p71

wave, to wave v 振る furu

waxing n ワックス wakkusu

weapon n 武器 buki

wear, to wear v 着る kiru

weather forecast n 天気予報
tenki yohō

Wednesday n 水曜日 sui yō
bi p15

week n 週 shū p4, 15

  this week 今週 konshū

  last week 先週 senshū

  next week 来週 raishū

weigh v 重い omoi

  I weigh ____. 私は体重が____
あります。watashi wa taijyū ga
____ arimasu.

  It weighs ____. これは____の
重さがあります。kore wa ____
no omosa ga arimasu. See p6
for numbers.

weights n 重さ omosa

welcome adv ようこそ yōkoso

  You're welcome. どういたしま
して。dō itashi mashite.

well adv よく yoku

  well done (meat) ウェル ダン
weru dan

  well done (task) よくやった
yoku yatta

  I don't feel well. 気分がよく
ありません。kibun ga yoku
arimasen.

western adj ウェスタンの
uesutan no

whale n 鯨 kujira

what adv 何の nan no / 何
nani p2

  What sort of ____? どんな種
類の____? donna shurui no
____.

  What time is ____? ____は何
時? ____ wa nan ji. p14

wheelchair n 車椅子 kuruma
isu p39

  wheelchair access 車椅子で
のアクセス kurumaisu deno
akusesu

  wheelchair ramp 車椅子用ス
ロープ kuruma isu yō surōpu

  power wheelchair 電動車椅
子 dendō kuruma isu

wheeled (luggage) adj 車輪付
き sharin tsuki

when adv いつ itsu p3

See p112 for questions.

where adv どこ doko p3

  Where is it? それはどこにあ
りますか? sore wa doko ni
arimasu ka.

which adv どれ dore p3

  Which one? どっち? docchi

white adj 白い shiroi

who adv 誰 dare p3

whose adj 誰の dare no

wide adj 広い hiroi p13

widow, widower n 未亡人
mibō jin やもめ, yamome
p103

wife n 妻 tsuma / 奥さん okusan
p101

wi-fi n ワイファイ wai fai

window *n* 窓 mado

windshield *n* フロントガラス furonto garasu

windshield wiper *n* ワイパー waipā

windy *adj* 風が強い kaze ga tsuyoi p111

wine *n* ワイン wain p42

winter *n* 冬 fuyu p17

wiper *n* ワイパー waipā

with *prep* ～と一緒に ～to issho ni

withdraw *v* 引く hiku

I need to withdraw money. お金を引き出したいのですが。okane o hiki dashi tai no desuga.

without *prep* ～なしで ～ nashi de

woman *n* 女性 josei

work, to work *v* 機能する kinō suru

This doesn't work. これは機能しません。kore wa kinō shimasen.

workout *n* ワークアウト wāku auto

worse ～よりも悪い ～yori mo warui

worst 最悪 sai aku

write, to write *v* 書く kaku

Would you write that down for me? 紙に書いていただけますか? kami ni kaite itadake masu ka.

writer *n* 作家 sakka p109

X

x-ray machine *n* レントゲン rentogen

Y

yellow *adj* 黄色い kiiroi

Yes. *adv* はい。hai.

yesterday *n* 昨日 kinō p4

the day before yesterday おととい ototoi p15

yield sign *n* 優先標識 yūsen hyōshiki

you *pron* あなた、あなた達 anata, anata tachi p3

your, yours *adj* あなたの、あなた達の anata no, anata tachi no

young *adj* 若い wakai p103

Z

zoo *n* 動物園 dōbutsu en p116

A

abura 油 *oil* n p77

adaputā puragu アダプター プラグ *adapter plug* n

afurete あふれて *overflowing* adv

afurika kei amerika jin no アフリカ系アメリカ人の *African-American* adj p105

ageru あげる *give, to give* v

ahiru アヒル *duck* n

ai suru 愛する *love, to love* v

ai suru 愛する *to love (family)*

ai suru 愛する *to love (a friend)*

ai suru 愛する *to love (a lover)*

ai 愛 *love* n

airurando no, airurando jin no アイルランドの、アイルランド人の *Irish* adj

airurando アイルランド *Ireland* n

aji 味 *taste (flavor)* n

ajia no, ajia jin no アジアの、アジア人の *Asian* adj p105

ajimi suru 味見する *taste, to taste* v

aka chan no 赤ちゃんの *baby* adj

bebī fūdo wa utte imasu ka. ベビー フードは売っていますか? *Do you sell baby food?*

aka chan 赤ちゃん p103/bebī ベビー p90 *baby* n

aka no 赤の *red* adj

akage 赤毛 *redhead* n p104

akarui 明るい *bright* adj

aki shitsu 空き室 *vacancy* n

aki 秋 *autumn* n p17

aki 秋 *fall (season)* n

akiraka ni suru 明らかにする *clear* v

ame ga furu 雨が降る *rain, to rain* v p111

ame ga furu yotei desuka. 雨が降る予定ですか? *Is it supposed to rain?*

ame no 雨の *rainy* adj

ame desu. 雨です。 *It's rainy.*

amerika no, amerika jin no アメリカの、アメリカ人の *American* adj

an nai jo 案内所 *information booth* n

an nai suru 案内する *guide, to guide* v

anata no, anata tachi no あなたの、あなた達の *your, yours* adj

anata, anata tachi あなた、あなた達 *you* pron p3

anda kami 編んだ髪 *braid* n p142

ano あの *that (far away)* adj

anzen na 安全な *safe (secure)* adj

kono chiiki wa anzen desu ka. この地域は安全ですか? *Is this area safe?*

ao jiroi 青白い *pale* adj p104

aoi 青い *blue* adj p105

appugurēdo アップグレード *upgrade* n p47

appurōdo suru アップロードする *upload, to upload* v p124

are v *See* be, to be.

arerugī han nō no アレルギー体質の / アレルギー反応の *allergic* adj p68

watashi wa _____ ni arerugī ga arimasu. 私は_____にアレルギーがあります。 *I'm allergic to _____.* p78,167 See p78 and 167 for common allergens.

arukōru アルコール *alcohol* n p79

arukōru wa dashite imasu ka. アルコールは出していますか? *Do you serve alcohol?*

arukōru nuki no bīru o kudasai. アルコール抜きのビールをください。 *I'd like nonalcoholic beer.*

aruku 歩く *walk, to walk* v

aruminiumu アルミニウム *aluminum* n

aruzenchin no, aruzenchin jin no アルゼンチンの、アルゼンチン人の *Argentinian adj*

asa himo 麻ひも / himo ひも *twine* n p126

asa 朝 / gozen 午前 *morning* n p14, 67

gozen 午前 *in the morning*

asai 浅い *shallow adj*

ashi 脚 *leg* n

ashi, futto 足、フット *foot (body part, measurement)* n

ashita 明日 *tomorrow* n p4

asobi ba 遊び場 *playground* n

asobi ba wa arimasu ka. 遊び場はありますか? *Do you have a playground?*

asupirin アスピリン *aspirin* n p162

atarashii 新しい *new adj* p125

atatakai 暖かい *warm adj* p111

ATM ki ATM 機 *ATM* n

ATM ki o sagashite imasu. ATM 機を探しています。 *I'm looking for an ATM.*

ato de あとで *later adv*

soreja, mata ato de. それじゃ、また後で。 *See you later.*

atsui 厚い *thick adj*

atsui 熱い *hot adj*

atsukau 扱う *handle, to handle* v

atsumeru 集める *collect, to collect* v

ayashisō ni 怪しそうに / yōsu ga hen 様子が変 *suspiciously adv* p44

B

bā バー *bar* n

baikingu バイキング *buffet* n

baiku バイク *motorcycle* n

baiorin バイオリン *violin* n

bājon バージョン *version* n

bakēshon / 休暇 kyūka バケーション *vacation* n p40, 44

kyūka de 休暇で *on vacation*

bakēshon ni dekakeru バケーションに出かける *to go on vacation*

bakkin 罰金 *fine (for traffic violation)* n p168

bakudan 爆弾 *bomb* n

ban バン *van* n

bangō annai 番号案内 *directory assistance (phone)* n

bara バラ *rose* n

baransu o toru バランスを取る *balance* v

barukonī バルコニー *balcony* n p60

basu バス *bass (instrument)* n

basu バス *bus* n p53, 55

basu tei wa doko ni arimasu ka. バス停はどこにありますか? *Where is the bus stop?*
_____ yuki no basu wa dore desu ka. _____行きのバスはどれですか。 *Which bus goes to _____?* p55

batā バター *butter* n p77

batterī バッテリー *battery (for car)* n

be, to be (permanent quality) v

bebī beddo ベビーベッド *crib* n p63

bebī kā ベビーカー *stroller* n

bebī kā wa rentaru deki masu ka. ベビーカーはレンタルできますか? *Do you rent baby strollers?*

bebī shittā ベビーシッター *babysitter* n

eigo o hanasu bebī shittā wa imasu ka. 英語を話すベビーシッターはいますか? *Do you have babysitters who speak English?*

beddo ベッド *bed* n p61

bejitarian ベジタリアン *vegetarian* n p38

benezuera no, benezuera jin no ベネズエラの、ベネズエラ人の *Venezuelan adj* p108

bengo shi 弁護士 *lawyer* n p108

benpi shita 便秘した *constipated adj*

benpi shite imasu. 便秘しています。 *I'm constipated.*

berī weru de ベリーウェルで *charred (meat) adj* p76

beruto ベルト *belt* n p41

beruto konbeyā ベルトコンベヤー *conveyor belt*

betsu no 別の *another adj* p43

bīchi ni noriageru ビーチに乗り上げる *beach* v

bīchi ビーチ *beach* n p62, 116, 152

bideo dekki ビデオデッキ *VCR* n

heya niwa bideo dekki ga oite arimasu ka. 部屋にはビデオデッキが置いてありますか? *Do the rooms have VCRs?*

bideo ビデオ *video* n

DVD matawa bideo wa doko de karirare masu ka. DVDまたはビデオはどこで借りられますか? *Where can I rent videos or DVDs?*

bijinesu ビジネス *business* n p37, 40

bijutsu ka 美術家 *artist* n

bijutsu kan 美術館 *art museum* n

bijutsu kan 美術館 *museum* n p116

bin ビン *bottle* n

dokoka de kono bin o atatameru koto ga deki masu ka. どこかでこのビンを温めることができますか? *May I heat this (baby) bottle someplace?*

binīru ビニール *vinyl* n p45

biriyādo ビリヤード *pool (the game)* n

bīru ビール *beer* n p42, 79

nama bīru 生ビール *beer on tap* p79

biza ビザ *visa* n

biza ga hitsuyō desu ka. ビザが必要ですか？ *Do I need a visa?*

bōi furendo ボーイフレンド *boyfriend* n p101

bokkusu seki ボックス席 p130/ bokkusu sīto ボックスシート p146 *box (seat)* n

boribia no, boribia jin no ボリビアの、ボリビア人の *Bolivian* adj

bōru ボール *ball (sport)* n

bōshi 帽子 *hat* n

bōto ボート *boat* n

boyaketa ぼやけた *blurry* adj p165

bubun 部分 *portion* n

budō en ぶどう園 *vineyard* n

budō ぶどう *grape* n

bujoku suru 侮辱する *insult* v

buki 武器 *weapon* n

bukkyōto 仏教徒 *Buddhist* n p113

burandē ブランデー *brandy* n p80

burausu ブラウス *blouse* n p135

burēki o kakeru ブレーキをかける *brake* v

burēki ブレーキ *brake* n p50

hijō burēki 非常ブレーキ *emergency brake*

burīchi ブリーチ *bleach* n

burīfu kēsu ブリーフケース *briefcase* n p44

burōdo bando ブロードバンド *broadband* n

buronzu sei no ブロンズ製の *bronze* adj

burunetto ブルネット *brunette* n p104

byōki no 病気の *sick* adj

kibun ga warui desu. 気分が悪いです。 *I feel sick.*

C

CD *CD* n p46, 124

CD purēyā CD プレーヤー *CD player* n p46

cha iro no 茶色の *brown* adj p106

chairudo shīto チャイルドシート *car seat (child's safety seat)* n

chairudo shīto o rentaru shite imasu ka. チャイルドシートをレンタルしていますか？ *Do you rent car seats for children?*

chakuriku suru 着陸する / tsuku 着く *land, to land* v p43

chātā suru チャーターする *charter, to charter* v p152

chekku auto suru チェックアウトする *check out, to check out* v p64

chekku auto チェックアウト *check-out* n

chekku auto no jikan チェックアウトの時間 *check-out time*

chekku auto wa nan ji desu ka.
チェックアウトは何時ですか？
What time is check-out?

chekku in チェックイン check-in
n p33

chekku in wa nan ji desu ka.
チェックインは何時ですか？
What time is check-in?

chekku no チェックの *checked
(pattern) adj*

chichi 父 / otōsan お父さん
father n p102

chihō no 地方の *local adj* p48

chiisai 小さい *little adj (size)*
sukoshi 、少し *(amount)*

chiisai 小さい *small adj* p13

chikai 近い *close (near)* p4

chikai 近い *near adj* p4

chikaku ni 近くに *nearby adj*
p73

chikatetsu 地下鉄 *subway n*
p57

chikatetsu no rosen 地下鉄の路
線 *subway line*
chikatetsu no eki 地下鉄の駅
subway station
_____ ewa dono chikatetsu de
ikeba yoi desu ka. _____ へはど
の地下鉄で行けばよいですか？
*Which subway do I take
for _____?*

chiketto uriba チケット売り場
box office n

chikin チキン *chicken n*

chīmu チーム *team n* p146

chippu チップ *tip (gratuity)*

chīzu チーズ *cheese n* p90

chizu 地図 *map n* p46

chōkaku shōgai no 聴覚障害の
hearing-impaired adj

chōkoku 彫刻 *sculpture n*

chōshoku 朝食 *breakfast n* p66

chōshoku wa nan ji desu ka. 朝
食は何時ですか？ *What time
is breakfast?*

chōwa suru 調和する *match, to
match v*

kono _____ wa watashi no fuku
to aimasu ka? この_____は私
の服と合いますか *Does this
_____ match my outfit?*

chūgoku no, chūgoku jin no 中
国の、中国人の *Chinese adj*
p107

chūishite atsukau 注意して扱う
Handle with care adj p141

chūkan no 中間の *middle adj*

chūmon suru 注文する *order, to
order (demand) v*

chūsha suru 駐車する *park, to
park v*

chūsha kinshi 駐車禁止 *no
parking* p51
chūsha ryōkin 駐車料金 *park-
ing fee* p51
shako 車庫 *parking garage*
p51

chūshoku 昼食 / ranchi ランチ
lunch n p73

D

daburu no ダブルの *double adj*
p61, 157

daburu beddo ダブル ベッド
double bed p61
nijū eizō 二重映像 *double
vision*

daigaku 大学 *college n*

daigaku 大学 *university n*

daigeki jō 大劇場 *coliseum n*

daku 抱く *hold, to hold v*

> te o nigiru 手を握る *to hold hands*
> kore o motte itadake masen ka. これを持っていただけませんか? *Would you hold this for me?*

dansei no 男性の *male adj*

dansei 男性 *male n* p41

dantai 団体 *party n*

dare ka 誰か *someone n* p42

dare no 誰の *whose adj*

dare 誰 *who adv* p3

dāsu ダース *dozen n* p13

dasu 出す *serve, to serve v*

daunrōdo suru ダウンロードする *download v* p125

de aru である *be*

de aru である *be, to be (temporary state, condition, mood) v*

de nai でない *no adv*

deguchi 出口 *exit n* p36

> deguchi nashi 出口なし *not an exit*

dekiru できる *able, to be able to (can) v*

dekiru できる *can (able to) v*

denchi 電池 *battery (for flashlight) n*

denki setsuzoku bu 電気接続部 *electrical hookup n* p71

denki 伝記 *biography n*

denwa no 電話の *phone adj*

> denwa chō wa arimasu ka. 電話帳はありますか? *Do you have a phone directory?*

denwa o kakeru 電話をかける yaru suru / ダイヤル dai *dial (a phone) v* p66

> chokutsū bangō ni kakeru 直通番号にかける *dial direct*

denwa 電話 *phone call n*

> korekuto kōru o shitai no desuga. コレクトコールをしたいのですが。 *I need to make a collect phone call.*
> kokusai denwa 国際電話 *an international phone call*

denwa 電話 *phone n* p62

> anata no denwa bangō o oshiete itadake masu ka. あなたの電話番号を教えていただけますか? *May I have your phone number?*
> kōshū denwa wa doko ni arimasu ka. 公衆電話はどこにありますか? *Where can I find a public phone?*
> denwa operētā 電話オペレーター *phone operator*
> puripeido denwa o utte imasu ka. プリペイド電話を売っていますか? *Do you sell prepaid phones?*

deru 出る *exit v*

dezainā デザイナー *designer n* p109

dezāto デザート *dessert n* p79

> dezāto no menyū デザートのメニュー *dessert menu*

disuco ディスコ *disco n* p114

do yō bi 土曜日 *Saturday n* p15

doa ドア *door n*

dōbutsu en 動物園 *zoo n* p116

dōbutsu 動物 *animal n*

dōbutsu 動物 *animal n*

bijutsu hin no tenji 美術品の展示 *exhibit of art*

doitsu no, doitsu jin no ドイツの、ドイツ人の *German adj*

doko demo どこへも *anywhere adv*

doko どこ *where adv* p3

sore wa doko ni arimasu ka. それはどこにありますか？ *Where is it?*

dokushin no 独身の *single (unmarried) adj* p102

anata wa dokushin desu ka? あなたは独身ですか？ *Are you single?*

dōmo arigatō どうもありがとう。 *Thank you.* p1

dorai kurīnā ドライ クリーナー *dry cleaner n*

dorai kuriningu ドライ クリーニング *dry cleaning n*

doramu ドラム *drum n*

dore どれ *which adv* p3

docchi どっち？ *Which one?*

doressingu ドレッシング *dressing (salad) n*

doresu ドレス *dress (garment) n*

dōro heisa chū 道路閉鎖中 *road closed sign n* p51

dōro 道路 *road n*

doru ドル *dollar n*

dōsei no 銅製の *copper adj*

dōzo どうぞ *please (polite entreaty) adv*

DVD DVD *n* p46

sono heya niwa DVD purēyā ga arimasu ka. その部屋にはDVD プレーヤーがありますか？ *Do the rooms have DVD players?*

DVD matawa bideo wa doko de karirare masu ka. DVD またはビデオはどこで借りられますか？ *Where can I rent DVDs or videos?*

E

E mēru Eメール *e-mail n* p110

anata no E mēru adoresu o itadake masu ka. あなたのEメールアドレスをいただけますか？ *May I have your e-mail address?*

ii mēru messēji Eメール メッセージ *e-mail message*

e 絵 *drawing (work of art) n*

e 絵 *painting n*

ebi 海老 *shrimp n* p92

eiga kan 映画館 *cinema n*

eiga 映画 *movie n* p115, 116, 128

eigyō chū 営業中 *open (business) adj*

eigyō shite imasu ka. 営業していますか？ *Are you open?*

eisei 衛星 *satellite n* p46

eisei rajio 衛星ラジオ *satellite radio* p46

eisei tsuiseki 衛星追跡 *satellite tracking* p46

eki 駅 / teisha eki 停車駅 *stop n* p58

koko wa watashi ga oriru eki desu ka. ここは私が降りる駅ですか? *Is this my stop?*

watashi wa nori sugoshite shimai mashita. 私は乗り過ごしてしまいました。*I missed my stop.*

eki 駅 *station n* p53, 57

koko kara ichiban chikai _____ wa doko desu ka. ここから一番近い_____はどこですか? *Where is the nearest_____?*

gasorin sutando ガソリン スタンド *gas station*

basu tei バス停 *bus station*

chikatetsu no eki 地下鉄の駅 *subway station*

eki 駅 *train station*

ekonomī エコノミー *economy n*

ekuadoru no, ekuadoru jin no エクアドルの、エクアドル人の *Ecuadorian adj*

enjin エンジン *engine n* p48

enjinia エンジニア *engineer n* p108

enseki 縁石 *curb n*

ensō suru 演奏する / **hiku** 弾く *play, to play (an instrument) v* p115

ensō 演奏 *band (musical ensemble) n* p155

erebētā エレベーター *elevator n* p59, 63

esa えさ *bait n*

esukarētā エスカレーター *escalator n*

esupuresso エスプレッソ *espresso n*

F

fakkusu ファックス *fax n* p67

fittonesu sentā フィットネス センター / **jimu** ジム *fitness center n* p60

fujinka i 婦人科医 *gynecologist n*

fukachiron no 不可知論の *agnostic adj*

fukai 深い *deep adj* p150

fukuro ni ireru 袋に入れる *bag v*

fukuro 袋 *bag n*

hikōki yoi no fukuro 飛行機酔いの袋 *airsickness bag* p43

watashi no baggu ga nusumare mashita. 私のバックが盗まれました。*My bag was stolen.*

watashi wa baggu o nakushi mashita. 私はバックを失くしました。*I lost my bag.*

fukusō 服装 *dress (general attire) n* p156

fukusō no kisoku wa nan desu ka. 服装の規則は何ですか? *What's the dress code?*

fun 分 *minute n*

sugu ni すぐに *in a minute*

funa yoi ni kiku kusuri 船酔いに効く薬 *seasickness pill n*

funa yoi 船酔い *seasick adj* p57

funa yoi shimashita. 船酔いしました。*I am seasick.*

fune de hakobu 船で運ぶ *ship, to ship v*

kore o _____ made fune de okuru niwa ikura kakari masu ka? これを_____まで船で送るにはいくらかかりますか? *How much to ship this to _____?*

fune 船 *ship* n p56

furaito フライト / ___bin __便 *flight* n p35

kokunai sen no shuppatsu / tōchaku basho wa doko desu ka. 国内線の出発/到着場所はどこですか? *Where do domestic flights arrive / depart?*

kokusai sen no shuppatsu / tōchaku basho wa doko desu ka. 国際線の出発 / 到着場所はどこですか? *Where do international flights arrive / depart?*

kono furaito wa nan ji ni shuppatsu shimasu ka. このフライトは何時に出発しますか? *What time does this flight leave?*

furansu no, furansu jin no フランスの、フランス人の *French* adj p107

furasshu フラッシュ *flush (gambling)* n

furikomi 振り込み *money transfer* p132

furonto garasu フロントガラス *windshield* n

furu hausu. フル ハウス! *Full house!* n

furu 振る *wave, to wave* v

furui 古い / sai no __歳の _ *old* adj p103

furumau 振る舞う *behave* v

furūto フルート *flute* n

furūtsu jūsu フルーツ ジュース *fruit juice* n

futatsu no 二つの *two* adj p10

fūtō 封筒 *envelope* n p127

futotta 太った *fat* adj p13

fuyu 冬 *winter* n p17

G

gādo ガード *guard* n

gaido bukku ガイドブック *guide (publication)* n

gaido tsuki tuā ガイド付きツアー *guided tour* n

gaido ガイド *guide (of tours)* n p131

gakkō 学校 *school* n

gakunen 学年 *grade (school)* n

garon ガロン *gallon* n p12

gāru furendo ガールフレンド *girlfriend* n p101

gasorin ガソリン *gas* n p48

nenryō kei 燃料計 *gas gauge*

gasorin ga haitte inai ガソリンが入っていない *out of gas*

geijutsu no 芸術の *art* adj

geki no kyakuhon 劇の脚本 *drama* n

gekijō 劇場 *theater* n

gengo 言語 *language* n

genki na 元気な *fine* p1

watashi wa genki desu. 私は元気です。 *I'm fine.*

genkin ni kaeru 現金に換える *cash, to cash* v

seisan suru 清算する *to cash out (gambling)* p161

genkin 現金 *cash* n p138

genkin nomi 現金のみ *cash only* p120

geri 下痢 *diarrhea* n p163

gēto ゲート *gate (at airport)* n p33

getsu yō bi 月曜日 *Monday* n p15

gin sei no 銀製の *silver* adj

ginkō 銀行 *bank* n p118

ginkō wa doko ni aruka oshiete itadake masu ka. 銀行はどこにあるか教えていただけますか? *Can you help me find a bank?*

girisha no, girisha jin no ギリシャの、ギリシャ人の *Greek* adj

girisha seikyō no ギリシャ正教の *Greek Orthodox* adj p113

gishi 義歯 *denture* n

gishi 義歯 *denture plate*

gitā ギター *guitar* n p115

go banme no 五番目の *fifth* adj

go gatsu 五月 *May (month)* n p17

gogo 午後 *afternoon* n p14

gogo ni 午後に *in the afternoon*

gojū no 五十の *fifty* adj p7

gōkei 合計 *total* n

合計でいくらですか? gōkei de ikura desu ka. *What is the total?*

gōru kīpā ゴールキーパー *goalie* n p146

gōru ゴール *goal (sport)* n

gorufu o suru ゴルフをする *golf, to go golfing* v

gorufu renshū jō ゴルフ練習場 *driving range* n

gorufu ゴルフ *golf* n p45

guatemara no, guatemara jin no グアテマラの、グアテマラ人の *Guatemalan* adj p107

gun 軍 *military* n

guramu グラム *gram* n

gurasu グラス *glass* n p76

gurasu de arimasuka. グラスでありますか? *Do you have it by the glass?*

gurasu de hitotsu onegai shimasu. グラスで一つお願いします。*I'd like a glass please.*

gurūpu グループ *group* n p152

gutai teki ni noberu 具体的に述べる *specify, to specify* v

gyūnyū 牛乳 / miruku ミルク *milk* n p78, 80

miruku sēki ミルクセーキ *milk shake*

H

ha ni kabusete iru mono 歯にかぶせているもの *crown (dental)* n

ha 歯 *tooth* n p167

ha ga ippon nuke mashita. 歯が1本抜けました。*I lost my tooth.*

hābu ハーブ *herb* n

hachi banme no 8番目の *eighth* n

hachi gatsu 八月 *August* n p17

hachi jū 八十 *eighty* n p7

hachi ハチ *bee* n

hachi ni sasare mashita. ハチに刺されました。*I was stung by a bee.*

hachi 八 *eight* n p6

haha 母 / okāsan お母さん *mother n* p101

hai iro no 灰色の *gray adj*

hai. はい。 *Yes. adv*

haikingu o suru ハイキングをする *hike, to hike v*

hairaito ハイライト *highlights (hair) n* p142

hairu 入る *enter, to enter v*

shinyū kinshi 進入禁止 *Do not enter.*

haisha 歯医者 *dentist n* p164

haisui 排水 *drain n*

haita 歯痛 *toothache n*

ha ga itami masu. 歯が痛みます。 *I have a toothache.*

hajimaru 始まる *begin v* p129

hajimaru 始まる *start, to start (commence) v*

hakike 吐き気 *nausea n* p163

hamaki 葉巻 *cigar n*

han zubon 半ズボン *shorts n* p75

hana 花 *flower n*

hana 鼻 *nose n* p142

hanasu 話す *speak, to speak v* p2

eigo o hanashi masu ka? 英語を話しますか? *Do you speak English?* p2

motto ōkina koe de hanashite kudasai. もっと大きな声で話してください。 / motto ōkina koe de hanashite itadake masen ka. もっと大きな声で話していただけませんか。 *Would you speak louder, please?* p2

motto yukkuri hanashite kudasai. もっとゆっくり話してください。 / motto yukkuri hanashite itadake masen ka. もっとゆっくり話していただけませんか。 *Would you speak slower, please?* p2

hanasu 話す *talk, to talk v*

hanbai in 販売員 *salesperson n* p108

hanbun 半分 *half n*

ni bun no ichi 二分の一 *one-half*

hangā ハンガー *hanger n*

hanka gai 繁華街 *downtown n* p133

hansamu na ハンサムな *handsome adj* p103

hareta 晴れた *sunny adj* p111

soto wa harete imasu. 外は晴れています。 *It's sunny out.*

haru 春 *spring (season) n* p17

hashi 橋 /ha no kyōsei burijji 歯の矯正ブリッジ *bridge (across a river, dental) n* p167

hashiru 走る *run, to run v*

hassha saseru 発車させる *start, to start (a car) v*

hayai 早い *early adj* p14

hayai desu. 早いです。 *It's early.*

hayai 速い *fast adj*

hazukashii 恥ずかしい *embarrassed adj*

heā doraiyā ヘアードライヤー *hair dryer n* p68

heā doressā ヘアードレッサー *hairdresser n*

heā katto ヘアーカット *haircut n*
kami no ke o kiri tai no desuga.
髪の毛を切りたいのですが。*I
need a haircut.*
katto wa ikura desuka. カットは
いくらですか? *How much is
a haircut?*
heddo hōn ヘッドホーン *head-
phones n*
heddo raito ヘッドライト *head-
light n*
hekomu へこむ *dent v* p48
kare / kanojo ga kuruma o
hekomase mashita. 彼 / 彼女
が車をへこませました。*He /
She dented the car.*
hekutāru ヘクタール *hectare
n* p11
henpin suru 返品する *return,
to return (something to a
store) v* p140
henshū sha 編集者 *editor n*
p109
hensoku ki 変速機 *transmis-
sion n*
ōto machikku オートマチック
automatic transmission
manyuaru マニュアル *standard
transmission*
heya 部屋 *room (hotel) n*
hitori /futari beya 1人 / 2人部
屋 *room for one / two*
rūmu sābisu ルームサービス
room service
hi 日 *day n*
ototoi ーおととい *the day
before yesterday* p15

koko nisan nichi ここ 2‐3日
these last few days
hi 火 *light (for cigarette) n*
p157
hi o kashima shō ka. 火を貸しま
しょうか? *May I offer you a
light?* raitā ライター *lighter
(cigarette) n* p158
hibi ware ヒビ割れ *crack (in
glass object) n*
hidari no 左の *left adj* p5
hidari ni 左に *on the left*
hifu 皮膚 *skin n*
hige ひげ *beard n*
hijō burēki 非常ブレーキ *emer-
gency brake n*
hijō deguchi 非常出口 *emer-
gency exit n* p37
hikōki no jōmuin 飛行機の乗務
員 *flight attendant*
hikōki yoi no fukuro 飛行機酔い
の袋 *airsickness bag n* p43
hiku 引く *pull, to pull v* p36
hiku 引く *withdraw v*
okane o hiki dashi tai no
desuga. お金を引き出したいの
ですが。*I need to withdraw
money.*
hikui 低い *low adj* p48
hinin 避妊 *birth control n*
hinin yaku ga nakunari
mashita. 避妊薬がなくなりまし
た。*I'm out of birth control
pills.*
motto hinin yaku ga hitsuyō
desu. もっと避妊薬が必要です。
*I need more birth control
pills.*

hinzū kyō no, hinzū jin no ヒンズ
ー教の、ヒンズー人の Hindu
adj p113

hippu hoppu ヒップホップ hip-
hop n

hiroi 広い wide adj p13

hitai 額 forehead n

hitotsu no 一つの one adj p10

hitotsu no 一つの single (one)
adj

shinguru beddo シングル ベッド
single bed

hiyake dome kurīmu 日焼け止め
クリーム sunscreen n

SPF ___ no hiyake dome
kurīmu wa arimasu ka. SPF
___の日焼け止めクリームは
ありますか? Do you have
sunscreen SPF ____? See
numbers p7.

hiyake shita 日焼けした tanned
adj

hiyake 日焼け sunburn n

watashi wa hidoku hiyake shimashita. 私はひどく日焼けしま
した。 I have a bad sunburn.

hodō 歩道 sidewalk n

hodō 歩道 walkway n

jidō idō tsūro 自動移動通路
moving walkway

hojū 補充 refill (of prescription) n

hoken 保険 insurance n p47,
125

hokōki 歩行器 walker (ambulatory device) n p39

hokōsha yō no 歩行者用の
pedestrian adj

hokuro ほくろ mole (facial
feature) n

hon ya 本屋 bookstore n p133

hon 本 book n p117, 139

honjurasu no, honjurasu jin no
ホンジュラスの、ホンジュラス人
の Honduran adj

hontō ni 本当に really adv

hōritsu 法律 law n

hōshi 奉仕 / reihai 礼拝 services
(religious) n p113

hoshii ～欲しい ～ want, to
want v

hoshii 欲しい need, to need v

hosuteru ホステル hostel n p60

hoteru ホテル hotel n p53, 60

jimoto no hoteru no ichiran
hyō wa arimasu ka. 地元のホ
テルの一覧表はありますか?
Do you have a list of local
hotels?

hotto chokorēto ホット チョコレー
ト hot chocolate n p80

hyaku 百 hundred n

hyōkō 標高 altitude n p148

hyūzu ヒューズ fuse n

I

ichi gatsu 一月 January n p17

ie 家 home n

igirisu jin, igirisu no, igirisu jin
no イギリス(の)、イギリス人(の)
English n, adj p168

eigo o hanashi masu ka. 英語
を話しますか? Do you speak
English? p2

igirisu イギリス England n

ii mēru suru Eメールする e-mail,
to send e-mail v

iin 医院 *doctor's office n*

iku 行く *go, to go v*

ikura いくら *how adv (how much)*, ikutsu いくつ *(how many)* p3, 35

ikutsukano いくつかの *some adj*

ima 今 *now adv* p3

inchi インチ *inch n* p11

insatsu suru 印刷する *print, to print v* p124

intānetto インターネット *Internet n* p34, 62

kōsoku intānetto 高速インターネット *High-speed Internet*

intānetto ni setsuzoku deki masu ka. インターネットに接続できますか? *Do you have Internet access?*

intā netto kafe wa doko ni arimasu ka. インターネットカフェはどこにありますか? *Where can I find an Internet café?*

inu 犬 *dog n* p166

kaigo ken 介護犬 *service dog* p39, 59, 64

ippai 一杯 *shot (liquor) n*

ippō tsūkō 一方通行 *one way (traffic sign) adj*

iriguchi 入口 *entrance n* p36

iro o nuru 色をぬる *color v*

iro 色 *color n*

isha 医者 *doctor n* p108, 163

ishō 衣装 *costume n*

isuramu kyō no イスラム教の *muslim adj* p113

itai. 痛い! *Ouch!*

itamu 痛む *hurt, to hurt v* p164

itai desu. 痛い!itai. 痛いです! *Ouch!That hurts!*

itaria no, itaria jin no イタリアの、イタリア人の *Italian adj* p107

itoko いとこ *cousin n*

itsu いつ *when adv* p3

See p112 for questions.

itsutsu no 五つの *five adj* p11

iu 言う *say, to say v* p100

iwau 祝う *celebrate, to celebrate v*

J

jaguchi 蛇口 *faucet n*

jazu ジャズ *jazz n* p114

ji 時 *o'clock adv* p4

ni ji 時 *two o'clock* 2

jidō hanbai ki 自動販売機 *vending machine n*

jiin 寺院 *temple n* p112

jikan 時間 *hour n* p124, 131

jikan 時間 *hours (at museum) n*

jikan 時間 *time n* p64

sore wa teikoku dōri desu ka. それは定刻通りですか? *Is it on time?*

nan ji ni. 何時に? *At what time?*

nan ji desu ka. 何時ですか? *What time is it?*

jiko 事故 *accident n* p52

jiko ni ai mashita. 事故にあいました。 *I've had an accident.* p52

jikoku hyō 時刻表 *timetable (train) n* p53

jimaku 字幕 *subtitle n*

jimu ジム *gym n* p143

jin ジン *gin n* p80

jinshu no majitta 人種の混じった *biracial adj* p105

jisho 辞書 *dictionary n*

jissai no 実際の *actual adj*

joggingu o suru ジョギングをする *jog, to run v* p145

jōhō 情報 *information n*

jōkyaku 乗客 *passenger n*

jōkyō 状況 *state n*

josei no 女性の *female adj*

josei 女性 *woman n*

jōshi 上司 *boss n*

jōtai 状態 *condition n*

yoi/warui jōtai 良い/悪い状態 *in good / bad condition*

jū ban me no 十番目の *tenth adj*

jū gatsu 十月 *October n* p17

jū hachi 十八 *eighteen n* p7

jū ichi gatsu 十一月 *November n* p17

jū ichi 十一 *eleven n* p7

jū ni gatsu 十二月 *December n* p17

jū no 十の *ten adj* p6

jū san no 十三の *thirteen adj* p7

jūden suru 充電する *charge, to charge (a battery) v* p59

jūgo no 十五の *fifteen adj* p7

jūgyō in 従業員 *employee n*

jūkyū no 十九の *nineteen adj* p7

junbi sareta 準備された *prepared adj*

jūni no 十二の *twelve adj* p7

junyū suru 授乳する *nurse v*

junyū dekiru basho wa arimasu ka. 授乳できる場所はありますか？ *Do you have a place where I can nurse?*

jūroku no 十六の *sixteen adj* p7

jūshichi no 十七の *seventeen adj* p7

jushin nin barai no 受信人払いの *collect adj*

korekuto kōru o onegai shimasu. コレクトコールをお願いします。 *I'd like to place a collect call.*

jūsho 住所 *address n* p110

jūsho wa nan desu ka. 住所は何ですか？ *What's the address?*

jūsu ジュース *juice n* p42

jūyon no 十四の / jū shi no 十四の *fourteen adj* p7

K

ka yō bi 火曜日 *Tuesday n* p15

kabā chāji カバーチャージ *cover charge (in bar) n* 156, 158

kādo カード *card n* p34

kurejitto kādo o tsukae masu ka. クレジットカードを使えますか？ *Do you accept credit cards?* p34

anata no meishi o itadake masu ka. あなたの名刺をいただけますか？ *May I have your business card?*

kado 角 /burokku ブロック *block n* p6

kagi o kakeru 鍵をかける *lock, to lock v*

doa ni kagi o kakeru koto ga dekima sen. ドアに鍵をかけることができません。 *I can't lock the door.*

doa ni kagi ga kakatte shimai heya ni hairu koto ga deki masen. ドアに鍵がかかってしまい部屋に入ることができません。 *I'm locked out.*

kagi 鍵 *lock n p143*

kai in 会員 *member n*

kai rui 貝類 *shellfish n p78*

kai 階 *floor n*

ikkai 1 階 *ground floor p63*
ni kai 2 階 *second floor*

kaidan 階段 *stair n*

kaidan wa doko desu ka. 階段はどこですか? *Where are the stairs?*

kaidan no kazu wa ōi desu ka. 階段の数は多いですか? *Are there many stairs?*

kaimono o suru 買い物をする *shop v p115*

shinshi fuku o kai ni kimashita. 紳士服を買いに来ました。 *I'm shopping for mens' clothes.*

fujin fuku o kai ni kimashita. 婦人服を買いに来ました。 *I'm shopping for womens' clothes.*

kodomo fuku o kai ni kimashita. 子供服を買いに来ました。 *I'm shopping for childrens' clothes.*

kairo purakutā カイロプラクター *chiropractor n p164*

kaisen sokudo 回線速度 *connection speed n p125*

kaisha 会社 *agency n p45*

rentakā gaisha レンタカー会社 *car rental agency*

kaji da. 火事だ! *fire! n*

kajino カジノ *casino n p60*

kakaku 価格 *price n*

kakeru かける *bet, to bet v*

kakin 家禽 *poultry n*

kaku 書く *write, to write v*

kami ni kaite itadake masu ka. 紙に書いていただけますか? *Would you write that down for me?*

kakunin suru 確認する *confirm, to confirm v p38*

yoyaku o kakunin shitai no desuga. 予約を確認したいのですが。 *I'd like to confirm my reservation.*

kami no ke 髪の毛 *hair n*

kami 紙 *paper n*

kanada no, kanada jin no カナダの、カナダ人の *Canadian adj*

kanada カナダ *Canada n*

kanashii 悲しい *sad adj p106*

kango shi 看護師 *nurse n p109*

kankō basu 観光バス *sightseeing bus n*

kankō 観光 *sightseeing n*

kankyō 環境 *environment n*

kanojo no 彼女の *her adj p3*

kansatsu suru 観察する *watch, to watch v*

kansō shita 乾燥した *dried adj*

kantorī ando wesutan カントリーアンドウェスタン *country-and-western n* p114

kanzen ni niete iai 完全に煮えていない *undercooked adj*

kanzume 缶詰 *can n*

kao 顔 *face n* p106

kapuchīno カプチーノ *cappuccino n*

kara tsuku rareta から作られた *made of adj*

kare no 彼の *his adj*

kare o 彼を *him pron* p3

karera (ni, o) 彼ら (に、を) *them (m/f)* p3

kariru 借りる *rent, to rent v*

kuruma o karitai no desuga. 車を借りたいのですが。 *I'd like to rent a car.* p45

kāru shita カールした *curly adj* p142

kāru カール *curl n*

kasa 傘 *umbrella n*

kashimiya カシミヤ *cashmere n*

katorikku kyō no カトリック教の *Catholic adj* p113

kau 買う *buy, to buy v* p121, 129, 134

kauntā カウンター *counter (in bar) n* p74

kawa 川 *river n* p150

kawa 皮 *leather n* p45

kawaita 乾いた *dry*

kono taoru wa kawaite imasen. このタオルは乾いていません。 *This towel isn't dry.*

kawakasu 乾かす *dry, to dry v*

watashi no fuku o kawakasu hitsuyō ga arimasu. 私の服を乾かす必要があります。 *I need to dry my clothes.*

kawari no mono 替わりのもの *substitution n*

kaze ga tsuyoi 風が強い *windy adj* p111

kaze カゼ *cold n* p98, 162

kaze o hiki mashita. カゼを引きました。 *I have a cold.*

kazoku 家族 / go kazoku ご家族 *family n* p3

kega けが *injury n*

keisatsu sho 警察署 / keisatsu no hashutsu sho 警察の派出所 *police station n* p33

keisatsu 警察 *police n* p33

keishoku 軽食 *snack n* p90

keitai denwa 携帯電話 *cell phone n* p121

kekkon suru 結婚する *marry, to marry v*

kengan shi 検眼師 *optometrist n*

kenri 権利 *rights n pl*

shimin no kenri 市民の権利 *civil rights*

kensa 検査 *search n*

te de kensa suru 手で検査する *hand search*

keshiki 景色 *landscape n*

keshō o suru 化粧をする *make up, to make up (apply cosmetics) v*

keshō 化粧 *makeup n*

ki o ushinau 気を失う *faint v*
p165

kicchin キッチン *kitchen n* p62

kichin to shita きちんとした *neat
(tidy) adj*

kieru 消える *disappear v*

kiiroi 黄色い *yellow adj*

kikai 機械 *machine n* p125

kiken 危険 *danger n* p51

kikon no 既婚の / kekkon shite
iru 結婚している *married adj*
p102

kiku 聞く *hear v*

kin en no 禁煙の *non-smok-
ing adj*

  kin en no 禁煙の *no smoking*
p36

  kin en no shitsu 禁煙の室 *nonsmoking room*

kin sei no 金製の *gold adj*

kin yō bi 金曜日 *Friday n* p15

kingaku ga kakaru 金額がかかる
cost, to cost v

  sore wa ikura shimasu ka. それ
はいくらしますか? *How much
does it cost?* p137

kinjo no hito 近所の人 / kinjo no
kata ご近所の方 *neighbor
n* p102

kinko 金庫 *safe (for storing
valuables) n* p68

  shitsu nai niwa kinko ga arimasu ka. 室内には金庫があり
ますか。*Do the rooms have
safes?* p68

kinkyū 緊急 *emergency n*

kinō suru 機能する *work, to
work v*

kore wa kinō shimasen. これは
機能しません。*This doesn't
work.*

kinō 昨日 *yesterday n* p4

  ototoi おととい *the day before yesterday* p15

kinpatsu no 金髪の *blond(e)
adj* p104

kinri 金利 *interest rate n* p119

kinzoku tanchi ki 金属探知機
metal detector n

kippu 切符 / chiketto チケット
ticket n p33, 35

  kippu uriba 切符売り場 /
chiketto kauntā チケットカウン
ター *ticket counter*

  katamichi kippu 片道切符 *one-
way ticket* p56

  ōfuku kippu 往復切符 *round-
trip ticket* p56

kireina きれいな *beautiful adj*
p137

kiri kizu 切り傷 *cut (wound) n*

  watashi wa hidoi kirikizu ga
arimasu. 私はひどい切り傷があ
ります。*I have a bad cut.*

kiri soroeru 切りそろえる /
soroeru そろえる *trim, to
trim (hair) v* p141

kiro guramu キログラム *kilo n*

kiro mētoru キロメートル *kilo-
meter n* p11

kiru 切る *cut, to cut v* p142

kiru 切る *hang up (to end a
phone call) v* p122

kiru 着る *dress v*

soko dewa seisō shinakereba nari masen ka. そこでは正装しなければなりませんか? *Should I dress up for that affair.*

kiru 着る *wear, to wear v*

kissa ten 喫茶店 *café n* p34, 74

intānetto kafe インターネット カフェ *Internet café* p124

kisu キス *kiss n*

kitsu en 喫煙 *smoking n* p61

kitsu en jo 喫煙所 *smoking area* p34

kin en 禁煙 *No Smoking* p61

kitsui きつい *tight adj* p136

kitte 切手 *stamp (postage) n*

kizu no aru 傷のある *scratched adj* p48

suri kizu no aru 擦り傷のある表面 *scratched surface*

kobosu こぼす *spill, to spill v* p43

kodomo tachi 子供たち *children n* p40,76

kodomo mo ii desu ka. 子供も いいですか? *Are children allowed?*

kodomo yō no puroguramu wa arimasu ka. 子供用のプロ グラムはありますか? *Do you have children's programs?*

kodomo yō no menyū wa arimasu ka. 子供用のメニュー はありますか? *Do you have a children's menu?*

kodomo 子供 *child n* p43

kodomo 子供 *kid n*

kodomo mo ii desu ka. 子供 もいいですか? *Are kids allowed?*

kodomo yō no puroguramu wa arimasu ka. 子供用のプロ グラムはありますか? *Do you have kids' programs?*

kodomo yō no menyū wa arimasu ka. 子供用のメニュー はありますか? *Do you have a kids' menu?*

kōen 公園 *park n* p116

kōgai 郊外 *suburb n*

kogitte 小切手 / chekku チェック *check n* p64, 118

toraberāzu chekku o tsukae masu ka. トラベラーズ チェッ クを使えますか? *Do you accept travelers' checks?* p64

kōhī コーヒー *coffee n* p81

aisu kōhī アイス コーヒー *iced coffee*

kōhisutamin zai 抗ヒスタミン剤 *antihistamine n* p162

kōi shitsu 更衣室 *changing room n*

kojin kyakushitsu 個人客室 / kyabin キャビン *private berth / cabin n*

kōka 硬貨 *coin n*

kōkai suru 航海する *sail, to sail v*

itsu shukkō shimasu ka. いつ 出航しますか? *When do we sail?* p150

kōkai 航海 *sail n*

kōkan rêto 交換レート *exchange rate n* p119

amerika doru/kanada doru no kōkan rēto wa nan desu ka. アメリカドル/カナダドルの交換レートは何ですか? *What is the exchange rate for US / Canadian dollars?*

kōkan suru 交換する *change (to change money, clothes) v*

koko ここ *here n* p4

kokonotsu no 九つの *nine adj* p11

kokuseki 国籍 *nationality n*

kōkyō gakudan 交響楽団 *symphony n*

kōkyūna 高級な *upscale adj*

kon nichi wa こんにちは *hello n* p1

kona miruku 粉ミルク *formula n*

bebī yō kona miruku wa utte imasu ka. ベビー用粉ミルクは売っていますか? *Do you sell infants' formula?*

kondoru コンドル *condor n*

konnan na 困難な / muzukashii 難しい *difficult adj* p148

kono この *this adj*

konomi 好み *taste (discernment) n*

konpyūta コンピューター *computer n*

konran shita 混乱した *confused adj*

konsāto コンサート *concert n* p116

konsento コンセント *plug n*

kontakuto renzu コンタクトレンズ *contact lens n*

kontakuto renzu o nakushi mashita. コンタクトレンズをなくしました。 *I lost my contact lens.*

konyakku コニャック *cognac n* p80

konyaku sha 婚約者 *fiancé(e) n* p102

konzatsu shita 混雑した *congested adj*

kopī o toru コピーを取る / kopī suru コピーする *photocopy, to photocopy v* p109

korera no これらの *these adj* p6

kōri 氷 *ice n* p78

koronbia no, koronbia jin no コロンビアの、コロンビア人の *Colombian adj*

kōsei busshitsu 抗生物質 *antibiotic n*

kōsei busshitsu o kudasai. 抗生物質をください。 *I need an antibiotic.*

kōshin suru 更新する *update, to update v*

kōsoku dōro 高速道路 *highway n*

kosutarika no, kosutarika jin no コスタリカの、コスタリカ人の *Costa Rican adj*

kotae 答え *answer n*

kotaeru 答える *answer, to answer (phone call, question) v*

kotaete kudasai. 答えてくださ
い。 *Answer me, please.*

kōto コート *coat n* p135

kōto コート *court (sport) n*

kotonaru 異なる / chigau 違
う / betsuno 別の *different
(other) adj p137 p69*

kōtsū 交通 *traffic n*

   kōtsū jōtai wa do desu ka. 交
通状態はどうですか？ *How's
traffic?*

   kōtsū kisoku 交通規則 *traffic
rules*

kowareru 壊れる *break v*

kōza 口座 *account n* p120

   tōza-yokin/futsū-yokin e/kara
furikaete tai no desuga. 当座
預金/普通預金口座へ/から振
り替えたいのですが。 *I'd like
to transfer to / from my
checking / savings account.*

kozutsumi 小包み *package n*
p125

ku gatsu 九月 *September n*
p17

kubaru 配る *deal (cards) v*

   watashi mo irete kudasai. 私も
入れてください。 *Deal me in.*

kuchi hige 口ひげ *mustache n*

kuchi 口 *mouth n*

kuda mono 果物 *fruit n* p90

kujira 鯨 *whale n*

kukkī クッキー *cookie n* p90

kūkō 空港 *airport n*

   kūkō made notte iku hitsuyō
ga arimasu. 空港まで乗って行
く必要があります。 *I need a
ride to the airport.*

   kūkō kara dono kurai no
tokoro ni arimasu ka. 空港か
らどのくらいのところにありま
すか？ *How far is it from the
airport?*

kumotta 曇った *cloudy adj*
p111

kunren suru 訓練する *train, to
train v*

kurabu ni odori ni iku クラブに踊
りに行く *go clubbing, to go
clubbing v*

kuragari 暗がり *dark n*

kurai 暗い *dark adj*

kurarinetto クラリネット *clarinet
n*

kurasshikku no クラシックの *classical (music) adj*

kurasu クラス *class n* p37

   bijinesu kurasu ビジネスクラス
business class

   ekonomī kurasu エコノミークラ
ス *economy class*

   fāsuto kurasu ファーストクラス
first class

kurejitto kādo クレジットカード
credit card n p119

kurejitto kādo o tsukae masu
ka. クレジットカードを使えます
か？ *Do you accept credit
cards?* p119

kuri kaesu 繰り返す *repeat, to
repeat v* p2

   mō ichido kuri kaeshite itadake
masu ka. もう一度繰り返して
いただけますか？ *Would you
please repeat that?* p2

kurīmu クリーム *cream* n p77

kurōbā クローバー *clover* n

kuroi 黒い /koku jin 黒人 *black* adj p104

kuruma isu 車椅子 *wheelchair* n p39

> kurumaisu deno akusesu 車椅子でのアクセス *wheelchair access*
>
> kuruma isu yō surōpu 車椅子用スロープ *wheelchair ramp*
>
> dendō kuruma isu 電動車椅子 *power wheelchair*

kuruma yoi 車酔い *carsickness* n

kuruma 車 *car* n

> rentakā gaisha レンタカー会社 *car rental agency*
>
> rentakā ga hitsuyō desu. レンタカーが必要です。 *I need a rental car.*

kurumi クルミ *nut* n

kutsu shita 靴下 *sock* n

kutsu 靴 *shoe* n p41, 133, 134

kutsurogu くつろぐ *lounge, to lounge* v

kyaku no ōi 客の多い (restaurant), hanashi chū de 話し中で (phone) *busy* adj

kyanbasu キャンバス (for painting)/ kyanbasu ji キャンバス地 (material) *canvas* n p45

kyanpā キャンパー *camper* n p71

kyanpu no キャンプの *camping* adj

kyanpu o suru kyoka ga hitsuyō desu ka. キャンプをする許可が必要ですか？ *Do we need a camping permit?*

kyanpu o suru キャンプをする *camp, to camp* v p115

kyanpu saito キャンプサイト *campsite* n p149

kyō 今日 *today* n

kyōdai 兄弟/go kyōdai ご兄弟 *brother* n p102

kyohi sareta 拒否された *declined* adj

> watashi no kurejitto kādo ga kyohi saretano desu ka. 私のクレジットカードが拒否されたのですか？ *Was my credit card declined?*

kyōiku sha 教育者 *educator* n p109

kyoka suru 許可する *permit, to permit* v

kyoka 許可 *permit* n

> kyanpu o suru kyoka ga hitsuyō desu ka. キャンプをする許可が必要ですか？ *Do we need a camping permit?*

kyōkai 教会 *church* n p112

kyū banme no 九番目の *ninth* adj

kyūjitsu 休日 *holiday* n

kyūjū no 九十の *ninety* adj p7

kyūkei 休憩 *intermission* n

kyūkyūsha 救急車 *ambulance* n

kyūmei yōgu 救命用具 *life preserver* n

M

macchi マッチ *match n*

macchi マッチ *book of matches*

machiai shitu 待合室 *waiting area n* p33

machigai 間違い *mistake n* p70

mado 窓 *window n*

mae motte 前もって *in advance* p129

magaru 曲がる *turn, to turn v* p50

hidari / migi ni magaru 左 / 右 に曲がる *to turn left / right* p50

kesu / tsukeru 消す / 付ける *to turn off / on*

mairu マイル *mile n* p11

māketto マーケット / ichiba 市場 *market n* p134, 137

furii māketto フリーマーケット *flea market* p134

aozora ichiba 青空市場 *open-air market*

makura 枕 *pillow n* p43, 67, 68

umō no makura 羽毛の枕 *down pillow* p68

manējā マネージャー *manager n*

manpuku ni natta 満腹になっ た *full, to be full (after a meal) adj*

manyuaru マニュアル *manual (instruction booklet) n* p48

massāji マッサージ *massage n* p66

matsu ge まつ毛 *eyelash n*

matsu 待つ *hold, to hold (to pause) v*

chotto matte. ちょっと待って! *Hold on a minute!*

pasu shimasu. パスします。 *I'll hold.*

matsu 待つ *wait, to wait v* p74

dōka omachi kudasai. どうかお 待ちください。 *Please wait.*

dono kurai machi masu ka. どの くらい待ちますか? *How long is the wait?* p74

mayonaka 真夜中 *midnight n*

mayu ge まゆ毛 *eyebrow n*

me no mienai 目の見えない *blind adj*

me 目 *eye n* p105

mēdo メード *maid (hotel) n*

megane 眼鏡 *eyeglasses n*

megane 眼鏡 *glasses (eye) n*

atarashii megane ga hitsuyō desu. 新しい眼鏡が必要です。 *I need new glasses.*

mei めい / meigo san 姪御さん *niece n* p102

mekishiko no, mekishiko jin no メキシコの、メキシコ人の *Mexican adj*

memai ga suru めまいがする *dizzy adj* p165

men 綿/kotton コットン *cotton n* p135

mendori 雌鶏 *hen n*

menkyo shō 免許証 *license n* p169

unten menkyo shō 運転免許証
driver's license

menyū メニュー *menu n* p74,
76

menyū o misete itadake masen
ka. メニューを見せていただ
けませんか? *May I see a
menu?*

kodomo yō no menyū 子供用の
メニュー *children's menu*

tōnyōbyō kanja yō no menyū
糖尿病患者用のメニュー *diabetic
menu*

kōsha ryōri no menyū コーシャ
料理のメニュー *kosher menu*

menzei no 免税の *duty-free
adj* p34

menzei ten 免税店 *duty-free
shop n* p34

mētoru メートル *meter n* p11

mezamashi tokei 目覚まし時計
alarm clock n p68

mibō jin 未亡人, yamome やもめ
widow, widower n p103

mibun shōmei sho 身分証明書
identification n p42

michi 道 *street n* p6

kono michi no mukō gawa こ
の道の向こう側 *across the
street* p6

kono michi (no saki) この道(の
先) *down the street* p6

dono michi. どの道? *Which
street?*

ato nan bon no michi ga
arimasuka? あと何本の道があ
りますか? *How many more
streets?*

midiamu rea ミディアム レア *me-
dium rare (meat) adj* p76

midiamu weru ミディアム ウェ
ル *medium well (meat)
adj* p76

midiamu ミディアム *medium
(size) adj*

midori iro no 緑色の *green adj*
p106

migi no 右の *right adj* p5, 50

migi gawa ni arimasu. 右側に
あります。 *It is on the right.*
p50

kado o migi ni magari masu. 角
を右に曲がります。 *Turn right
at the corner.*

mijikai 短い *short adj* p12

mikon no 未婚の *maiden adj*

sore wa watashi no kyūsei
desu. それは私の旧姓です。
That's my maiden name.

mimi ga kikoenai 耳が聞こえない
deaf adj

minato 港 *port (for ship) n*

minshu shugi 民主主義 *democ-
racy n*

miri mētoru ミリメートル *mil-
limeter n*

miri rittoru ミリリットル *milliliter
n*

miru 見る *look, to look(to
observe) v*

tada miteiru dake desu. ただ
見ているだけです。 *I'm just
looking.*

koko o mite. ここを見て! *Look
here!*

miru 見る *see, to see v*

misete itadake masu ka? 見せて
いただけますか? *May I see
it?*

miryō sareta 魅了された
charmed adj

mise 店 *shop n*

mise 店 *store n*

miseru 見せる *show, to show v*

misete itadake masen ka. 見せ
ていただけませんか? *Would
you show me?*

misuterī ミステリー *mystery
(novel) n*

mīto bōru ミートボール *meat-
ball n*

mitsukara nai 見つからない
missing adj

mitsukeru 見つける *find v*

mizu 水 *water n* p42

kono mizu wa nome masu ka.
この水は飲めますか? *Is the
water potable?*

koko ni suidōsui wa arimasu
ka. ここに水道水はありますか?
Is there running water?
p71

mizuqi 水着 *swimsuit n*

mochi kaeri yō no menyū 持
帰り用のメニュー *takeout
menu n*

modoru 戻る *return, to return
(to a place) v*

mōfu 毛布 *blanket n* p43

moguru もぐる *dive v*

sukyūba daibu スキューバダイ
ブ *scuba dive* p151

moku yō bi 木曜日 *Thursday
n* p15

mondai 問題 *problem n*

mosuku モスク *mosque n*

motsu 持つ *have v*

motte imasu. 喘息を持っていま
す。 *I have asthma.* p167

motto sukunia もっと少ない
less adj

mottomo chiisai, mottomo
sukunai 最も小さい、最も少な
い *least adj*

murasaki no 紫の *purple adj*

mushi yoke 虫除け *insect repellent n* p163

mushi 虫 *bug n*

mushiba 虫歯 *cavity (tooth
cavity) n*

mushiba ga aru yō nandesu. 虫
歯があるようなんです。 *I think
I have a cavity.*

mushinron sha 無神論者 *atheist
n* p113

mushiro むしろ *rather adv*

musuko 息子 / musuko san 息子
さん *son n* p103

musume 娘/ojōsan お嬢さん
daughter n p103

muttsu no 六つの *six adj* p11

muzukashii 難しい *hard adj
(difficult)* / katai 堅い *(firm)*
p45

myūjishan ミュージシャン *musi-
cian n* p109

N

nagai 長い *long adj* p12

nagaku 長く *long adv*

dore kurai nagaku. どれくらい長く? *For how long?*

nagame 眺め *view n*

bīchi no nagame ビーチの眺め *beach view*

shigai no nagame 市街の眺め *city view*

nagareru, nagasu 流れる、流す *flush, to flush v*

kono toire wa nagare masen. このトイレは流れません。*This toilet won't flush.*

naibu 内部 / naka 中 *inside* p74

naito kurabu ナイトクラブ *nightclub n*

nakusu 失くす *lose, to lose v*

watashi wa pasupōto o nakushi mashita. 私はパスポートを失くしました。*I lost my passport.*

watashi wa saifu o nakushi mashita. 私は財布を失くしました。*I lost my wallet.*

watashi wa mayotte shimai mashita. 私は迷ってしまいました。*I'm lost.*

namae 名前 *name n* p101

watashi wa ___ to mōshimasu. 私は___と申します。*My name is ___.* p1

anata no namae wa nan desu ka. あなたの名前は何ですか? *What's your name?* p101

nan demo 何でも *anything n*

nan no 何の / 何 nani *what adv* p2

donna shurui no ___. どんな種類の___? *What sort of ___?*

___ wa nan ji. ___は何時? *What time is ___?* p14

nana ban me no 七番目の *seventh adj*

nana jū no 七十の *seventy adj* p7

nanatsu no 七つの *seven adj* p11

nani ka 何か / nani 何 *something n* p75, 124

nanika 何か /nanimo 何も / *any adj*

nanimo nai 何もない / sukoshi mo nai 少しもない、全くない mattaku nai *none n* p13

nanpa sen 難破船 *shipwreck n*

naosu 直す *correct v*

napukin ナプキン *napkin n*

nashi de 〜なしで 〜 *without prep*

natsu 夏 *summer n* p17

nebiki 値引き *discount n*

watashi wa nebiki no taishō ni narimasuka. 私は値引きの対象になりますか? *Do I qualify for a discount?*

neko ねこ *cat n*

nesshin na 熱心な *enthusiastic adj* p106

nettowāku ネットワーク *network n*

nezumi ねずみ *mouse n*

ni gatsu 二月 *February n* p17

ni kakoku go o hanasu 二ヶ国語を話す *bilingual adj*

niban me no 二番目の *second adj*

sekyuritī chekku pointo セキュリティチェックポイント *security checkpoint*

sekyuritī gādo セキュリティガード / keibi in 警備員 *security guard* p33

nichi yō bi 日曜日 *Sunday n* p15

nihon no, nihon jin no 日本の、日本人の *Japanese adj* p107

nijū no 二十の *twenty adj* p7

nikaragua no, nikaragua jin no ニカラグアの、ニカラグア人の *Nicaraguan adj* p107

nikibi にきび *acne n* p163

niku 肉 *meat n* p78, 90

nimotsu 荷物 / ryokō kaban 旅行カバン *luggage n* p34, 52

ryokō kaban no funshitsu wa doko ni hōkoku shimasu ka. 旅行カバンの紛失はどこに報告しますか? *Where do I report lost luggage?*

funshitsu shita ryokō kaban o uketoru basho wa doko desu ka. 紛失した旅行カバンを受け取る場所はどこですか? *Where is the lost luggage claim?*

nin niku にんにく *garlic n* p97

ninki ga aru 人気がある *popular adj* p155

ninshin shita 妊娠した *pregnant adj*

nioi o kagu 匂いをかぐ *smell, to smell v*

no hō o konomu の方を好む *prefer, to prefer v*

no mukō gawa の向こう側 *across prep* p6

kono michi no mukō gawa この道の向こう側 *across the street* p6

no yō ni mieru のように見える *look, to look (to appear) v*

kore wa dō mie masu ka. これはどう見えますか? *How does this look?*

noboru 登る *climb, to climb v*

yama ni noboru 山に登る *to climb a mountain*

kaidan o noboru 階段を昇る *to climb stairs*

nomi komu 飲み込む *swallow, to swallow v*

nomi mono 飲み物 *drink n* p75, 76, 157

nomi mono o kudasai. 飲み物をください。 *I'd like a drink.*

nomu 飲む *drink, to drink v*

nori sokonau 乗りそこなう *miss, to miss (a flight) v* p39

notte iku 乗っていく *ride, to ride v*

nozomu 望む *like, desire v (to please)*

ga suki desu. ＿＿が好きです。 *I would like ＿＿.*

nuno 布 *fabric n*

nuru 塗る *paint, to paint v*

nusumareta 盗まれた *stolen adj* p44

nusumu 盗む *steal, to steal v*

nuu 縫う / saihō o suru 裁縫をす
る、to sew v p116

nyūjirando no, nyūjirando jin no
ニュージーランドの、ニュージー
ランド人の New Zealander
adj

nyūjirando ニュージーランド
New Zealand n

nyūjōryō 入場料 admission fee
n p131

nyūkō suru 入港する board v

o

oba おば / obasan おばさん
aunt n p102

ōbāhīto suru オーバーヒートする
overheat, to overheat v

kuruma ga ōbāhīto shimashita.
車がオーバーヒートしました。
The car overheated.

ocha お茶 / cha 茶 tea n p88

ochido 落ち度 fault n p52

watashi ni ochido ga arimasu.
私に落ち度があります。I'm at
fault. p52

sore wa kare ni ochido ga
arimasu. それは彼に落ち度が
あります。It was his fault.

ochiru 落ちる fall v

odoru 踊る /dansu o suru ダンス
をする dance v p116, 159

ofuro ni hairu お風呂に入る
bathe, to bathe oneself v

ofuro お風呂 bath n

ōgoe de yobu 大声で呼ぶ
shout v

oi おい / oigo san 甥御さん
nephew n p102

oji おじ / ojisan おじさん uncle
n p102

okane お金 money n

okawari お替わり refill (of beverage) n

ōkii 大きい big adj p13

ōkii 大きい large adj p137

okkē オッケー okay adv

okotta 怒った angry adj

oku 置く place, to place v

oku 置く put, to put v

okure 遅れ delay n

dono kurai okurere imasu ka.
どのくらい遅れていますか?
How long is the delay?
p36, 39

okuri mono 贈り物 gift n

okuru 送る send, to send v
p125, 127

okyaku お客 guest n

omocha おもちゃ toy n

omocha ya おもちゃ屋 toy
store n

kodomo no omocha wa ari-
masu ka. 子供のおもちゃはあ
りますか? Do you have any
toys for the children?

omoi 重い weigh v

watashi wa taijū ga _____
arimasu. 私は体重が_____あり
ます。I weigh _____.

kore wa _____ no omosa ga
arimasu. これは_____の重さ
があります。It weighs _____.
See p7 for numbers.

omosa 重さ weights n

omutsu おむつ *diaper n*

omutsu wa doko de kaerare masu ka. おむつはどこで替えられますか? *Where can I change a diaper?*

ongaku 音楽 *music n* p114

nama ensō 生演奏 *live music*

onna no ko 女の子 *girl n*

onsei no 音声の *audio adj* p132

opera オペラ *opera n* p114

operētā オペレーター *operator (phone) n*

ōpun kā オープンカー *convertible n*

orenji iro no オレンジ色の *orange (color) adj*

orenji jūsu オレンジ ジュース *orange juice n* p42

orību オリーブ *olive n*

oshaburi おしゃぶり *pacifier n*

osoi 遅い *late adj* p14

dōka okure naide kudasai. どうか遅れないでください。 *Please don't be late.*

osoi 遅い *slow adj*

osou 襲う *mug, to mug (someone) v*

osowareta 襲われた *mugged adj*

osu 押す *push, to push v* p36

ōsutoraria no, ōsutoraria jin no オーストラリアの、オーストラリア人の *Australian adj*

ōsutoraria オーストラリア *Australia n*

oto ga urusai 音がうるさい *noisy adj*

otoko no ko 男の子 *boy n*

otoko 男 *man n*

otsuri おつり *change (money) n*

otsuri o kudasai. おつりをください。 *I'd like change, please.*

kono otsuri wa tadashiku arimasen. このおつりは正しくありません。 *This isn't the correct change.*

otto 夫 / shujin 主人 / go shujin ご主人 *husband n* p101

oushi 雄牛 *bull n*

oya 親 *parent n*

oyogu 泳ぐ *swim, to swim v* p143

koko dewa oyoge masu ka. ここでは泳げますか? *Can one swim here?*

P

painto パイント *pint n* p12

pan パン *bread n* p78, 90

panama no, panama jin no パナマの、パナマ人の *Panamanian adj*

paraguai no, paraguai jin no パラグアイの、パラグアイ人の *Paraguayan adj*

parēdo パレード *parade n*

pasu suru パスする *hold, to hold (gambling) v* p161

pasu suru パスする *pass, to pass v*

pasu shimasu. パスします。 *I'll pass.* p160

pasupōto パスポート *passport n*

watashi wa pasupōto o nakushi mashita. 私はパスポートを失くしました。 *I've lost my passport.*

pātī パーティー *party n*

seitō 政党 *political party*

pātonā パートナー *partner n*

perū no, perū jin no ペルーの、ペルー人の *Peruvian adj*

piano ピアノ *piano n* p115

pīnattsu ピーナッツ *peanut n*

pinku no ピンクの *pink adj*

pittari au ぴったり合う *fit (clothes) v* p136

pittari atte iru yō ni miemasu ka. ぴったり合っているように見えますか? *Does this look like it fits?*

piza ピザ *pizza n* p72

pondo ポンド *pound n*

ponpu ポンプ *pump n*

poppu myūjikku ポップ ミュージック *pop music n*

posuto kādo ポストカード *postcard n*

pōtā ポーター *porter n* p33

pōto wain ポートワイン *port (beverage) n*

puerutoriko no, puerutoriko jin no プエルトリコの、プエルトリコ人の *Puerto Rican adj*

purasuchikku プラスチック *plastic n* p45

purei suru プレイする *play, to play (a game) v*

purei プレイ *play n*

purofesshonaru na プロフェッショナルな *professional adj*

puroguramu プログラム *program n*

puroguramu o itadake masu ka. プログラムをいただけますか? *May I have a program?*

purotesutanto プロテスタント *Protestant n*

pūru プール *pool n* p60

R

rabendā iro no ラベンダー色の *lavender adj*

rajio ラジオ *radio n*

eisei rajio 衛星ラジオ *satellite radio* p46

ramu shu ラム酒 *rum n* p80

ranpu ランプ *light n (lamp)* p50

rappu toppu ラップトップ *laptop n* p140

raunji ラウンジ *lounge n*

rea no レアの *rare (meat) adj* p76

regē レゲー *reggae adj* p114, 155

reibō 冷房 p128 /eakon エアコン p46, 62, 68 *air conditioning n*

reibō o sagete/agete itadake masen ka. 冷房を下げて/上げていただけませんか? *Would you lower / raise the air conditioning?*

rekishi teki na 歴史的な *historical adj*

rekishi 歴史 *history n*

remonēdo レモネード *lemonade n*

ren ai shōsetsu 恋愛小説 *romance (novel)* n

rentogen レントゲン *x-ray machine* n

reshīto レシート *receipt* n p119, 120

ressha 列車 / densha 電車 *train* n p53, 54

tokkyū ressha 特急列車 *express train*

futsū ressha 普通列車 *local train*

kono densha wa _____ e iki-masu ka. この電車は_____へ行きますか? *Does the train go to ___?*

densha no jikokuhyō o itadake masu ka. 電車の時刻表をいただけますか? *May I have a train schedule?*

eki wa doko ni arimasuka. 駅はどこにありますか? *Where is the train station?*

ressun レッスン *lesson* n p154

resutoran レストラン *restaurant* n p34

yoi resutoran wa doko ni arimasu ka. よいレストランはどこにありますか? *Where can I find a good restaurant?*

rihatsu ten 理髪店 *barber* n

rikai suru 理解する *understand, to understand* v

wakari masen. わかりません。 *I don't understand.* p2, 100

wakari masu ka. わかりますか? *Do you understand?*

rikon shita 離婚した *divorced* adj

rimujin リムジン *limo* n p53

rippa na 立派な *great* adj

rittoru リットル *liter* n p12

riyōken 利用券 *voucher* n p40

roiyaru furasshu ロイヤル フラッシュ *royal flush* n

rōka 廊下 *hallway* n

rokkā ロッカー *locker* n p143

hokan rokkā 保管ロッカー *storage locker*

rokkā rūmu ロッカールーム *locker room* p144

rokku kuraimingu ロッククライミング *rock climbing* n

rokku ロック *rocks (ice)* n p79

rokku de onegai shimasu. ロックでお願いします。 *I'd like it on the rocks.*

rokkun rōru ロックンロール *rock and roll* n

roku gatsu 六月 *June* n p17

rokujū no 六十の *sixty* adj p7

romanchikku na ロマンチックな *romantic* adj

rōpu ロープ *rope* n p147

ryō 量 *amount* n

ryōgae 両替 *currency exchange* n p34, 119

koko kara ichiban chikai ryōgae jo wa doko ni arimasu ka. ここから一番近い両替所はどこにありますか? *Where is the nearest currency exchange?*

ryōkin puran 料金プラン *rate plan (cell phone)* n

ryōkin 料金 *fare* n

ryōkin 料金 *fee* n

ryōkin 料金 *rate (for car rental, hotel)* n p47, 64

> ichi nichi atari no ryōkin wa ikura desu ka. 一日当たりの料金はいくらですか? *What's the rate per day?*
> isshūkan atari no ryōkin wa ikura desu ka. 一週間当たりの料金はいくらですか? *What's the rate per week?*

ryokō kaban 旅行カバン *(luggage)* p49, toranku トランク *(in car) trunk* n

ryokō suru 旅行する *travel, to travel* v p38, 40

ryokō 旅行 *trip* n p98

ryōri suru 料理する *cook, to cook* v

> ryōri suru koto ga dekiru heya o onegai shimasu. 料理することができる部屋をお願いします。 *I'd like a room where I can cook.*

ryōri 料理 *dish* n p77

S

sābisu ryō サービス料 *service charge* n p64, 119

sābisu サービス *service* n

> kaisō 回送 *out of service*

sāfin suru サーフィンする *surf* v p152

sāfu bōdo サーフボード *surfboard* n

sagasu 探す *look for, to look for (to search)* v

pōtā o sagashite imasu. ポーターを探しています。 *I'm looking for a porter.*

sai aku 最悪 *worst*

saibā kafe サイバー カフェ *cybercafé* n

> saibā kafe wa doko ni arimasu ka. サイバー カフェはどこにありますか? *Where can I find a cybercafé?*

saiban sho 裁判所 *court (legal)* n p52,168

saifu 財布 *purse* n

saifu 財布 *wallet* n p42

> watashi wa saifu o nakushimashita. 私は財布を失くしました。 *I lost my wallet.*
> dareka ni saifu o nusumare mashita. 誰かに財布を盗まれました。 *Someone stole my wallet.* p42

saigo ni 最後に *last* adv

saikō no 最高の *best*

saisho no 最初の *first* adj

saishō 最小 *least* n

saizu サイズ *size (clothing, shoes)* n p134

sake 酒 *liquor* n p40

saki e 先へ / mae e 前へ *forward* adj p5

sakka 作家 *writer* n p109

samui 寒い *cold* adj p166

> samui desu. 寒いです。 *I'm cold.*
> soto wa samui desu. 外は寒いです。 *It's cold out.*

san bai no 3 倍の *triple* adj

san banme no 3番目の *third adj*

san gatsu 三月 *March (month)* n p17

san rūfu サンルーフ *sunroof* n p17

san 三 *three* p6

sango shō さんご礁 *reef* n p151

sangurasu サングラス *sunglasses* n

sanjū no 三十の *thirty adj* p7

sanka suru 参加する/shusseki suru 出席する *attend* v p104

sanso tanku 酸素タンク *oxygen tank* n

sarada サラダ *salad* n

sarubadoru no, sarubadoru jin no サルバドルの、サルバドル人 の *Salvadorian adj* p108

sashi komu 差し込む *plug, to plug* v

sasu 指す *point, to point* v p2

____ no hōkō ni sashi shimeshite itadake masen ka. ____の方向に指し示していた だけませんか? *Would you point me in the direction of____?*

sayōnara さようなら *goodbye* n p99

sedan セダン *sedan* n p46

see months of the year *month* n p17

seibetsu 性別 *sex (gender)* n

seigen sokudo 制限速度 *speed limit* n p51

seigen sokudo wa nan kiro desu ka. 制限速度は何キロですか? *What's the speed limit?* p51

seihin 製品 *product* n

seikatsu 生活 *living* n

nani o shite seikatsu shite imasu ka. 何をして生活してい ますか? *What do you do for a living?*

seiketsu na 清潔な *clean adj*

seikyū suru 請求する *bill* v p123

seikyū suru 請求する *charge, to charge (money)* v p123

seikyū 請求 *claim* n

baishō o seikyū shimasu. 賠償 を請求します。 *I'd like to file a claim.*

seki o suru 咳をする *cough* v p162

seki 咳 *cough* n p162

sekken 石鹸 *soap* n

sekyuritī gādo セキュリティ ガー ド / keibi in 警備員 *security guard* p33

semai 狭い *narrow adj* p13

sen 千 *thousand* p7

senaka o sasuru 背中をさする *back rub* n

senaka 背中 *back* n

senaka ga itami masu. 背中が痛 みます。 *My back hurts.*

senchi mētoru センチメートル *centimeter* n

senkyo 選挙 *election* n p112

senmen dai 洗面台 *sink* n

senmen yōhin 洗面用品 *toiletries* n p90

senpūki 扇風機 *fan* n

sensō 戦争 *war* n p112

sentaku / randori 洗濯 *laundry* n p67

serufu sābisu no セルフサービス
の self-serve adj

sētā セーター sweater n p41,
135

setsudan sareta 切断された
disconnected adj

opēreta san, denwa ga kirete
shimai mashita. オペレータさ
ん、電話が切れてしまいました。
Operator, I was discon-
nected.

setsumei suru 説明する explain
v

sewa o suru 世話をする mother,
to mother v

shakō dansu 社交ダンス ball-
room dancing n p129

sharin tsuki 車輪付き wheeled
(luggage) adj

shatoru basu シャトル バス
shuttle bus n

shatsu シャツ shirt n

shawā o abiru シャワーを浴びる
shower, to shower v

shawā シャワー shower n p62

sore niwa shawā ga tsuite
imasu ka? それにはシャワー
が付いていますか? Does it
have a shower?

shi gatsu 四月 April n p17

shi 市 / machi 街 city n p62

shiai 試合 match (sport) n

shiawase na 幸せな / ureshii 嬉し
い happy adj p106

shichaku shitsu 試着室 fitting
room n

shichaku suru 試着する try, to
try on (clothing) v

shichi gatsu 七月 July n p17

shichimenchō 七面鳥 turkey n

shīfūdo シーフード / gyokai rui 魚
介類 seafood n p91, p78

shiharau 支払う pay, to pay v

shihei 紙幣 bill (currency) n
p118

shikaku shōgai no 視覚障害の
visually-impaired adj

shikke no aru 湿気のある humid
adj p111

shima no 縞の striped adj

shimai 姉妹 / go shimai ご姉妹
sister n p102

shimatta しまった!/zan nen 残念!
Damn! expletive

shinbun uriba 新聞売り場 news-
stand n p139

shinbun 新聞 newspaper n

shindai 寝台 berth n

shindai 寝台 sleeping berth n

shinkoku suru 申告する declare
v p40

shinkoku suru mono wa
arimasen. 申告するものはあり
ません。 I have nothing to
declare.

shinpai na 心配な / shinpai
shiteiru 心配している anx-
ious adj p106

shinseki 親戚 relative (family) n

shinsen na 新鮮な fresh adj p77,
90, 91

shinzō hossa 心臓発作 **heart attack** n p164

shinzō 心臓 **heart** n p164

shio no nagare 潮の流れ **current (water)** n

shio 塩 **salt** n p97

> sore wa gen en desu ka. それは減塩ですか? *Is that low-salt?*

shiraberu 調べる **check, to check** v

shiraberu 調べる **search, to search** v

shiroi 白い **white** adj

shiruku シルク **silk** n p135

shiryoku 視力 **vision** n

shishoku suru 試食する **try, to try (food)** v

shita ni 下に **down** adj

shita no 下の **below** adv p70

shitagi 下着 **underwear** n

shitataru 滴る **drip** v

shitate ya 仕立て屋 **tailor** n p67

> yoi shitate ya o susumete itadake masen ka. よい仕立て屋を勧めていただけませんか? *Can you recommend a good tailor?*

shite yoi してよい **may** v aux

> _____ shitemo yoi desu ka. _____してもよいですか? *May I _____?*

shītsu シーツ **sheet (bed linen)** n

shitsumon suru 質問する **ask a question** v

shitsunai gaku 室内楽 **chamber music** n

shitte iru 知っている **know, to know (someone)** v

shitte iru 知っている **know, to know (something)** v

shiyō kanō na 使用可能な **available** adj

shiyōryō 使用料 **toll** n

shizuka na 静かな **quiet** adj p74

shō ショー **show (performance)** n

> sho wa nanji desuka? ショーは何時ですか? *What time is the show?*

shōgai sha ni taiō shita 障害者に対応した **handicapped-accessible** adj

shōgai 障害 **disability** n

shōgo 正午 **noon** n p14

shohōsen 処方箋 / shohōyaku 処方薬 **prescription** n p40

shōka furyō 消化不良 **indigestion** n

shōkai suru 紹介する **introduce, to introduce** v p101

> anata o _____ ni shōkai shimasu. あなたを_____に紹介します。 *I'd like to introduce you to _____.*

shoku nin 職人 p109/kōgeika 工芸家 **craftsperson** n

shokuji 食事 **meal** n p40, 43

shokuryō hin 食料品 **groceries** n

shomei 署名 **sign, to sign** v p120

> doko ni shomei sureba ii desu ka? どこに署名すればいいですか? *Where do I sign?*

shōnika i 小児科医 *pediatrician n*

osusume no shōnika i wa imasu ka. お勧めの小児科医はいますか? *Can you recommend a pediatrician?*

shoppingu sentā ショッピングセンター *mall n* p133

shori suru 処理する *process, to process v*

shōsetsu 小説 *novel n*

shōyō de 商用で *business adj* p103

bijinesu sentā ビジネス センター *business center* p66

shōzō ga 肖像画 *portrait n*

shū 週 *week n* p4, 15

konshū 今週 *this week*
senshū 先週 *last week*
raishū 来週 *next week*

shufu 主婦 *homemaker n*

shumi 趣味 *hobby n*

shuppansha 出版社 *publisher n*

shuppatsu suru 出発する *leave, to leave (depart) v* p35

shuppatsu 出発 *departure n*

shurui 種類 *kind (type) n*

sore wa donna shurui desu ka. それはどんな種類ですか? *What kind is it?*

sobakasu そばかす *freckle n*

sobo 祖母 / obāsan お祖母さん *grandmother n* p102

sōda sui ソーダ水 *seltzer n* p79

sōda ソーダ *soda n* p42

daietto sōda ダイエット ソーダ *diet soda*

sodatsu 育つ *grow, to grow (get larger) v*

doko de sodachi mashita ka. どこで育ちましたか? *Where did you grow up?*

soe mono 添え物 *side n*

yoko ni soete 横に添えて *on the side (e.g., salad dressing)* p77

sofu 祖父 / ojīsan お祖父さん *grandfather n* p102

sofubo 祖父母 *grandparent n*

sofuto uea ソフトウェア *software n*

sōji suru 掃除する *clean, to clean v*

kyō, heya o sōji shite kudasai. 今日、部屋を掃除してください。 *Please clean the room today.*

soko ni そこに (nearby) / asoko ni あそこに (far) *there (demonstrative) adv*

arimasu ka. ありますか? *Is / Are there?*

asoko ni あそこに *over there*

sokudo kei 速度計 *speedometer n*

sokudo o otosu 速度を落とす *slow, to slow v* p53

sokudo o otoshite kudasai! 速度を落としてください! *Slow down!* p53

sono その *that (near) adj*

sonshō shita 損傷した *damaged adj* p44

sorerano それらの *those adj*

sōsu ソース *sauce n*

soto 外 *outside* n p74

subete no すべての *all* adj p13

itsumo いつも *all of the time* ijō desu. dōmo arigatō. 以上 です。どうもありがとう。 *That's all, thank you.*

subete すべて *all* n p13

sugiru 〜過ぎる 〜 *too (excessively)* adv

sui yō bi 水曜日 *Wednesday* n p15

suiei pantsu 水泳パンツ *swim trunks* n

sūji 数字 / bangō 番号 *number* n p54, 66, 110

heya wa nan ban. 部屋は何番? *Which room number?*

anata no denwa bangō o oshiete itadake masu ka. あなたの電話番号を教えていただけますか? *May I have your phone number?*

sukejūru スケジュール *schedule* n

suki de aru 好きである *like, to like* v (*to please*)

watashi wa koko ga suki desu. 私はここが好きです。 *I like this place.*

sukoshi 少し *bit (small amount)* n

sukottorando no, sukottorando jin no スコットランドの、スコットランド人の *Scottish* adj

sukūtā スクーター *scooter* n p46

sukyan suru スキャンする *scan, to scan (document)* v p124

sukyūba daibingu o suru スキューバダイブをする *scuba dive, to scuba dive* v p151

sumi masen すみません *excuse (pardon)* v p50, 77

sumi masen すみません *Excuse me.*

sumi masen すみません *sorry* adj

sumi masen. すみません。 *I'm sorry.*

sumi 隅 *corner* n

sumi no 隅の *on the corner*

sumu 住む *live, to live* v

anata wa doko ni sunde imasu ka. あなたはどこに住んでいますか? *Where do you live?*

sunēku ai da! スネークアイだ! *Snake eyes!* n p160

sunōkeru スノーケル *snorkel* n

sūpā māketto スーパーマーケット *supermarket* n

supa スパ *spa* n p60

supaisu スパイス *spice* n

supea taiya スペア タイヤ *spare tire* n

supein no, supein jin no スペインの、スペイン人の *Spanish* adj p107

supein スペイン *Spain* n

supesharu スペシャル *special (featured meal)* n

supōtsu スポーツ *sports* n p116

sūpu スープ *soup* n

suramu gai スラム街 *slum* n

surōpu, kuruma isu スロープ、車椅子 *ramp, wheelchair* n p59

suru する *do, to do v*

susumeru 勧める *recommend, to recommend v*

sutaffu スタッフ *staff (employees) n* p70

sutajiamu スタジアム *stadium n* p145

sutēki hausu ステーキハウス *steakhouse n* p72

suteki na すてきな *nice adj*

sutoresu o kanjite iru ストレスを感じている *stressed adj*

sutorēto no ストレートの / chokumō 直毛 *straight (hair) adj* p142, p104

koko o saki massugu ここをまっすぐ *straight ahead* p5

sutorēto de ストレートで *straight (drink)* p79

massugu ikimasu. まっすぐ行きます。 *Go straight. (giving directions)* p50

sutorēto ストレート *straight (gambling) n* p161

sūtsu kēsu スーツケース *suitcase n* p44

sūtsu スーツ *suite n*

suwaru 座る *sit, to sit v*

T

tabako o suu タバコを吸う *smoke, to smoke v* p158

tabako タバコ *cigarette n*

tabako hito hako タバコ 1 箱 *a pack of cigarettes*

tabe mono 食べ物 *food n*

taberu 食べる *eat v*

gaishoku suru 外食する *to eat out*

tadashii 正しい *correct adj*

watashi wa tadashii densha ni notte imasu ka. 私は正しい電車に乗っていますか? *Am I on the correct train?*

taishi kan 大使館 *embassy n*

taiya タイヤ *tire n* p48

taiya ga panku shima shita. タイヤがパンクしました。 *I have a flat tire.*

taiyō 太陽 *sun n*

takai 高い / se ga takai 背が高い *tall adj* p105

takai 高い *expensive adj* p73, 156

takai 高い *high adj*

takaku nai 高くない *inexpensive adj* p73

takuji sho 託児所 *nursery n*

takuji sho wa arimasu ka. 託児所はありますか? *Do you have a nursery?*

takusan no 多い ōi / 沢山の *many adj* p13

takushī タクシー *taxi n* p36, 52

takushī. タクシー! *Taxi!*

takushī o yonde itadake masen ka. タクシーを呼んでいただけませんか? *Would you call me a taxi?*

tamari ba 溜まり場 *hangout (hot spot) n*

tamesu 試す *try, to try (attempt) v*

tāminaru ターミナル *terminal (airport) n* p36

tamotsu 保つ *keep, to keep* v

tanomu 頼む *ask for (request)* v

tanomu 頼む *order, to order (request)* v

tanoshimu 楽しむ *enjoy, to enjoy* v

taoru タオル *towel* n

> motto taoru o itadake masu ka. もっとタオルをいただけますか? *May we have more towels?*

taryō 多量 / takusan no 沢山の *much* n p131

tasukeru 助ける *help, to help* v

tasukete. 助けて! *Help!* n

tatsu 立つ *stand, to stand* v

tazuneru 訪ねる *visit, to visit* v

te 手 *hand* n

tebukuro 手袋 *glove* n p153

tēburu テーブル *table* n p74

> futari yō no tēburu 2人用のテーブル *table for two*

tegoro na nedan no 手頃な値段の *moderately priced* adj p60

teikyō suru 提供する *offer, to offer* v

teinei na ていねいな / shinsetsuna親切な *courteous* adj p70

tekuno テクノ *techno* n p114

tenimotsu no 手荷物の *baggage* n

> tenimotsu hikiwatashi jo 手荷物引き渡し所 *baggage claim* p44

tenimotsu 手荷物 *baggage* n p34, 44

tenisu テニス *tennis* n p61

> tenisu kōto テニス コート *tennis court* p61

tenji 展示 *exhibit* n

tenji, amerika no 点字、アメリカの *braille, American* n

tenki yohō 天気予報 *weather forecast* n

tento テント *tent* n

terebi テレビ *television* n

tetsudai 手伝い /ashisutansu アシスタンス *assistance* n p59

tetsudau 手伝う *assist* v p39

to issho ni 〜と一緒に 〜 *with* prep

tōchaku suru 到着する *arrive, to arrive* v p35, 36

tōchaku 到着 *arrival(s)* n

tōgyū shi 闘牛士 *bullfighter* n

tōgyū 闘牛 *bullfight* n

toire トイレ *bathroom (restroom)* n p33, 59

> koko kara ichiban chikai kōshū toire wa doko ni arimasu ka. ここから一番近い公衆トイレはどこにありますか? *Where is the nearest public bathroom?*

toire トイレ *restroom* n p33

> kōshū toire wa arimasu ka. 公衆トイレはありますか? *Do you have a public restroom?*

toire トイレ *toilet* n

toire no mizu ga afurete irun desu. トイレの水が溢れているんです。*The toilet is overflowing.* p69

toire ga tsumatte imasu. トイレがつまっています。*The toilet is backed up.*

toiretto pēpā トイレット ペーパー *toilet paper n*

toiretto pēpā ga naku nari mashita. トイレット ペーパーがなくなりました。*You're out of toilet paper.*

tojiru 閉じる *close, to close v*

tojita 閉じた *closed adj*

tōjō ken 搭乗券 *boarding pass n* p41

tōjō 搭乗 *board n* p39

tōjō shite 搭乗して *on board*

tōkei 闘鶏 *cockfight n*

tokkyū no 特急の *express adj*

tokubetsu yūsen chekku in 特別優先チェックイン *express check-in*

tokudai no 特大の *extra-large adj*

tōkuni 遠くに / tōi 遠い *far* p5

made wa doredake tōku hanarete imasu ka. ＿＿＿ まではどれだけ遠く離れていますか？ ＿＿＿ *How far is it to ＿＿＿?*

tokuten 得点 *score n*

tomaru 停まる *stop, to stop v*
tomatte kudasai. 停まってください。*Please stop.*

tomare 止まれ *STOP (traffic sign)*

tomare, dorobō. 止まれ、泥棒！ *Stop, thief!*

tomaru 泊る / taizai suru 滞在する *stay, to stay v* p64, 70

＿＿＿ nichi kan taizai suru yotei desu. ＿＿＿日間滞在する予定です。*We'll be staying for ＿＿＿ nights.* p64 Numbers, p7.

tōmei na 透明な *clear adj* p151

ton トン *ton n*

tōnyōbyō no 糖尿病の *diabetic adj*

toraberāzu chekku トラベラーズ チェック *travelers' check n*

toraberāzu chekku o genkin ni kōkan deki masu ka. トラベラーズチェックを現金に交換できますか？ *Do you cash travelers' checks?*

tori kesu 取り消す *cancel, to cancel v* p38

watashi no furaito wa kyanseru saremashita. 私のフライトはキャンセルされました。*My flight was canceled.*

tori 鳥 *bird n*

nante subarashii torihiki da. なんてすばらしい取引だ！ *What a great deal!*

torihiki 取引き *deal (bargain) n*

torinozoku 取り除く / nugu 脱ぐ *remove, to remove v* p41

toshi 歳 *age n*

nan sai desu ka. 何歳ですか？ *What's your age?*

totemo とても *very* p78

tozan 登山 *climbing* n p147

tozan dō 登山道 / toreiru トレイ ル *trail* n p149

tozan dō wa arimasuka. 登山 道はありますか？ *Are there trails?*

tranpetto トランペット *trumpet* n

tsuā ツアー *tour* n

gaido tsuki tsuā wa arimasu ka. ガイド付きツアーはあります か？ *Are guided tours available?*

onsei gaido tsuki tsuā wa arimasu ka. 音声ガイド付きツ アーはありますか？ *Are audio tours available?*

tsugi 次 *next* prep

no tsugi の次 *next to*

tsugi no eki 次の駅 *the next station*

tsukareta 疲れた / tsukarete iru 疲れている *tired* adj p106

tsukareta 疲れた *exhausted* adj

tsukau 使う *use, to use* v

tsukuru 作る *make, to make* v

tsuma 妻 / okusan 奥さん *wife* n p101

tsumatte iru つまっている *backed up (toilet)* adj

toire ga tsumatte imasu. トイレが つまっています。 *The toilet is backed up.*

tsuno 角 *horn* n

tsureteiku 連れて行く *take, to take* v

eki made tsurete itte kudasai. 駅まで連れて行ってください。 *Take me to the station.*

_____ made iku niwa ikura kakari masu ka. _____まで行く にはいくらかかりますか？ *How much to take me to _____?*

tsuri zao 釣竿 *fishing pole* n

tsūro 通路 *aisle* n

tsūyaku 通訳 *interpreter* n p168

tsūyaku ga hitsuyō desu. 通 訳が必要です。 *I need an interpreter.*

tsuzukeru 続ける *continue, to continue* v

tsuzuku 続く *last, to last* v

tsuzuru つづる *spell, to spell* v p100

tsuzuri o itte kudasai. つづりを 言ってください。 / tsuzuri o itte morae masu ka. つづりを言っ てもらえますか。 *How do you spell that?* p100

U

ubau 奪う *rob, to rob* v

gōtō ni aimashita. 強盗に遭いま した。 *I've been robbed.*

ude 腕 *arm* n p165

ue ni 上に *up* adv p5

ue no 上の *above* adj p70

ueitā ウエイター *waiter* n

ueku appu kōru ウェークアップ コ ール *wake-up call* n

uesutan no ウェスタンの *western adj*

ugoku 動く *move, to move v*

uke ireru 受け入れる *accept, to accept v*

kurejitto kādo o tsukae masu ka. クレジットカードを使えますか? *Do you accept credit cards?* p34

uketoru 受け取る *receive, to receive v*

uma 馬 *horse n*

ume awase o suru 埋め合せをする *make up, to make up (apologize) v*

unten shu 運転手 *driver n* p52

unten suru 運転する *drive v*

uokka ウオッカ *vodka n* p80

ureshii 嬉しい *delighted adj*

urikire 売り切れ *sold out adj*

uru 売る *sell, to sell v*

uruguai no, uruguai jin no ウルグアイの、ウルグアイ人の *Uruguayan adj* p108

urusai うるさい *loud adj* p70

urusaku うるさく *loudly adv*

usagi うさぎ *rabbit n*

USB pōto USB ポート *USB port n*

ushi 牛 *cow n*

ushiro no 後ろの *behind adv* p5

usu chairo no 薄茶色の *hazel adj* p106

usui 薄い *thin adj*

uta 歌 *song n* p159

utau 歌う *sing, to sing v*

utsusu 移す *transfer, to transfer v*

okane o idō shitai no desuga. お金を移動したいのですが。 *I need to transfer funds.*

uwagi 上着 *jacket n* p41, 75

V

vendaje m, bando eido バンドエイド *band-aid n*

W

wai fai ワイファイ *wi-fi n*

wain ワイン *wine n* p42

waipā ワイパー *windshield wiper n*

waipā ワイパー *wiper n*

wakai 若い *young adj* p103

wakareta 別れた / bekkyo shite iru 別居している *separated (marital status) adj* p103

wakeru 分ける *split (gambling) n*

wakkusu ワックス *waxing n*

wāku auto ワークアウト *workout n*

ware yasui 割れやすい / waremono chūi 「割れ物注意」 *fragile adj* p126

watashi tachi (ni, o) 私達(に、を) *us pron* p3

watashi wa 私は *I pron*

Y

yaki (ni) sugita 焼き(煮)すぎた *overcooked adj*

yaku 焼く / yaki tsukeru 焼きつける *burn v*

koko de CD ni yakitsuke (kakikomi) deki masu ka. ここで CD に焼きつけ（書込み）できますか？ *Can I burn a CD here?* p124

yakubutsu chiryō 薬物治療 *medication n*

yama 山 *mountain n*

   tozan 登山 *mountain climbing* p147

yasai 野菜 *vegetable n*

yasui 安い *cheap adj* p47, 146

yatoi nushi 雇い主 *employer n*

yawarakai 柔らかい *soft adj*

yoake 夜明け *dawn n* p14

   yoake ni 夜明けに *at dawn*

yobidasu 呼び出す *page, to page (someone) v* p34

yobu 呼ぶ *(shout)* denwa o kakeru 電話をかける *(phone) call, to call v* p66

yobun no 余分の *extra (additional) adj*

yoi よい *good adj* p60, 72

yōkoso ようこそ *welcome adv* dō itashi mashite. どういたしまして。 *You're welcome.*

yoku deiri suru よく出入りする *hang out (to relax) v*

yoku よく *well adv*

   weru dan ウェルダン *well done (meat)*

   yoku yatta よくやった *well done (task)*

   kibun ga yoku arimasen. 気分がよくありません。 *I don't feel well.*

yokusō 浴槽 *bathtub n* p62

yomu 読む *read, to read v*

yon banme no 四番目の *fourth adj*

   yon bun no ichi 四分の一 *one-fourth*

   yonbun no ichi 四分の一 *quarter adj*

   yon bun no ichi 四分の一 *one-quarter*

yonjū no 四十の *forty adj* p7

yori mo warui ～よりも悪い *～worse*

yori yoi より良い *better*

yorokobaseru 喜ばせる *please, to be pleasing to v*

yorokobi 喜び *pleasure n* ureshii desu. 嬉しいです。 *It's a pleasure.*

yoru 夜 *night n* p14

   yoru ni 夜に *at night* ippaku atari 一泊当たり *per night* p64

yosan 予算 *budget n*

yottsu no 四つの *four adj* p11

yoyaku 予約 *appointment n* p141,164

   yoyaku ga hitsuyō desu ka. 予約が必要ですか？ *Do I need an appointment?* p164

yoyaku 予約 *reservation n* ____ no yoyaku o shitai no desuga. ____の予約をしたいのですが。 *I'd like to make a reservation for ____.* p64 See p7 for numbers.

yūbin de dasu 郵便で出す *mail v*

yūbin kyoku 郵便局 *post office n*

　yūbin kyoku wa doko ni arimasu ka. 郵便局はどこにありますか? *Where is the post office?*

yūbin 郵便 / tegami 手紙 *mail n* p67

　kōkūbin 航空便 *air mail* kakitome 書留 *registered mail*

yudaya kyō no, yudaya jin no ユダヤ教の、ユダヤ人の *Jewish adj* p113

yūjin 友人 / tomodachi 友達 *friend n* p101

yūki no 有機の *organic adj*

yuki saki 行き先 *destination n*

yukkuri ゆっくり *slow(ly) adv*

　motto yukkuri hanashite kudasai. もっとゆっくり話してください。 *Speak more slowly.* p100

yurui ゆるい *loose adj* p136

yūsen hyōshiki 優先標識 *yield sign n*

yūshoku 夕食 *dinner n* p117

Z

zandaka 残高 *balance (on bank account) n* p120

zaseki 座席 p37, 38/ seki 席 *seat n* p42, 43, 54

　chairudo shiito チャイルドシート *child seat* p46

zasshi 雑誌 *magazine n*

zeikan 税関 p36/kanzei関税 p125 *customs n*

zeikin 税金 *tax n* p64, 138

　fuka kachi zei 付加価値税 *value-added tax (VAT)* p138

zenpō no 前方の *front adj* p38

　furonto desuku フロント デスク *front desk* p66

　furonto doa フロント ドア *front door*

zensoku 喘息 *asthma n* p167

　zensoku ga arimasu. 喘息があります。 / zensoku o

zutsu 頭痛 *headache n* p165

急ぐ *hurry v* p52, 53

　watashi wa isoide imasu.. 私は急いでいます。 *I'm in a hurry* isoide kudasai. 急いでください! *Hurry, please!*

NOTES

NOTES

NOTES

NOTES

NOTES

NOTES

This book belongs to:

_____

_____

Holly and Hope Prayer Book

© 2014 Christian Art Gifts, RSA
Christian Art Gifts Inc., IL, USA

Written by Carolyn Larsen

Designed by Christian Art Gifts

Images used under license from Shutterstock.com

Printed in China

ISBN 978-1-4321-1291-2

16 17 18 19 20 21 22 23 24 25 – 12 11 10 9 8 7 6 5 4 3

Prayer Book

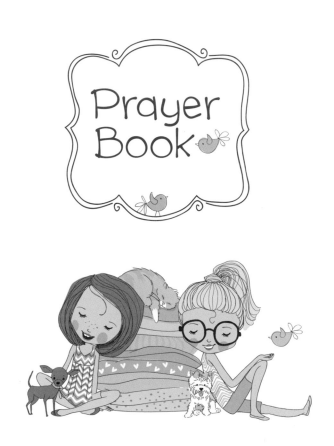

christian
art gifts®

Contents

Prayers for the Future

Prayers for When I'm Scared

Prayers to Help Me Obey

Prayers for How Awesome God Is

Contents

Prayers to Help Me Be Strong 105

Prayers to Know God Better 113

Prayers When I Don't Understand 121

Prayers
for My
Family

Maybe
I Should Be Nicer

Dear God,

Sometimes my family makes me so mad. Then I say not very nice things. You know what though, even when I'm fighting with them, I still love them. Maybe I should try to be nicer. Please help me to be nicer so that we don't fight so much.

Amen.

"Do to others whatever you would like them to do to you."

Matthew 7:12

Bless
Mom and Dad

Dear God,

Mom and Dad work hard to take care of our family. I'm really thankful for all that they do. Will You take care of them? Please help them find time to just have fun. Please keep them healthy and bless them, Lord.

Amen.

The person who trusts in the Lord will be blessed. The Lord will show him that He can be trusted.

Jeremiah 17:7

Giggles and Belly Laughs!

Dear God,

I love my family.
I love it when we act silly and
make each other laugh.
We make the best memories by having
so much fun together. Thank You for
my family. You knew which family would
be exactly the right one for me!

Amen.

*If you are cheerful,
you feel good; if you are sad,
you hurt all over.*

Proverbs 17:22

The Best Grandparents

Dear God,

My grandma and grandpa are the best. I really love them. It's so cool to listen to their stories about when Mom and Dad were kids. I love when Grandpa takes me fishing and Grandma makes yummy cookies. God, please be sure they know how much I love them.

Amen.

Grandparents are proud of their grandchildren, and children should be proud of their parents.

Proverbs 17:6

13

Obeying
Is the Hardest

Dear God,

AAHHH!!!
Why is obeying so hard?
I don't mean to disobey, but I keep
doing it. I need Your help with obeying
because I want to do better. Please help
me to stop and think before I do stuff
that is going to get me into trouble.

Amen.

*Jesus says, "If you love Me,
obey My commandments."*

John 14:15

Not Enough Time

Dear God,

I love Mom and Dad. They work hard and always seem so busy. I wish I could spend more time with them. Please help them with their work so that they have more time to relax and spend with me.

Amen.

Those who look to the Lord for help will be radiant with joy.

Psalm 34:5

15

Prayers
for My

Friends

17

My Friends Are Awesome!

Dear God,

Thank You for my friends. Everything I do is more fun when I share it with them. My friends laugh with me. They cry with me. They forgive me when I mess up. I know my friends really care about me and I care about them, too!

Amen.

A friend loves at all times.

Proverbs 17:17

I Miss My Friend

Dear God,

I had a fight with my best friend.
I said some really mean things to her.
I didn't mean any of it. I'm going to tell her
I'm sorry and ask her to forgive me.
Lord, I just pray that she will forgive me.
I miss her.

Amen.

*Confess your sins to each other
and pray for each other so God can
heal you. When a believing person
prays, great things happen.*

James 5:16

New Friends for My Friend

Father,

My friend is moving away. We've been friends forever and I'm going to miss her. But, right now I'm going to ask You to help her. She's scared about going to a new school. Help her to make new friends quickly and to be happy in her new home.

Amen.

Let us continue to love one another, for love comes from God.

1 John 4:7

Courage = New Friend

Dear God,

There's a new girl in my class.
It must be hard to not know anyone.
She's probably lonely.
It's scary to talk to someone I don't know,
but I know You'll help me.
Please give me the courage to say hello
and maybe I'll make a new friend!

Amen.

*"Don't ever be afraid or discouraged!
I am the Lord your God,
and I will be there to help
you wherever you go."*
Joshua 1:9

I Am Sad about My Friend

Dear God,

My feelings are hurt. All of a sudden my friend is ignoring me. I don't know what happened, but I miss her. Will You help me find out what happened and help me to make it better?

Amen.

Friends come and friends go,
but a true friend sticks by you like family.

Proverbs 18:24

My Friend
Knows You!

Dear God,

My friend and I had so much fun today. We spent all day talking about You! We talked about all the wonderful things You made for us to enjoy. Thank You that my friend knows You, too. It's awesome that we both believe in You.

Amen.

God-friendship is for God-worshipers; they are the ones He confides in.

Psalm 25:14

Lost Stuff

Dear God,

I saw on TV that people lost their homes in a flood. I feel so bad for them. I pray for the children who lost their stuff. Be really close to all of them, God. Please help them find a place to stay. Please help them to not be too sad.

Amen.

The Lord is good, a strong refuge when trouble comes. He is close to those who trust in Him.

Nahum 1:7

Saying Goodbye

Dear God,

I didn't know my heart could
hurt so much. Someone I love died.
I'm sad because I'll miss them a lot.
I know that, because of You, I will see
them again someday in heaven.
But, for right now — I'm sad.

Amen.

God blesses those people who grieve.
They will find comfort!

Matthew 5:4

Sin Makes
Me Sad

Dear God,

Can I tell You what makes
me sad? It's when I do things
that make You sad. Like when I say
mean things or I fight with my friends.
The Bible tells me not to do those things,
so please forgive me. Please help me
to stop doing those things.

Amen.

*Sin will not be your master, because you
are not under law but under God's grace.*

Romans 6:14

I Don't Know What to Do

Dear God,

I lost my school book today. I have no idea where I put it and I need it for school tomorrow. I looked everywhere for it but couldn't find it! I don't know what to do. Please help me find it, Lord. Thank You.

Amen.

God always helps in times of trouble.

Psalm 46:1

Aching Heart

Oh God,

It feels like I'll never stop crying. I'm just so sad. My friend is sick. I haven't seen her in a while. I feel so alone without her at school. Please help her. Please make her feel better so that she can come back to school.

Amen.

The Lord heals the brokenhearted and bandages their wounds.

Psalm 147:3

30

Bad Weather

Dear God,

It's raining outside. Dad and I were supposed to go for a walk in the park today, but Mom said the weather is too bad to go outside. Dad promised we could go tomorrow, but I'm still sad. Please let the sun shine tomorrow so that Dad and I can go for our walk together.

Amen.

The Lord watches over everyone who obeys Him, and He listens to their prayers.

1 Peter 3:12

Prayers of

"I Messed Up and I'm Sorry"

A
Grumpy Day

Dear God,

I was grumpy all day today.
I talked back to Mom. I was mean
to everyone. I love my family. I don't
know why I acted like that. I'm sorry.
I'll ask them to forgive me, but first
I wanted to ask You. Please forgive me.

Amen.

If we confess our sins to God,
He can always be trusted
to forgive us and take our sins away.

1 John 1:9

Blabbermouth

Dear Father,

I messed up.
My friend told me something
that was top secret. She didn't
want me to tell anyone. But ... I did.
She's mad and I guess I don't blame her.
I'm really sorry. I feel bad. Please
help her to forgive me.

Amen.

*You will say the wrong thing if you talk
too much — so be sensible and
watch what you say.*

Proverbs 10:19

Ignoring God

Dear God,

I've been ignoring You. I don't know why but all of a sudden I just didn't feel like reading my Bible or praying. I know it's important and I feel better when I do those things. I'm sorry. Help me to do better, please.

Amen.

There's nothing like the written Word of God for showing you the way. Every part of Scripture is God-breathed and useful one way or another — showing us truth, correcting our mistakes, training us to live God's way.

2 Timothy 3:15-17

Telling
the Truth

Dear God,

I was doing stuff Mom told me
not to do and I broke something.
Even worse, I lied about how
it got broken. I'm going to be in
so much trouble. I know I need
to tell Mom the truth.
Help me, please.

Amen.

Tell each other the truth.

Zechariah 8:16

37

Using Time Better

Dear God,

I have work for school but it's not finished.
Instead of working on it this weekend
I played with friends. I'm going to get
a bad grade. I know it's my own fault.
Please help me to learn from this
and to use my time better
from now on.

Amen.

Teach us to use wisely
all the time we have.

Psalm 90:12

Blaming Others

Dear God,

I got someone into trouble. I told Mom that they did something that they didn't really do. Now they are in a bunch of trouble. I don't know why I did it, but I'm sorry. Please forgive me and please help them to forgive me, too.

Amen.

You must not tell lies about your neighbor.

Exodus 20:16

Prayers
for the

Future

41

Someday ...

Dear God,

Someday I'm going to be grown up.
I don't know what I want to do — be a
nurse or a teacher or an astronaut.
But I know I want to still be a Christian.
I want everyone to know that I love You!
That's the most important!

Amen.

*"I know what I am planning for you,"
says the Lord. "I have good plans
for you, not plans to hurt you.
I will give you hope
and a good future."*

Jeremiah 29:11

Changing Schools

Dear God,

I have to change schools next year. It's kind of scary to think about it. I'll go to a bigger school with different teachers. I'm kind of nervous about finding my way around and stuff. Will You please stop the butterflies in my tummy? Please take the nervousness away.

Amen.

Give your worries to the Lord, and He will take care of you. He will never let good people down.

Psalm 55:22

The Big Show!

Dear God,

There is a play coming up and everyone is coming to watch! What if I forget my words or get stage fright? Please hold my hand when the time comes for me to walk out onto the stage and help me to remember all of the words.

Amen.

*Christ gives me the strength
to face anything.*

Philippians 4:13

Summer Worries

Dear God,

There's a Sunday school camp coming up. I have to go, but I'm scared. I don't know anyone there. Please help me to not be scared and to make friends quickly. Let me have fun with others who believe in You, too. Thank You.

Amen.

God gives His people peace.

Psalm 29:11

Test Drama

Dear God,

I have a big test coming up and I don't know if I'm ready. I know I've been working hard, but what if the test is too difficult? What if I disappoint my mom and dad? Please help me to work hard and prepare so that I am ready when the test comes.

Amen.

In all the work you are doing, work the best you can. Work as if you were doing it for the Lord, not for people.

Colossians 3:23

Party Time!

Dear God,

My friend's birthday party is coming up, but I'm scared to go. She's invited so many people who I don't know and don't really fit in with. What if I can't find anyone to talk to or play with? What if they don't like me? Please let them accept me. I don't want to feel left out.

Amen.

"God does not see the same way people see. People look at the outside of a person, but the Lord looks at the heart."

1 Samuel 16:7

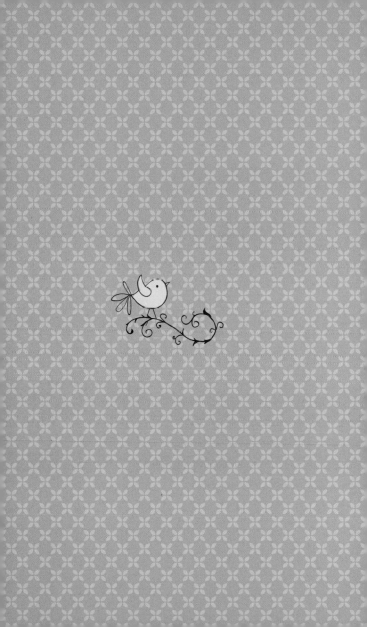

Prayers
for when I'm

Scared

I Don't Like Storms

Dear Lord,

I'm scared. The wind is blowing hard and the thunder is super loud. It hurts my ears. Lightning keeps flashing and rain is pounding against the windows. I know that You control the wind, rain and lightning, so I don't need to be afraid because You are much stronger than these.

Amen.

"Don't worry, because I am with you. Don't be afraid, because I am your God. I will make you strong and will help you; I will support you with My right hand that saves you."

Isaiah 41:10

Moving to a New City

Dear God,

Help! We are moving. What if I don't make any new friends? What if I don't get how the new school works? This is super scary. Please help me. Help me to be calm. Help me to make new friends and fit in well. Thank You.

Amen.

You, Lord, give true peace to those who depend on You, because they trust You.

Isaiah 26:3

Nightmares

Dear God,

I keep having really scary dreams. I wish they would stop. Please, help me to remember that these dreams are not real. Help me to remember that You are with me so I don't have anything to be scared of. Thank You for sticking super close to me.

Amen.

I lay down and slept, yet I woke up in safety, for the Lord was watching over me.

Psalm 3:5

Trusting
God Completely

Dear Lord,

It scares me when I hear Mom
and Dad talk about all the accidents
on the road. About people getting hurt.
Please don't let Mom or Dad get hurt.
Please keep them safe. Help me to
completely trust You with their lives.

Amen.

*Trust in the Lord
with all your heart.*

Proverbs 3:5

53

Stop Fighting

Dear God,

Mom and Dad fight a lot.
It's scary when they yell at each other.
I wish they could always be happy.
Please help them to figure out what's
wrong and to fix it. Please
make them happy again.

Amen.

*If you search for God with all your
heart and soul, you will find Him.*

Deuteronomy 4:29

Help for Others

Dear God,

Mom says there are a lot of people out there who do not have homes or food or loving families. Please help the people who are scared and all alone with no homes or food. Please take care of them and thank You for taking such good care of us.

Amen.

Our help is from the Lord, who made heaven and earth.

Psalm 124:8

Prayers
to Help Me

Obey

57

Sharing Is Hard

Dear God,

I want to obey, but some things are hard —
like sharing stuff. I'm not so good
at sharing. I like to play with my own stuff.
Mom says it is really important to learn
to share. Please help me to be
better at that. Thanks.

Amen.

*"Give, and you will receive.
Your gift will return to you in full."*

Luke 6:38

Obeying
Helps Me Learn

Dear God,

Someone is always telling me stuff to do. I can't wait to be grown up so that they can't tell me what to do anymore. I guess all the things I learn by obeying will help me learn to be a good grown up. So ... please help me to obey.

Amen.

Children, obey your parents because you belong to the Lord, for this is the right thing to do.

Ephesians 6:1

Not Obeying Is Sin

Dear God,

Sometimes I don't feel like obeying. Something inside makes me want to do exactly the opposite of what I'm supposed to do. I guess that "something" is sin. I don't like it. Please forgive me for not obeying. Help me to not sin and always obey. Thanks.

Amen.

Offer praise to God our Savior because of our Lord Jesus Christ! Only God can keep you from falling and make you pure and joyful in His glorious presence.

Jude 1:24

Controlling
My Words

Dear God,

Talking back to Mom and Dad gets me into trouble. I know I'm not supposed to — they've told me plenty of times. But sometimes things pop out of my mouth before I can stop them. Please help me to stop those words before they come out. Thank You.

Amen.

You must all be quick to listen, slow to speak, and slow to get angry.

James 1:19

The Bible
Is Important

Dear God,

Thank You for the Bible.
The Bible tells us what You want
us to do and how You want us to live.
I want to obey You, so please help me to
learn the Bible and understand it. Thanks.

Amen.

*All Scripture is inspired by God
and is useful to teach us what is true
and to make us realize what is wrong
in our lives. It corrects us when we are
wrong and teaches us to do
what is right.*

2 Timothy 3:16

Breaking the Rules

Dear God,

I know Mom told me not to run around in the kitchen, but I did. I accidently knocked over a glass and it broke. Mom was mad. I'm sorry I disobeyed. I promise to listen next time ... please help me to listen and to not break the rules.

Amen.

Children, always obey your parents, for this pleases the Lord.

Colossians 3:20

Prayers
for How

Awesome
God Is

Prayer
Is Awesome

Dear God,

It's so awesome that You care about what I care about. I can tell You anything! Thank You for hearing my prayers when I'm worried or scared. Thank You for listening when I just need to talk. I think prayer is a wonderful thing that You invented.

Amen.

I will exalt You, my God and King, and praise Your name forever and ever.

Psalm 145:18

Creation Is Awesome

Dear God,

Wow, You really had good ideas for making stuff. Thank You for the beautiful trees, the colorful flowers, the big blue ocean and all the animals! You have made everything around us so wonderful. Thank You for it all!

Amen.

In the beginning God created the heavens and the earth.

Genesis 1:1

Awesome Stuff

Dear God,

Some stuff You made is just stuff — like rocks and dirt. But some stuff that You made is full of surprises. Like how a caterpillar turns into a beautiful butterfly. That's awesome! You must have had lots of fun thinking of that. Thanks for surprises!

Amen.

Let all things praise the name of the Lord, because they were created at His command.

Psalm 148:5

The Bible Is Awesome

Dear God,

The Bible is awesome! The stories in it teach us about people who lived for You. They show us how You took care of them. That helps us know that You'll always take care of us, too. Thank You.

Amen.

Your word is a lamp to guide my feet and a light for my path.

Psalm 119:105

Forgiveness Is Awesome

Dear God,

Do You know what one of my favorite things is that You do? It's when You forgive me. I make a lot of mistakes so I think it's pretty awesome that when I ask You to, You will forgive me and even forget about my mistakes. Thanks for that!

Amen.

The Lord says, "I will treat them with kindness, even though they are wicked. I will forget their sins."

Hebrews 8:12

God's Strength Is Awesome

Dear God,

You are the strongest and most powerful ... more awesome than anything! I am thankful to know that my God can do anything and that You are the boss of everything, and even with all that power and important stuff to do, You love me!

Amen.

Lord, Your power is great, and Your glory is seen everywhere in heaven and on earth. You are King of the entire world.

1 Chronicles 29:11

Prayers of Thanks

Thankful
for My Family

Dear Father,

Thank You for my family.
I know they love me and would do
anything for me. I would do anything
for them, too. Thank You for giving me
my family. Thank You for the way
they love me and make me laugh.
They're wonderful.

Amen.

*Give thanks for everything to
God the Father in the name of our
Lord Jesus Christ.*

Ephesians 5:20

Thankful for Help

Dear God,

Thank You for places that get food and water for people around the world who really need it. It's so sad when people don't have enough food to eat or clean water to drink. Please help them and show me how I can help them, too.

Amen.

Make sure you don't take things for granted and share what you have with others. God takes particular pleasure in acts of worship that take place on the streets.

Hebrews 13:16

Thankful for Friends

Dear God,

I have the best friends in the whole world! We like to do the same kinds of things. We laugh at the same things. We talk about stuff and best of all is that we pray for each other. Thanks for my friends!

Amen.

You are better off to have a friend than to be all alone, because then you will get more enjoyment out of what you earn. If you fall, your friend can help you up.

Ecclesiastes 4:9-10

Thank You
for Rainbow Promises

Dear God,

Thank You for rainbows.
They are one of my favorite things
to look at. I know that rainbows go all
the way back to Noah and the big flood.
Thank You for promising to take care of us.
I know that means You love people a lot.

Amen.

*"I have placed My rainbow in the clouds.
It is the sign of My covenant with you
and with all the earth ... never
again will the floodwaters
destroy all life."*

Genesis 9:13, 15

Thankfulness for Music

Dear Lord,

I love to sing because it makes me happy. My favorite songs to sing are ones about You and how much You love me. The words of the song usually say things in a better way than I can. Thank You for thinking of music.

Amen.

*Sing out your thanks to the Lord:
sing praises to our God
with a harp.*

Psalm 147:7

Thankful for Laughter

Dear Lord,

Thank You for all the things that make me laugh. Thank You for Mom who tickles me till I laugh and Dad who tells me funny stories just to see me smile. Thank You for my friends who I have fun with every day.

Amen.

The Lord will once again fill your mouth with laughter and your lips with shouts of joy.

Job 8:21

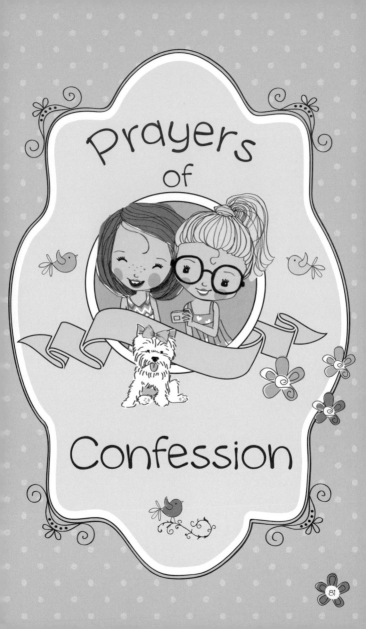

Prayers
of
Confession

Saying
Mean Things

Dear God,

I feel awful. I said some really
mean things to my friend.
She didn't deserve what I did.
I don't know why I do things like that.
Please forgive me. Please give me the
courage to apologize to her and help
her to forgive me.

Amen.

*When you talk, do not say harmful things,
but say what people need — words that
will help others become stronger.*

Ephesians 4:29

What's Most Important?

Dear Lord,

I love sport. I'm good at it, too.
But, I think it is too important to me.
I think about it all the time and being the
best is more important than serving You.
I'm sorry, please help me to get
things in the right order.

Amen.

*"Your heart will be where
your treasure is."*

Matthew 6:21

Honoring God's Name

Dear God,

I said Your name,
but not in praise.
I often hear people say Your name
almost like a swear word. I guess
I hear it so much that I did it, too.
I'm so sorry. I love You and I respect You.
Please forgive me.

Amen.

*You must not misuse the name
of the Lord your God. The Lord will not
let you go unpunished if you
misuse His name.*

Exodus 20:7

Temper Tantrums

Dear God,

I lost my temper ... again.
Sometimes I get so mad and
I can't control myself. I start throwing
things and yelling and stuff. I know
that's not a good example of
living for You. I'm sorry. Please
help me to not get so mad.

Amen.

*Don't get so angry that you sin.
Don't go to bed angry.*

Ephesians 4:26

Trust
God More

Dear God,

I don't think I trust You enough.
I worry about stuff and I'm scared
about things. These are things that
I should trust You to take care of.
Did You know that it's hard sometimes?
Please help me learn to trust You more.

Amen.

*Trust God, my friends, and always
tell Him each one of your concerns.
God is our place of safety.*

Psalm 62:8

Jealousy

Dear God,

My friend got the best gifts for
her birthday. I wish Mom and Dad
would buy those things for me.
I know that You don't like it when people
are jealous of others. Please help me
to not be so jealous, but rather to be
happy for my friend. Help me, please.

Amen.

*It's healthy to be content,
but envy can eat you up.*

Proverbs 14:30

Prayers About

God's Love

Thankful for God's Love

Dear God,

Thank You for loving me so much.
It's amazing that the God who
made everything there is ...
the God who has everyone in
the world to take care of ...
loves me! I know You do.
I love You, too.

Amen.

*Nothing in all creation will ever
be able to separate us from
the love of God.*

Romans 8:39

90

God's Amazing Forgiveness

Dear God,

I'm so thankful for Your forgiveness.
I don't do wrong things on purpose, but I'm so thankful that when I tell You I'm sorry You will forgive me and never even think of it again. That makes me love You even more.

Amen.

Our God, You are merciful and quick to forgive; You are loving, kind, and very patient.

Nehemiah 9:17

God's Word Teaches Me

Dear God,

The Bible tells me so much
about You. I read how You helped
Your people. I read about Your love.
The Bible shows how You teach us
to live for You and be kind and loving
to others. Thank You for the Bible.

Amen.

*Young people can live a clean life
by obeying Your Word.*

Psalm 119:9

Prayer Is a Privilege

Dear God,

Thank You that I can pray!
I can pray about anything and at
any time and I know that You will hear
my prayer. I know that You cannot
always give me what I ask for in prayer.
But I also know that You will give
me something much better than I
could ever dream of. Thank You!

Amen.

Never stop praying.

1 Thessalonians 5:17

Staying Close to God

Dear God,

Some days I feel sad for no reason. I know that's when Satan will try to wiggle into my heart and tell me that no one cares how I feel. I'm thankful that I can ask You to push him out of the way — and You do! Thanks!

Amen.

Give yourselves completely to God. Stand against the devil, and the devil will run from you.

James 4:7

Full of Joy!

Dear God,

Today I just feel like singing and dancing and spreading happiness all around. What a great feeling! Thank You for giving me so much to be happy about. Thanks for sunshine and flowers and music and friends and family. Most of all thanks for YOU!

Amen.

This is the day that the Lord has made. Let us rejoice and be glad today!

Psalm 118:24

Prayers
to Help Me

Learn

More
like Jesus

Dear God,

I need help learning to be more like You. Please teach me to be as kind, loving, forgiving and caring as You. Help me to live so that everyone around me can see that I believe in You.

Amen.

Imitate God in everything you do, because you are His dear children. Live a life filled with love, following the example of Christ.

Ephesians 5:1-2

Loving Everyone

Dear Lord,

Some people are easy to love. Some people are not. I need Your help to learn to love a girl at school who I don't really like. Help me see the good in her. Help me see that maybe she just needs someone to be her friend. Thank You.

Amen.

May the Lord make your love for one another and for all people grow and overflow.

1 Thessalonians 3:12

Forgiving
When I Don't Want To

Dear God,

Okay, I'm not so good at
forgiveness. I know that.
When someone hurts me I don't
always want to forgive them.
Help me learn to forgive when someone
hurts me. Help me to forgive and forget —
just like You do for me.

Amen.

*"If you forgive those who sin against you,
your heavenly Father will forgive you.
But if you refuse to forgive others,
your Father will not forgive your sins."*

Matthew 6:14-15

Memorizing Bible Verses

Dear God,

I want to memorize Bible verses.
I think it would help me to have them
in my mind when I'm scared or need help
with remembering that You love me.
It's hard for me to memorize,
so please help me to get
Your Word in my mind.

Amen.

*I have hidden Your Word in my heart,
that I might not sin against You.*

Psalm 119:11

Stop and Think!

Dear Lord,

I am not good at obeying — even when I know that the rules are just there to keep me safe or to help me treat others better. Please help me to learn to stop and think before I do or say things that might hurt someone else.

Amen.

Wise people think before they act.

Proverbs 13:16

A Caring Heart

Dear God,

Help me learn to be more caring. Help me to want to help when someone needs food or water, or just a friend. Help me to always keep other people in my prayers and to never take for granted what I have. There are so many people out there who need help more than I do. Please give me a caring attitude and a loving heart.

Amen.

Dear children, let's not merely say that we love each other; let us show the truth by our actions.

1 John 3:18

Prayers
to Help Me Be

Strong

Being Strong

Dear God,

Sometimes when I'm playing with friends they want to do things that I know would be wrong. Help me be strong to keep from doing wrong things. Also help me be kind in how I speak to my friends so I don't sound like a know-it-all.

Amen.

God taught us to give up our wicked ways and to live decent and honest lives in this world.

Titus 2:12

Truth Is Best

Dear God,

I need Your help with something. Sometimes I tell little lies so I don't look like the guilty one. Sometimes I tell lies to make myself look good or more important than others. I know it isn't right to do this. Please help me to stop lying.

Amen.

God can't stomach liars;
He loves the company
of those who keep
their word.

Proverbs 12:22

Kids Who
Don't Know God

Dear God,

Some of the kids in my school don't think much of You. They make fun of me for going to church and praying. Please help me to be strong enough to tell them that, "Yeah, I love and obey God." Help me be strong but kind. Thanks.

Amen.

People who do not believe are living all around you and might say that you are doing wrong. Live such good lives that they will see the good things you do and will give glory to God on the day when Christ comes again.

1 Peter 2:12

Cheaters Never Win

Dear God,

I cheat. I do. When I'm playing a game or something, I want to win so bad that I will cheat. That's not nice, is it? It doesn't show others that I love You. I need Your help to be a good loser and not a cheating winner.

Amen.

"Whoever can be trusted with very little can also be trusted with much, and whoever is dishonest with very little will also be dishonest with much."

Luke 16:10

Help Me Get Well

Dear Father,

I don't feel good. I'm crabby because I feel bad. I know that's hard for Mom. She's just trying to take good care of me and I'm being mean. Help me to be more patient and kind to her. Thanks.

Amen.

*Be joyful because you have hope.
Be patient when trouble comes,
and pray at all times.*

Romans 12:12

The Promise
of Heaven

Dear God,

Thank You, Lord, for heaven.
I know that when we die we will go
up to heaven with You. Thank You for
getting heaven ready so that we
can come and live there with
You forever.

Amen.

*"There is more than enough room
in My Father's home. If this were not so,
would I have told you that I am going
to prepare a place for you?"*

John 14:2

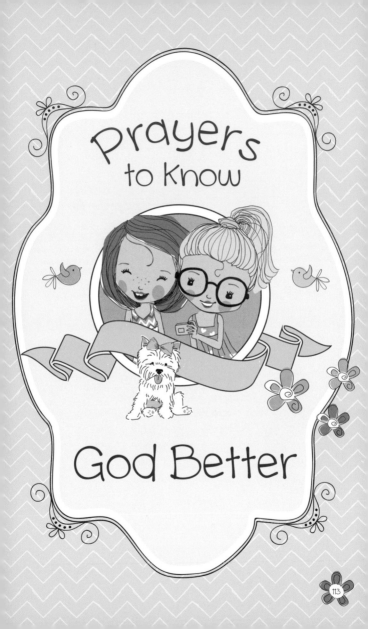

Prayers
to Know
God Better

Learning
God's Word

Dear God,

I want to get to know You better
and better. I think one of the ways
to do that is to read the Bible.
I need help understanding it, though.
Please help me with that. If I understand
it then I'll understand You better.

Amen.

*Don't be like the people
of this world,
but let God change the
way you think.
Then you will know how
to do everything
that is good and
pleasing to Him.*

Romans 12:2

Knowing God

Dear God,

Some of my friends just goof off in Sunday school and church. I've done that, too. But, I think that if I want to know You better, I should pay attention and learn from the lessons and messages. Please help me to pay attention in Sunday school so that I can get to know You better.

Amen.

No one can have faith without hearing the message about Christ.

Romans 10:17

Commanded
to Pray

Dear Father,

I don't really understand prayer.
I do it, but don't know if my prayers
change things. Even if it doesn't,
Your Word says to pray and ... it feels
good to pray. So, thanks for hearing my
prayers and for doing what's best for me.

Amen.

Never give up praying.
And when you pray,
keep alert and be thankful.

Colossians 4:2

Blessing of Teachers

Dear God,

Thank You for the people in my life who have known You for a long time. They teach me how to live for You. I see how they trust You and that helps me to trust You, too. I'm glad I have them to help me learn more about You.

Amen.

Jesus prayed, "I pray for all those who will believe in Me because of their teaching. Father, I pray that they can be one. As You are in Me and I am in You, I pray that they can also be one in Us. Then the world will believe that You sent Me."

John 17:20-21

Making
Good Choices

Dear God,

Thank You for giving us a choice
in what to do. Sometimes though,
I don't make good choices. I usually
know what's right, but sometimes I'm not
strong enough to make the right choice.
I need Your help to be strong and make
good choices. Please help me.

Amen.

*The Lord says,
"I will make you wise
and show you where
to go. I will
guide you and
watch over you."*

Psalm 32:8

Strong
Enough to Forgive

Dear God,

Some things I'm not so good at,
like forgiving my friends when
they hurt my feelings. Even if they say
they are sorry, I hold a grudge for a while.
For some reason I cannot seem to always
let things go. Please help me to be
strong enough to forgive instead of
being so selfish about it. Thank You.

Amen.

*Love is patient and kind.
Love is not jealous or boastful or
proud or rude. It does not demand its
own way. It is not irritable, and it
keeps no record of being wrong.*

1 Corinthians 13:4-5

Prayers When I Don't Understand

Helpful,
Not Just Sad

Dear God,

It's okay to be sad when
bad things happen. But, I don't
want to just be sad, I want to help.
I don't understand why some people
have such hard things in their lives.
Please show me how to be
a friend who helps when
someone has a problem.

Amen.

*He comforts us in all our troubles so
that we can comfort others. When they
are troubled, we will be able to give
them the same comfort God
has given us.*

2 Corinthians 1:4

Be An Example

Dear God,

I don't understand why some people don't care about You. They don't think about praying or reading the Bible. I pray that I can show them how special You are and how much You love them by how I live my life.

Amen.

Don't let anyone think less of you because you are young. Be an example to all believers in what you say, in the way you live, in your love, your faith, and your purity.

1 Timothy 4:12

Treating Others as I Want To Be Treated

Dear God,

Why do some people
hurt other people?
How can someone be so mean?
Don't they know how bad that is?
I pray for people who are mean to stop
and think about how sad it is to hurt
others in any way.

Amen.

*Jesus says, "Do to
others as you
would like them
to do to you."*

Luke 6:31

Wanting To Do Good

Dear God,

I don't get it. I try to be good but I keep doing the same bad things over and over. I wish I could stop. But, I can't unless You help me. Please help me to be better and to listen when You say that it is wrong to do something.

Amen.

The moment I decide to do good, sin is there to trip me up. I truly delight in God's commands, but it's pretty obvious that not all of me joins in that delight. I've tried everything and nothing helps. The answer, thank God, is Jesus Christ.

Romans 7:21-25

Never Give Up

Dear God,

So many people just never give up. Even when everyone tells them to, they just never stop believing. Please give me the strength and courage to never give up, no matter what people say. Because I know that with You by my side anything is possible.

Amen.

Jesus said, "All things are possible for one who believes."

Mark 9:23

Needing Comfort

Dear God,

There are kids at school who are mean to me. I don't know why. I didn't do anything to them. Please let them stop being so mean and please help me to be strong when they are.

Amen.

The Lord upholds all who fall and lifts up all who are bowed down.

Psalm 145:14

127

CONTENTS

LIST OF ILLUSTRATIONS

The tall windows of the Hall of Mirrors, extending almost the full width of the palace, allowed the king and his courtiers to enjoy spectacular views over Louis XIV's beloved Lenotrian gardens.

INTRODUCTION

The king had hardly said that there should be a palace
than a wondrous palace emerged from the earth . . . [1]

THIS SOUNDS LIKE A FAIRY TALE—AND INDEED
the words are those of Charles Perrault, the
author of 'Little Red Riding-Hood', 'Cinder-
ella', 'Puss in Boots' and many other classic fairy stories. The
creation of the Palace of Versailles, to which he was referring,
was not quite as instantaneous as a fairy tale might require.
But it was not far off. For within a matter of years after 1660,
an obscure hunting lodge was transformed into a huge and
magnificent set of buildings, commandingly placed in ornate
gardens. For posterity, as much as for his contemporaries in
France and across Europe Versailles redefined what a royal
palace should be.

The claim that all this was the work of a single man—
Perrault's master, in fact—was exaggerated, but it was not

mere flattery by a sycophantic courtier. The Bourbon king Louis XIV (ruled 1643–1715), absolute monarch and ruler by divine right, selected the location (of which his father Louis XIII had been fond), conceptualised the kind of palace he wanted built and, for decades—right up to the moment of his death—devoted all his imaginative powers to its realisation. Versailles was the considered brainchild of a king who wanted a monument that could glorify, commemorate, inspire and command. Created on royal orders, constructed and decorated to royal-approved design, the palace was made at a gallop to the measure of a single man, who flaunted himself to his courtiers and his subjects as 'Louis the Great'.

As the author of fairy tales suggested, this enchanted site functioned through sheer dazzlement. Scale and beauty worked in tandem to compel respectful awe from all who encountered it—courtiers, noblemen, diplomats, travellers, merchants and artisans, and ordinary Frenchmen and women. The greatest artists in French history were tasked to produce an overwhelming, decorative spectacle. The project extended beyond the walls of the palace, for Louis also took an obsessive interest in its gardens; and a thriving new town was conjured out of a tiny adjacent village. Versailles was not just a

This powerful ceremonial portrait of Louis XIV was commissioned from the painter Hyacinthe Rigaud in 1701 as a gift to his grandson on his accession to the Spanish throne as Philip V. But the king admired it too much to let it go. Placed in the state apartments on public view it became the most widely known image of 'Louis the Great'.

power-building: it comprised a whole landscape of power. There was a cosmic dimension to it, too: one of the principal allegorical motifs of power woven into the palace's fabric was the image of Louis as the Sun King, *le Roi soleil*,* benignly radiating the warmth of his influence over his subjects, as the universe revolved around him.

The prestige of Versailles was at its zenith after 1682, when Louis moved his whole court to the site. He brought his government bureaucracy in tow as well, effectively turning his back on Paris, the largest and most prestigious city in continental Europe. Versailles was henceforth in substance the French monarchy's court, capital and seat of government.

Only the king of the greatest and richest power in Europe could have possibly imagined (and resourced) a scheme as majestic, as ambitious and as demanding as Versailles. Its prestige grew exponentially as the eighteenth century unfolded: the palace stimulated fellow monarchs across Europe into emulation; its grounds exemplified the 'French garden' style, whose popularity swept Europe; and even the town of Versailles, in effect a Louis-Quatorzian creation with its wide straight roads, provided a model that prefigured Haussmann's nineteenth-century redevelopment of Paris and, more immediately, inspired Washington in the United States and Portugal's post-earthquake Lisbon.

---

* Although the phrase 'the Sun King' or *le Roi soleil* is very widely used in writing about Louis XIV, it was not in fact common under the *ancien régime*. Since, as we shall see below, the sun motif was only one among many ascribed to Louis XIV, I have eschewed using it much in this volume.

This characteristic boiserie incorporates at its centre Louis XIV's sun motif.

Yet the Versailles project put severe strains on Louis XIV's treasury and placed his successors, Louis XV (ruled 1715–74) and Louis XVI (ruled 1774–92), in a paradoxical situation. Neither wanted to change what seemed to be the winning Louis-Quatorzian formula for greatness, based on displays of power abroad as well as at home. Yet the task of living up to their predecessor's standards was challenging, and neither monarch found Louis XIV easy to imitate. To some extent they could only become themselves by diverging in certain ways from the Louis-Quatorzian ideal. This was even more the case for Louis XVI's queen, Marie Antoinette, who loved the palace's splendour—but wanted it to be focused mainly on herself. Increasing public unease—echoing a 'Black Legend' that went back to Louis XIV's ruinous wars and his repression of Protestantism—highlighted the glaring contrasts between the luxury of the court and the living conditions of the rest of the nation. By 1789 Versailles had become a national bone of contention rather than a symbol of unity under the Bourbon dynasty.

There were thus already questions in the air about the role of Versailles in the political system prior to the French Revolution, when the French monarchy descended swiftly into a terminal crisis. From the declaration of the First Republic (1792–1804) onwards, it was asked whether a palace complex made to measure for the greatest monarch in early modern Europe could be accommodated within a modernised political system. Could Versailles be 'de-Bourbonised'? And what exactly was Versailles *for* in a post-absolutist age? Successive governments—including Napoleon, whose empire (1804–14) followed the demise of the First Republic, and a restored Bourbon monarchy between 1815 and 1830—grappled with this conundrum, but failed to supply a durable answer in what was a highly volatile political atmosphere.

The most substantial response came from King Louis-Philippe (ruled 1830–48), a member of the collateral, Orléans branch of the Bourbon dynasty. His cherished idea was to make the palace a commemorative site for the whole history of France from earliest times to his own 'July Monarchy', including republic and empire as well as monarchy. For this purpose, he created an extensive set of historical galleries, dedicated to 'all the glories of France'. Following Louis-Philippe's fall from power, the galleries were retained and adapted under the Second Republic (1848–52) and Napoleon III's Second Empire (1852–70)—and indeed are still in existence today.

Versailles was thus transformed from a place in which history was made into one where history was remembered. Yet two linked flashbulb moments returned the palace briefly but strikingly to centre stage in France's national story. The first was in 1871, when Louis XIV's famous Hall of Mirrors was designated as the site for the declaration of the German Empire, following France's defeat in the Franco-Prussian War. For a short period thereafter—up to 1879—Versailles became the seat of national government under the Third Republic (1870–1940). The second moment came forty years later, in 1919, when the treaty that ended the First World War was signed in Versailles; the stage-managed signature of Germany's defeat took place in the Hall of Mirrors—an ostentatious French riposte to the national humiliation of 1871.

Henceforward, Versailles was an iconic site in the republican as well as the monarchist tradition. The palace was incorporated in the French political mainstream, republicanised and even depoliticised. It has gone on to play a small but significant ceremonial role in the Fourth and Fifth Republics (1946–58; 1958 to the present). The political debates which divided the nation across the nineteenth century have, however, lost their relevance and bite.

The minimal role of Versailles in contemporary politics is most definitely not the reason why up to six or seven million individuals currently visit the palace and its grounds each year. These crowds are drawn by Versailles's distant past, not its political present. A crucial stimulus for that attraction has been the establishment of a quite different role for the palace, developed since the late nineteenth century by a line of visionary curators. These individuals realised that Versailles in the modern age could never match the historical Versailles for glory and influence, and that the future of the palace therefore lay in its past. But its new role was conceived less as a chauvinistic history lesson on the nationalistic lines sketched by Louis-Philippe, than as a memory site, which allows visitors to experience in some way the greatest moments and cultural achievements of the palace prior to 1789. This change of vocation has involved a combination of preservation, conservation, commercialisation and infectious imagination, so as to allow an extraordinary historical moment and the artistic and cultural achievements associated with it to appear to speak for themselves.

This book thus tells a three-stage story of this remarkable monument. First, how an abandoned location with no history was transformed into a fairy-tale palace which made history

(Chapter 1). Second, how Versailles functioned during its age of grandeur (Chapters 2, 3 and 4). And third, how that palace, after struggling to adapt to the modern age, eventually found a vocation as a memory palace and cultural hub (Chapters 5 and 6).

This magnificent bust of Louis XIV was the work of the Italian sculptor and architect Gian-Lorenzo Bernini, who spent 1665 in France at the king's invitation.

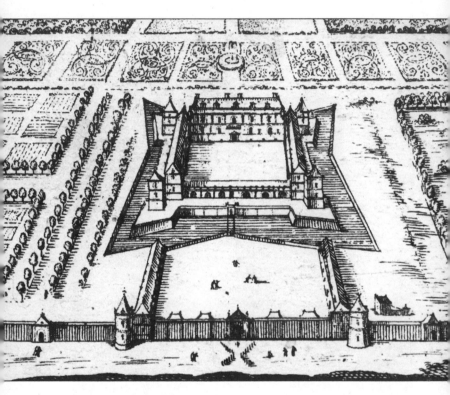

This image of Louis XIII's Versailles by the map-maker
Jacques Gomboust captures the chateau as it was following
embellishment by the king in the early 1630s.

CREATING

From House of Cards to Fairy-tale Palace

LOUIS XIII'S HUNTING LODGE

HE GRANDEUR OF VERSAILLES HIDES THE fact that it represented a triumph of Culture over Nature at its least prepossessing. The Duc de Saint-Simon (1675–1755), who lived in the palace as a courtier under Louis XIV for more than a decade, was admittedly no friend of the monarchy. Writing his memoirs many years after the event, he was damning in his judgement on the site of the palace: it was, he said 'the saddest and most unrewarding of places, with no view, no woods, no water and no earth; for it is all shifting sand and marsh, and the air is consequently bad'.[1] From valley slopes, water ran down to a boggy and marshy plain, full of ponds and stretches of stagnant water which made the area unhealthy and malodorous, especially during the hot summer months. It attracted high winds, too, producing a kind of soggy bleakness.

A matter of years before the birth of Louis XIV, Versailles was little more than a geographical expression. It denoted a thinly populated site on the southern flank of the Val de Galie, some twelve miles to the south-west of Paris. The site's history was as undistinguished as its geography. The discovery in 2006 of a Merovingian cemetery lying to the south of the present-day palace suggests habitation as early as the eighth century, but written records start to mention 'Versailles' only from the mid-eleventh century. The place name derives from the Old French *versail*, meaning a ploughed field. Though dominated by thick woods and low-lying marshland, the medieval landscape did, in fact, include, alongside vines and orchards, open fields where grain was cultivated; this was ground at a windmill located on a mound where Louis XIV would later create his palace.

In the middle of the sixteenth century, the village and its outlying farms probably housed fewer than a couple of hundred individuals, living in modest thatch- and slate-roofed cottages. Any prosperity the area enjoyed derived from the fact that it lay at the intersection of a number of roads, including a major artery linking Paris and Normandy. Versailles saw a lot more cattle passing through to be slaughtered in Paris than it did human beings. Yet by the mid-sixteenth century, wealthy Parisians started investing in property here. One Martial de Loménie, an influential state financier, built a manor house and petitioned the Crown to allow the village to have a weekly market and four annual fairs. Loménie fell victim to the Saint Bartholomew's Day Massacre of Protestants in Paris in 1572, and his property passed into the hands of Albert de Gondi, a Tuscan by birth who had established himself in the entourage of the French Queen Regent, Catherine de Medici. Gondi was too busy in affairs of state to improve the area, but, along with other members of his family, he continued to buy land here. By the turn of the century, when the kings of France started taking an interest in Versailles, the Gondis were its most powerful family.

King Henry IV passed this way with his army in 1589, en route to besiege the city of Paris towards the end of the French Wars of Religion. Maybe it stuck in his mind, for he returned here to hunt on several occasions from 1604 onwards. Thick woodland made it an ideal spot for hunting game, notably deer, boar, wolves and hare. Situated close to Saint-Germain-en-Laye—where Renaissance kings had established a stylish chateau that became a favoured royal residence—Versailles was a convenient destination for a day-long hunting trip, but Henry IV sometimes passed the night here, too, normally in the Gondi manor house. In 1607 he took his five-year-old son on his first hunting expedition here. The boy came away with 'a hare, five or six quail and two partridges'[2]—and, seemingly, an enduring passion for the place.

In 1610, following Henry IV's assassination, the boy became king. The reign of Louis XIII (ruled 1610–43) was perturbed by religious conflicts, provincial revolts and urban commotions, and then, from 1635, open warfare with Austria and Spain in

VERSAILLES

the Thirty Years War. The king was engaged in a seemingly endless sequence of campaigns across the country, and when he returned to the Île-de-France, his preferred choice of residence was Saint-Germain-en-Laye. In the late 1610s he began to make hunting trips out to Versailles. Shy, ungregarious and mildly misogynistic, Louis seemingly preferred the company of a small group of male hunting cronies to his court at Saint-Germain. In 1623 he confirmed his leisure priorities by deciding to construct a small hunting lodge here on the elevated ground by the village windmill.

This little dwelling, in which he stayed for the first time in 1624, was situated exactly on the spot now occupied by the *cour de marbre* at the heart of Louis XIV's palace. But its antecedent was humble and rudimentary: the building housed only around a dozen men and a few followers. Louis fortified it with a moat and a ten-foot-high wall with turrets at the corners, as befitted a kingdom still troubled by provincial feuding. Its style was somewhat archaic: in the capital the fashion for constructing in white Parisian stone was gaining ascendancy, but Louis's lodge at Versailles was built of red brick, with the occasional Doric column and with black slate roofs. According to Saint-Simon, this gave the place the attributes of a 'house of cards'[3]—coloured red, white and black and very fragile-looking. It gained a little by the demolition of the adjacent windmill.

Many at the royal court found the monarch's passion for Versailles baffling. Apart from abundant sport for hunting, there was very little about the location to recommend it. The

14

shortcomings of the site, which Saint-Simon remarked on so acidly,* were all the more striking when compared with the Louvre and Tuileries Palace complex in Paris and the chateau of Saint-Germain-en-Laye, which enjoyed lovely views over the Seine. For the Marquis de Bassompierre, Versailles was a 'puny chateau' that not even a country gentleman would take pride in. When Louis reminded a courtier of the demolition of the Versailles windmill, the courtier riposted that while the mill had gone, the wind remained.[4] And so did the summer stench. Yet Louis saw the environmental issues less as a hindrance than a challenge. From the late 1620s he started to make his lodge habitable for longer periods than overnight stays. Newly acquired properties in and around the village also allowed him to lay out extensive gardens to the rear.

In 1630 Versailles witnessed the 'Day of the Dupes', which saw the thwarting of an attempted factional coup against Louis's principal minister, Cardinal Richelieu. Thereafter, Louis based himself and his court at Saint-Germain-en-Laye, which allowed him to escape to Versailles or to other royal residences such as Fontainebleau and Compiègne, while Richelieu was installed as the king's principal adviser at nearby Rueil. Except in cases of major state business, this arrangement allowed Louis to stay away from Paris and the Louvre, for neither of which he felt much affection.

Further building at Versailles between 1631 and 1634 helped transform the miniscule hunting lodge into something

---

* See p. 11.

resembling a country house—and even a tourist destination. In 1639 Claude de Varennes's *Le voyage de France* urged visitors to the Paris region to pay a visit to Versailles: this was the first of very many guidebook recommendations.[5] The king, moreover, was inordinately proud of his new possession. He arranged rendezvous there so that he could show it off to eminent foreign dignitaries. (These included in 1641 the papal envoy Giulio Mazzarini, who, as Cardinal Mazarin, would succeed Richelieu as the king's principal minister in 1642.) Louis entertained his queen, Anne of Austria, here too and constructed rooms for her—though he never allowed her to spend the night. Even in 1641, when an outbreak of smallpox at Saint-Germain prompted Louis to transfer to Versailles his son and heir, the three-year-old Louis XIV, Anne was ordered to stay away and to take shelter elsewhere. Versailles was a very male preserve.

As a baby, Louis XIV was said to have been terrified of his lugubrious father and screamed whenever he saw him. Despite this early aversion, the child would inherit from his father a deep love of Versailles. This element of affective continuity overlay a disjunction between the two monarchs' use of the site. Louis XIII valued the small size of Versailles, the privacy it offered away from the court, its highly masculine ambiance and its fortress-like appearance. From the first years of his personal reign, following the death of Mazarin in 1661, however, Louis XIV sought to demilitarise the chateau, to feminise its denizens, to publicise its activities and then, finally, in 1682, massively to increase it in size, by relocating his whole court and government here. He would turn a modest country house into a palace.

THE MAKING OF A FUN PALACE

Louis XIV waited until he was a young man before turning his mind to Versailles. When his father died in 1643 he was only four years old and power passed into the hands of his mother, Anne of Austria, who ruled as Regent, advised by Cardinal Mazarin. Anne based the court in Paris, preferring the Palais-Royal, the former home of Cardinal Richelieu, to the cramped accommodation of the Louvre. Versailles was effectively abandoned and fell into disrepair for a decade. In 1651, during a quiet period of the turbulent civil wars known as the Fronde (1648–52), Louis made a visit to the site. Once the wars were ended, he started hunting more regularly in its environs. He seems to have seen potential in the semi-abandoned building, ordering its renovation in 1660 and visiting it with his new queen, Marie-Thérèse.* These events took place just before he overthrew Mazarin's successor, Nicolas Fouquet, and determined to rule directly and without a principal minister.

---

* Maria Teresa (1638–83) was the daughter of King Philip IV of Spain, and Queen Elisabeth, who was herself the daughter of Henry IV of France. Maria Teresa married Louis and adopted the French version of her name in 1660.

The chateau at Vaux-le-Vicomte constructed between 1658 and 1661 by Louis XIV's ill-fated finance minister Nicolas Fouquet was in a sense a proto-Versailles. It showcased the talents of painter Charles Le Brun, architect Louis Le Vau and garden designer André Le Nôtre, all of whom became centrally involved in the king's plans for Versailles.

Louis appears to have been nurturing this political strategy in advance of a celebrated moment in July 1661 when he visited Fouquet in his sumptuous chateau of Vaux-le-Vicomte, some 56 kilometres (35 miles) south-east of Paris. Fouquet's star had risen very high and the sheer splendour of Vaux—its buildings, its gardens and the magnificence of Fouquet's festive reception for his ruler—must have dazzled Louis. The 'audacious luxury' that Louis charged Fouquet with displaying only confirmed suspicions about Fouquet's probity and ambitions that Louis had already developed. In September 1661 Louis ordered d'Artagnan, the Commander of the King's Musketeers, to arrest Fouquet and cast him into a prison from which he would never emerge. Louis now held his destiny in his own hands.

If Fouquet's corruption was no surprise for Louis, what appears to have opened his eyes on his visit to Vaux was the handiwork of the creative triad behind it: architect Louis Le Vau, garden designer André Le Nôtre, and painter Charles Le Brun. Almost straight away, Louis conscripted these men to the project he had developed for Versailles in his mind's eye. At this stage, his ideas were still more than a little hazy, and Versailles did not yet fully monopolise his attention: he was simultaneously commissioning important new work for the Louvre and the Tuileries, as well as at the Château de Vincennes. Jean-Baptiste Colbert, Louis's new post-Fouquet ministerial factotum, was also hatching plans to make a magnificently redesigned Louvre the centrepiece of a new Paris that would match ancient Rome for grandeur. Yet it was soon apparent that Louis's overall plans for Versailles were far bigger and better than his father's. In addition, with the outstanding creative talents of Le Vau, Le Nôtre and Le Brun at his disposal, Louis wished not simply to emulate his finance minister's achievement at Vaux-le-Vicomte, but far to surpass it.

Louis XIII had started expanding Crown property around the Versailles chateau, ending the Gondi clan's local influence. Louis XIV followed this lead, consolidating Bourbon holdings so as to enlarge the park and gardens. By the time that Louis brought his queen back to Versailles in 1663, change was well under way. Yet the queen was increasingly out of the picture at Versailles. From 1662 Louis was escaping here with the numerous mistresses he was to enjoy over the following years. In May 1664 he staged a themed festival in the palace grounds, *Les Plaisirs de l'Île enchantée*. Ostensibly in honour of his mother, the Regent Anne of Austria, the event also marked a stage in his newly hatched love affair with teenage lady-in-waiting Louise de La Vallière. The three days of festival events, attended by several hundred courtiers, and showcasing gardens in which Le Nôtre was already hard at work, included *La Princesse d'Élide*, a new comedy-ballet by Molière with music by Jean-Baptiste Lully, tournament jousting, dancing, pageants, firework displays and sumptuous, candle-lit banquets.

The pace of festivity relented in the mid-1660s: the War of Devolution of 1667–8 attracted most of the king's attention. But military victory only strengthened Louis's desire to expand and make further embellishments. He celebrated victory with a further lavish fête in 1668, the so-called *Grand Divertissement royal*, with further contributions from Molière and Lully (which he planned as a homage to another new mistress, Madame de Montespan). Louis XIII's private hunting lodge was being transformed into a Fun Palace where Louis could ostentatiously take his pleasure.

Managing the expansion of Versailles proved to be a fraught process. Louis XIII's original chateau was in increas-

This panoramic view by painter Pierre Patel shows how ambitiously
the young king had already developed his father's chateau by 1668.

ingly bad shape, and royal advisers argued that it was imprac-
tical to retain it. But the king, driven partly by filial fidelity
to his father's memory, and partly too by a realisation that
complete renovation would put Versailles out of commission
for some time, dug in his heels. He threatened, 'with some
feeling', that even if it were demolished entirely, 'he would

have it rebuilt unchanged in its entirety'.[6] Architect Louis Le Vau devised the ingenious solution of not only retaining it, but also expanding it considerably by loosely encasing it on three sides with extensive further building, disposed around two new courtyards. The buildings of this 'envelope', as it was called, were designed in a more classical manner, thereby meeting the criticism that a brick-and-slate palace had become laughably anachronistic. Le Vau's 'envelope' thus kept Louis XIII's hunting lodge as the symbolic and actual centre of a complex primed for even further expansion. It was from around this time too that Louis XIII's little open courtyard was tiled in marble and received the name the *cour de marbre*.

The wave of expansion around this period was partly functional. The new space opened up by Le Vau's 'envelope' allowed more apartments to be created for a larger group of individuals. In addition, the wings around the *cour de marbre*, which initially performed service functions (kitchens, stables, administrative offices) were extended outwards to create a larger and wider courtyard (the *cour royale*). A further development was the creation of space for the government's ministerial team: Louis realised that stays in Versailles were protracted enough for him to need to have ministers at hand. In 1670–72, four pavilion-style buildings were created in the chateau's forecourt. They would be joined into two large, forward-jutting blocks—the 'ministers' wings'—later in the 1670s.

Despite the pragmatism of these new arrangements, high priority was also given to decorative grandeur and the organisation of royal leisure. Visitors to the chateau were

This view from the capacious Orangerie that Louis XIV constructed between 1683 and 1685 faces south across ornate parterres towards the *pièce d'eau des Suisses*, a huge lake which watered the nearby royal kitchen garden.

highly impressed by the decorative changes that Louis was introducing. After visiting in 1670, for example, the Bishop of Fréjus commented that Versailles was 'even greater and more beautiful than Rome'.[7] A taste for the exotic was increasingly evident: Le Vau constructed an Orangerie in 1663 for a range of non-native plants (including many pillaged from Fouquet's

Vaux-le-Vicomte), and a Menagerie for the display of captive birds and animals from all over the globe. In 1668 he purchased the hamlet of Trianon, which was situated within the estate, razed the buildings, rehoused the inhabitants and ordered Le Vau to begin work on a one-storey summer house, which was planned to be 'convenient for spending a few hours a day during the summer heat'.[8] Designed in a self-consciously oriental style, the building was faced with blue-and-white tiles (in fact from Delft and French provincial manufactories rather than from Japan). These gave the building its name: the 'Porcelain Trianon'.*

The building, decorative and land-development schemes that Louis XIV undertook from the 1660s did not come cheap. Funds dedicated to Versailles on this scale meant less money for other major schemes, for which Louis's right-hand man Colbert constantly chided his royal master. Plans for the site, Colbert had claimed in 1662, amounted to nothing more than 'patchwork'. Versailles, he maintained, 'more concerns Your Majesty's pleasure and entertainment than his glory'. 'What a shame if the greatest and most virtuous of kings should be judged by the measure of Versailles!' The minister had contrasting ambitions for the Louvre, which he accounted 'the most superb palace that ever was'. In 1665 he brought to Paris the great Italian sculptor and architect Gian-Lorenzo Bernini with plans (never to come to fruition) to design a new eastern façade for it.[9]

---

* The reference is to the huge porcelain tower of Nanjing, one of the wonders of the Orient, which was destroyed in the nineteenth century.

Louis resisted—or ignored—such entreaties. His apparent indifference towards Paris may date back to the humiliations the city had heaped on him and his Queen Regent mother during the Fronde: on two separate occasions, he had been effectively held prisoner there by rebels against royal authority. Post-Fronde, Louis's mother had established the royal court in the Palais-Royal in the capital, but in 1661 Louis donated this to his brother Philippe, duc d'Orléans. At the same time, work was undertaken on the Louvre and Tuileries to make them grander and more habitable. But while this took place, Louis decamped to the palace of Saint-Germain-en-Laye. This allowed multiple brief outings to Versailles, especially in the summer months (though there were long stays in his Fontainebleau palace, too, and occasional visits to places such as Chambord in the Loire Valley). The last time that the king overnighted in Paris was in 1666: his reign still had nearly fifty years to run! Day visits largely for ceremonial purposes continued, but became increasingly rare: there were only eight royal visits to Paris between 1682 and 1715.

Louis was also spending time away from the Île-de-France on military campaigns at the front. The War of Devolution of 1667–8 was followed by Louis's Dutch War of 1672–8. The king really needed an uninterrupted period of peace to oversee the kind of changes he was envisaging for Versailles. As chance would have it, this is what he got: France would fight no wars between 1678 and 1688; a decade of tranquility allowed Louis's Versailles plans to blossom.

MONARCHICAL HUB

In 1677 the normally secretive Louis XIV revealed to the world that Versailles would become the home of both his court and his government. The chateau would not lose its earlier vocations as hunting lodge and palace of pleasures: far from it, for Louis remained an avid huntsman and Versailles would continue for many years to be celebrated for the splendour of its festivities. Yet Louis's announcement marked a quantum leap in his thinking. The five years after 1677 would be spent on the huge operation of readying the site for its new role as monarchical hub and governmental nerve centre. This would involve a substantial part of the government bureaucracy and the entire royal court (not simply certain choice members) being relocated, installed, accommodated and entertained.

For this work, Louis could count on the continued guidance of Le Brun and Le Nôtre, both still at the height of their powers, although the other member of his original creative triad, architect Louis Le Vau, had died in 1670. His role was assumed by an equally imaginative and effective operator, Jules Hardouin-Mansart. Mansart would make significant contributions to the task of remoulding Versailles for its new vocation.

The expansion of the Versailles complex proved a convenient canvas for the display of royal symbolism. Louis's youthful enthusiasm for Alexander the Great, whose military exploits he admired, led to early decorative references to the Greek commander. But in 1662 Louis chose as his personal emblem the sun, giver of life and centre of the universe. It represented, the king opined, 'assuredly the loftiest and finest image of a monarch'.[10] Emblems of the sun and the sun god Apollo (also the patron of peace and the arts) began to appear throughout the royal estates. Le Brun, whom Louis ennobled in 1662, then made *Premier peintre du Roi* two years later, worked with his team to decorate the great Apollo Room (Salon d'Apollon), at the heart of the enfilade of state rooms disposed along the northern side of the chateau. The other ceremonial rooms in the suite were named after planets that rotated around the sun (Venus, Mars, etc.). 'Since the sun is the king's device and since poets conflate the sun with Apollo,' antiquarian (and royal sycophant) André Félibien wrote in 1674, lauding the ubiquity of the solar leitmotiv, 'so there is nothing in this superb residence which does not relate to this divinity'.[11] Louis's Fun Palace was becoming a Sun Palace.

The solar fixation was also evident in the chateau's gardens. Particularly striking in this respect was the Grotto of Tethys, constructed in the 1660s around one of the chateau's reservoirs as a private royal bathing suite, and decorated with shells, stones and mirror fragments. The decorative conceit here was of Apollo the sun god bathing in the waters of Tethys, the water goddess wife of Oceanus, at the end of his passage through the skies. The Apollo link was also referenced in key fountain displays established at the heart of the gardens.

Yet notwithstanding these flights of allegorical fantasy, Louis's thinking remained at bottom pragmatic and functional. A key part of his forward planning revolved around his recognition that the glittering performance of kingship which he was developing in the palace* required a greatly expanded support system and service sector to sustain it. The erstwhile village of Versailles was accordingly tailored for this purpose.

The king had a largely free hand here, since his father's and his own property acquisitions meant that the Crown owned most of the village and its environs. Le Nôtre laid out for him three wide, tree-lined avenues converging on the chateau from the eastern, town side. These followed the model that the king was starting to use in Paris for the creation of boulevards on the site of demolished city walls—though, in fact, it would take 200 years for the capital to boast a boulevard as grand as the central, 100-yard-wide Avenue de Paris leading up to the Palace of Versailles.† Rectilinear streets and squares divided the terrain into lots and the king stimulated the building of new private residences (*hôtels particuliers*) for members of the high court nobility.

Versailles needed workers as well as aristocrats, and Louis encouraged the formation of a new neighbourhood on the northern flank of the chateau, where a migrant army of building workers and artisans of every description came to reside. Colbert was tasked with purchasing old houses, demolishing them and then encouraging new housing developments. A royal charter in 1671 offered all comers a plot of land in addition to a range of inducements, on condition they

---

* See Chapter 4, p. 82.

† Opened in 1854, the Avenue Foch (then Avenue de l'Impératrice) was the first Parisian boulevard to exceed this width.

built a dwelling that used approved building materials and conformed to the style and height of the chateau. The building of the huge administrative block on the southern side of the chateau known as the Grand Commun (1682–4) involved the destruction of the village's parish church of Saint-Julien and its neighbourhood. The area would be reconstructed around the chateau and subsequently endowed with the parish church (now cathedral) of Saint-Louis, while the northern neighbourhood was restructured around the new parish of Notre-Dame. By the last years of Louis's reign, the urban population of Versailles was some 45,000.

Such expansion meant that by the 1680s the chateau no longer stood in splendid isolation in the midst of the unpropitious terrain that Louis XIII had found when he constructed his hunting lodge. While new housing was sprouting up all over the northern and southern sides of the chateau, there were also significant developments behind the chateau to the west. Louis XIII had carved out of the wild forest a sizeable space for a park and gardens. It needed to be mastered, its combination of hilly terrain and aquatic marsh regulated and made fit for purpose. Louis XIV set in train a massive project of earth removal, using military engineering techniques usually employed in fortification works. Soon, little trace was left of the mound on which had stood a windmill whose sails had once cast a shadow over the rooms of the chateau. Neatly levelled and terraced space offered a perfect environment for garden development. Between 1668 and 1672 some 130,000 trees were planted on the estate.

These gardens, however—together with an expanding royal court and a mushrooming adjacent service town—simply guzzled water. And therein lay a huge problem, which highlighted the scale of the difficulty of subordinating Nature to Culture in such a barren site. Oddly, considering how water-logged the soil in the region was, water was a rare commodity here and water supply the long-running Achilles heel of Versailles. The Val de Galie in which Versailles was set had no major river running through it, only a number of small streams. Louis set his engineers to work in draining the marshland in ways that created a number of large reservoirs fed by the natural watercourses of the locality. The engineers lent Nature a helping hand by skilfully constructing pumps and watermills and installing subterranean aqueducts and piping. Marshy land adjacent to the south side of the chateau—the colourfully named 'Stinking Pond' (*Étang puant*)—was drained so as to provide a water supply to the royal kitchen garden or *Jardin potager*, created here between 1678 and 1682, and also to source the huge nearby lake known as the *pièce d'eau des Suisses*.*

It was soon apparent, however, that the water problem could not be solved locally and would necessitate going further afield. In the late 1660s the river Bièvre, which flowed into the Seine in Paris, was dammed to produce an inflow and this technique was then tried elsewhere. Notorious among such projects was the diversion of the waters of the

---

* So called because it was dug by a regiment of Swiss guards.

Seine near Marly-le-Roi—about 9 kilometres (6 miles) away from Versailles, but also, more problematically, some 150 metres (490 feet) lower. This was an engineering challenge that was begun in the 1680s and involved the creation of the so-called '*machine de Marly*', a huge and ingenious set of pumps of pharaonic scale. The results it achieved were, however, meagre. Nevertheless, the Marly scheme encouraged Louis to consider an ambitious plan to bring water from the river Eure, some 80 metres (50 miles) distant. The idea proved chimerical and had to be abandoned after France went back to war in 1688.

Ellis Veryard, an Englishman who visited Versailles in 1701, remarked that he 'could not but admire that so much money should be spent in beautifying a Bogg'.[12] This was a back-handed compliment. The water problem at Versailles never entirely disappeared; the disadvantages of the site that Saint-Simon and others pilloried were a continuing and unwelcome backdrop to Louis XIV's performance of power. Even so, the environmental problems that had augured so ill for the Versailles project constituted a chronic rather than an acute condition and, by 1682, when the court moved to Versailles, these challenges had largely been met.

Colbert once remarked to Louis XIV that 'except brilliant campaigns, there is nothing that signals the grandeur and intelligence of princes more than buildings'.[13] Louis XIV had more than lived up to the implicit injunction. And his achievement at Versailles appeared all the more striking to contemporaries, precisely *because* of the scale of the physical problems (more or less) solved along the way. Even Saint-Simon had grudgingly to admit that Louis 'delighted in tyrannising nature and taming it by dint of arts and treasures'.[14] Louis's fairy-tale castle, sprung magically from barren soil, thus accrued all the more emphatically to his renown. In his own as well as many of his contemporaries' eyes, such apparent miracles justified the sobriquet the king acquired in the 1670s of 'Louis the Great'.

MYTHOLOGISING

The Golden Era (1682–1715)

OUIS THE GREAT'S TRANSFER OF COURT AND government to the site on 5–6 May 1682 signalled the creation of the enduring myth of Versailles that was to be endlessly celebrated by royal propagandists, historians and art connoisseurs from that moment to the present day. Yet the construction of that myth was less straightforward than it is often made to seem. The palace of Louis the Great did not spring into life fully formed as though from the head of Zeus. Learned philologists sometimes claimed that the name of the palace of the Louvre in Paris derived from the word *'l'oeuvre'* ('the work')—signifying that it was never finished but always a work in progress. Much the same could be said of Louis XIV's Versailles. It was the result of compromise and negotiation, tinkering and amending, new directions and second thoughts. The royal chapel, for example, was housed in four different locations around the palace before a permanent home was found for it in the North Wing—and then only in 1710, five years before Louis's death. Moreover, some of the king's plans—for an opera house, for example—were never fulfilled. Construction stopped and started according to the king's micromanaging whim—but also sometimes in a rhythm dictated by the state of the royal treasury at times of war. Louis changed his mind ceaselessly, forcing work to stop and then restart in a different direction. The palace swarmed continuously with building workers, decorators and artisans as much as with courtiers and government clerks. There was not a single spot in the whole enterprise, the Princesse Palatine, second wife of Louis's brother Philippe, duc d'Orléans (who lived here for over thirty years), complained, with an exaggeration born of frustration, 'which hasn't been modified ten times'.[1] For more than half a century Versailles was probably the biggest building site in Europe—and on the king's death in 1715 was still not complete. Even so, it was indubitably the period from 1682 down to the king's death in 1715 that represented the Golden Age of Versailles, in which the palace took on the shape and *éclat* that visitors and tourists encounter today.

ANATOMY OF A BUILDING COMPLEX

As late seventeenth-century tourists approached Versailles along the wide Avenue de Paris that led, up a slight incline, towards the palace, their eye-line was invariably drawn towards the *cour de marbre* at its heart. This initial glance paid involuntary homage to Versailles's origins. The courtyard's outline exactly traces that of Louis XIII's little hunting lodge, which his son had insisted should be retained as his palace's focal point. The combination of red (brick), white (marble and stone) and blueish-black (tiles) reproduces the colours that first triggered the comment that the original building was little more than a 'house of cards'.* The same design scheme was followed in the wings jutting forward at both sides of the *cour*. (The latter would only be transformed into stone-faced, neoclassical structures in the late eighteenth and early nineteenth centuries.†)

The rustically archaic façade of Louis XIII's original buildings around the *cour de marbre* was thoroughly worked over from the late 1670s by architect Jules Hardouin-Mansart, who added the sculpture busts and the clock ensemble—each overflowing with political and allegorical messages. When the clock struck the hour, a statue of Louis XIV appeared, which was crowned with laurel by a passing goddess. The balcony, too, was Mansart's creation: it was located in what towards the end of his life became the king's bedroom at the very heart of the palace, thus giving the retiring 'Sun King' an appropriately majestic sunrise. It also allowed him to look down familiarly, for example, on Parisian market-women and fishwives (*poissardes*), who customarily came to the *cour de*

---

* See Chapter 1, p. 14.
† See Chapter 3, p. 78.

The famous *cour de marbre* at the heart of the palace complex.

marbre in delegation to congratulate the king at various ceremonial moments. Such encounters symbolised the axiom, as Louis XIV was to instruct his son, that 'free and easy access of subjects to the king' was an ancient singularity of the French monarchy—and one he desired that Versailles should always observe.[2]

The Avenue de Paris took the visitor approaching the ornate outer gate of the palace complex between two magnificent stable blocks that Mansart had completed in 1681. On the right side of the Avenue, the Grande Écurie housed ceremonial and royal mounts, as well as a riding school and the school of royal pages, while the Petite Écurie to the left provided stabling for draught horses and included the palace blacksmith (the *maréchalerie*). Passing through the Écuries, any well-dressed individual (beggars, monks, prostitutes and recent smallpox victims were specifically excluded) could enter the palace gates from the huge parade ground (the Place d'Armes) into the Ministers' Court in front of the palace itself. This was bounded to left and right by two long buildings jutting out from the palace façade, containing the offices of royal ministers. These structures partially hid from view the very considerable lateral palace extensions on the garden side of the inner courtyard, the South Wing (to the left on entering) and the North Wing (to the right).*

---

* These were completed by Mansart only in the late 1680s (see p. 53).

Visitors advanced to the gate leading into the *cour royale*. Here, if they were wearing a sword denoting gentility (and they could hire one on the spot if necessary), they could enter the palace and its grounds. Once within, they might catch sight of the king or queen on their way to daily Mass in the chapel, or perhaps exercising in the gardens. Louis ordained the daily schedule in Versailles—in much the same way that he micromanaged everything else in the palace—in a highly ordered and ritualistic manner.* Although only select courtiers were allowed to witness some of those rituals—notably the *lever* and the *coucher,* the moments of the king's day in which he rose and retired—the general public were admitted to others, including the so-called *grand couvert,* the moment at which the king ate his evening meal. As this example suggests, visitors to Versailles were there not as participants in but as spectators of court life. Their assigned role was to goggle and be awestruck.

Tourist hotspots within the chateau always included the great Hall of Mirrors (Grande Galerie or Galerie des Glaces). An open terrace originally designed by Le Vau to look over the gardens had not been a success: it was useable only in the summer and it leaked. The Hall of Mirrors thus started as an elaborate repair job. Constructed by Mansart in 1678 and then decorated by sundry painters, sculptors and skilled artisans over the next five years, it stretches for some 73 metres (80 yards) and is flanked at each end by the superbly appointed

---

* For discussion of this point, see Chapter 4 (pp. 85–89).

The Hall of Mirrors—usually then called Grande Galerie—soon became one of the most celebrated and admired features of the palace.

Salon de la Guerre and Salon de la Paix. The rich, multi-coloured marble, silver furnishings, exquisite Boulle* mar-quetry and parquet flooring paled when set against the huge floor-to-ceiling mirrors stretching down one wall, with which French artisans threw down a challenge to the Venetian

---

* André-Charles Boulle (1642–1732) was a cabinet-maker who fulfilled numerous commissions for Louis XIV. Four of his sons became *ébénistes du roi*.

masters who had formerly dominated the glass-making craft. On the ceilings the *Premier peintre du Roi* (First Painter to the King) Charles Le Brun composed a series of paintings that depicted eighteen years of the king's victories between his assumption of personal power in 1661 and the Treaty of Nijmegen in 1678. This iconography needed clearance by the royal council, for there were some who feared (probably rightly) that its chest-banging triumphalism would be taken amiss by other European powers.

Aesthetically, Le Brun's ceiling paintings marked a significant representational shift. Hitherto, Louis's claims to greatness at Versailles had been expressed through comparisons with mythological figures or else through the iconography of the sun. Now, however, it was Louis in person who dominated each image (albeit dressed in Roman military cuirass, with bare arms and legs, together with an improbable combination of wig and fleur-de-lys mantle). The shift from myth to history implied that Louis's actions were elevating him to the status of legend. The central image, moreover, was captioned 'Louis governs by himself', and commemorated the moment in 1661, following the overthrow of Fouquet, when he decided to dispense with a principal minister and govern by direct personal rule. Versailles was irredeemably Louisocentric.

Despite the aura of openness and accessibility which Louis encouraged in the palace, strict hierarchy was the rule, and life was dictated by unwritten but strictly observed rules about access to the royal presence. The state apartments—the *Grands Appartements*—could be strolled through in normal times, but they were closed to outsiders for special events and for the private parties that the king held for his courtiers in the evenings—the so-called *soirées d'appartement*. Similarly, only the closest and most trusted members of the court—his own family, the most august aristocrats and maybe some favoured hunting companions—were admitted to the royal presence in more informal settings. Private accommodation was also out of bounds. The royal apartments were thus split into two: the state rooms for display and formal business, and a smaller and more intimate set of rooms in which the king could feel simply *chez soi*. Yet solitude and close intimacy were not really Louis's style. On one occasion when the Dauphine, complaining of the vapours, asked to be excused from attending a ball, Louis replied sternly: 'We are not like private individuals. We owe ourselves entirely to the public.' As Jean de La Bruyère, satirist of court life, noted, 'A king lacks in nothing, save only the charms of a private life.'[3]

If Louis felt that he owed himself in some way primarily to the public, he also believed that the courtiers housed in Versailles owed everything of value in their lives to him as reigning monarch. There was nothing new about a royal court—kings had long had them, though much about their ceremonies and protocols had emerged from the Renaissance onwards. What Louis did at Versailles was, however, genuinely innovative: he planned the court as a place which his mightiest subjects would feel compelled to attend and which would also, as Saint-Simon put it, make them feel 'in certain disgrace for not being present'. As the Italian envoy Primi

Visconti, writing in the 1670s, noted: 'the passion of courtiers to make themselves noticed by the king is unbelievable'.[4]

Three factors incentivised courtiers to adapt so eagerly to the new Versailles. First, the court was the main source of state patronage, and presence at the new palace was viewed as a *sine qua non* of royal favour. Both honour and income were involved. Moreover, the expensive court lifestyle led high nobles increasingly into dependence on handouts from the state treasury. Second, the court offered an exciting and unmatchable social and cultural life.* Third, there was the fact that Louis provided them with lodgings at the state's expense. Initially, Louis's encouragement to relocate in Versailles had been targeted at getting the high nobility to build *hôtels particuliers* in the town. The construction of the Écuries in the 1670s and early 1680s had, in fact, involved the destruction of several aristocratic residences opposite the palace gates. Although many courtiers retained town lodgings, all state and court officials were in theory housed in the palace and its dependencies. Courtiers were non-paying guests at Versailles.

The more successful this Versailles formula was, the more space it required, particularly as government ministries were now also based in Versailles. Building programmes were instituted in order to produce more suites of rooms. This had been the motivation behind Le Vau's 'envelope',† whose encasing of the original chateau more than doubled available space.

---

* See Chapter 4 (page 89).
† See Chapter 1 (page 22).

Mansart then followed this up by building a lateral southern wing between 1679 and 1682, with an identical northern wing bringing the requisite symmetry from the late 1680s. Space for lodgings was also created by relocating service functions. The wings of the *cour royale,* for example, had housed stables, kitchens and offices in the 1660s. Stables were subsequently moved to the new Écuries on the Avenue de Paris, while the massive quadrangular Grand Commun was constructed behind the southern ministry wing for administrative staff and for service functions, as well as providing overflow lodgings. With these bulky new structures in place, it was clear that Louis had established Versailles as a new kind of monarchical institution: a hub of government, a brilliant artistic and architectural showcase, and home of the high aristocracy.

PARK AND GARDENS

Versailles is a palace of two faces. Anyone approaching it from the town side in the east along the Avenue de Paris immediately observed the traces of the original Louis XIII structure. Despite some modernisation, the façade as a whole retained its red, white and blue palette. Yet for the visitor who successfully ran the gauntlet of gateway checks on entry, and then ventured into the gardens, a completely different Versailles opened up. The style imposed by Louis Le Vau on the western side of his 'envelope' structure—and continued by Mansart for the exterior of the Hall of Mirrors and for the façade of the two lateral wings—was more in accordance with classical precepts: stone replaced brick and no roof was visible behind an ornamental balustrade. The extraordinary width of the palace, partly obscured from the town perspective, was very apparent from the garden side: the 'enveloped' original chateau together with the wings stretched more than a quarter of a mile in all. It was majestically imposing—as well as quite unmissable—from vantage points in a garden and adjoining park that stretched out to the horizon across huge expanses of open land and reflective expanses of ornamental water.

The gardens were encompassed within the area that Louis XIV and his father had pieced together through purchases and acquisitions and which became known as the *Grand Parc* (Great Park). A terrain that came to extend to 15,000 hectares, it incorporated more than 20 villages with an overall population of several thousands, contained within a 10-foot-high wall 25 miles long, with 24 points of access.* Louis XIII had come to Versailles in the first place to hunt, and the *Grand Parc* was where he and his successors did just that. Within this sprawling terrain of the *Grand Parc*, Louis XIV marked out the so-called *Petit Parc*. Its roughly 1,700 hectares were less wild and more manicured than the *Grand Parc*, though less ornate and punctiliously designed than the formal gardens nearest the house.

The Hall of Mirrors presents a grandstand view of the gardens, with the eye ranging from Culture (the gardens) to wild

---

* By way of comparison, the *boulevard périphérique* which now runs around Paris is only 36 kilometres (22 miles) long.

Nature (the Grand Parc) by way of tamed Nature (the Petit Parc). A striking visual feature of the latter was the Grand Canal. The principal arm of this cruciform feature extends a mile in length (the transverse arm is slightly shorter) and is in a direct line with the central avenue (the Grande Allée), which symmetrically divides the gardens in two for the viewer standing at the middle of the Hall of Mirrors. The dimensions and depth of the canal were sufficient for it to take all manner of craft, including galleys, gondolas (the gift of the Doge of Venice), Neapolitan feluccas, English yachts, Dutch barges and replicas of French battleships. A small village on the edge of the canal, known as La Petite Venise, housed shipworkers and their families.

The Grand Canal was laid out by the mastermind behind the whole setting of the palace, namely André Le Nôtre. A powerful figure who won the personal friendship and respect of the monarch (who uncharacteristically greeted him with an affectionate bear hug), it was Le Nôtre who laid out the 'boulevardised' avenues that approached the palace from the town side. He also ensured that the gardens were not a secondary feature of the palace but integral to its design and impact. Their importance was established early: indeed, the most brilliant moments in Versailles's early history had precisely been those Arcadian fêtes such as the *Les Plaisirs de l'Île enchantée* (1664) and the *Grand Divertissement royal* (1668), which had revealed the gardens's charms.

The gardens adopted the classicising aesthetic that was dominating the palace interiors. As we have noted,* they also echoed the allegorical solar theme important in the early stages of Louis's reign. An early example of this, the Grotto of Tethys, fell victim to the palace's expansion, the building of the North Wing in the 1680s, leading to its demolition. Yet some of the Grotto's statuary was moved to a grove in the main garden, which took the appropriately solar name of Bosquet des Bains d'Apollon, and there were many other solar echoes around the gardens. (Other themes, such as war and peace, were evident in trophies and ornamental vases.)

Louis showed the importance that he attached to the gardens in 1679 by sending Le Nôtre, who was already over sixty years old, on a tour of Italy, hitherto regarded as the acme of garden design, to cherry-pick ideas to import to Versailles. On his return, Le Nôtre worked closely with the other principal players in the king's artistic team, initially ministerial factotum Jean-Baptiste Colbert, Charles Le Brun and Jules Hardouin-Mansart. Water-engineers, most famously the Florentine Francini dynasty, played a role in the placement and functioning of fountains that from the 1660s became one of the king's special passions. The profusion, variety and height of the Versailles fountains became a thing of wonderment for all visitors.

In what became celebrated as the very archetype of the formal 'French garden' style that swept Europe thereafter,

---

* See Chapter 1 (p.27).

Le Nôtre made sure that the Versailles gardens showed Nature disciplined as a kind of mini-kingdom under Bourbon control. They were symmetrically organised around the axis provided by the Grande Allée, which divided the site. Around this, unilinear paths were set out between geometrically shaped parterres and flowerbeds where flowers were displayed to advantage behind box-border hedging and topiarised shrubs. The tight grip over nature was relaxed slightly in places—notably in the areas given over to groves or *bosquets*. These were confined modular spaces, multimedia installations combining artfully arranged vegetation with hydraulically controlled water effects, sculptures, follies and garden furniture. Although disciplined shaping and pruning were never far away, they were set in designs planned to surprise, intrigue and delight by their apparent spontaneity. The Bosquet du Labyrinthe, for example, was a maze with thirty-nine mini-fountains (it gave way to the Bosquet de la Reine in 1778). The Bosquet de la Colonnade was made up of an assemblage of Ionic columns, and the Bosquet de la Salle de Bal comprised a cunningly disposed series of waterfalls around a dance floor. From the 1680s, especially as Mansart took a more controlling hand in the design of the *bosquets*, the solar theme went into decline (as was the case in the Versailles interiors) and references became historical and naturalistic rather than mythical, allegorical or cosmological. Thus the Bosquet de l'Arc de Triomphe had a mini–triumphal arch and a cascade of fountains memorialising the king's military victories.

The Bosquet du Théâtre d'Eau, depicted by Jean Cotelle in 1688, had been created by André Le Nôtre between 1671 and 1674 and featured some of the numerous fountains associated with the Francini dynasty of water engineers. It could serve as an open-air theatre. It was destroyed and replaced by a *bosquet* less demanding of water supply in the 1770s.

Many visitors were also forcefully struck by the profusion and quality of the statues located in the gardens, within the *bosquets* and without. More than a hundred sculptures, ranging from antique specimens to examples from the very finest contemporary artists, and fashioned in stone, iron, lead and other media, they made (and make) the gardens a huge open-air sculpture museum. Although many were free-standing, they often formed an integral part of the water features and *bosquets*. From the Hall of Mirrors, for example, the visitor looked down along the Grande Allée towards the famous Bassin de Latone, a complex water feature with dozens of sculptures around the central figure of Latona, daughter of Apollo. Beyond, the eye tracks along a unilinear lawn (the Grand Tapis) to the line of the Grand Canal. Just in front of this lies the Bassin d'Apollon with Apollo on his chariot marking the rising of the sun.

The king's fondness for the Versailles gardens was signalled by the fact that between 1689 and 1705 he wrote no fewer than six versions of a personal guide to them, the *Manière de montrer les jardins de Versailles*.[5] He visited them almost daily and, when gout restricted his mobility in the 1680s, had a little wheelchair specially constructed. He seemed quite as exercised by what his visitors thought of the gardens as by their views of the palace itself. The guidebook included no invitations to linger or to daydream, and permitted no games, picnics or fishing trips. Visitors were there to be impressed and to admire: out of obedience to the king's command, therefore, their progress around the gardens was to be brisk, disciplined and respectful.

The spectacle that visitors witnessed was designed to mark the king's mastery and display of Culture as well as Nature in all their richness and superabundance. The range of works of artistic genius from the modern as well as the ancient world, in a dazzling array of forms and media, seemed to endeavour to recapitulate and condense western culture within a single site. Nature, too, was commanded by human ingenuity into miraculous forms. Water—so problematic a presence at Versailles, as we have seen*—had been managed and channelled so that brilliant water features could decorate the site. The earth had been reshaped by human heft into geometrical regularity. The menagerie contained a copious collection of fauna from around the globe—ostrich, flamingo, elephant, camel, lion, parrot, gazelle (a rhinoceros would follow in the eighteenth century). Parterres displayed plants and shrubs gathered from across France (Norman daffodils, Provençal roses, Languedocian maples), while the new Orangerie designed by Mansart in 1686 to replace Le Vau's earlier model acclimatised exotic fruits from around the world (incidentally displaying the reach of French global commerce), as well as the largest collection of orange trees in Europe, 2,000 in all. And the *Potager du Roi* contrived to provide the king with figs in springtime and strawberries at Christmas. Nature seemed to genuflect to the Bourbon will.

---

* See above, Chapter 1, p. 30.

THE PASSING OF AN ERA

As time went on, signs appeared that Louis was tiring of his self-assigned task of ceaseless publicity, and of the constant stream of gawping visitors it brought to his palace and grounds. In 1685 he closed the gardens to public access, reopening them only in 1704.* Already in 1679—even before the court's formal relocation to Versailles—he had started work on a major new project, the building of a chateau at Marly, which was intended as a more relaxed retreat for him and a select group of his closest courtiers. Situated towards the perimeter of the Grand Parc, Marly was over five miles distant from the palace. Even closer at hand was the blue-tiled 'porcelain' Trianon which Louis had designed in 1670 as a kind of summer house. In 1687–8 Mansart was commissioned to raze it and to create a much more splendid structure on the site. This was the Marble Trianon (Trianon de marbre), which became known as the Grand Trianon. Louis devoted a huge amount of attention to its superb gardens, which became famous for their flower displays.

The new Trianon was not decorated quite as sumptuously as one might have anticipated. There was a new emphasis on lightness, notably through the use of mirrors and white paint, which was both a financial and an aesthetic choice. The heavy, sumptuous, polychromatic look of early Versailles was

---

* It is worth noting that travel accounts suggest that the order was only fitfully carried out. Jeroen Duindam, *Vienna and Versailles: The Courts of Europe's Dynastic Rivals, 1550–1780* (Cambridge, 2003), p. 167.

coming to be seen as *dépassé*. In addition, the royal treasury was feeling the pinch. To the expenditure on the main house and garden, and then on Marly and the Trianon, were added the huge demands of European warfare. The extensive make-over of the palace and its gardens had been facilitated by the decade of peace between 1679 and 1688. But the outbreak of the War of the League of Augsburg (1688) inaugurated an international landscape that would remain sombre for France right through to Louis's death in 1715. Peace in 1697 would be followed by the ruinously expensive War of the Spanish Succession (1701–14). Moreover, meteorological disasters in 1693–4 and 1709–10 (the 1709 winter was so cold that wine froze in glasses, ink on pens and birds to boughs) produced near-famine conditions throughout the country, massively reducing the tax take. With warfare increasingly tying the king's hands, plans for new projects were put on hold and the buildings budget for Versailles was severely reduced. In 1689, as much out of financial desperation as from national solidarity, the king despatched all his palace silverware from Versailles to be melted down for coin.

In these last decades of Louis's reign there were still moments when the financial vice relaxed enough for the king to envisage substantial initiatives. Changes to the king's apartment included the creation—partly out of his former bedroom—of a large antechamber, the Salon de l'Œil de Boeuf (named after the bulls-eye shape of its main window). This allowed the king's bedroom, the Chambre du Roi, to be relocated in 1701 to the exact centre of the first-floor apart-

Louis XIV's final chapel, completed in 1710, marked a stylistic transition away from sumptuous polychromatic splendour to an elegant and more discreet whiteness, that presaged the decorative trends of the later eighteenth century.

ment in what had formerly been his dressing room. The most significant structural change in this period was the decision to complete the construction of the chapel. Plans had been readied by Mansart in 1687, but it was only consecrated in 1710, two years after Mansart's death. This huge structure was the fifth chapel in the palace's brief history—and was to be its last. No time or money was available to fill the site of the old chapel with a planned Salon d'Hercule.

It was not only financial constraints that led to a fading of the splendours of the palace. The change of mood was also linked to Louis's own temperament and disposition. Following the death of Queen Marie-Thérèse in 1683, his almost immediate secret marriage to Madame de Maintenon—the former nanny to his illegitimate children with Madame de Montespan—was critical in this respect. She encouraged the king towards domestic calm and sober piety and away from profligate expenditure, sexual adventures and court gaiety. The festive schedule dwindled, partly also owing to the king's frequent extended absences from the palace. 'The king doesn't seem to like Versailles as once he did,' remarked one courtier in 1698. 'Every Tuesday he goes to Marly or Meudon and sometimes to the Trianon, which is only at the end of the garden, and he only returns on Saturday evening.'[6] In the last years of his reign, Louis was spending up to half of his time in Marly.

Louis was still able to push the boat out occasionally— the reception for an envoy of the Shah of Persia in February 1715 saw him staggering under the weight of a gold costume studded with over 12 million livres' worth of diamonds. But courtiers sensed that his heart had not been in it for some time: court routines were becoming exceptional rather than quotidian, as Louis lingered elsewhere. Versailles seemed to be losing its charm—and to a degree its *raison d'être*.

A terrible wave of mortality within the royal family in the last years of the king's reign added to the air of melancholy. The king lost successively and in short order no fewer than three Dauphins: his son Louis (1711), his grandson, the duc de Bourgogne (whose wife also died around the same time, 1712) and his great-grandson, the duc de Bretagne (1712). The only heir left standing was another great-grandson, the infant duc d'Anjou, born in 1710.

3

CONTINUING

The Bourbon Succession (1715–1789)

HE DEATH OF LOUIS XIV IN 1715 BROUGHT to the throne his only surviving offspring and great-grandson, the five-year-old duc d'Anjou—frail survivor of a bout of measles that carried off his parents and his older brother in a matter of months—who took the title of Louis XV. Power passed almost at once to the ex-king's least-favourite nephew, the *bon vivant* reprobate Philippe II, duc d'Orléans, who became Regent for the infant king. On his deathbed, Louis XIV had counselled that the child should live away from Versailles to protect his health—there was a general suspicion that the unhealthiness of the site had been linked to the deaths over the previous few years of many of his closest relatives. The old king had proposed Vincennes, but Orléans thought otherwise, and, in

September 1715, the whole court and government shipped out of Versailles to Paris. The young king took up residence in the Tuileries Palace, while Orléans preferred to stay in his own dwelling, the Palais-Royal.

Versailles was so closely and inextricably connected with 'Louis the Great' that this wilful removal from his palace cast doubt on whether it would ever again be the principal residence of his Bourbon successors. Pending a decision, the palace, deprived of governmental and court personnel, remained an empty shell. The palace's governor took advantage of the situation to undertake a Herculean cleaning operation and also ensured that the fountains in the grounds played at regular intervals to attract sightseers. When Czar Peter the Great of Russia visited in 1717 he looked avidly around the palace and gardens with little by way of supervision or diplomatic escort.

In Paris the growing Louis XV still clearly nurtured nostalgic feelings for the house where he was born. In June 1722 the twelve-year-old monarch took the decision to move court and government back to Versailles. On arriving at the palace, after visiting the chapel, the boy romped excitedly around palace and gardens, leaving his followers panting in his wake, before he collapsed in a heap on the parquet flooring of the Hall of Mirrors to admire the ceiling paintings of Charles Le Brun representing the illustrious career of Louis XIV. This final gesture was a revealing augury for the future. The young king saw it as his mission to command Versailles to wake, Sleeping Beauty–like, from its slumbers and to stay true to the spirit of its founder.

CLOSING AN ERA, CONTINUING TRADITIONS

'Louis XIV was still there,' was the astonished reaction of the minor Breton nobleman and future Romantic poet François-René de Chateaubriand, who was presented to King Louis XVI at Versailles in 1786.[1] If the old king's spirit seemed still to hover over the royal court on the eve of the Revolution, this was hardly by accident. Both Louis XV and, from 1774, his successor Louis XVI showed punctilious respect for the founder of Versailles and all his works. Throughout the six decades of Louis XV's reign the great clock on the palace's *cour de marbre* was made to show the exact moment that Louis XIV had died. Louis XV's palace ran on Louis XIV-time.*

Early in his reign Louis XV formally outlined his intentions with the words, 'I wish to follow in everything the example of the late king, my great-grandfather,'[2] a lapidary statement that also proved a programme for action—or inaction. Over his long reign he changed very little in the basic structure of the site. Versailles was certainly not set in aspic: the new king had a passion for building and spent hours poring over architectural drawings and discussing them with his architects, and the palace endlessly buzzed with building work. Yet this was only advanced tinkering and more radical plans stayed on paper. The main mark he left on the palace took the form of three projects, all of which were directly inspired by Louis XIV. Firstly he undertook the completion of the Salon

---

* The clock changed in 1774 to the time when Louis XV had died and remained like this down to the Revolution.

Maurice Quentin de La Tour's portrait of Louis XV as military commander captures the king's confidently saturnine good looks.

d'Hercule, which was located in the space formerly occupied by the chapel. Louis XIV had started the project in 1712 and work resumed in the early 1720s. By the time it was finished it was viewed as the most magnificently appointed reception room in the whole palace, with fine marble decorations matched by François Le Moyne's superbly detailed ceiling and a huge Veronese canvas on one wall (where it can still be seen). The room was formally inaugurated in 1739 by the marriage of the king's daughter Elisabeth to the Spanish royal heir.

Louis was as respectful of his predecessor's gardens as he was of his palace. His second significant achievement, the Bassin de Neptune—the most elaborate and brilliant combination of aquatic sculpture and fountain in the whole estate—was again essentially finishing work initiated by Louis XIV in the 1680s. Louis had a bigger task with the third project, namely the construction of an opera house. Louis XIV had adored opera and ballet and only the impact of warfare had prevented his creating an opera house in the late 1680s. Later hostilities—notably the War of the Austrian Succession (1740–48) and the Seven Years War (1756–63)—would delay Louis XV's plans also, but building finally got under way in 1768. Designed by Premier Architect Ange-Jacques Gabriel,* and constructed in a rush for the marriage in 1770 of Louis's grandson and heir, the duc de Berry, the future Louis XVI, with the Austrian princess Marie Antoinette, Gabriel's construction was generally regarded as the finest opera house in Europe.

Gabriel worked hard in the last years of Louis's reign to overcome the king's entrenched reverence for the Versailles of his predecessor. In particular, he wished to modernise the palace exterior facing the town in line with contemporary, neoclassical tastes, which would bring it closer in style to the

---

* Ange-Jacques Gabriel (1698–1782) followed his father Jacques Gabriel into the post of *Premier Architecte du Roi* in 1742.

garden façade. The king funded the construction of the new ministerial offices for War and Foreign Affairs between 1759 and 1762 in this style—though both were located in the town. By the end of his life Louis had assented to Gabriel's plans for the makeover of the palace's frontage, too, but it was too late in the day to lead to a complete transformation. Work began in 1771, but by the time of Louis's death in 1774 only a new façade for the northern, governmental wing (renamed the Gabriel Wing in the architect's honour) had been finished.

Louis's reluctance to change the public face of Louis XIV's Versailles was matched by his dogged maintenance of court traditions that Louis had sanctified. Generally speaking, etiquette was more rigidly followed under Louis XV than it had been under Louis XIV. The bedroom ritual of rising and retiring was retained, as were the other choreographed acts of state. At the *grand couvert*, the public widely admired the king's deft handling of a boiled egg, as he removed its top by a single, stage-managed strike with his fork.[3] Despite its continuing air of exclusiveness, the palace remained, in line with the constitutional adage about the accessibility of the ruler, wide open to the general public too—to the extent that beggars were sometimes found wandering around bedrooms. In 1757 a deranged domestic servant, Robert-François Damiens,* was able to get close enough to the king to stab him as he was stepping into his carriage (the wound proved only slight).

---

* Damiens would be tortured and savagely executed for his attack on Louis XV, outraging Enlightenment opinion.

While Louis XV revered the grandeur and customary practices of monarchy established by his great-grandfather, one specific facet of his character differentiated him markedly from his predecessor. This was his deep-dyed desire to live a life of his own for at least some of the time. Louis XIV had, as we have seen, regarded himself as in a sense 'belonging' to his people,* and chose to conduct his life in and for the public, making ostentatious state rituals of the most banal of individual occurrences, and blurring the line between public and private acts. Yet if La Bruyère had maintained that a king of France could have anything he liked except a private life, Louis XV proved him wrong.†

A consistent thread throughout Louis XV's reign was his determination to carve out a private space for himself. Madame de Ventadour, his childhood nanny, remarked of his feeling of 'relief at not having to play the king all the time'.4 He retained a melancholic disposition—in part the inevitable emotional legacy of his losing so many of those he loved in the first few years of his life. But he was neither monk nor hermit, and relished close and friendly relations with a select group of those he trusted. Above all, he didn't want to live simply by and for the public.

This binary cast of mind, which valued privacy as much as publicity, had an impact on the architecture, material culture and quotidian routines of Versailles life. One of its

---

* See Chapter 2 (p. 41).
† Ibid.

The great ceremonial bedroom that Louis XIV had created at the centre of the palace in 1701 was rebarbatively glacial and from 1738, Louis XV created a new more intimate space where he slept—passing into the ceremonial bedroom for the day's ceremonies.

most distinctive expressions was Louis's move to create living quarters for himself at the heart of the palace that distanced him from court rituals and official state business. Louis XIV's Grands Appartements were kept pristine and intact, but from the late 1730s Louis XV devoted his energies to creating an inner sanctum within a private suite of rooms in which he could largely shut himself off.

Louis XIV had managed to spend at least some time in his private quarters, free from the attentions of courtiers. Under both Louis XV and Louis XVI, these rooms swelled in dimension to become sizeable suites, little houses even, extending over several floors. Both men spent a much greater proportion of their time there. They granted admittance to the inner sanctum to only a very few distinguished visitors and some favoured courtiers. Many of the masterpieces in the royal collections—notably Leonardo da Vinci's *Mona Lisa*— were located here, and Louis XV also boasted collections of curiosities and of coins and medals, plus a personal library and study (the king was 'always writing', the Marquis d'Argenson claimed),[5] a map room, chemistry and physics laboratory, a kitchen (he enjoyed cooking) and a lathe for wood- and ivory-carving. If we remain less knowledgeable about these rooms than about any part of the palace, this is largely because so few people ever went there—and indeed hardly anyone suspected their existence. A tell-tale sign of expansion, however, was Louis's construction of additional rooms above the level of the palace frontage, including an observatory and access to a terrace leading out over the Hall of Mirrors where he liked to take night walks. Louis XVI inherited this suite and made changes to it in line with his own interests, including creating a locksmith workshop.

These changes were linked to emergent notions of elegance, intimacy and comfort to which Louis XV proved keenly attached. He seems to have felt less at home in the majestic, multi-purpose rooms of Versailles than in his private suite where he developed a new aesthetic in line with ideas gaining traction among Parisian elites, notably the lighter, airier, more curvaceous forms of the rococo. Lower ceilings, wall spaces that were less vast, busy ornamentation and *boiseries**

showcasing white with gold detail were especially popular, while more artful illumination and space-producing mirrors were increasingly favoured. By the end of the period, wallpaper was making inroads on the dominance of tapestry wall-hangings, while the lighter Riesener† furniture increasingly pushed out the old heavy Boulle‡ pieces. The environments thus adorned showed a growing trend towards comfort: lower ceilings made rooms cosier; portable porcelain stoves gained preference over huge draughty chimney hearths; screens and blinds controlled light and kept prying eyes at bay; food trolleys and dumbwaiters (*tables volantes*) were preferred to the heavy apparatus of food preparation and presentation; and servant bells were installed to reduce the need for constant staff presence.

A new concern with hygiene made itself felt as part of this trend towards greater comfort. Tales of the abysmal levels of sanitation at Versailles continue to abound, their persistence encouraged by the gutting of the living quarters of the court

---

* Ornate and intricately carved wood panelling.

† Jean-Henri Riesener (1734–1806) was a royal cabinet-maker (*ébéniste du roi*), whose furniture typified the neoclassicism of the era of Louis XVI.

‡ See footnote on p. 39.

nobility in the mid-nineteenth century,* which has led historians to lose sight of hygienic improvements. Running in sordid counterpoint to the palace's reputation for splendour and magnificence, the myth has highlighted the omnipresence of insanitary practices in Louis XIV's Versailles: the absence of baths; the king receiving visitors seated on his close-stool; the contents of chamber pots hurled out of windows on to passing pedestrians; urination in corridors and alcoves; and so on.

Some of these practices continued right through to 1789. Marie Antoinette was said to have received the defenestrated contents of a chamber pot on one occasion. The redolent smell of urine in public places around the palace would be remarked on in Proustian tones by courtiers returning there after the Revolutionary and Napoleonic periods.[6] Of course, any institution which regularly attracted thousands of public visitors on a regular basis was destined to suffer in this respect before the invention of public conveniences in the nineteenth-century city. But it does appear that shifting notions of personal cleanliness and bodily comfort were transforming behaviour as the eighteenth century progressed, and Louis XV himself was in the vanguard of such change. His private suite contained at one time or another no fewer than seven bathrooms, and they were furnished not only with copper baths but also with *chaises anglaises* (water closets). Louis also improved the palace's sewer system, so that its underground pipes deposited rubbish and faecal matter well away from the living quarters.

---

* See Appendix, pp. 177–178.

Another adjunct to bodily hygiene that became increasingly popular across this period was the bidet; on the eve of the Revolution even royal guardsmen possessed them.

Louis XV's private suite allowed him to get on with the business of state in peace, but it also provided a more informal setting in which he could spend time with family members. Although he showed affection for his children, the king excluded Queen Marie Leczinska from all family get-togethers. Louis had married the Polish princess in 1725 and she bore him nine children over the following twelve years. He renovated the Queen's Apartments to provide more spacious living space for their growing family. But in time, the queen's apartments cut her off from her husband. Relations between them cooled rapidly from the late 1730s, and the two increasingly saw each other only on public court occasions. Marie found solace in piety and in music—she sponsored the finest musicians in the land—Louis, in the arms of other women. From 1745 he made one of his many lovers, Madame de Pompadour, official mistress or *maîtresse en titre*—a role that had not been seen at court since the Montespan and Maintenon era of the late 1670s and 1680s. After a spell in the palace attics (quarters less Spartan than they sound), Pompadour was given rooms on the ground floor of the main block of the palace, with a connecting staircase to the king's apartment. She would remain the king's official mistress until her death in 1764. Long before this her sexual relations with the king had ceased and, like the queen, she had to accept Louis's indulgence in a series of mistresses. These were drawn now more from commoner than aristocratic stock, and assignations often took place outside the palace in a private residence in the town, the so-called Parc aux Cerfs. His affairs became less frequent over time, but did not cease—even after 1768 when Louis took the courtesan Madame du Barry as his new *maîtresse en titre*.

KINGS ON THE MOVE AND OUT OF REACH

Keeping the king happy by keeping him constantly engaged and interested was the main reason for Madame de Pompadour's longevity in Louis's favours. She appears from the start to have made a shrewd appraisal of the king's melancholic disposition and his need for a life away from the public glare. For nearly two decades she worked tirelessly to share his interests and to make him happy in a constant round of diversions. She knew, courtiers remarked, how to cheer up the morose monarch and keep his boredom at bay. She organised private theatrical performances, in which princes of the blood competed with high aristocrats for the best roles. She sponsored musical events—the infant Mozart played in her and the king's presence; she showed interest in Louis's obsession with architecture; she encouraged his patronage of the fine arts. Porcelain was a particular shared passion: she was partly responsible for the king's establishing the state-owned Sèvres porcelain manufactory, situated a stone's throw from her favoured Bellevue country residence near Meudon. Each year, she and Louis held an auction of the new Sèvres crockery for the courtiers.

This contrived whirligig of activity entailed constant mobility. In one way, Louis XV was a sedentary monarch compared to his predecessors: apart from a fortnight's visit to Reims for his coronation in 1722, a couple of campaigning seasons on the Flanders front in 1744–5, and a swift, week-long visit to Normandy in 1751, he never left the Paris/Versailles region. Yet within these circumscribed bounds, he was markedly itinerant. Like Louis XIV he made regular seasonal visits to his palaces at Compiègne in summer and Fontainebleau in autumn, in each of which some degree of ceremonial life was upheld. What was new about this pattern of royal displacement was the amount of time he spent at smaller chateaux and other residences, where he shut himself off from public view and from the company of more than a handful of courtiers. Evident before 1745, this trait was reinforced by Madame de Pompadour: as well as using royal residences at Choisy, Meudon and La Muette, Louis was also a frequent visitor to the country houses that Madame de Pompadour acquired.

In the Versailles estate, Louis overhauled the Grand Trianon as a private retreat. After neglecting it completely, he suddenly—again at Pompadour's prompting—saw its potential. Louis made no structural changes to the Grand Trianon, though in the 1750s he created a set of botanical gardens and greenhouses in its park. After 1763, however, he instructed Premier Architect Gabriel to build an entirely new residence on the site of these gardens, which became known as the Petit Trianon. A masterpiece in the neoclassical style, completed in

1768, the Petit Trianon would be enjoyed not by Pompadour, who died in 1764, but rather by Madame du Barry (and later by Queen Marie Antoinette).

Louis XV's hypermobile schedule meant that he tended to be more absent from than present at the actual Palace of Versailles: he spent the night there only fifty-two times in 1750 and sixty-three times in 1751. Later in his reign he was a little less itinerant, but even so he rarely spent half the week fulfilling his formal ceremonial duties in the palace. Versailles was still a showcase of the glory of the Bourbon monarchy, but for much of the time the Bourbon monarch had left the building.

Louis's disdain for places outside his charmed circle of favoured residences extended to an indifference towards France's capital city (and the city of his boyhood). A fortnight spent in Paris in 1744—during which, in a rare moment of enthusiasm, Parisians dubbed him 'the Well-Beloved' ('*le Bien-Aimé*')—was the last time he stayed there overnight. Thereafter he kept his visits to a minimum—maybe one or two trips a year on average for ceremonial events. Parisians had always set great store by the accessibility of their king—public entry to Versailles and its grounds was a significant token of this attachment. Yet this counted for very little given that Louis XV had so massively diminished his physical presence there. Under Louis XIV, Parisians regretted that the king was based in Versailles rather than in Paris; under Louis XV, they grew irritated that the king was generally *not* in Versailles—and when he was, he was more often than not hidden away at the Trianon or in the comfort of his private apartments.

THE MARIE ANTOINETTE MOMENT

In 1774 Louis XV died in his bed at Versailles, as his predecessor had done. Few could fault the strength of his attachment to the traditions that Louis XIV had created. And there was much about Versailles in 1774 that remained fully in keeping with Louis XIV's vision. Louis XV's performances of majesty were convincing and effective: the duc de Lévis commended his monarch for 'his exact observance of court civilities, [and] the maintenance of ancient forms and of the paraphernalia which surround the throne'.[7] Versailles continued to be seen, at home and abroad, as the most magnificent royal court in Europe, a fitting symbol for a France still generally regarded as Europe's 'Great Nation'. Versailles remained synonymous with royal style, protocol and *éclat*: as the Marquise de La Tour du Pin noted, its name 'resonated like a magic spell' at all levels of French society'.[8] Tourists from new worlds and old, equipped with guidebooks in numerous languages, beat a path there to ogle and admire. The court's support system, namely the town of Versailles, was prospering, too, and had grown to some 70,000 souls by 1789, making it one of France's largest conurbations.

By the time of his death, however, Louis XV had become personally unpopular, lurid tales of his sexual dissipation circulating widely. One of the first acts of his grandson-successor Louis XVI was to eradicate all signs of the king's mistresses and sex life. This pledge of a new start was widely and warmly welcomed. But it was not long before enthusiasm tailed off. Louis XVI's dedication to the idea of Louis XIV's Versailles was as staunch as his predecessor's. In any case, he lacked the funds to do more than tinker and plan ahead. As it turned out, for many of his fifteen years as ruler in Versailles, he was caught up in matters of foreign policy, especially relating to the American War of Independence (1776–83). The overseas military adventures of his predecessors had built up the national debt to dizzying proportions, and Louis XVI reaped the whirlwind they had sown. Overall, France was losing out to Britain in a global commercial and colonial struggle. The American colonists' defeat of Britain, therefore, achieved with the assistance of French arms and materiel, was a heartening success for France; the peace ending the war was signed at Versailles in 1783. The downside of military victory, however, was the staggering cost of the war. By the 1780s around half of French government outgoings were on the armed forces and on servicing debts run up in wars fought over the previous century. Court expenditure, in contrast, hovered around 5 per cent annually.

The war and its financial aftermath left little time or money for anything substantial to be achieved at the palace. Louis undertook a complete overhaul of tree cover in the palace gardens—the trees planted under Louis XIV were now in bad shape. But there was no mood for radical change: 'we could not respect too much,' it was noted as the work of replanting trees got under way, 'everything that was done under the reign of Louis XIV.[9] Within the palace Louis implemented a structural change to his private apartments that revealed much about his character: this was the creation of a special corridor—known as the *passage du roi*; this allowed him to move discreetly from his own suite of rooms to and from the queen's apartments without passing through a series of public rooms where he might encounter groups of nudging and winking courtiers.

As this sexual timidity suggests, Louis XVI was excessively nervous and retiring, characteristics which made him ill-suited for the public role that Versailles historically demanded. Louis XV had proved constitutionally incapable of matching Louis XIV's ability to live his daily life in public, yet he knew how to 'play king' (as his nanny had put it) when it was necessary.* But Louis XVI failed both tests: he could neither feel confident of his own worthiness for a public role, nor play-act his way convincingly through royal rituals specifically designed for Versailles. While professing—like his predecessor—absolute fidelity to the traditions established by Louis XIV, he simply went through the motions with the *lever*, the *coucher* and the rest. Awkward and flat-footed, he exuded the impression that he would rather be anywhere else.

As Louis XV had done, Louis XVI reduced his formal presence in Versailles by circling ceaselessly around royal palaces and country houses in the Île-de-France. He nurtured great plans for Versailles—he purchased residences at

---

* See Chapter 3 (p. 79).

Saint-Cloud and Rambouillet where he planned to stay while it was given a complete overhaul. But they were never realised. In the year of his accession, he passed more nights away from Versailles than he spent in the palace. He emulated the habits of his predecessors by venturing into his capital city only for ceremonial occasions. His queen visited Paris more frequently, to attend the opera. Louis left the Île-de-France on just three occasions: once in 1775 to Reims for his coronation, again in 1786 to visit Cherbourg for the ceremonial opening of new port facilities, and then finally in 1791 as he fled Paris to escape the clutches of the Revolution, only to be stopped near the eastern frontier at Varennes.*

Louis XVI's reign also continued the trend towards a more 'privatised' form of life. More time and attention were devoted to improvements in the royal couple's private living arrangements than in the public buildings. Queen Marie Antoinette played the leading role in this. A new vision of Versailles seemed to impose itself on the palace—or rather in its margins, since life went on drably and intermittently in the main buildings as if to show that the old Louis XIV clockwork still functioned. On arriving from the Austrian court in 1770, this daughter of Holy Roman Empress Maria Teresa had seemed attracted by the splendour and beauty of Versailles. Her taste for fashion made her something of a celebrity, and her activities were enthusiastically reported in the pages of the burgeoning popular press. The honeymoon did not last,

* See Chapter 5 (p. 113).

however. Marie Antoinette soon found court protocol to be overly formal and mind-numbingly dull; furthermore, she was treated with condescension and contempt by anti-Austrian factions within the court. Her instinct was to turn away from the public life of the court—and also from her husband, to a certain degree—and to fashion a private world of style and luxury. She worked with the neoclassical architect-designer Richard Mique to recreate entirely the environment in which she lived.

Their earliest projects were focused on the queen's suite of rooms in the palace, which were splendidly redesigned. But it was in their renovation of the Petit Trianon that Marie Antoinette and Mique left their most indelible mark. Louis had made Marie Antoinette a gift of the Petit Trianon on his accession to the throne, and she proceeded to treat the estate as her personal domain, scandalizing court opinion by having her servants wear her own livery and issuing instructions headed 'By Order of the Queen'. It was said that even the king had to ask her permission to visit (and he never spent the night there with her). Marie Antoinette found in the Petit Trianon a safe haven in which she could be herself with little regard for her royal duties. With Mique's help, she experimented with new projects and new tastes. While Louis retained the Le Nôtrian formality of the palace gardens, at the Trianon his queen replaced Louis XV's beloved botanical gardens with a so-called 'Anglo-Chinese' landscape garden; in keeping with the contemporary vogue of sensibility towards nature, it was ornamented by a grotto, a belvedere with accompanying rocky waterfall feature

The thatched and decorative watermill was one of the most attractive
features of Marie-Antoinette's 'hamlet'. A stream did turn the water
wheel, but too slowly for it ever to function as a mill.

inspired by Hubert Robert,* and a soulful monument to love.
(The queen also employed Robert to reimagine the Bosquet
des Bains d'Apollon in the main Versailles gardens in what was
a strikingly pre-Romantic statement.) She and Mique went on

* Hubert Robert (1733–1808) was best known as a painter of landscapes and ruins,
with what is often seen as a pre-Romantic sensibility. In royal service he also
extended his work into garden design.

The Bosquet of the Bains d'Apollon (the Baths of Apollo) was designed
by the painter and landscape designer Hubert Robert between 1778 and
1781. The statues at the centre had once been housed in the old grotto of
Tethys. Robert placed them, unusually for Versailles, within a fashionably
pre-Romantic English garden style setting.

to extend the Petit Trianon estate so as to create a hamlet (the
Hameau de la reine). Besides a working farm with a domestic menagerie, this included a range of buildings both rustic
(mill, fishpond, dovecote, chicken-run) and urbane (billiard

room, gambling salon, dining room). One of her courtier-critics remarked: '*C'est à grand frais qu'on s'est attaché à donner au hameau de la Reine l'aspect d'un lieu pauvre*' ('Giving the Hameau de la Reine the appearance of an impoverished spot has been very costly').[10]

Money was funnelled into the queen's fantasy world, while essential work on the main body of the chateau was endlessly deferred. The approach from the town side in particular gave a depressing impression of neglect: 'a great part of the front next the town . . . with its shabby, half-brick walls and broken windows' offered a spectacle of advanced disrepair, Benjamin Franklin observed in 1767.[11]

Since its inception, the Versailles project had been centred on the person of the king; it depended on his playing the role set out by Louis XIV and working hard to maintain the unique allure of the palace and its traditions. By 1789, however, Louis XVI seemed to be bringing a new level of dysfunctionality to the role, as court life was thrown out of gear by the impact of his queen.

4

LIVING

Styles of Versailles life

ENIZENS OF VERSAILLES OFTEN SPOKE OF their living in '*ce pays-ci*'—a faintly propri-etorial, in-group way of referring to their social world. Outsiders might regard such individuals as '*gens de la cour*' ('court people'), indicating that, regardless of exact rank, being attached to and frequenting Versailles was the basis of their social identity. Ways of speaking and acting, of walking and talking, of dressing and addressing were different in 'this land' (*ce pays-ci*), this little world, from what the rest of humanity experienced. One never spoke of 'gifts' ('*dons*') in court society, for example, only 'presents' ('*cadeaux*'); one drank not 'champagne' but '*vin de champagne*'; one elided the 'c' at the end of certain words ('*sac*', meaning 'bag', was thus pro-nounced '*sa*') and inserted a lazy 'z' in odd places ('*avant hier*' meaning 'the day before yesterday', became '*avant z'hier*'); one knew a dozen ways of nodding, bowing and showing respect; women deployed a special sliding walk on Versailles parquets which involved not lifting their feet, so as to avoid treading on the trains of other court ladies. The sense of pampered exclusivity and entitlement which resulted is summed up by the celebrated words of Talleyrand, the aristocratic archbishop (and future Revolutionary and Napoleonic foreign minister): '*Qui n'a pas vécu dans les années voisines de 1789 ne sait pas ce que c'est que la douceur de vivre*' ('Whoever was not alive around 1789 simply does not know the pleasure of living').[1]

Yet life at Versailles had two sides to it. What Talleyrand's words failed to note is that the enviable *douceur de vivre* was highly dependent on the efforts of others. Alongside the world of king and courtiers was a sprawling and heterogeneous service class that constructed the material environment and ensured the smooth running of the myriad activities of court life. The lives of courtiers and of the human infrastructure that made the court tick were inextricably intertwined. Versailles was not just a palace and a set of buildings, then, but a distinctive style of life—and that style of life floated on top of a world of service and labour. Moreover, by 1789, its *douceur* seemed to be coming under threat.

BEING KING IN 'CE PAYS-CI'

The rules that '*gens de la cour*' were obliged to follow in '*ce pays-ci*' had been created by Louis XIV, their king and master.

The original choice of the site of the palace may have been his father's, and, in creating the material and social world of Versailles, he borrowed extensively from other cultural models and collaborated extensively, but in essence the material and social world of Versailles was Louis XIV's own work. He called the tune—as did his successors. Yet Louis XIV was probably the only one of the six monarchs to inhabit the palace (five of them named Louis, in fact) who wholeheartedly relished the experience. Louis XIII, who founded the site and built the embryonic chateau, conceived it as a refuge and retreat from the court rather than its home. At the other extreme, Louis XV and Louis XVI accepted the Versailles that Louis XIV had created and were loyal to its ways—but only managed to tolerate the place by regularly shutting themselves away from its demands. Louis XVI's heir ('Louis XVII') died in a revolutionary prison, and both Louis XVIII and Charles X (Louis XVI's brothers and post-Revolutionary, post-Napoleonic successors), who had lived in Versailles as the comtes de Provence and d'Artois up to 1789, did not have the political will to reinhabit the palace after 1815.*

Louis XIV consciously developed the court as a political and diplomatic statement and as a means of producing social harmony after the troubles of the Fronde at the beginning of his reign. Once he had settled on the palace as home for his court and government, his strategy was to use scale and splendour as a means of dazzling his subjects and monarchical

---

* See Chapter 5 (p. 121).

rivals into acceptance of his greatness. His wager was that the very visibility of the glories of the site—maintained by a policy of accessibility to all his subjects—would benefit and stabilise his regime.

It was not simply greatness that was on show at Versailles; it was *French* greatness. Despite some borrowings from Italian court culture, the artistic glories of the palace were largely home-produced. Colbert, Le Vau, Mansart, Le Nôtre and Le Brun provided the framework within which French painters, sculptors, decorative artists and skilled artisans displayed their wares, massively elevating the esteem in which French art was held across Europe. Almost every French artist of eminence alive in the last 150 years of the *ancien régime* contributed to Versailles in some way, their names too numerous to list. But Versailles also showcased some of the greatest examples of the decorative arts of the period by anonymous or little-known artisans providing glass from Saint-Gobain, Savonnerie carpets, Gobelins tapestries, marble from quarries across the country, elegant furniture from Paris cabinet-makers, Sèvres porcelain—and, latterly, fancy wallpapers and Paris dress fashions. Being surrounded by his own commissions reflected further glory on the king. Italian ambassador Primi Visconti noted an actorly quality in Louis XIV's self-presentation that expressed itself as performing 'as though he were on the stage'.[2] Versailles was the theatre of Louis XIV's majesty and cultural primacy.

The brilliance of the art and architecture of Versailles was plain enough to those who visited the palace—but it was also endlessly thematised in the different forms of royal propaganda in which Louis and his officials engaged. The print media reproduced and diffused a plethora of images of the palace, its gardens and artworks and the doings of the court. Coins and medals served as propaganda tools for king and palace alike. Thus the *idea* of Versailles and its wonders inveigled its way into the consciousness of ordinary French men and women who never ventured near it. The site itself developed as a tourist location, drawing visitors from across the Île-de-France.

Versailles was also Louis XIV's private home, but the king's private life was always subsumed under his public role—and indeed he made intimate details of his personal life into ritualised public performances. The schedule of his day was followed by the court as a whole; courtiers, on his orders and under his surveillance, observed pervasive ceremonial rituals. The king's rising from and retiring to his bed in the Chambre du Roi—the *lever* at around 8 a.m. and the *coucher*, normally at around 10.30 p.m. or later—were the subject of complex mini-ceremonies involving scores of courtiers and palace servants. These individuals, numbering up to a hundred, entered the royal bedroom from the antechamber—after 1701, this was the Salon de l'Œil-de-Bœuf. The king would then pass into the room symmetrically placed on the other side of his bedchamber, the Salle du Conseil. Here he would spend the morning working on affairs of state, with a changing cast of ministers and other officials. At 12.30 p.m., or sometimes earlier, the king attended chapel for Mass, passing through the Hall of Mirrors, where large groups were usually gathered, conversing and gossiping—and awaiting the royal presence.*

The king's meals were public affairs, too. He ate the so-called *petit couvert* at 1 p.m. with courtiers standing in his presence. The *souper au grand couvert* was an altogether grander and more public affair, served with gold tableware and eaten in the queen's apartments at around 10 p.m. with close members of his family in the presence of a gawking group of courtiers and members of the general public. Afternoons could be taken up with visits to the Trianon or Marly, or promenades in the palace gardens, or else with hunting.

Most elements of this daily schedule were broadly followed by Louis XIV's successors—at least when they were in the palace. They were also unwavering in their commitment to hunting; it was, after all, the sport of Bourbon kings that had brought Louis XIII to Versailles in the first place. Louis XV was attached to a particular set of hunting rituals: the so-called *botté* (booting) and *débotté* (debooting) ceremonies, which the king hosted in the Chambre du Roi and which involved punctilious observation of stylised courtesies. The forms of hunting had changed over time: Louis XIII had hunted wolves and practised falconry, but wolves had been

---

* Historians' accounts of the timing of these morning events differ. It seems that the king either went to Mass early or later in the morning and fitted his council meetings around this. See, for example, Béatrix Saule, *Versailles triomphant: une journée de Louis XIV* (Paris, 1996), pp. 62, 82; and Antoine Amarger et al., *The Hall of Mirrors: History and Restoration* (Dijon, 2007), p. 60.

killed off in the Île-de-France by the early eighteenth century, while falconry had become a colourful anachronism. Louis XIV was associated with a rise in the popularity of shooting game. In 1708 alone, 63 of the 118 days on which he hunted were spent with shooting parties, usually followed by a carriage, as his physical mobility lessened—the rest comprised 49 stag hunts, 5 falconry sessions and a single boar hunt. Louis XV hunted three days a week, and, on hunting days when female courtiers came along, he hosted a private party for them in the evening in his rooms. But he would probably be outdone in his enthusiasm by Louis XVI, who between 1775 and 1791 killed 1,274 stags.

Court life involved a range of other, more intermittently occurring but similarly ritualised, performances of royalty. These included family and court-related events such as the births, marriages and deaths of members of the royal family and official presentations of aspiring courtiers. There were religious events too, such as the touching for the 'King's Evil' (it had been believed since the Middle Ages that the reigning monarch could channel God's healing power to those suffering from scrofula, a form of tuberculosis). There were ceremonies involving the main orders of chivalry over which the king presided, as well as those relating to religious festivals like Easter. Pomp and ceremony attended the presentation of new ambassadors and—to an even greater extent—official state visits. The presentations of the Doge of Genoa (1685) and embassies from Siam (1686) and Persia (1715)—all,

A diplomatic delegation from Siam led by the statesman Kosa Pan visited
Versailles in 1686 to explore possible trade links with France. The delegation was received, exceptionally, in the Hall of Mirrors, and had to run
the gauntlet of hordes of courtiers before arriving at the far end where
the king sat, on a specially constructed dais. This sketch was by Premier
peintre Charles Le Brun for a painting he never executed.

exceptionally, hosted in the Hall of Mirrors—became legend-
ary for their sumptuousness.

Ritualised ceremony—seemingly ever-present from Louis
XIV's rising in the morning to his retiring at night—was, in
fact, relaxed under certain circumstances. These included the

moments of leisure, usually in the early evening, when the king shut himself away from his courtiers in his private rooms. In the later years of his reign he spent increasing amounts of time in the suite of Madame de Maintenon, though he did much state business there also.

In addition, Versailles enjoyed the king's organised leisure. There were afternoon promenades of various types, while evening entertainments included concerts and operatic and theatrical performances. Louis arranged weekly visits by the Comédie-Française troupe (specialising in tragedies) and the more light-hearted Comédie-Italienne. These might be incorporated within the private royal parties known as *soirées d'appartement*, which happened three times a week— normally on Mondays, Wednesdays and Thursdays—between the hours of 6 and 10 p.m.* The *soirées* took place along the enfilade of splendidly appointed ceremonial rooms of the *Grands Appartements*, extending down the northern side of the chateau and leading into the Salon de la Guerre and the Hall of Mirrors. In some rooms there was music and dancing, in others gambling and billiards; towards the far end tables were laden with the finest food and drink. On these occasions the king waived requirements of formal etiquette and seemed more relaxed in his demeanour. As he aged, Louis attended the *soirées* less frequently, but he insisted that other members of the royal family continue to do so.

---

* See Appendix 2, pp. 166–167.

Louis's diminishing commitment to courtly entertainment in his declining years was evident in the amount of time he spent in Marly. This absenteeism would be taken further by his successors. Louis XV could not get back to Versailles quickly enough in 1722, following the court's relocation to Paris during the Regency, and was assiduous in his maintenance of Louis XIV's rituals. Yet both he and Louis XVI rebalanced the public and private aspects of court life in the direction of the latter. This shift in court schedules had important consequences for the main audience for the monarch's performance of kingship at Versailles, namely his courtiers.

PLAYING THE COURTIER

> The court was magnificent to excess; nothing
> was meagre in regard to furnishings, dress,
> carriage, expenses on the table, livery and the
> number of servants. The great lords emulated
> each other in prodigious expenditure . . . [3]

The words of François Hébert, curé of the town of Versailles, written in 1686, are evidence of the extent to which France's aristocracy committed themselves to a regime of excess and splendour at Versailles. And they demonstrate Louis XIV's success in domesticating a group that at the start of his reign, in the Fronde (1648–52), had threatened to tear his kingdom apart. An important element in Louis XIV's strategy for

Versailles was that it offered the high nobility the chance to participate in its spectacle and enjoy its rewards. By basing not only his court but also the principal elements of his government in Versailles, and in encouraging the high nobles to establish themselves there, the king was centralising state patronage in a way that was genuinely new. He was at the apex of two networks that were more interlocking and more porous than is often claimed. One network comprised court and military office (and was dominated by the older 'Sword' nobility), the other government civil office (the purview of the 'Robe' nobility).*

Louis's intention was never to bring all of the kingdom's nobility to 'ce pays-ci', only the nobles that counted—princes of the royal blood, dukes and peers, the cream of the old nobility from the provinces—and to locate them on the same site as his government ministers. The total number of nobles based in the palace at any one time varied, but was probably between 6,000 and 7,000 individuals, maybe up to 3,000 of whom had lodgings in the palace and its dependencies.† The spirit of emulation mentioned by Hébert meant that anyone

---

* *Noblesse d'épée* (nobles of the sword) denotes the oldest class of French nobility, descended from the knightly class of the medieval era, who owed service to the king in exchange for ownership of landed estates; *noblesse de robe* ('nobles of the robe) refers to those nobles who owed their advancement to holding legal or administrative positions.

† Historians' estimates on numbers vary, sometimes quite wildly. I have followed Matthieu da Vinha, an authoritative source, who suggests 7,000 *logeants*: see his *Le Versailles de Louis XIV*, p. 47. It is even more difficult to estimate servant numbers. See also pp. 98–100.

who was anyone in France would wish to be present. Dynastic honour, individual careers, appointments in all branches of civil and military service now flowed as never before through the hands of the monarch.

To be a courtier at Versailles meant to be obsessed with the need for 'appearance' ('*paraître*'). Determined to bring the aristocracy together en bloc, Louis liked his court to be large and distinguished. Absence was regarded as folly or worse. 'He is a man I never see' was the king's crushing comment on a courtier whom he disfavoured for his absences.* But *paraître* signified not only being physically present in the pool of patronage, but also keeping up appearances, behaving in a manner consonant with one's rank within society and within the king's favours, and policing respect for status and precedence. Conspicuous consumption on their part was conjoined with emulative anxieties. As the king swept past in the Hall of Mirrors, for example—for all its glamour, a glorified corridor—courtiers jockeyed restlessly for position. In the Chambre du Roi, distinguished families competed for the opportunity for one of their number to be accorded a favour—holding the king's shirt for him to don, for example, or grasping the candle lighting his way to bed—that might seem pifflingly banal but which was loaded with honour and therefore potential for patronage in Louis's ceremonial regime.

In this febrile world of favour, anxiety and aspiration hovered around the issue of lodgings in particular. As we have

* See Appendix 4, p. 169.

noted, one of Louis's innovations at Versailles was to undertake to accommodate all those who held an office or a position within the court and government. This had happened
in no other royal palace. It was a considerable undertaking,
involving much time and effort on the part of the king and
those of his officials who dealt with the palace buildings. The
expansion of the palace that Louis undertook in the 1670s and
1680s was targeted particularly at creating more living space
for courtiers. Even so, the more the court boomed, the more
the lodging issue became a matter of squeezing a quart into a
pint pot. Very few courtiers—the royal family, plus those who
held the highest and/or most honorific posts—had a suite
of rooms. Most courtiers' lodgings comprised two rooms,
invariably lacking basic cooking facilities or even a hearth,
with draughty windows and smelly latrines along the hall or
down the staircase. By the end of the *ancien régime* the size
of the royal family was adding significantly to the problem
of space: Louis XVI's extensive family all had separate house-
holds, whose office-holders required accommodation. The
number of rooms available for the nobility shrank by a quarter
in a matter of decades, increasing tensions and resentments.

These problems meant that living conditions for most
nobles outside this charmed royal circle were far below
the quality that such individuals would enjoy in their own
homes. The widespread and growing taste for comfort over
the course of the century made this increasingly irritating.
We know from the comte de Noailles, who served as governor of the palace in the eighteenth century, that because of

pressure on space, Louis XIV had frowned on even the highest aristocrats having more than a couple of servants lodged in the palace—far fewer than they would have had in their own homes.[4] This explains why many courtiers ensconced in the palace chose to have separate lodgings—or even, for the great, an *hôtel particulier*—in the town of Versailles. Here they could keep most of their servants plus their carriage, a key item of ostentatious emulation. The town also housed many courtiers who had not—or not yet—managed to secure a lodging in the palace. Then there were the so-called *galopins* (the gallopers), who made day trips from Paris to attend the court.

Despite their poor quality, and uncertainties over possession, palace lodgings were viewed as preferable to other quarters. They were a convenient and safe option for courtiers attending events early or late in the day. And they were also places where a change of clothes could be carried out expeditiously. The court had strict expectations regarding dress: women could be obliged to change three or four times a day; Louis XIV himself set the tone by donning up to four different wigs in a single day. In addition, having a lodging in the palace helped foster new bonds of sociability and patronage among courtiers. Although the king offered lodgings, he did not provide food for his courtiers save at festive or key ceremonial occasions (such as the *soirées d'appartement*). Meals had to be brought in by caterers (*traiteurs*), or eaten by invitation to the tables of great nobles, or of certain court officials who were paid to offer hospitality. Mealtime sociability spread to other forms of leisure—parties, gambling, concerts and dances. These informal networks gave vitality to court life on those occasions when the king was absent or not holding court. They helped forge, despite the divisions, dissensions and coteries, a shared courtier culture adapted to the needs of '*ce pays-ci*'.

Despite the king's emphasis on visibility and access to his person, most courtiers found their monarch difficult to get hold of—whether for discussion of matters of accommodation or other issues. A favoured few had informal dealings with him that facilitated requests for favours. At the *soirées d'appartement* the king was approachable—but not to talk about business. Outside of this less formal context, moreover, ushers and guards of various descriptions watched doors and entrances, regulating individual approaches to the monarch.

The very sizeable royal military household was composed of a congeries of different troops, including musketeers, light cavalry and French Guards. Some units, such as the *Cent-Suisses** and the *Garde Écossaise* (Scottish company), were manned by foreign mercenaries. Each had its own often bewildering protocols and traditions. When closing the royal courtyard at night, for example, the *Garde Écossaise* (founded in the fifteenth century, the company in fact boasted very few Scots by Louis XIV's time) cried out '*Hhay hha Mier*'— seemingly a rendering of 'I am here' in a French version of a Scottish accent.[5] Wherever he went in the palace, Louis was

---

* The Swiss guard was originally created as personal bodyguard by Louis XI in 1480.

accompanied by twelve Swiss guards and twelve other soldiers from the household regiments. This level of security was sufficient to deter casual approaches to the monarch, though the complexity of the guards' organisation could militate against their effectiveness. They were, for example, unable to prevent Robert-François Damien's assassination attempt on Louis XV in 1757.* And, despite their presence, theft and vandalism in the palace and gardens were sometimes rampant.

Gaining access to the monarch—difficult at the best of times—became impossible when the king absented himself, as was increasingly the case over the course of the century. Even when he was in residence, Louis XV frequently (and often at short notice) replaced public meals with dining with small groups of favourites away from public gaze.† He also spent time with his mistresses: after particularly heavy nights he would keep courtiers waiting for hours for a *coucher* and a *lever* whose timing Louis XIV had always observed punctiliously. Louis XVI had no mistresses, but a wife whom he adored. However, she was even more disenchanted with court rituals than he, and chose to spend most of her time in her redesigned private suite in the palace or out at the Petit Trianon.

Marie Antoinette took up with a select company of young, high-living nobles and noblewomen without much Versailles pedigree behind them. This became a problem because she

---

* See Chapter 3 (p. 78).
† See Appendix 5, p. 170.

Born in 1755, the Austrian princess Marie Antoinette was only fourteen years-old when in 1770 she married Louis XV's heir, the future Louis XVI, and still a teenager when in 1774 her husband acceded to the crowd. She found the French court stuffy, condescending, convention-bound—and old.

showed herself keenly interested in dispensing patronage, and not solely within her own household. Royal mistresses had acted as poles of patronage in the past, but had sought to integrate themselves within existing networks. The patronage dispensed by Madame de Pompadour, for example, worked best after she had been legitimated by becoming lady-in-waiting to Queen Marie Leczinska. In contrast, Marie Antoinette not only interfered with her husband's patronage network but also operated her own, based on individual favourites who were essentially court nobodies. This was to have serious consequences.

SERVICING THE COURT

The 6,000 to 7,000 wealthy, demanding and conspicuously consuming nobles who formed the royal court at Versailles were the tip of a demographic iceberg. Below the waterline—and attracting very little attention, either then or now—was a formidably large body of non-nobles whose function was to keep afloat the noble denizens of '*ce pays-ci*'.

The size and composition of this service sector varied over time. It was probably at its height in the second half of the seventeenth century, when the palace was being built, the gardens laid out and basic infrastructural work was under way. Informed estimates in the early 1680s, when the whole location was a huge building site under scaffolding, suggested over 20,000 workers were employed in construction. This number doubled if one counted those workers, including

The Flemish painter Adam Frans Van der Meulen was based in Paris from the 1660s and won many commissions from Louis XIV. This 1668 canvas of Versailles as a building site shows the enormity and complexity of the king's plans for the chateau.

soldiers from more than forty regiments, who were tasked with extending the water supply to the chateau from the river Eure, some 50 miles distant. This was not only back-breaking work, it was also dangerous. The summer months in this region full of swampy pools were notorious for producing epidemics of various kinds of fever. In the 1670s it was whispered that the government was deliberately hushing up the high mortality rate.[6] The 'Black Legend' that the splendour of Versailles had been callously built with scant concern for the lives of the king's subjects gained wider currency. It was further diffused by the Protestant diaspora across Europe that Louis instigated by the reintroduction of religious intolerance in the 1685 revocation of the Edict of Nantes.*

Once the major phase of construction was out of the way, probably the largest group of workers at Versailles (and certainly the least prestigious) were the domestic servants. One estimate suggests that there were some 3,000 individuals servicing Crown officers, most of whom were in royal employment. Yet alongside these were vast numbers of servants working for courtiers, and usually housed outside the palace. It is telling that as soon as the court left the palace in 1789 and noble emigration began, the population of the town slumped by more than half, from around 70,000 to 26,000. Many of these missing tens of thousands had been servicing the palace prior to 1789.

_____

* The Edict of Nantes, signed in 1598 by Henri IV, had granted a number of civil rights to France's Calvinist Protestants (or Huguenots).

The number of abandonments in 1789 extended beyond the domestic service grouping into the hospitality, building, clothing and luxury goods sectors of the urban economy. Louis XIV had wanted Versailles to showcase the work of the finest artists and skilled artisans from across the nation, and to demonstrate its international prestige. Many artisans—furniture-makers, workers in marble, goldsmiths, jewellers, scientific instrument-makers, craftsmen in specialist and luxury trades and the like—will have been based in palace or town, though again a high proportion were, like their masters and clients, *galopins* who resided in Paris and came to the palace for specific tasks. Elite practitioners secured niches on the Crown payroll, but demand in the 'private' sector for employment with courtiers was also very buoyant. Courtiers had residences in town to furnish, which created yet more work for skilled tradesmen and artisans. The old aristocracy were increasingly embracing the new practices of personal hygiene—and their associated accoutrements—which Louis XV was pioneering in Versailles. Courtiers attempted to introduce them into their quarters, but with only partial success: space considerations and questions of cost for the royal treasury inhibited their spread throughout the palace. Courtiers' cramped living quarters were much inferior to those they enjoyed in their own private residences. The palace seemed to belong to another age.

The management of Versailles and its grounds also seemed anachronistic. In theory, this was under the charge of a single Intendant appointed by the king. In practice, the running of operations was anything but centralised. Aspects of court life were tended to by some twenty fairly autonomous functional administrations. These operated like silos in their respective areas of competence. The *Bouche du Roi*, for example, one of the largest such units, was responsible for food provisioning and was divided up into numerous sub-units—mini-silos in effect—some of which were for particular supplies (bread, fruit, wood, etc.), while others had different remits (such as for the king's table, as against those of his courtiers). There were separate administrations for buildings, lodgings and furnishing. The *Menus Plaisirs* looked after most aspects of ceremony and entertainment, but also liaised with three separate administrations for different aspects of the chapel, plus other units for music and wardrobe. Then there were the six units devoted to hunting matters—two for the stables (*Écuries*), and one each for kennels (*Chenil*), falconry (*Fauconnerie*), wolves (*Louveterie*) and boars (*Vautrait*).

A great many of the posts in the royal employ—at court and in government, and at both high and low levels—operated under a system known as *vénalité* (venality). This meant that the candidate paid a lump sum to the state treasury, which then produced an annual interest payment to the holder, very often of around 4 per cent. The generalisation of this practice in the seventeenth century is widely credited with reducing noble factionalism by centralising patronage and giving office-holders an investment in stable government. But there were three important consequences of this system, all of which involved inefficiencies that worsened in the eighteenth century. First, the capital outlay encouraged holders to seek to recoup their expenditure at an accelerated rate, partly through extending their activities entrepreneurially or else—maybe more commonly—through rank corruption. Kick-backs were an integral part of the way the patronage system worked. Second, the system encouraged place-holding and the exclusion of talent. Certain posts became hereditary fiefdoms. Three generations of the Padelin family served as royal chimney sweeps, for example, while the Martigny and Gerard window-cleaning dynasties could each boast over a hundred years of devoted service. Such stalwart service was far from rare. Finally, the system tended towards stasis and thus discouraged reform. Posts were difficult to get rid of, partly because of the dynastic investment and partly because the removal of a post necessitated that the post-holder be reimbursed his capital sum. The post of Bearer of the Royal Chamberpot (*Porte-chaise d'affaires du Roi*) continued to receive his salary long after Louis XV had started using a water closet instead. There was a captain for mule harnesses, even though mules were no longer found at Versailles. Government would, however, make swingeing cuts only under duress. Indeed, a greater temptation was to double the number of officials for a particular function and impose alternating periods of service. There were, however, structural limits to how far such practices could continue. And under Louis XVI, those limits seemed to have been reached.

VERSAILLES MALFUNCTION

Louis XIV had made the management of patronage crucial to the functioning of Versailles. But he had created a system that proved inflexible and difficult to control. Louis XVI in particular did not manage it well. Under his reign, Versailles had less to offer because the king had less to offer. This was mainly because the state's finances were in a mess and there was less surplus to fuel the pumps of patronage. The royal court was the third most expensive item in the state budget—but its size (some 5 per cent) was dwarfed by spending on war and debt maintenance linked to past wars. Financially, the court was not really the big problem; politically, however, it was perceived to be so.

Part of the king's solution to his escalating financial problems—starting in the 1770s and continuing intermittently through the 1780s—was to make economies. The ceremonial schedule created by Louis XIV continued, but events became fewer in number. This reduced the already diminishing *éclat* of court culture, and was linked to Louis XV and Louis XVI's moves towards the privatisation of their lives at Versailles. Under Louis XVI the number of nights devoted to the *soirées d'appartement* was considerably reduced. The king held court only on Sundays, occasional Tuesdays and on days of great

The setting, posture and symbols of royalty in this official portrait of Louis XVI consciously quote Rigaud's swagger portrait of Louis XIV (page 3). Characteristically, Louis XVI cuts an altogether meeker and less imperious figure than his distinguished forebear.

festivals or ceremonies. Courtiers might still turn out in force for major events, but the court itself was often almost embarrassingly empty. Louis XVI's awkward and self-conscious demeanour in court ceremonies did not help. Courtiers got into the habit of attending court to perform the duties of posts they held or else attended weekly entertainments and balls—but pointed their carriages Paris-wards at the end of the day.

The decline of Versailles's cultural reputation during this period was thrown into stark relief by the rise of Paris, which was enjoying one of the most brilliant eras in its history. The home of the intellectual movement of the Enlightenment, its book and newspaper industries flourished, its luxury goods and fashion trades boomed, and its cultural trends were mimicked across the globe. Paris had a brilliance that made Versailles look almost drab and unfashionable. The high nobility whom Louis XIV had entertained so lavishly in the past, now twiddling their thumbs at court, found the delights of France's capital city more alluring than the gilded but semi-deserted palace of 'Louis the Great'. Indeed the Palais-Royal, Paris home of the duc d'Orléans—who was treated with contempt at court—became a hub for printing and pamphleteering, generating lively political debates that were often critical of Versailles; in some respects the Palais-Royal became a kind of counter-Versailles.

Living at court in Versailles was thus no longer the enviable option for the high nobility, especially as the squeeze on space tightened. Furthermore, court economies caused by the state's financial problems saw a drastic fall in opportunities for preferment. Swingeing cuts in the 1770s and especially in the 1780s to posts in state service both in Versailles and throughout the monarchy's civil and military arms comprised a severe blow to an increasingly alienated court nobility. Attempts to reduce sinecures enjoyed a measure of success: one-third of all posts on the royal payroll in 1750 had been abolished by 1789. But there was less patronage to be had. In these straitened circumstances, courtiers did not take kindly to Marie Antoinette setting up her own pyramid of patronage, which largely excluded the most venerable court dynasties. Louis XIV had conceived Versailles as a means of keeping the high nobility unified, delocalised, under his surveillance, in his debt—and happy. But it was no longer working that way.

Discontented courtiers started to react antagonistically towards the royal family. Malicious gossip started by disgruntled courtiers would dog the king and queen right up until their deaths: that Louis was sexually impotent, politically incompetent and a drunkard; while Marie Antoinette was an insatiable Messalina who used her independence from the weakling monarch to pursue an endless round of sexual gratification. The queen was also said to favour Austrian influence in government, to dominate her husband, to pour money into the pockets of wealthy and idle hangers-on, and to fritter away state revenue on her beloved hamlet at the Petit Trianon.

Criticism directed at the conduct of Marie Antoinette inevitably found a wider target in the royal court as a whole. Most courtiers, though resentful towards the king, wanted a better-funded and more fairly managed Versailles to continue.

But those outside the system in an increasingly buoyant public sphere—notably in Paris—began a more urgent questioning of the desirability of an absolute monarchy and of the place of Versailles within it. Lurid tales of royal (especially queenly) extravagance at Versailles were disseminated in the public sphere by illicit scandal sheets, which revelled in dragging the name of Versailles through the mud.

The conviction grew that the palace was largely responsible for the state of near-bankruptcy that threatened France from 1786. Versailles was represented less as a symbol of French prosperity and grandeur than as a drain on national resources; it was harming the public rather than benefiting them. Courtiers were viewed not as the backbone of the state but as heartless parasites. In the late 1780s, for example, it seemed almost obscene for the queen to dress the part of a humble milkmaid in her fantasy village in the Petit Trianon while bread prices rocketed across France, causing mass hunger. To some extent, Versailles had become the victim of its own boosterish propaganda. Its hubristic scale made it appear less a blessing than a blight on the French nation, a handicap for the monarchy, and an anachronism that needed either to be destroyed—or else to be brought radically up to date.

5

REPUBLICANISING

In Search of a New Role

HE 5TH AND 6TH OF MAY WERE RED-letter days in the history of Versailles. On 5 May 1682 the final excited preparations had been made for the arrival the following day of King Louis XIV, his court and his administration, to take residence and inaugurate one of the most brilliant chapters in the history of the French monarchy. One hundred and seven years later, 5 May 1789 marked the opening by his great-great-great-grandson Louis XVI of the Estates General, France's ancient representative body, which had last met in 1614. At that earlier date, the Estates had met in Paris; Versailles had then been little more than a hamlet. Holding the meeting here in 1789 was an acknowledgement of how the monarchy—and Versailles—had changed.

No space within the palace itself could accommodate the 1,200 elected deputies, so the Estates met in the airy and revamped Salle des Menus Plaisirs, built in 1786 on the Avenue de Saint-Cloud. Louis's speech to the assembled throng stressed the need for them to work harmoniously together to solve the financial crisis that threatened the solvency of the state. Yet when the deputies met next day to start business, they were unable to decide how to proceed. The commoner deputies of the Third Estate feared they would be ganged up on by the two other 'privileged' orders (the clergy and the nobility). They also detested the nobility's condescending use of court ceremonial to promote their interests. So they resolved to sit tight and refuse to get down to business, even as bankruptcy loomed.

The procedural wrangle initiated on 6 May 1789, the anniversary of Louis XIV's Versailles 1682 installation, mushroomed spectacularly into a major political crisis, which in turn initiated a revolutionary process. In mid-June the Third Estate declared itself to be the National Assembly, offering nobles and clerics the opportunity to join with them. When, on 20 June, the king attempted a new initiative, closing the Salle des Menus Plaisirs, the Assembly decamped to a real tennis court (*jeu de paume*) close to the palace. Here its members took 'a solemn oath never to separate and to come together wherever circumstances may dictate until the constitution of the kingdom shall be established and placed upon a firm foundation'. On 9 July the Assembly renamed itself the National Constituent Assembly and requested that the king

Louis-Léopold Boilly's painting shows the Versailles Jeu de Paume—best known as the location of the famous 'Tennis-Court Oath' of 20 June 1789—in its habitual guise, as a court for real tennis.

stand down the large numbers of troops who had been gathering around Versailles and Paris from the last days of June.

The lurch towards revolution quickened with the storming on 14 July of the fortress of the Bastille in Paris, widely seen as a symbol of Bourbon abuse of power. Louis XVI himself could still attract a measure of popularity, however. On his entry into Paris on 17 July 1789, in an attempt to quell the disturbances, he was greeted rapturously by Parisians, who cheered him on as the 'restorer of French liberties' and were enthused at his agreeing to wear the tricolour cockade, just invented to signal the union between the city and the monarchy (red and blue were the ceremonial colours of Paris, white that of the Bourbon dynasty).

Most opposition to the Crown still tended to spare the king and to channel its anger against putatively 'evil counsellors' among his courtiers. This was indeed the context for the so-called October Days (5–6 October 1789), which led to the royal family's removal to Paris. In late September and early October discontent over high bread prices—which were attributed to the influence of speculators and hoarders with links to the royal court—erupted in the capital. Journalists and pamphleteers argued that Versailles wanted to starve Paris out of its revolutionary views. Matters came to a head on 1 October when a banquet for the royal guards got out of hand with soldiers and courtiers allegedly trampling tricolour cockades underfoot and engaging in counter-revolutionary sabre-rattling. Indignation in Paris triggered a mass march of Parisians out to Versailles. There was open riot and the threat of attacks on the royal family; Marie Antoinette, whom some now viewed as the most evil of Louis's evil counsellors, was particularly at risk. Ironically, she only avoided what might have been a lynching by escaping a threatening mob along the *passage du roi* that Louis XVI had once created to get to her bedroom.* Further disorder was quelled by the decision to

---

* See Chapter 3 (p. 74).

remove king, royal family and indeed the National Assembly to Paris. As he stepped into the carriage that would bear him to the capital, Louis turned to the comte de La Tour du Pin, governor of the palace, and said, wistfully, as though only too well aware of the enormity of the changes under way, 'You remain in charge here. *Tâchez de me sauver mon pauvre Versailles*' ('Try to save my poor Versailles for me').[1]

In Paris the royal family were installed in the run-down and fusty Tuileries Palace. It was quite a comedown. 'It is very ugly here, Mummy,' said the six-year-old Dauphin, to which Marie Antoinette replied, with a resigned air that was not her forte, '*Mon fils*, Louis XIV once lived here and found it very comfortable.'[2] Removed from their Versailles element, the royal family struggled to adapt—and almost at once felt like prisoners. On 20 June 1791 Louis XVI and Marie Antoinette fled revolutionary Paris in an attempt to link up with counter-revolutionary elements of the army at Montmédy, close to France's eastern frontier. They were arrested the following day at Varennes, just 48 kilometres (30 miles) from their destination. The incident soured Louis's relations with Parisians and indeed with the country as a whole. Once war against *ancien régime* Europe began in 1792, the king's failure fully to commit to the Revolution appeared treasonous. With military humiliation at the hands of Austria and Prussia staring France in the face, a popular insurrection in Paris on 10 August 1792 forced the National Assembly to announce the king's abdication and then, on 21 September, to declare a republic.

As plain Citoyen Louis Capet ('Citizen Louis Capet'), stripped of his titles, Louis was tried for high treason and collusion with the invading Prussian forces (who had been repelled by a French revolutionary army at Valmy on 20 September). Sentenced to death on 15–17 January 1793 by the new National Assembly, the Convention, which had been elected in autumn 1792, Louis was guillotined in the Place de la Révolution (now Place de la Concorde) on 21 January. The king's failure to adapt to the Revolution was unsurprising. One could take Louis XVI out of Versailles; but it was much more difficult to take Versailles out of Louis XVI.

BOURBONS WITHOUT VERSAILLES, VERSAILLES WITHOUT THE BOURBONS

For over a hundred years, from 1682 to 1789, the tempo of French history had been set from Versailles. After 1789, Versailles would always be (as it still is) on the receiving end of national history—and, for most of that time, most of that history would be made from Paris. The fairy-tale castle, the icon of supreme monarchical power, crashed ignominiously to earth with an almighty bump in 1789. Paris took revenge for its political emasculation by Louis XIV and his heirs.

A good deal of the public hostility that had grown up against Versailles in the last decades of the *ancien régime* had been directed against the royal court. The costs of the court had been, it was held (albeit on the basis of information that was wildly exaggerated) a major cause of the Revolution.

What now was Versailles *for*? The question was all the more pressing following the king's removal from his palace in October 1789 and then the overthrow of the monarchy and the establishment of a republic in August–September 1792. What was to be done with an institution created by the monarchy to serve and glorify the interests of monarchy? How could Versailles be rethought for a modern, post-absolutist, republican age?

France's very chequered political and constitutional history ensured that there would be a wide range of responses to this fundamental question over the next two centuries. Since the Revolution, France has had two spells of monarchy (1815–30, 1830–48), two empires (1804–15, 1852–70) and the unclassifiable Vichy regime during the Nazi occupation of 1940–44. In the long term, the republican mode of government has prevailed, though there have been no fewer than five instantiations (1792–1804, 1848–52, 1870–1940, 1946–58, and 1958 to the present). In these successive regimes, the question of Versailles's future was viewed from many perspectives. Yet it is also true that for all of them it was not a very important question. Versailles had suffered a catastrophic demotion in 1789–92. Over the next centuries it would suffer less from active antagonism than from sheer neglect. Decay, dispersal and often half-hearted efforts at readaptation would be the destiny of Versailles for the next century and more.

Without the king at the helm, both the palace and town of Versailles sank fast. The Republic had other, more urgent tasks in hand, not least the war against Europe. In 1789 the court had almost instantaneously dissolved into nothing: a few courtiers still attended the monarch at the Tuileries, but most either emigrated or else returned to their provincial estates. The administrative shell of the palace and its domains continued as if on autopilot, but income from the domain fell catastrophically as tenants took a rent holiday. The return of the court to Versailles seemed increasingly implausible once the palace's furniture started to be transferred to the Tuileries. The hammer blow to the artisanal and service sector of the urban economy caused the population to fall like a stone. The city, so long the support service of the palace, had lost its *raison d'être*—there was nothing much left to support or service. Instead of being a commanding national icon, in 1790 Versailles suffered the reduced status of being named departmental *chef-lieu* (capital) of the new *département* of Seine-et-Oise.* For most of the nineteenth century Versailles was 'a sad place', as the novelist Stendhal put it, 'in which one yawns before dying of boredom'.[3] Its reduced, small-town status was confirmed by the fact that it only topped the 70,000 population level of 1789 as recently as 1936.

Deterioration in the palace's fortunes was even more rapid. Over the next few years there would be continuing discussion over what to do with the site, its collections and its

* The eighty-three *départements* created in 1790 replaced the old *ancien régime* provinces and were intended as a rational method of enhancing national unity. There are now ninety-five *départements* in metropolitan France. Seine-et-Oise was abolished and divided into three smaller *départements*—Yvelines, Val-d'Oise and Essonne—in 1968. Versailles is in the *département* of Yvelines.

moveable property. A decision in late 1792 to relocate most paintings, sculptures, tapestries and other artworks to the Louvre helped swell the holdings of what was already being destined as the nation's art collection. In the same spirit, new national institutions also benefited from the palace's books (the Bibliothèque nationale), scientific objects (the Arts et Métiers conservatory), and musical instruments and sheet music (the Opéra). The wild animals of the Menagerie were moved out to a new site, too, in the Jardin des Plantes in south-eastern Paris.

The Russian author Nikolay Karamzin sadly noted the resulting transformation: 'Versailles without the court,' he opined, 'is like a body without a soul; the city is a kind of melancholy orphan.' A German traveller in the mid-1790s was to concur: 'Versailles has lost 30,000 inhabitants. It is wretched and deserted. The chateau is uninhabited. Most of the park . . . is neglected. The chateaux and houses of the Trianon are empty, ruined or destroyed . . . A doleful, tomb-like solitude surrounds the wanderer in these sites that were formerly so animated.'[4]

Excited demands that the palace be razed to the ground, as had happened to the Bastille in 1789, became more insistent as the Revolution moved to the left. One deputy in the National Assembly suggested posting a placard at Versailles reading 'For Sale or Rent', while another demanded that the palace be ploughed under.[5] But the palace was saved—'nationalised' was the term used—by the decree of 5 May (that date again!) 1794. It stated that Versailles (along with a number of other former palaces) was to be 'conserved and maintained at the expense of the Republic for the enjoyment of the people and to create institutions useful for agriculture and the arts'.

In this context, mere survival was an achievement. Other royal palaces and chateaux were less fortunate: Marly was sold off as a manufactory for cotton goods and blankets and Meudon was turned into a test site for military balloons. Much of the Versailles estate suffered, too. Marie Antoinette's Petit Trianon was sold off in lots, with a tavern and a dance hall moving in. An arms manufactory was set up in the Grand Commun; in the early nineteenth century it would become a military hospital. In the gardens, many of Le Nôtre's floral parterres were given over to vegetables and fruit trees. The Grand Canal was filled in and turned to pasture.

In the late 1790s more imaginative attempts were made to utilise Versailles for a number of broadly pedagogic and conservationist purposes. The most successful of these were a secondary school and, in particular, from 1797, the Musée spécial de l'école française, which was developed as a complementary museum to the Louvre, specialising in French artists, with an art school attached.

The 'nationalisation' decree of 1794, however, had come not a moment too soon for the palace. To overcome Nature's deficiencies, Louis XIV had established Versailles by a tremendous effort of will, backed up with enormous amounts of state money. His successors had proved equally and doggedly committed to the work of maintenance and expansion. Now and throughout the 1790s, neither political will nor state money was much in evidence. And it showed. Versailles fell into disrepair and a general air of shoddiness came to reign. Nature fought back. Visitors queued up, moreover, to see what they were encouraged to think of as a monument to monarchical vanity, selfishness and despotism. Lack of adequate policing meant that many went home with memorabilia snatched from the largely unsupervised house and gardens. Politics also had a part to play in the story of decay: the National Assembly decreed the 'de-royalisation' of public buildings, with the result that all symbols of monarchy (fleurs-de-lys, crowns, sceptres, imperial busts, etc.) were removed or destroyed. In addition, cash-strapped governments ran a series of auctions that dispersed many artworks and material objects not grand enough to augment national collections. There were 17,000 lots in the 1793–5 sales alone and they included even everyday objects like beds, mattresses, candlesticks, curtains, bottles of wine and kitchen utensils. In terms of its collections and its quotidian material culture, as well as in human terms, Versailles was disintegrating.

UNTHINKABLE TO DESTROY, DIFFICULT TO SAVE

The notorious political fixer, the abbé Siéyès, when asked what he had done during the most turbulent years of the French Revolution, stated simply, '*J'ai vécu*' ('I survived'). Much the same could have been said of Versailles. There was a case that it was too big and important to fail. But in the long term, survival probably did require more than the limited and constrained uses that the Republic had found for it in the late 1790s. This sizeable quandary puzzled the two regimes that followed the First Republic: the Napoleonic regime (1804–15) and the Bourbon Restoration (1815–30). Neither formed a new vocation for the palace.

One might have thought that Napoleon would have revelled in the splendour of Versailles. Linking his regime to the Bourbons (as well as, paradoxically, to the Revolution) was one of his standard strategies for claiming political legitimacy: in 1799 he selected the rooms of Louis XVI when he installed himself at the Tuileries Palace, for example, and re-established a code of etiquette for a revived court (albeit based in Paris, not Versailles) that drew on the Bourbon tradition. But it may simply have been that Versailles was not big enough for him: 'Better not do anything,' he noted, 'if one cannot do something that rivals what Louis XIV has done.'[6] Second-best was not Napoleon's style. His input at the main palace was limited to some minimal work of restoration, including the creation of decorative 'N's on certain exteriors. Just getting the house and garden's maintenance under control was highly expensive. And, of course, in war Napoleon had another distraction. Pending a decision on the palace's future, which he never made, he closed down the Musée spécial, dispersing its collections to the Louvre and to provincial galleries.

Napoleon did, however, engage with the Trianon, which he found less overblown and more congenial than the main palace. He spotted its potential in 1805, but only took it seriously as his separation from the Empress Josephine led him to seek an alternative country retreat to Malmaison, where the couple had been installed. Work of restoration on both Trianon sites was given a boost by Napoleon's marriage to Marie-Louise of Austria in 1810.

The niece of Marie Antoinette took an unlikely shine to the site, and she stimulated Napoleon to restore the very dilapidated former queen's Hameau as well as the main Trianon buildings, furnishing them in a style of 'fairy-tale luxuriousness', according to one visitor.[7] He organised fêtes in the palace grounds, too: fountains played as he conspicuously punted his empress around a newly restored Grand Canal in a gondola.

If Napoleon was never more than a fleeting presence in Versailles, his Bourbon successors—Louis XVI's brothers, Louis XVIII (ruled 1815–24) and Charles X (ruled 1824–30)—were scarcely more engaged. Both had spent their youth in Louis XVI's court. Louis XVIII had followed Louis XVI to Paris in October 1789, residing in the Luxembourg Palace. He fled the city at the same time as the king's abortive flight to Varennes in June 1791. He had spent his life since then dragging sadly around Europe—as had his brother, who had fled the Revolution even earlier, leaving Versailles just a day or so after the fall of the Bastille in 1789.

The townspeople of Versailles were immensely cheered to see signs of life and the bustle of business returning with the restored monarch in 1814. New staff were hired and a full-scale assault was launched on decay: the old symbols of

royalty were reinserted into paintings, sculptures and decorative features, and rooms were spruced up, bringing into the
light of day, a contemporary noted, 'all the glory of the great
age of Louis XIV, hidden by dust and enveloped in spiders-
webs'—though it was also noted that one only had to sneeze
to bring plaster cupids raining down.[8]

Any lingering thoughts that the restored Bourbon
dynasty might return to Versailles in anything like the style of
the *ancien régime* were swiftly crushed by the circumstances
of Louis XVIII's accession in 1814. When he entered Paris in
May, following Napoleon's defeat in the War of the Sixth Coa-
lition, he showed little sense of compromise. Less than a year
later, however, Louis was forced by Napoleon's return from
exile to leave the city *à toute vitesse* with his tail between his
legs. A brief period of civil war saw the palace occupied by
Prussian troops, breathing fire and issuing blood-curdling
threats. But after Napoleon's defeat at Waterloo in 1815, peace
returned, as did the old king. Entering Paris, as it was said, 'in
the baggage train' of the allied armies, Louis was now a wiser
man. Realising that any attempt at evoking the absolutist style
would stir up national resentment and could topple him, he
made liberal concessions in a new constitution. He decided
not to stay in Versailles and installed himself at the Tuileries
instead. He contented himself with some minor changes to
his old home, notably rebuilding the 'Old Wing' in the palace forecourt, renamed the Dufour Wing, to be symmetrical
with the Gabriel Wing that faced it. Versailles-type splendour

was far too expensive for the restored regime to contemplate: Napoleonic France had lived off the proceeds of conquest, but now, forced back to its 1792 frontiers, the country was in straitened circumstances—and also had to pay war reparations to the allies who had defeated Napoleon.

Louis's heir and successor, Charles X, was far less liberal than his brother, and his taste for *ancien régime* traditions was symbolised by a full-throttle coronation in 1825, complete with the ceremony of touching for the King's Evil. But even this hyper-reactionary ruler recoiled from the bother and expense of making Versailles a central feature of his reign. He combined residence in the Tuileries with country visits to Saint-Cloud. He even permitted a further round of sales of precious objects from the royal collections, recalling the auctions of the Revolutionary decade. His last contact with Versailles was poignant. Chased out of Paris by popular insurrection in July 1830, he paused to hold his final council of ministers in the Trianon, before realising the cause was hopeless and heading for exile. The Bourbon link with its Versailles creation had ended for ever.

SALVATION THROUGH HISTORY

Louis-Philippe's ascent to power in the 1830 Revolution finally killed off the notion that Versailles might provide a home for a dynasty and a court, or continue to play an active part in French political life. The July Monarchy's new king was a member of the Orléans dynasty.* The Orléans had no nostalgic attachment to Versailles. It was a duc d'Orléans who had moved the court to Paris in the Regency of 1715–22, only for Louis XV to move it back.† The duc d'Orléans who was Louis-Philippe's father had had an apartment in Louis XVI's palace and played the courtier when he wished. But he made his home his official residence in the Palais-Royal in Paris, where he preferred to court public opinion rather than curry his cousin's favours out at Versailles. The black sheep in the Bourbon fold, much reviled by his cousins and their factions, he showed enthusiasm for the Revolutionary cause, being elected to the National Assembly in 1792. Despite republicanising his name as Philippe-Égalité (Philip-Equality) and voting for Louis XVI's execution, he ended up being guillotined himself (November 1793). His father's fate caused the young Louis-Philippe, who as duc de Chartres had been serving in the republican armies, to flee to the enemy for self-protection. Despite all this, the king shared a liberal version of Revolutionary principles and this had endeared him to elite opinion enough to secure him the crown.

This was not, however, a track record to encourage the thought that the new king might restore the old Versailles, to which he was temperamentally ill-disposed. Louis-Philippe did have a court at the Tuileries Palace, but he ended the old rules of etiquette. Glorying in the role of 'bourgeois monarch',

---

* The junior royal house descended from Philippe I, duc d'Orléans, younger brother of Louis XIV.

† See Chapter 3 (p. 58).

Horace Vernet's 1846 painting of King Louis-Philippe with his sons outside the gates of Versailles features in the background the Gabriel Wing, on which can be read the phrase '*À toutes les gloires de la France*' ('To all the glories of France'). This served as motto for the Museum of the History of France which the king created here.

he breathed a spirit of conciliation and compromise. He wanted his regime to be seen as one that brought the different political traditions of France together in harmonious unity. This notion stimulated a vision for Versailles that would transform the site and resolve the quandary regarding its purpose: shortly after his accession, Louis-Philippe decided to turn the site into a narrative history lesson for the nation and about the nation. Versailles's future, he thought, would only be guaranteed if it was accepted that the palace's role as an active force in political and cultural life was over, and that its destiny could only be secured as a site not of monarchical power but of national memory, as the Musée de l'histoire de France.

Once the decision was made, Louis-Philippe took a keen personal interest in reshaping the site, visiting regularly, week in, week out, during the works and spending prodigiously on it from his own account. Once the transformation of Versailles was complete, he took enormous pride in his handiwork and loved to take groups of schoolchildren around the galleries. At the core of his vision was the creation of a visual chronicle of France in paintings and sculptures from earliest times to the present. The framework was set by the holdings still extant in the palace, but he also scoured the museums and galleries of France for pictures that could be incorporated. There remained gaps in the chronology, however, and Louis-Philippe commissioned paintings to fill them—commissioning by the square metre, critics unkindly called it. Alongside the central chronicle of French history, there were a number of parallel histories—the history of the Crusades was highly popular, along with the chronicle of coronations—but the *pièce de résistance* was the Gallery of Battles, which depicted the great French military victories from the Frankish king Clovis's triumph at Tolbiac in 496 through to Napoleon's at Wagram in 1809. The Musée also included a painting of the battle of Valmy in 1792, the First Republic's first victory, at which Louis-Philippe had himself fought. As this range suggests, the ideological fusion of political traditions—monarchical, republican and imperial—was evident, with Louis-Philippe's own regime implicitly identified as the summation and happy ending of French history.

The ceremonies inaugurating Louis-Philippe's Museum of the History of France in 1837 focussed on the famous Gallery of Battles, depicting French victories from earliest times.

The inauguration of the new galleries, dedicated '*À toutes les gloires de la France*' ('To All the Glories of France') took place in June 1837, and was an initial success. Crowds flocked to Versailles, and Victor Hugo congratulated the king warmly for having 'made a national monument of a monarchical monument'.[9] It was not long, however, before criticisms started raining down—as indeed they have continued to this day. The king's valiant efforts to harmonise the different political traditions satisfied none of them (especially the revolutionists, who felt massively short-changed). The hagiographical tone to a national story told in terms of kings, heroes and battles left wider social forces and the whole realm of ideas out of the story. The king's mildly monomaniacal focus on the historical galleries also had a negative impact on the rest of the site. Surprisingly little was done to restore the royal apartments, for example, while hundreds of paintings throughout the palace were affected by a distinctive, disfiguring mould. Although the king devoted time and effort to modernising the Trianons as a family retreat, he rarely spent the night there.

Far more serious was the work of destruction that Louis-Philippe's creation entailed. He chose to situate the galleries in the wing of the palace that had been inhabited by the Princes of the Blood, and set about simply cleansing all the variegated and multi-sized rooms of their historic decorative features and producing drably monotonous long galleries. 'Before Versailles could be restored,' he confided to a friend, 'partitions had to be knocked down, these rats' nests destroyed and the usurped space reconquered.'[10] These 'rats' nests' had belonged to the former comtes de Provence and d'Artois, on whom he thus exacted posthumous, Orléanist revenge. In addition, the priority that the king showed for producing a coherent national story over the artistic merit of images used resulted in an aesthetically uneven effect, with much pretty mediocre work. ('My successors will replace the canvasses,' Louis-Philippe argued in his own defence. 'I simply wanted first to provide the picture frames.')[11]

Whatever the failings of taste and the collateral damage wrought by the historical galleries, Louis-Philippe had none-theless supplied Versailles with a new vocation. Turning the palace into a glorified history lesson had the additional effect of fashioning it as tourist attraction in an age of growing mass leisure. This was helped by the arrival of the railways: two lines from the French capital to Versailles were opened in 1839–40, facilitating access for Parisians and Paris-based tourists alike. And the tourist trade gave the economy of the town of Versailles a shot in the arm. Although the hotel busi-ness did well, in practice the railway service also encouraged day trips from Paris (as it still does).

Although the storyline of the history galleries had under-lined the July Monarchy as a civilisational and national end-point, the regimes that followed in swift succession did little to change their layout. The Second Republic (1848–51), which came into being following the overthrow and flight to England of Louis-Philippe, was too short to allow visionary thinking.

And little of the latter was evident during Napoleon III's Second Empire.* The Emperor established additional galleries to celebrate the French conquest of Algeria after 1830 and victories in the Crimea in the 1850s. But, generally, he showed less interest in the site than his wife did: Empress Eugénie developed an obsessive passion for Marie Antoinette, collected furniture and memorabilia of the queen on the international art market, and in 1867 sponsored an exhibition devoted to her life. For his part, Napoleon III used the palace to host a number of state visits that gave it a sporadically festive air. Especially notable was the visit of Queen Victoria in 1855, which incidentally produced the first photographic images of the site. This new medium would enhance Versailles's status as a tourist attraction, particularly from the last decades of the century, as the picture postcard came into its own.

THE THIRD REPUBLIC: NEW DIRECTIONS

Louis-Philippe's historical gallery had seemed to confirm that Versailles was now nothing more than a theatre of memory. But, after the fall of the Second Empire, as a result of Napoleon III's defeat in the Franco-Prussian War of 1870–71 and the subsequent declaration of the Third Republic, the palace found itself once more at the centre of national politics. Over the winter of 1870–71 Paris was besieged by the Prussian army, which set up its headquarters in Versailles. German troops

---

* Louis-Napoleon, nephew of Napoleon I, transformed himself from elected president of the Second Republic into Napoleon III, Emperor of the French.

Anton von Werner's painting of the moment at which Bismarck declared
the German Empire in the Hall of Mirrors on 18 January 1871 was commissioned as a gift for the seventieth birthday in 1885 of the Chancellor.
Highly propagandistic, the painting is full of historical errors: that day,
for example, Bismarck was not wearing the white jacket here shown and
was fourteen years younger than he appears.

drilled in the Place d'Armes, while the Hall of Mirrors housed hospital beds for wounded German soldiers. King Wilhelm I of Prussia, who had visited Versailles as a teenager at the time of the Prussian occupation in 1814, lodged in the Prefecture in the town, while his Chancellor Otto von Bismarck was put up in one of the high-end hotels. On 18 January 1871—the anniversary of the declaration of the Prussian monarchy in 1701—the two men combined in an astonishing *coup de théâtre*: Wilhelm was proclaimed Kaiser (Emperor) of a unified Germany in the Hall of Mirrors. A month later France signed a peace treaty whose terms included the payment of a massive war indemnity and the ceding to Germany of the provinces of Alsace and Lorraine.

The scene in Versailles's iconic Hall of Mirrors opened a period of seventy-five years in which Franco-German antagonism was the principal axis around which European history revolved. For France it represented a humiliation that cut deep into the national psyche. When France and its allies defeated Germany in the First World War, the government insisted—in a second flashbulb moment—that the peace treaty of 1919 should be signed in the same location. If this did something to lift French morale and restore national pride, the history of Franco-German hostility still had more chapters to unfold . . .

By 1919, as this vignette suggests, Versailles had acquired an accepted place within republican political culture. The First Republic had been perplexed about what to do with the site; the Second Republic was too brief to be able to get its head around the problem; it was the Third Republic that succeeded in incorporating Versailles into regular political life. This process, however, started anything but happily. Indeed in 1870–71 Versailles for a moment seemed in total opposition to the politics of the nation's capital, and the Versailles population appeared heartless reactionaries completely at odds with the republican tradition.

When elections to the shakily established Third Republic in early 1871 produced a strong monarchist majority, Paris protested in its traditionally rebellious manner. The Paris municipal government formed itself into a 'Commune' that embraced radical social policies, which led the newly elected national assembly to remove itself to Versailles. A stand-off between national government and Paris Commune developed, which escalated into violent conflict when the former besieged the mutinous capital in the spring of 1871. In the 'Semaine sanglante' ('Bloody Week') of 21–28 May, government troops entered Paris and suppressed the Commune with brutal efficiency. Some 20,000 Communards and others were summarily executed in Parisian streets and parks, and an additional 40,000 were arrested. Many of the latter would be deported to New Caledonia. At Versailles itself, the Orangerie and the Grandes and Petites Écuries were turned into gaols for wounded Communards, and firing squads operated within the park.

The situation in 1871 was far too tense for the government to return to Paris. In addition, the fires that had swept through the capital in the aftermath of the suppression of the Commune had destroyed many public buildings, including the

Tuileries Palace, the Hôtel de Ville and the law courts. It was agreed that the national parliament and government should continue to be based at Versailles at least pro tem. The ministries moved into the main buildings of the palace—causing more disruption than the Prussian officer class had managed. The two elected chambers were also found a home: ultimately the Senate would sit in the Opera house, while a special conference chamber was established for the lower house in the South Wing. This was made large enough to host joint sessions of the two bodies.

The choice of Versailles as the home of the French government was a product of the extraordinary circumstances of 1870–71. It was given support by the fact that monarchists were temporarily the dominant force in national politics following the Paris Commune. However, the monarchist threat soon dissipated. As republicans won more seats in the two elected chambers a return to Paris grew more likely. In 1879 the republican majority voted to move the government back to the French capital.

Versailles's latter-day engagement with national politics had been short and anything but sweet. But the return of the government to Paris in 1879 left little residual anti-Versailles feeling among the republican deputies, who had come to accommodate themselves quite well within the palace and the town. And the constitution allowed the palace to retain a small but not insignificant role within the Republic. Notably, the two elected chambers convened in Versailles to elect a president. This was a practice which continued through the

Third Republic down to 1940 and was subsequently adopted under the Fourth Republic after 1944. René Coty was the last president to be elected at Versailles, in 1953.

This convention for the election of the president passed into abeyance under the 1958 constitution of the Fifth Republic, in which presidents were elected by the population as a whole. Yet by then it was clear that Versailles had established a kind of supra-political role as a republican palace: it was where constitutional amendments were agreed by the two assemblies. And here, too, peace treaties were signed (as in 1919), state banquets were held, visiting dignitaries were hosted and international conferences were convened. But was this all that Versailles had come to? Happily not. A new imaginative vision of a Versailles open to France and the wider world had already started to emerge.

The curatorship of Pierre de Nolhac between 1892 and 1920 marked a turning point in the post-Bourbon life of the Palace of Versailles.

6

CONSERVING

Versailles, Curation and Heritage

N 1892 THE PALACE OF VERSAILLES ACQUIRED
a new director, Pierre de Nolhac. De Nolhac was
still in his early thirties and his experience of
museums amounted to little more than five years as *adjoint*
(assistant) in the same institution. Despite this relative lack
of experience, de Nolhac would remain in post until 1920.
His influence over the institution lasted in some ways even
after his death in 1936. More than any other individual, he was
responsible for bringing Versailles into the modern era. Paradoxically, that would involve, as we shall see, looking back
rather than forward.

The question that had first puzzled the revolutionaries of 1789—what was Versailles, dynastic seat of the
Bourbon dynasty, nerve-centre of the French state, *for,* in a

post-absolutist age?—had received a variety of responses. None of the regimes that followed—including the restored Bourbon monarchs who ruled between 1815 and 1830—considered a return to its earlier functions. The Orléanist monarch had come up with an answer of sorts: turning the palace into a museum of the glories of French history. Versailles would thus serve the patriotic cause, dissolving political barriers in a unified celebration of France's greatness. After a few wobbles in the early 1870s, when the nature of the regime suggested that a monarchist restoration might be on the cards, the Third Republic had largely accepted this nationalistic approach and added a largely depoliticised ceremonial role for the former palace of the Bourbons. From the late nineteenth century, Versailles was no longer the focus of political debate; it had been effectively republicanised.

Yet if it had latterly acquired an acceptance of sorts within national life, a challenging physical monument like Versailles also required substantial material support, which the Third Republic, like its predecessors, was loath to extend. By 1892, despite some efforts of reconstruction, Versailles was visibly dilapidated. The problem was all the more acute in that there were some who liked it that way. *Fin-de-siècle* aesthetes like Robert de Montesquiou, who relished crumbling façades and overgrown monuments, urged that institutions like Versailles should be left 'to die well'. Proust, a friend of de Montesquiou, largely concurred, bemoaning efforts at modernisation and relishing the site as 'a great name, sweet and tarnished, royal cemetery of leafy glades, vast lakes and marbles'.[1] The palace seemed so linked to its distant, glorious past that when, just after 1900, two English lady tourists claimed to have experienced unearthly visions of Marie Antoinette and her circle in the Trianon grounds, the perception of a palace haunted by its former denizens gained widespread traction.[2]

Such 'change-nothing' attitudes echoed the approach of the curators and archivists in place when de Nolhac began work as director of Versailles. Their view of conservation, de Nolhac wryly noted, amounted to leaving unfound treasures unfound. Their career advice for their new colleague was 'leave well alone a museum that no longer interests anyone'.[3]

THE DE NOLHAC PARADIGM

The title that de Nolhac later gave his memoir of his days as director, *La résurrection de Versailles* (1937), showed just how opposed he was to such a conservative, defeatist view. It also indicated the scale of his ambitions. His analysis of the problems the institution faced was prophetically on the mark: first, Versailles lacked financial resources; second, it was not attracting enough visitors; and third, the historical research and curatorial care it offered were not sufficiently professional. His answers to these issues sketched out guidelines that all his successors would follow. While pressurising public authorities for more money, he argued that curators should also seek to diversify income streams, notably from private philanthropy; that they should deploy increased income so as to improve the quality of what was on offer, while also using modern media to increase the palace's popularity with the general public; and that they needed to bring the institution into the mainstream of professional historical research and curation.

This approach implied that Versailles was a monument classified as worth conserving. Symptomatically, for most of the period since 1789 this had not been the case: it was a government building, a civil building (*bâtiment civil*), and did not count as a historical monument. Notions of historical conservation had emerged during the 1790s, as revolutionaries sought to distinguish between what was and was not worth preserving of the *ancien régime*. In 1838 a national Historical Monuments Commission was established and the listing of historic buildings began. The commission's notion of conservation and heritage—concepts now brought under the heading of the word *patrimoine*—had a strong period-specific aesthetic element. Buildings were thought worth conserving not just because they were old, but because they were attuned to current canonical views of beauty and historical value. Throughout the nineteenth century, priority was thus given to monuments from Antiquity and—especially once a taste for the Gothic emerged—the medieval period. Buildings from the seventeenth and eighteenth centuries tended to be downgraded. Much the same had been true, moreover, of the canons of art history: the high valuation given to medieval and especially Renaissance works completely overshadowed French classical art. Even a figure such as Louis XIV's court painter Charles Le Brun, central to the Versailles story, was widely disparaged or ignored. Only in the late nineteenth century had this begun to change, with seventeenth- and eighteenth-century French art from the Versailles period being viewed more admiringly. This was evident in the *fin-de-siècle* development of museums and art galleries across Europe. It also registered in the decision in 1906 to place the buildings and estate of Versailles on the national conservation list for the first time.

This change in status played strongly into de Nolhac's hand. He staked Versailles's claims for conservation not simply on the grounds of its historical significance but also and above all for their artistic value. As de Nolhac stated, a depoliticised Versailles stood as 'a decorative arts museum [that was] unique in the world'.[4] It followed that the pro- gramme for action was absolutely not to try to imagine a future for Versailles grounded in modernity. The Louis- Philippe museum approach had been based on the idea of representing the national past rather than incarnating it. Now it looked like passé propaganda for the Orléanist regime. For de Nolhac, Versailles's viability in the modern world involved establishing its value through reframing for future genera- tions what could be seen as 'a moment of perfection in French art'.* De Nolhac's 'resurrection' of Versailles involved recreat- ing the spirit of its glory days under the Bourbons—giving up the nineteenth century's quest for modernisation and instead

---

* To use the title of a 1974 exhibition at the Hôtel de la Monnaie in Paris: *Louis XV: un moment de perfection de l'art français.*

turning the clock back rather than forward, thus allowing the palace's initial identity to reassert itself.

Nolhac's approach also implied that the destiny of Versailles, now shorn of its former political context, would depend in future less on rulers and statesmen than on museum curators and historians. De Nolhac himself was both. Originally destined for a career as a scholar of the Italian Renaissance, he had discovered unknown manuscripts by Petrarch in the Vatican Library before taking up his post at Versailles. His studies had been influenced by the professionalisation of historical scholarship taking place in this period. In particular, the École pratique des hautes études, created in 1868, placed an emphasis on archival research by professionally trained cadres of historians. Work in archives could not only reveal hidden facets of the past, but also dispose of myths that had built up over time and been disseminated widely enough to give them credence. This positivistic approach had its limitations, but also produced a powerful impact, revolutionising the study of the history of the monument and its denizens. De Nolhac had trained at the École pratique and fully subscribed to its tenets. An early discovery, for example, was a document mapping out the accommodation of individuals across the palace under the *ancien régime*, which allowed him completely to revise existing assumptions about court hierarchy.

Between 1898 and 1931 de Nolhac would write over a dozen careful scholarly works on Versailles and the figures most associated with its history. He also held regular historical conferences and seminars at the site, his academic status enhanced by his becoming a professor at the Sorbonne in 1910. His work reveals, moreover, that he had not restricted his researches to manuscripts, but had also scoured the stores and attics of the chateau for unexpected treasures. In writing the history of Versailles, the rediscovery of the material culture of its past was to be as important as its written records.

This revitalised scholarly approach was very much to the fore in de Nolhac's reform of Louis-Philippe's historical galleries, which were showing their age and no longer fired the imagination of visitors. De Nolhac realised that the old king had placed the creation of an unbroken historical record over any notion of authenticity. He therefore transformed the ordering principles and contents of the galleries. Much dross in the form of anachronistic reimaginings of great battles was removed, and gaps filled with finds of superior artistic quality that de Nolhac had made within the palace. In the palace as a whole, paintings were wherever possible placed alongside other artworks from the same period.

De Nolhac was no respecter of entrenched opinion: his radical changes to the underlying philosophy and layout of the historical galleries—and the palace collections in general—risked alienating supporters of old ideas about Versailles. He countered this by embarking on a concerted and enduring charm offensive, targeted at key figures in the political and cultural elite. From titled luminaries (including the duc d'Aumale, son of Louis-Philippe, and Napoleon III's venerable widow, the former empress Eugénie, who had a personal investment in the old Versailles) to literary figures such as the Goncourt brothers and Anatole France—all were bombarded with de Nolhac's seriousness, courtesy and discreet zeal. He also drew on his finds to organise annual exhibitions dedicated to underrated artists such as Jean-Marc Nattier, who had painted portraits of the women of Louis XV's court. These attracted a broader public that could now appreciate great artworks without feeling they were thereby demonstrating royalist sympathies. For much of the nineteenth century, anxiety had focused on the possibility of the restoration of the Bourbon dynasty; from now on, it would instead focus on the restoration of the site and its furniture.

Although initially anxious that it could inhibit his authority, de Nolhac also welcomed the establishment in 1907 of the Société des Amis de Versailles, on the lines of a similar 'friends' group that had been created for the Louvre in 1897. It originated following a campaign by the journalist Eugène Tardieu in the *Écho de Paris* newspaper, which had deplored the crumbling, uncared-for state of much of the palace. The Society's founding committee included two future Presidents of the Republic (Alexandre Millerand and Raymond Poincaré), cultural celebrities—the Society's first president was the famous dramatist Victorien Sardou—and, significantly, Francophile North American millionaires.

The outbreak of war in 1914 interrupted de Nolhac's directorship and brought its own problems. In the face of a threatened German breakthrough in the autumn of 1914, some precious artworks were evacuated and others walled-in in the cellars below the Gabriel Wing. In 1918 fear of air raids led to further emergency measures. But, for the most part, life at Versailles went on as usual, though fundraising charity events for patriotic causes were added to the usual round of visits, conferences and seminars.

The signing in the Hall of Mirrors of the treaty that ended the Franco-Prussian War in 1871 stripped France of the provinces of Alsace and Lorraine, and marked the inauguration of the German Empire. The decision to hold the ceremonial signature of the peace treaty ending the First World War in 1919 in the same location was an unequivocal riposte, and marked a key moment in soldering together the history of Versailles and the history of the Third Republic. Versailles would henceforth signal a republican triumph as well as an absolutist creation. This also proved the moment—following a final exhibition, dedicated to France's contribution to the American War of Independence, which had ended in another Treaty of Versailles in 1783—that de Nolhac retired. Under his watch, Versailles had become republicanised and his vision for the palace's future established as curatorial orthodoxy.

FROM DE NOLHAC TO VAN DER KEMP

One of the principal points of de Nolhac's approach to the conservation of Versailles was that state funding would never suffice, and that private philanthropy would always be needed to provide the funds that so complex a monument required. This was to remain true in the decades that followed his retirement, partly because of a huge increase in the number of listed monuments throughout France—there were 1,702 of them when de Nolhac came to Versailles in 1887, but by 1920 they numbered 4,400. Moreover, the war had wreaked destruction and damage on many of these, especially those near the Western Front, greatly increasing demands on state coffers. Help was, however, at hand: by 1918–19 one of the principal sources of Versailles's financial salvation, US philanthropy, had already made its presence felt.

The decision to hold the 1919 signing ceremony in Versailles might be accounted as an act of chauvinistic triumphalism quite as provocative as Charles Le Brun's famous series of Louis XIV's victories that graced its ceilings.* Yet, in fact, French Premier Georges Clemenceau's proposal of the site was warmly supported by US President Woodrow Wilson. This highlighted the extent to which Versailles had become an icon of Western civilisation in the anglophone world, and most strikingly in North America.

Before the war, de Nolhac had already enjoyed a measure of success in drawing financial support from Francophile millionaires. Versailles was one of the models that Gilded Age American tycoons used in designing their residences. The Vanderbilt Marble House constructed between 1888 and 1892 in Rhode Island, for example, a pastiche of the Trianon, is but a single example of a whole wave of similar acts of architectural homage. Gordon Bennett, super-rich publisher of the *New York Herald*, exemplified a complementary

---

* See Chapter 2, p. 55.

War artist William Orpen was commissioned by the British government to paint the signing of the Versailles Peace Treaty in the Hall of Mirrors on 28 June 1919, ending hostilities and setting out terms for the peace. The international figures around the table form a collective portrait that is dwarfed by the surroundings. This effect is enhanced by Le Brun's famous painting, *Le Roi gouverne par lui-même*, which is visible at the top of the painting: the grandeur of the king's reputation contrasted with the often petty squabbling that marked the peace conference.

trend, that of wealthy figures building pieds-à-terre in the town of Versailles in imitation of Mansart and Mique. Such individuals also often sent their children to finish their education through 'civilisation' courses in Paris, and they also trawled the international art market to collect works from the period of Versailles's former glories. The Third Republic played up to this infatuation: the French pavilion at the Universal Exposition held in St Louis in 1904 was dripping with Sèvres porcelain, Gobelins tapestries and the like. From this perspective, de Nolhac's final exhibition in 1919 on the American War of Independence was artfully contrived as millionaire bait.

These transnational exchanges prepared the ground for a surge of US philanthropy from the interwar period onwards. It had become essential, in fact. The buildings and especially the gardens of Versailles were in very bad shape. The government decision in 1922 to allow the palace to impose an entry charge for visitors seemed almost an act of financial desperation. Then, in 1924, out of the blue, the President of the Republic Raymond Poincaré received the offer of a donation of a million dollars from the Standard Oil heir John D. Rockefeller, Jr. Rockefeller had toured cultural sites in France the previous year and now chose Versailles along with the chateau of Fontainebleau and Reims Cathedral as the targets of his largesse. He would add a further $1.85 million to his gift in 1927. Three-quarters of the money he donated went to Versailles, funding a whole host of works of restoration.

Scholarly research into the monument continued in the interwar years, and was given extra impetus by the discovery—by the curator Pierre Verlet—that much of the Versailles furniture, dispersed after 1789, was still to be found in museums, galleries, depositories and warehouses across France—and could therefore be both identified and, it was hoped, returned to their home. De Nolhac's successors followed his approach in consistently seeking to publicise and promote individual projects over the interwar period. An exhibition in 1937 to celebrate the centenary of Louis-Philippe's historical galleries met with great success. So, too, did the 1939 exhibition marking the 150th anniversary of the French Revolution. It was, however, forced to close its doors early when the Second World War broke out in September of that year. Versailles had already begun to prepare for a war in which the risks of devastation were incalculably higher than ever before: windows were boarded up, rafters fireproofed, artworks placed in storage and many items sent to safe havens in the provinces—as was the table on which the 1919 peace treaty had been signed. In the event, the Nazi occupying forces were gentle towards Versailles. After all, the Germans were ultra-respectful of a historic site in the creation of the Reich and the Hall of Mirrors became a place of pilgrimage for German soldiers on leave in Paris (who customarily aimed a kick at the spot where the 1919 Versailles treaty had been signed). Fortunately, plans to give the collaborationist Vichy regime's President, Marshal Pétain, an official residence here fell through: such an

German troops occupied Versailles from 1940 to 1944. The popularity of the Hall of Mirrors where the German Empire had been declared in 1871 helped to protect the palace in bad times.

act would have repoliticised the site in a harmful way for the palace's future. The relative calm of these years was broken momentarily in 1944, when Versailles seemed at risk from Allied bombing associated with the Normandy landings. In the event, although there were casualties in the town, the palace and estate were untouched.

The Nazi occupation had, however, been damaging in another way. For it had interrupted the Sisyphean task of repair and reconstruction that Versailles always demanded. Lack of manpower during the war years, along with lack of funds and shortages of raw materials and combustibles, which left many rooms to freeze in hard winters in the 1940s, had done their work. In 1951 a heavy snowstorm led to water leaking into the Hall of Mirrors. Warned that disaster was at hand, the minister for the Fine Arts, André Cornu, took the unexpected step in 1952 of launching a public appeal for funds on the radio. 'To tell you that Versailles is at risk of ruin,' he told listeners, 'is tantamount to saying that Western civilisation is on the point of losing one of its flagships. It is not only an artistic masterpiece that France must fear seeing disappear, but in each of us an irreplaceable image of France.'[5]

This was a real challenge that tested the success of the rehabilitation of the public image of Versailles since the days of Pierre de Nolhac and the impact was highly positive. A public subscription struck a resounding chord at every level of society, not only in France but across its colonies and indeed internationally. The national committee of the Sauvegarde de Versailles campaign, stuffed full of prominent political, social and cultural dignitaries, was replicated by scores of local committees brimming with enthusiasm for the task in hand.

Two other notable cultural events at around the same time consolidated Versailles's place in French national affections: first, the creation in 1953 of the new technique of *son et*

lumière in the palace, which was hugely popular; second, in the following year, the release of Sacha Guitry's film production of the romanticised history of the palace under the Bourbons, *Si Versailles m'était conté* (known in English as *Royal Affairs in Versailles*), featuring such stars as Gérard Philippe, Jean Marais, Orson Welles, Claudette Colbert, Edith Piaf and Brigitte Bardot. Some of the profits of the film were funnelled into the Sauvegarde campaign.

The year 1953 marked a turning point in another way, too, for it also witnessed the appointment as director of Versailles of the young and dynamic Gérald Van der Kemp, who was to remain in post until 1980. Personally charismatic, 'VDK' had joined the Foreign Legion in his youth; as a young curator during the Second World War he was said to have once kept the Mona Lisa under his bed to prevent it from falling into Nazi hands. In post, he proved a shrewd political operator. His overtly Gaullist sympathies provided him with excellent political links after the declaration of the Fifth Republic in 1958, which he utilised to the advantage of Versailles. In 1966 he negotiated with Charles de Gaulle the cession of a wing of the Trianon estate—the so-called Trianon-sous-Bois—for presidential purposes. Versailles was also placed at the permanent disposition of the President of the Republic for state ceremonies and for receptions of heads of state. The visit of Britain's Elizabeth II in 1957, which also inaugurated the

Advertising poster for Sacha Guitry's 1954 blockbuster. The image evokes the march on Versailles in 1789 and the *journées* of 5 and 6 October.

newly restored opera house, was a glittering early example—
and was followed by visits from, among others, the Soviet
leader Nikita Khrushchev in 1960 and US President John F.
Kennedy in 1961.

But Van der Kemp was far more than a political fixer.
Immediately grasping the need for Versailles to retain its place
in national affections, he prioritised improvements in visiting
conditions. Visitors were allowed for the first time to wander freely rather than to follow guided tours, and restaurants
and modern toilet facilities were provided on-site for the first
time. It all helped: the exhibition of 1954 devoted to Marie
Antoinette drew a quarter of a million visitors. In the late
1930s annual visitor numbers had reached a million (yet only
4,000 overnight stays in Versailles hotels were recorded). By
the 1980s they would be approaching two million and rising.

For the Marie Antoinette exhibition, Van der Kemp had
secured the financial aid and logistical support for loans of
Baroness Élie de Rothschild. Such a link was symptomatic.
While being aware of the crucial need to cater to the public and to rethink the visitor experience, Van der Kemp also
borrowed from de Nolhac's happy formula of seeking philanthropic support for the institution. The Sauvegarde de Versailles movement had supplied a host of new potential donors
that he nurtured. North American Francophiles, still legion,
were a particular target. The five sons of John D. Rockefeller,
Jr. contributed a quarter of a million dollars to the Sauvegarde campaign. Van der Kemp's exploitation of this rich vein
of patronage was further facilitated by his marriage to the

American heiress Florence Harris, giving the couple an *entrée* into global philanthropic networks. In 1970 Harris created the Versailles Foundation, which operated at a more rarefied level and complemented the work of the Amis de Versailles.

The philanthropic network was absolutely vital for Van der Kemp in achieving his greatest ambition—to decorate the rooms of the palace with their original furniture. This objective was in line with the challenge made by Pierre Verlet in the 1930s, but it also linked to Pierre de Nolhac's earlier wish to seek a future for Versailles by taking it back in time to its days of glory under the *ancien régime*. In 1961 Van der Kemp was able to go part of the way towards realising the idea by securing a government commitment that public bodies throughout France be obliged to return to Versailles any works from the palace that were found to be in their possession. Although some holders were powerful enough to resist—the Louvre, for example, is unlikely ever to hand over the Mona Lisa, though it has made some prize transfers—there was a significant flow of works back to the palace via this route. But it was international philanthropy that proved the most important source of 'lost' Versailles artworks. Van der Kemp drew from international donors not just huge sums of money but also artworks they had purchased on the art market and which they freely donated to the chateau. David Rockefeller, for example, made the gift of a piece of needlework material done by Marie Antoinette at Versailles and the Tuileries Palace.

These donations were highlighted in a series of mediatised inaugurations that punctuated Van der Kemp's tenure:

ranging from the opening of the opera house in 1958 (which featured in Queen Elizabeth's 1957 visit) to the reopenings of the Grand Trianon (1966), the suites of Madame de Maintenon and of the queen (1975), the Hall of Mirrors and the Chambre du Roi (both in 1980). Critics expressed horror that to complete the 'look' of certain rooms, Van der Kemp had recourse to the work of local teams of skilled artisans, and he was not above discreetly using plastic instead of crystal in some rooms. Nevertheless, the achievement was huge.

In 1978 a group of Breton nationalists planted a bomb in the historical galleries. It caused a certain amount of damage, but was more important for the loud and unanimous public outrage that it provoked. This showed the extent to which Versailles was now accepted as an icon of national unity that transcended political boundaries. Artfully directed by a series of visionary directors, Versailles had secured a cherished place in the republican sun.

CONCLUSION

ÉRALD VAN DER KEMP'S TENURE—ONE IS tempted to say reign—at Versailles between 1953 and 1980 consolidated and updated the formula for Versailles's survival and prosperity identified at the turn of the century by his predecessor Pierre de Nolhac. That formula is essentially still in place, though the character of and balance between the different elements—reliance on private philanthropy as well as state subventions, commercial acumen and awareness of visitor satisfaction, and professional standards regarding the history of Versailles—have shifted in a number of respects.

The biggest changes have been to the context in which Versailles operates. When VDK came on the scene, the palace was scarcely keeping its head above water financially, and was finding it hard to establish contemporary relevance. By the time he left the palace, dramatic change was evident in levels of public and state investment in the idea of national heritage (*patrimoine*). From the 1960s and 1970s the notion had expanded to embrace natural and more broadly conceived cultural sites as well as individual historical monuments. Culture Minister André Malraux's law of 1962 introduced protection for so-called *secteurs sauvegardés,* historical and cultural sites that could include entire neighbourhoods such as the Marais in Paris. Sites no longer had to pre-date 1800 to be considered historical monuments—the Eiffel Tower was thus listed for the first time in 1964. The international heritage movement stimulated further development in France: the year of European heritage in 1975 was important in international consciousness-raising, as was the listing of World Heritage Sites begun by UNESCO in the early 1970s. Versailles was UNESCO-listed in 1979. By 2017 France, with forty-three sites, had become the country with the fourth highest number of such sites (behind Italy, China and Spain). A telling sign of how much resonance the heritage movement had achieved was the sharp growth in visitor numbers to all French museums: from 5 million in 1960, the number nearly tripled to 14 million by 1992. This upward trend was reflected in the number of visits to Versailles: by 2000 the 2 million mark was being regularly achieved.

The heritage movement has also boosted scholarship, an important part of the de Nolhac paradigm. The notion of *lieux de mémoire* (sites of memory), coined by publisher and historian Pierre Nora, initiated fertile and imaginative explorations of the links between national history, collective memory and individual institutions.[1] From the late 1980s and early 1990s Versailles became the subject of exciting new research, which has continued to the present day. After 2006 much of this work was channelled through the Centre de recherche du château de Versailles, which sets the history of the palace in the broader context of court culture across Europe.[2]

The second major contextual change was the government decision in 1995 to give the Versailles estate a considerable measure of administrative unity and autonomy through the creation of the Établissement public du château, du musée et du domaine national de Versailles (EPV for short) under the tutelage of the Ministry of Culture.[3] As its title suggests, the EPV's remit extends to both the estate and the buildings, enabling a more coherent unified approach. The body has used its autonomy to pursue a dynamic policy of expansion. This has involved taking back parts of the palace and grounds that were in the hands of central government. The Trianon-sous-Bois wing conceded to General de Gaulle in 1966 for state visits was returned to the EPV in 2005. In the same year, the legislative chamber created in the South Wing in the early 1870s, which had since 1879 been administered from Paris, also passed into the EPV's hands. With the exception of the small hunting lodge, the Pavillon de la Lanterne, situated near the site of the old Menagerie—which President Sarkozy took over in 2007 as a presidential retreat—the Versailles estate is now fully managed by the EPV.

The second way the EPV has expanded has been through taking on and developing as tourist destinations those properties within the town of Versailles that had links with the palace in the past. The *Jeu de Paume*, situated a short distance from the palace entrance, which was the site of the dramatic Tennis Court Oath of June 1789, a key moment in the Revolutionary drama of that year, was listed by the Second Republic in 1848—more than half a century before the palace. Restored for the Revolutionary bicentenary in 1989 after decades of gentle vegetation, it now forms part of the Versailles visits. Similarly, the Hôtel des Menus Plaisirs—the Estates General's normal meeting place—came under the purview of the EPV. Since 1996 it has hosted the Centre for Baroque Music. Also in 1996 the Grand Commun, which had remained a military hospital until 1986, was reincorporated into the palace and is currently being prepared as the service hub for the whole domain. Modernisation of the Écuries on the doorstep of the palace has also made them part of the Versailles visitor experience: since 2012 the Petite Écurie has housed a sculpture museum; and in 2016 a modernised museum of carriages reopened within the Grande Écurie.

The efforts of expansion and modernisation since 2003 have taken place within a state-sponsored scheme, known as 'Le Grand Versailles', planned to continue until 2020. A key aim has been work of restoration and renovation, the most eye-catching of which was the complete refit of the Hall of Mirrors in 2007. The scheme provides for the state to make an annual subvention to the EPV of 25 million euros—roughly a quarter of the total budget. Income from tickets and commercial activities makes up nearly 50 per cent of the overall

budget. A considerable part of the rest comes from philanthropy and sponsorship in various forms.

The EPV's autonomy has allowed it to woo new cohorts
of benefactors even more aggressively than in the past. The
Versailles Foundation and an American branch of the Amis
de Versailles founded in 1999 keep alive the US contribution. It is noticeable that while around 20 per cent of visitors to the palace and gardens are French, the next largest
national cohort is from the United States with 14 per cent
(Britain, in contrast, only manages about 3 per cent of the
total). Since 2003 the EPV has diversified its income from
the revenue stream derived from private philanthropy into
innovative forms of sponsorship with businesses and international firms. The VINCI construction group were the
main partners, for example, in the restoration of the Hall
of Mirrors and went on to support the renovation of the
Dufour Wing of the palace. The Bréguet watch company is
currently playing a similar role in restoration work in Marie
Antoinette's Hameau. Revenue from sponsorship is variable,
but often amounts to 15 to 20 million euros annually. It was
largely through such sponsorship links that the EPV sur-
mounted the terrible devastation caused in 1999 by a storm
which destroyed 10,000 trees throughout the estate.

Versailles has prospered under the EPV and the state-
backed 'Le Grand Versailles' scheme. In the first decade of
its existence, visitor numbers rose from 2.9 to 4 million—
and continued to rise. The 6.7 million visitor level achieved

in 2016 made Versailles the third most visited museum in France, behind the Louvre and the Eiffel Tower.* The EPV has also been shrewd in keeping the palace in the public eye, notably by collaborating with film-makers on location shooting. Versailles has appeared in hundreds of feature films and TV dramas. Sofia Coppola's highly popular *Marie Antoinette* (2006) had historians picking holes in the script as the Versailles turnstiles whirled. The EPV showed little interest in artistic values or quality: Coppola seemed to suggest that Louis XVI's queen was a fashion-shoe fetishist, for example, while the popular 2015 TV series *Versailles* presented Louis XIV's palace as the site of improbably frequent couplings.

No doubt, on considering these aesthetic lapses, the EPV would have been crying all the way to the bank. A more serious way of building new audiences was the decision to hold an annual exhibition featuring a modern artist—with an apparent preference for outrageous ones. The Michael Jackson statue and balloon sculptures of Jeff Koons dominated the first show in 2008 and controversy has never seemed far away, with the work of Takashi Murakami (2010), and then Anish Kapoor (2015), infuriating Versailles traditionalists. Indeed Kapoor's *Dirty Corner*, which he unwisely compared to Marie Antoinette's vagina, attracted anti-Semitic graffiti and personal attacks.[4]

---

* The fact that Disneyland Paris claims double that number is a reminder of changing tastes in mass leisure.

If Versailles stays in the news as a result of such exhibitions, the incident also highlighted some of the issues the palace faces as a result of its strategic successes in wooing the media and attracting public attention.[5] The sheer number of visitors to Versailles creates its own strains: being endlessly jostled by tourist hordes in the state rooms and the Hall of Mirrors can be a mildly scary experience. Weight of visitor numbers has caused deterioration in some furnishings and some parts of the gardens, while having the fountains play much more frequently than in the past has caused damage to the statuary on some installations. Lack of surveillance in parts of the gardens has led to a surge in cases of vandalism. There are tensions, too, between the work of conservation by curators and the business models beloved of EPV management. These have surfaced in recent years over the decision to orientate strategic restoration for the palace buildings around the year 1789 (the Marie Antoinette moment) and around 1715 for the gardens (the Le Nôtre moment, so to speak). The discrepancy is problematic: some of the most striking *bosquets*, such as Hubert Robert's pre-Romantic Bains d'Apollon, were created after 1715, while long-destroyed seventeenth-century features have been essentially recreated, prompting charges that this risks making the whole estate a version of 'Versailles-Land'. The policy also effaces nineteenth-century features of the garden, so often neglected in the work of conservation. The desire to provide period furnishings for palace rooms has led to a scandal of a different sort. Accusations of forgery have been made against dealers who have seemingly exploited the palace management's desire to find 'forgotten' pieces by providing counterfeit furniture at huge expense to the palace—and ultimately to the public purse.

On balance, however, the problems Versailles currently faces shrink into insignificance in comparison with those it confronted in the immediate aftermath of 1789. The palace and gardens probably look better now than they have for decades—indeed possibly for centuries. Versailles's place in the national affections seems unchanged—and indeed appears to have been enhanced. The use of the palace in 2017 as a stage for newly elected President Emmanuel Macron to flex his political muscles suggests that politicians are once again becoming alert to the cultural capital of this extraordinary world-historical site of memory.

ACKNOWLEDGEMENTS

I warmly thank my former student, Gabriel Wick, for allowing me to draw on his expertise on Versailles. David McCallam kindly supplied a translated version of the Chénier poem cited on pages 174–6—though I have tried to rework it in my own way, probably for worse. My thanks also go, as ever, to my agent, Felicity Bryan. Georgina Blackwell and Richard Milbank gracefully guided the text through the editing process. Thank you to Katie Lambright and Sandra Beris for their help in shepherding the book to completion. And my wife, Josephine McDonagh, is a constant and loving inspiration for all I do.

APPENDICES[1]

1. Designing Versailles

In his memoirs, royal adviser (and author of fairy tales) Charles Perrault (1628–1703) gives fascinating glimpses into the king's involvement in the early development of Versailles.

The king had ordered the construction of the grotto at Versailles, and I thought that, since His Majesty had taken for his emblem the words *Nec pluribus impar* ('Not unequal to many'), with a globe underneath the words, and since most of the decorations at Versailles had adopted the fable of Apollo and the Sun, it would be good to situate, at the other end of the park to the grotto (which since has been destroyed), Apollo coming to rest with Thetis after having encompassed the earth. This would represent the king coming to rest at Versailles after having worked to do good to all the world . . .

After examining plans to demolish the old chateau and replace it with an entirely new one, the king still wished to preserve the little chateau. It was pointed out that it threatened to collapse and was buckling in a number of places. Suspecting a plot, the king said loudly and with some feeling, 'Do as you like, but if you demolish it I will have it rebuilt unchanged in its entirety.'

2. Louis XIV entertains

Louis XIV's sister-in-law the Princesse Palatine, duchesse d'Orléans (1652–1722), was one of the great letter-writers of her age. Here she gives an eye-witness account of the king's habitual round of entertainments, the so-called *soirées d'appartements*.

Every Monday, Wednesday and Friday, the *soirées d'appartement* take place. All the men at court gather in the royal antechamber at 6 p.m., while the ladies gather in the Queen's chamber. All then proceed to the salon [which forms part of the still-unfinished Hall of Mirrors]. There is a large room there where there are violins for those who wish to dance. Beyond is the royal throne room, where there are all kinds of vocal and instrumental music. Then beyond, there is the royal bedroom where three card-tables have been set up for the king, his brother and the queen. Beyond that is a grand room in which there are twenty gaming tables covered with green velvet cloth with golden fringes, and then a large antechamber containing the king's billiards table. Beyond that is another large room with four long tables with all sorts of dishes, fruit tarts and confitures and so on. People then go onwards into a room with four tables, this time weighed down with carafes and glasses and all sorts of wines. After eating, people return to the gaming rooms. Those who do not gamble—including myself and many others—wander around from one room to another, listening to music or watching the gaming, for one can go where one wishes. All this lasts until 10 p.m., at which time people go off to have supper. It is certain that all this is worth seeing. It would all be magnificent and entertaining if one could bring to the occasion a happy heart.

3. A royal guide to the gardens

Louis XIV's personal guide for visitors to his beloved gardens—his *Manière de montrer les jardins de Versailles*—provided a strict itinerary aimed to ensure admiration for his achievements.

1. On leaving the chateau by the vestibule in the *cour de marbre*, one goes onto the terrace. One must stop at the top of the steps to consider the situation of the parterres, the water features and the fountains.

2. Next, one turns left and descends the Sphynx steps. At the top of them one pauses to consider the Parterre du Midi, and from there one proceeds to the balustrade of the Orangerie, from which point one can see the parterre of the orange trees and the Swiss lake (*piece d'eau des Suisses*).

3. One turns right to go up to the terrace, and proceeds to the part where one can see the Bacchus and Saturn statues.

4. One then proceeds onto the terrace near to the Cleopatra statue, and then to the top step by the Latona fountain; one can there see the fountains and the water-jets around it, the lizards, the ramps, the statues, the *allée royale*, the *bassin d'Apollon*, and the canal; and then one must turn around to look at the parterre and the chateau.

5. Next one goes down the slope . . .

4. Louis XIV and his courtiers

The duc de Saint-Simon was a denizen of Louis XIV's court in the last years of his reign, and this passage from his memoirs shows the persistence of the king's commitment to attracting the nobility to Versailles.

The king looked to the left and the right at his *lever*, *coucher* and at his meals, in passing through his rooms, and in the Versailles gardens in which only courtiers were allowed to follow him. He saw and noticed everyone, and no one escaped his gaze, even those who were hoping not to be seen. He remarked by himself the absences of those who were always at court and those of the transients who came more or less frequently. He combined the particular and general reasons for these absences, and never lost the slightest occasion to behave appropriately as a consequence. He regarded it as a demerit both to himself and to all distinction not to make the court one's normal residence for the first group, and for others to come rarely while it was certain disgrace for those who came never or almost never. When it was a question of some benefit for them, he proudly replied, 'He is a man I never see.' Above all, he could not abide people who enjoyed themselves in Paris. He tolerated fairly easily those who preferred the countryside, although one had to be moderate in this or else to have taken precautions before residing elsewhere for some time.

5. Versailles under Louis XV

Wenzel Anton, Prince von Kaunitz-Rietberg, was Austrian Empress Maria Theresa's ambassador to France in 1751–2, before becoming Austrian Chancellor and negotiating the Franco-Austrian treaty of alliance in 1756. Kaunitz's view of Versailles under Louis XV, however, showed a certain asperity, and highlighted courtiers' growing preference for Paris over Versailles.

> Versailles is a real desert when the king is absent, as he is for ten months of the year. At such times, only those who are obliged to remain do so. When he is present, the courtiers who attend him hunt with him and take supper in his private apartment—or else, if they don't sup, they return as fast as they can to Paris to hide their shame and despair. At these times, one commonly sees a score of ladies present, and no men at all, except for a few decrepit old seigneurs. For the fortnight when it is not their turn on the rota of service, the ladies-in-waiting spend their time in Paris, while those who remain have the painful duty of taking the saddest supper in all the world with Queen Marie Leczinska . . .
>
> In the midst of all the splendour and studied grandeur, one is surprised to note from time to time certain practices quite out of keeping with the court. People throng all the apartments at Versailles at all times. The men who have the honour of doing court to the queen are allowed to enter even into her bedroom. In the queen's antechamber, one sees serving girls sitting down with ladies-in-waiting, in a way that makes it difficult to distinguish them.

6. An English traveller is
unimpressed by Versailles

The English agronomist Arthur Young (1741–1820) toured France on the eve of the Revolution. *His Travels in France* (1792) revealed a down-to-earth approach which had little truck with the purported splendour of the palace.

The ceremony of the king's dining in public is more odd than splendid. The queen sat by him with a cover before her, but ate nothing; conversing with the duke of Orleans and the duke of Liancourt who stood behind her chair. To me it would have been a most uncomfortable meal, and were I a sovereign I would sweep away three-fourths of these stupid forms . . .

The palace of Versailles, one of the objects of which report had given me the greatest expectation, is not in the least striking. I view it without emotion; the impression it makes is nothing. What can compensate the want of unity? From whatever point viewed, it appears an assemblage of buildings; a splendid quarter of a town, but not a fine edifice; an objection from which the garden front is not free, though by far the most beautiful.—The great gallery is the finest room I have seen; the other apartments are nothing; but the pictures and statues are well known to be a capital collection. The whole palace except the chapel seems to be open to all the world; we pushed through an amazing crowd of all sorts of people to see the procession [of a royal ceremony] many of them not very well dressed, whence it appears that no questions are asked.

7. Queen Marie Antoinette's smile

Chateaubriand was one of France's leading Romantic poets and writers in the early nineteenth century. As a young noble-man, he gained privileged entry to the royal court just as the Revolution was starting in July 1789. At the end of this pas-sage, he refers here to his role in 1815 under the Bourbon Res-toration when he would be involved in the exhumation of the remains of the royal family guillotined during the Terror.

A Breton poet who had just arrived in Paris begged me to take him to Versailles. There are people who visit gardens and fountains while empires are being over-thrown . . . I took my Pindarus to the Hall of Mirrors at the time of the royal Mass . . . The queen passed by with her two children; their fair hair seemed to be awaiting crowns. The virginal dignity of the eleven-year-old Mme the duchesse d'Angoulême, who com-bined nobility of rank with the innocence of a mere girl, drew the gaze of all. The little Dauphin walked un-der his sister's protection, and M. Du Touchet followed his pupil. He noticed me and kindly pointed me out to the queen. She glanced at me with a smile, the gracing salutation that she had made me on the day of my presentation at court. I will never forget this smile, that soon afterwards would be no more. In smiling, Marie Antoinette formed her mouth in such a way that the memory of the smile (horrid to relate) allowed me to recognise the jaw-bone of this daughter of kings when the head of the poor woman was discovered in the exhumations of 1815.

8. A plan to destroy Versailles in 1789

In recounting his role in the Revolution in his *Le Nouveau Paris* (1798) the celebrated Parisian author, journalist and politician Louis-Sébastien Mercier (1740–1814) justified his failed proposal to destroy Versailles altogether at the start of the Revolution.

As long as it was still standing, the palace of Versailles gave courage to all the slaves of the royal court and nurtured their treachery. Since people hold great store by symbolism, had the home of kings been destroyed, as political prudence demanded, the king and his court would have realised that the act of insurrection was serious and decisive, and they would have joined with it, and all the blood that later flowed would have remained in the veins of the generous-hearted French nation . . .

The palace of Versailles was the vestment of a great
king, of a proud and powerful king; and there were to be
no more proud and powerful kings. In these unique circumstances, people should have harkened to the voice
of a dreamer strongly convinced of the real dangers that
resulted from allowing to subsist a palace that was the
centre of all kinds of political machinations and whose
name stirred ideas, from near and far, that were wholly
discordant with an order of things that was so novel.

9. Elegy to a lost Versailles, 1794

The young poet André Chénier (1762–94) took a pro-
monarchist position in 1789, and his 'Ode to Versailles', written as the Terror was unfolding in Paris, has a powerfully
elegiac tone. He would be guillotined a matter of days before
the overthrow of Robespierre in July 1794.

Ô Versaille, ô bois, ô portiques,
Marbres vivants, berceaux antiques,
Par les dieux et les rois Élysée embelli,
A ton aspect, dans ma pensée,
Comme sur l'herbe aride une fraîche rosée,
Coule un peu de calme et d'oubli.
Paris me semble un autre empire,
Dès que chez toi je vois sourire
Mes pénates secrets couronnés de rameaux,

D'où souvent les monts et les plaines
Vont dirigeant mes pas aux campagnes prochaines,
Sous de triples cintres d'ormeaux.
Les chars, les royales merveilles,
Des gardes les nocturnes veilles,
Tout a fui; des grandeurs tu n'es plus le séjour:
Mais le sommeil, la solitude,
Dieux jadis inconnus, et les arts, et l'étude,
Composent aujourd'hui ta cour.

[. . .]

Ah! témoin des succès du crime,
Si l'homme juste et magnanime
Pouvait ouvrir son coeur à la félicité,
Versailles, tes routes fleuries,
Ton silence, fertile en belles rêveries,
N'auraient que joie et volupté.

℁ ℁ ℁ ℁ ℁ ℁

O Versailles, your woods and porticos,
Your living marble, your ancient bowers,
Elysium enhanced by gods and kings;
At your prospect in my mind
As fresh dew on dry grass
Calm and forgetfulness gently flow.
Paris seems a different realm
Whenever I see my secret retreats
Smiling and crowned with branches;

The plains and hills lead me further
Through nearby countryside
Under triple vaults of elms.
Cavalcades and royal marvels,
The nightly watch of guards—all has fled
Where greatness no longer finds its home,
Today your court only holds
Sleep, solitude; study, the arts
Gods unknown here hitherto.

[. . .]

Any man of just and generous mind
On seeing crime's success
Could open his heart to happiness.
Ah! Versailles! your flowery alleys
Your silence, fertile in sweet reveries
Would offer only joy and sensual delight.

10. Insanitary memoirs of the old Versailles

The celebrated nineteenth-century architectural theorist Eugène
Viollet-le-Duc (1814–79) here records an unusual form of nostal-
gia for the *ancien régime* Versailles among the court's erstwhile
denizens.

We freely admit that our ancestors had none of the conveniences in their homes, palaces and chateaux that to-

day we cannot do without . . . At Versailles the seigneurs of Louis XIV's court were obliged, for lack of latrines, to relieve themselves in the corridors . . . We remember the odour that lingered, during the reign of Louis XVIII in the corridors of Saint-Cloud, since Versailles traditions were scrupulously observed there . . . One day when I was young we visited Versailles with a respectable lady from Louis XV's court. Passing a stinking corridor, she could not withhold an exclamation of regret: 'This odour recalls for me a very wonderful time!'

11. The strengths and weaknesses of Louis-Philippe's Museum of French History

Delphine de Girardin (1804–55) wrote journalism under a male pseudonym, then published her best pieces under her own name as *Lettres parisiennes* in 1843.

[Louis-Philippe's museum] is Louis XIV's Versailles, that rats and politicians were going to destroy and that Louis-Philippe has saved. Doubtless it is sad to see walls of oak where once only marble was allowed; no doubt this refectory of the marshals of France lacks the splendour of the golden rooms on the first floor; but whose fault is that? It is not the king's but rather the current age. Versailles today is no longer the work of a monarch's munificence, it is the fruit of his ruler's economies ... The first duty of a sovereign is to understand his age; the first duty of a monument is to represent it. It seems to me that in this respect Louis-Philippe and the new Versailles have fulfilled their responsibilities. It is not their fault if the age is not as beautiful, if in our day plaster replaces mouldings, or if cardboard replaces bronze, or if bald-headed deputies replace long-wigged ambassadors ...

12. *Pierre de Nolhac on the 'resurrection' of Versailles*

In his 1937 posthumous memoirs Pierre de Nolhac, the visionary curator who led the recovery of the palace and gardens in the early twentieth century, associated the poor condition of the buildings and estate with the indifference of its curators when he joined the museum in 1886.

[Louis-Philippe's museum], more or less accommodated in what had been a working palace, was full of unsuspected riches; but the public had lost its taste for them—or at least the part of the public not attracted to the military paintings which seemed to fill it completely. In the gallery of battles, people only looked at the zouaves of Horace Vernet and the Napoleons. The great canvases by which the Second Empire had just continued a pictural tradition dating back to Louis

XIV no longer spoke to French hearts that had been crushed by the defeat at Sedan [in the Franco-Prussian War in 1870]. Versailles suffered from an understandable disdain that seemed justified by the circumstances of the time . . .

The indifference of the state for Versailles was also evident in the state of dilapidation in which the *bosquets* had been left. The fountains were falling into ruin one by one. The park—or rather the garden, to use the old term—was very little visited by outsiders and belonged solely to the inhabitants of the town . . .

The museum stores were full of uncertainty. The residue of the collections not utilised by Louis-Philippe were mixed together with pictures moved there when the chambers for the deputies were built in the palace. All sorts of sculptures were crowded together here and it seems that there would be some interesting finds here. In my naive, beginner's view, all this was scandalous, as I informed the curator for whom I worked.

Should we not perform a triage? We could present and maybe save some priceless pieces in these galleries that the state of the service does not allow to be opened to the public?

Young man, said my manager, don't get carried away. I am not unaware of the riches that we have up in the stores; but there is no way we can display them. And don't go talking about this either, for our job is to conserve them and it is easiest to do this if they conserve themselves.

But, I said, they are in a poor state of conservation: the stores in the attics are almost unheated in winter and get too hot in the summer . . .

. That is Louis-Philippe's fault, and not ours. There is no immediate danger and if I brought up such a serious question, the administration would hold it against me. Don't be zealous, young man. Write books about Versailles if you like, but leave in peace this museum that no longer interests anyone.

13. *The iconic beginnings of US philanthropy towards Versailles*

This letter from the US millionaire philanthropist John D. Rockefeller, Jr. (1874–1960) to French President Raymond Poincaré, which became widely known when published in the newspaper *Le Figaro* on 30 May 1924, marks an iconic moment in the history of the conservation of Versailles.

3 May 1924

Dear Mr President,

Returning to France last summer after an interval of 17 years, I was impressed anew with the beauty of her art, the magnificence of her architects and the splendor of her parks and gardens. Many examples of these are not only national but international treasures, for which France is trustee; their influence on the art of the world will always be full of inspiration.

That some of these great national monuments should be showing the devastating effects of time because current repairs could not be kept up during the war and that others should still bear silent witness to the ravages of war stirred in me feelings of deep regret. I realize that this situation is only temporary and will eventually right itself as the people of France are able to turn from other more pressing tasks and resume that scrupulous maintenance of their public monuments for which they have established so enviable a reputation. In the meantime I should count it a privilege to be able to help towards that end and shall be happy to contribute one million dollars, its expenditure to be entrusted to a small committee composed of Frenchmen and Americans.

It would be my thought that the money should be used for the reconstruction of Rheims Cathedral; for the reconditioning of the buildings, fountains and parks of Versailles; and for the purpose of making repairs that are urgently needed in the palace and gardens of Fontainebleau.

I am moved to make this proposal, not only because of my admiration for these great outstanding products of art, the influence of which should be continued unimpaired through the centuries to the enrichment of the lives of succeeding generations, but also because of the admiration which I have for the people of France, their fine spirit, their high courage and their devotion to home life.

With sentiments of high regard, I am, my dear Mr President,

JOHN D. ROCKEFELLER, JR.

FURTHER READING

There has been a remarkable flowering of research into and scholarship about Versailles in the last several decades. Unfortunately, only a very small proportion of it is available in English. An excellent introduction and state of the field is Mathieu da Vinha and Raphaël Masson (eds), *Versailles: histoire, dictionnaire et anthologie* (Paris, 2015). Notable themes covered in recent years include Louis XIV's day (Béatrix Saule), Versailles's iconography (Gérard Sabatier, Dominique Poulot, Jean-Pierre Neraudeau), rooms and lodgings (William Newton), the world of the court (Frédérique Laferme-Falguières, Alexandre Maral), court festivities (Marie-Christine Moine), the estate (Vincent Maroteaux, Thierry Sarmant, Frédéric Tiberghien), the park (Thierry Bosquet and Philippe Beaussant) and Louis-Philippe's Versailles museum (Thomas Gaehtgens). Though now outdated, Jean-François Solnon, *Histoire de Versailles* (several re-editions since first publication in 1997) remains the best accessible single-volume account. Émile and Madeleine Houth, *Versailles aux trois visages* (Versailles, 1980) is still the best treatment of the town of Versailles. Two valuable works covering periods on which there is surprisingly little other overall coverage are Jean-Claude Le Guillou, *Versailles avant Versailles: au temps de Louis XIII* (Paris, 2011) and Franck Ferrand, *Versailles après les rois* (Paris, 2003). On aspects of art and architecture, see the excellent catalogues of exhibitions held at the palace in recent years. Finally, the institutional website of the chateau is excellent, outguns any tourist guide, and is consultable in English-language version at http://en.chateauversailles.fr/.

Nearly all works in English start with Louis XIV and finish with the French Revolution. This is also true of Tony Spawforth, *Versailles: A Biography of a Palace* (New York, 2008), the most accessible and useful general account.

Claire Constans, *Versailles: Absolutism and Harmony* (New York, 1988) is excellent and also beautifully illustrated. Other useful English-language references are:

Amarger, Antoine, *The Hall of Mirrors: History and Restoration* (Dijon, 2007)

Baridon, Michel, *A History of the Gardens of Versailles* (Philadelphia, PA, 2008)

Berger, Robert W., *Versailles: The Château of Louis XIV* (University Park, PA, 1985)

Berger, Robert W., *In the Garden of the Sun King: Studies on the Park of Versailles under Louis XIV* (Washington, DC, 1985)

Burke, Peter, *The Fabrication of Louis XIV* (New Haven, 1992)

Duindam, Jeroen, *Vienna and Versailles: The Courts of Europe's Dynastic Rivals, 1550–1780* (Cambridge, 2003)

Dunlop, Ian, *Versailles* (London, 1970)

Goldstein, Claire, *Vaux and Versailles: The Appropriations, Erasures, and Accidents that Made Modern France* (Philadelphia, PA, 2007)

Hibbert, Christopher, *Versailles* (New York, 1972)

Himelfarb, Hélène, 'Versailles, Functions and Legends' (2001), in *Rethinking France: Les lieux de mémoire*, ed. David P. Jordan, 3 vols (Chicago, 2001–2009), I

Le Roy Ladurie, Emmanuel, *Saint-Simon and the Court of Louis XIV* (Chicago, 2001)

Levron, Jacques, *Daily Life at Versailles in the Seventeenth and Eighteenth Centuries* (London, 1968)

Mansel, Philip, *The Court of France, 1789–1830* (Cambridge, 1988)

Mukerji, Chandra, *Territorial Ambitions and the Gardens of Versailles* (Cambridge, 1997)

Pommier, Edouard (1998): 'Versailles: The Image of the Sovereign', in *Realms of Memory: The Construction of the French Past*, ed. Lawrence D. Kritzman, 3 vols (New York, 1997–1998), III

Richard, Pascale, *Versailles, the American Story* (Paris, 1999)

Thompson, Ian, *The Sun King's Garden: Louis XIV, André Le Nôtre and the Creation of the Gardens of Versailles* (London, 2006)

NOTES

Introduction

1 Charles Perrault, cited in Frédéric Tiberghien, *Versailles: le chantier de Louis XIV, 1662–1717* (Paris, 2002), p. 91.

1. Creating: From House of Cards to Fairy-tale Palace

1 Saint-Simon, *Mémoires*, 8 vols, ed. Yves Coirault (Paris, 1983–8), V, p. 532.

2 Jean Héroard, *Journal*, 2 vols, ed. Madeline Foisil (Paris, 1989), I, p. 1287.

3 Saint-Simon, *Mémoires*, V, p. 522.

4 Bassompierre, *Journal de ma vie*, 4 vols, ed. Marquis de Chantérac (Paris, 1870–77), III, pp. 285–6; windmill anecdote: Jean-François Solnon, *Histoire de Versailles* (Paris, 1997), p. 17.

5 Claude de Varennes, *Le voyage de France* (Paris, 1639), p. 195.

6 Jean-Baptiste Colbert, *Lettres, instructions et mémoires*, 10 vols (Paris, 1861–82), V, p. 266, fn. 1.

7   Cited in Solnon, *Histoire de Versailles,* p. 83. The bishop was, of course, exaggerating.

8   Pierre Verlet, *Versailles* (Paris, 1961), pp. 119–20 (citing André Félibien).

9   Colbert, *Lettres,* V, pp. 282–4, 268–9.

10 Louis XIV, *Mémoires pour l'instruction du Dauphin* [1806], ed. Pierre Goubert (Paris, 1992), p. 137.

11 André Félibien, *Description sommaire du chasteau de Versailles* (Paris, 1674), pp. 11–12.

12 Ellis Veryard, *An Account of Divers Choice Remarks . . . taken in a Journey Through the Low Countries, France, Italy and Part of Spain. . . .* (London, 1701), p, 67. Cited in Hendrik Ziegler, *Louis XIV et ses ennemis: image, propagande et contestation* (Paris, 2013), p. 331.

13 Colbert, *Lettres,* V, pp. 268–9.

14 Saint-Simon, *Mémoires,* V, p. 532.

2. Mythologising: The Golden Era (1682–1715)

1   Solnon, *Histoire de Versailles,* p. 120.

2   Louis XIV, *Mémoires,* p. 133.

3   Solnon, *Histoire de Versailles,* p. 141; Jean de La Bruyère, *Les caractères* (Paris, 1841), p. 262.

4   Primi Visconti, *Mémoires sur la cour de Louis XIV, 1673–1681* (Paris, 1988), p. 147.

5   There are several modern editions of Louis XIV's *Manière de montrer les jardins de Versailles.* See Appendix 3, pp. 167–68.

6   Cited in Solnon, *Histoire de Versailles,* p. 219.

3. *Continuing: The Bourbon Succession (1715–1789)*

1   Chateaubriand, *Mémoires d'outre-tombe*, 2 vols, ed. Jean-Claude Berchet (Paris, 1989–98), I, p. 248.

2   Cited in Michel Antoine, *Louis XV* (Paris, 1989), p. 162.

3   Madame Campan, *Mémoires sur la vie privée de Marie-Antoinette*, 2 vols, 3rd edn (Paris, 1823), p. 16.

4   Cited in Antoine, *Louis XV*, pp. 46–7, 52 ('*soulagement à ne plus faire le Roi*').

5   Antoine, *Louis XV*, p. 447.

6   See Mathieu da Vinha, *Le Versailles de Louis XIV* (Paris, 2009), p. 112. See Appendix 10, pp. 176–77.

7   Gaston de Lévis, *Souvenirs et portraits, 1780–1789* (Paris, 1815), p. 143.

8   Henriette-Lucy de La Tour du Pin, *Journal d'une femme de cinquante ans, 1778–1815*, 2 vols, ed. Comte Aymar de Liedekerke-Beaufort (Paris, 1913), p. 177–72.

9   Cited in V. Maroteaux, *Versailles, le Roi et son domaine* (Versailles, 2000), p. 148.

10 Marquis de Bombelles, *Journal*, 8 vols, ed. Jean Grassion and Frans Durif (Paris, 1977–2013), pp. 151–2.

11 Cited in Christopher Hibbert, *Versailles* (New York, 1972), p. 145. See too the comments of the English tourist Arthur Young, cited in Appendix 6, pp. 171-72.

4. *Living: Styles of Versailles Life*

1   François Guizot, *Mémoires pour servir à l'histoire de mon temps*, 8 vols (Paris, 1858), I, p. 6.

2   Visconti, *Mémoires*, pp. 43–4.

3   François Hébert, *Mémoires du curé de Versailles*, ed. Georges Girard (Paris, 1927), p. 18.

4   William Ritchey Newton, *Derrière la façade: vivre au château de Versailles au XVIIIe siècle* (Paris, 2008), p. 235.

5   Da Vinha, *Le Versailles de Louis XIV*, p. 269.

6   For these stories and their relationship to worker numbers, see Thierry Sarmant, *Les Demeures du Soleil: Louis XIV, Louvois et la surintendance des bâtiments du roi* (Seyssel, 2003), pp. 179ff.

5. Republicanising: In Search of a New Role

1   La Tour du Pin, *Journal*, p. 232.

2   Cited in John Hardman, *The Life of Louis XVI* (London, 2016), p. 349.

3   Pierre Breillat, *Versailles, ville nouvelle, capitale modèle* (Versailles, 1986), p. 12, citing a character in one of Stendhal's novels.

4   Both cited in Mathieu da Vinha and Raphaël Masson (eds), *Versailles: Histoire, dictionnaire et anthologie* (Paris, 2015), pp. 813, 818.

5   Michel Beurdeley, *La France à l'encan, 1789–1799: exode des objets d'art sous la Révolution* (Paris, 1981), p. 94; Odile Caffin-Carcy and Jacques Villard, *Versailles et la Révolution* (Paris, 1988), p. 40.

6   Cited in Claire Constans, *Versailles: Absolutism and Harmony* (New York, 1998), p. 244.

7 Visitor cited in Jérémie Benoît, 'Napoléon à Trianon', at https://www.napoleon.org/histoire-des-2-empires/articles/napoleon-a-trianon/

8 Franck Ferrand, *Versailles après les rois* (Paris, 2012), p. 99; Constans, *Versailles*, p. 246.

9 Ferrand, *Versailles après les rois,* p. 139.

10 Munro Price, *The Perilous Crown: France between Revolutions, 1814–1848* (London, 2007), pp. 274–5.

11 Cited in Ferrand, *Versailles après les rois,* p. 127.

6. Conserving: Versailles, Curation and Heritage

1 See the passages by Montesquiou in da Vinha and Masson, *Versailles*, pp. 904ff.; and Marcel Proust, *Les Plaisirs et les jours* (1916: Paris, 1924), p. 176.

2 The tale may be consulted through Charlotte A. E. Moberly and Eleanor F. Jourdain, *An Adventure*, with a preface by Edith Oliver (London, 1931). This edition includes learned opinion which claimed the visions were due to 'retrocognition'. See also Terry Castle, 'Contagious Folly: *An Adventure* and Its Skeptics', *Critical Inquiry* 17, no. 4 (Summer, 1991), pp. 741–72.

3 Pierre de Nolhac, *La Résurrection de Versailles* (Paris, 1937), p. 13. See Appendix 12, p. 180.

4 Pierre de Nolhac, *La Création de Versailles* (Paris, 1925), pp. xxxi–xxxii.

5 André Cornu, cited in Ferrand, *Versailles après les rois,* p. 284.

Conclusion

1   Pierre Nora (ed), *Les lieux de mémoire*, 3 vols (Paris, 1997). There
     have been English translations of various essays from the collec-
     tion. The relevant Versailles essays are: Helène Himelfarb, 'Ver-
     sailles: Functions and Legends', in *Rethinking France: Les Lieux
     de mémoire*, ed. David P. Jordan, 3 vols (Chicago, 2001–2009), I;
     and Edouard Pommier, 'Versailles: The Image of the Sovereign',
     in *Realms of Memory: The Construction of the French Past*, ed.
     Lawrence D. Kritzman, 3 vols (New York, 1997–1998), III.

2   http://chateauversailles-recherche.fr/.

3   See http://www.chateauversailles.fr/etablissement-public#nos
     -missions (includes annual reports back to 2003).

4   Anish Kapoor, *Versailles* (Paris, 2015).

5   A useful vantage-point for such issues is *La Tribune de l'art*:
     http://www.latribunedelart.com. See, for example, Didier Ryk-
     ner, 'Domaine de Versailles, ou Versailles-land?' (25 March
     2007), http://www.latribunedelart.com/domaine-de-versailles
     -ou-versailles-land.

Appendices

1   Many of these passages are drawn from the rich anthology
     of texts about Versailles included in Mathieu da Vinha and
     Raphaël Masson (eds), *Versailles: histoire, dictionnaire et an-
     thologie* (Paris, 2015). All translations are my own.

INDEX

Colin Jones teaches at Queen Mary University of London and the University of Chicago. He is the author of many books on French history, including *Paris: The Biography of a City* and *The Smile Revolution in Eighteenth Century Paris*.

Photograph by Ron Jautz